To my dearest

From Mab.

ALDGATE
No 29
INSTITUTE.

D0989804

THE LIFE OF BENJAMIN DISRAELI
EARL OF BEACONSFIELD

Mrs Wyndham Lewis.
from a miniature at Hughenden.
painted in 1829 by Rochard.

THE LIFE OF
BENJAMIN DISRAELI
EARL OF BEACONSFIELD

BY WILLIAM FLAVELLE MONYPENNY

VOLUME II.
1837—1846.
WITH PORTRAITS AND ILLUSTRATIONS

Read no history, nothing but biography, for that is life without theory.—CONTARINI FLEMING.

LONDON
JOHN MURRAY, ALBEMARLE STREET, W.
1912

THE LIBRARY
University of Saskatchewan
REGINA CAMPUS

CONTENTS OF VOL II.

LIST OF ILLUSTRATIONS TO VOL. II.

PREFACE

The period covered by this volume, the preparation of which has been delayed by reasons of health, is a period of critical importance in Disraeli's career, and one with regard to which there has been much misunderstanding. It is also, as it seems to me, the period when his genius was at its greatest height and vigour. These are the justifications, if any are needed, for what may seem at first sight the disproportionate length at which it has been treated.

I have again to thank Lord Rothschild and the other trustees of the Beaconsfield estate for their constant kindness and encouragement. Outside the Beaconsfield papers my main reliance, as in the previous volume, has been on published material; but I have once more to record my obligations to Captain Lindsay for the originals of many of Disraeli's letters to his sister, and I am also under obligations to the Duke of Rutland, Lord Lansdowne, and Mr. Leopold de Rothschild, in the case of a few other documents. For most of the illustrations I am again indebted to Mr. Coningsby Disraeli, but the portraits of Lord George Bentinck, Mr. Henry Hope, and Lord John Manners, are owing, respectively, to the

Duke of Portland, Mr. Adrian Hope, and Lady Victoria Manners.   Lastly, my best thanks are due to Mr. G. E. Buckle and my publisher, Mr. Murray, for their kindness in reading the proof-sheets and for many helpful suggestions.

W. F. M.

October, 1912.

CHAPTER I.

THE MAIDEN SPEECH.

1837–1838.

On November 15, 1837, Queen Victoria's first Parliament assembled for its first session, and Disraeli began the career in the House of Commons which was to last without a break for nearly forty years.

To Sarah Disraeli.

[*Nov.* 15, 1837.

MY DEAREST,

I took my seat this morning : I went down to the House with Wyndham [Lewis] at two, and found it very full, the members standing in groups and chatting. About three, there was a cry of ' Order, order,' all took their seats (myself on the second bench, behind Sir Robert Peel), and a messenger summoned the Commons. The Government party was very strong in consequence of an article in *The Times* about two days back, which spread a panic through their ranks, but which I think was a hoax. Shaw Lefevre proposed, and Strutt of Derby seconded, Abercromby.[1] Both were brief, the first commonplace, the other commonplace and coarse ; all was tame. Peel said a very little, very well. Then Abercromby, who looked like an old laundress, mumbled and moaned some dullness, and was then carried to the chair, and said a little more amid a faint, dull cheer. To me of course the scene was exciting enough, but none could share my feelings except new members.

[1] The Speaker in the late Parliament, who at its opening in 1835 had been put forward by the Whigs against his Tory predecessor Manners Sutton, and elected by a majority of six after a fierce party struggle. The article in *The Times* had hinted that the Opposition might follow the example set them by the Whigs in 1835, and oppose Abercromby's re-election.

Peel came to the Carlton yesterday, and was there a great deal. He welcomed me very warmly, but all indeed noticed his cordial demeanor ; he looks very well, and shook hands with me in the House. He asked me to join a small dinner at the Carlton on Thursday ' A House of Commons dinner purely,' he said ; ' by that time we shall know something of the temper of the House.'

O'Connell came in very late ; many members on both sides arrived only this morning. I did not recognise Bulwer, but as he is in town I think he must have been there.

My love to all,

D.

The old Palace of Westminster had been partly destroyed by fire in 1834, and Lords and Commons were still in the temporary chambers[1] which they occupied while Barry's stately pile was rising from the ruins. The House of Commons of which Disraeli now found himself a member has a remarkable roll of fame. Lord Melbourne, the Whig Prime Minister, had his place in the House of Lords, but, with the exception of Lord Aberdeen, every one of his successors in the highest office under the Crown down to the time when Lord Salisbury formed his first Government, nearly half a century later, was in the new House of Commons. Sir Robert Peel, who had been Prime Minister for a short period already, and now led the Opposition, was in a very few years to be Prime Minister again. Lord John Russell, who was now Home Secretary and leader of the House, was twice to be at the head of Whig administrations ; but in the interval between them he was to revert to second place, yielding the primacy to his present colleague, Lord Palmerston, the Foreign Secretary, who, over fifty as he was, and with a very long career in office behind him, had as yet given little promise of the fame and popularity he was afterwards to win. Lord Stanley, Peel's neighbour on the front Opposition bench, who had begun life as a Whig, was to be three times Prime Minister as the leader of the Tories ; and on the same bench sat Mr. Gladstone, who, though not yet

[1] The Lords in the Painted Chamber, and the Commons in the old House of Lords.

twenty-eight, had now been five years in Parliament and had held subordinate office in Peel's short administration, and who on no less than four occasions was to find himself at the head of a Government of the opposite party. The new member for Maidstone, conspicuous by his Jewish appearance and highly dandified dress, completes the number of our future Prime Ministers; though, as he moved into his place behind Peel and Stanley and Gladstone, none probably but himself had a thought of the high destiny that awaited him.

After Russell and Palmerston, the most notable occupants of the front Ministerial bench were Spring Rice, the Chancellor of the Exchequer; Poulett Thomson, the President of the Board of Trade, who a few years later, under the title of Lord Sydenham, was, as Governor-General of Canada, to leave his mark on the history of our colonial administration; Cam Hobhouse, the friend of Byron, President of the Board of Control; the Attorney-General, Sir John Campbell, afterwards Lord Chancellor; and Lord Morpeth, the popular Chief Secretary for Ireland, of which Thomas Drummond, the Under-Secretary, was now the real ruler. Macaulay was still in India, but within two years was to take his place in the Whig Cabinet. Sir Henry Hardinge, who had been Irish Secretary in Peel's short administration, but who is better remembered as a soldier and Governor-General of India, was among those who had seats on the front Opposition bench, as were also Sir Edward Sugden, who had been Irish Lord Chancellor, and was later, as Lord St. Leonards, to sit on the English Woolsack; Goulburn, who had been Peel's Home Secretary in 1835; and Herries—' old, grey-headed, financial Herries '[1]—who had begun his career under Pitt, and had been Chancellor of the Exchequer without a Budget in the brief Ministry of Goderich. Sir James Graham had lost his election in Cumberland, and, when Parliament met, was not in his place by Lord Stanley, with whom he had seceded from the Whigs in

<hr />

[1] See Vol. I., p. 205.

1834 ; but he was soon to return to the House as member
for another constituency.

Outside the two front benches there were many noteworthy figures. Most conspicuous of all was the burly
form of O'Connell, the real, though not exacting, master
of the Government. Close to him, but sharply contrasted in the matter of bulk and stature, was his lieutenant, Richard Lalor Sheil. On the Tory side of the
House there were Disraeli's friends, Lord Chandos and
Sir Francis Burdett ; Mackworth Praed, member for
Aylesbury, already nearing the close of his too brief life ;
Lord Ashley, afterwards famous as the philanthropic
Earl of Shaftesbury ; and two notable personalities in the
representatives of King's Lynn, Lord George Bentinck,
then an invincibly silent member, and Sir Stratford
Canning, who had won celebrity in the diplomatic world
long before he entered Parliament. Among the Whig
members were the witty and vivacious Charles Buller,
and a boyish figure, Lord Leveson, who during Disraeli's
time was to play a conspicuous part on the political stage
as Lord Granville. The little band of Radicals, though
attenuated by the elections, was, in proportion to its
numbers, richer in talent and personality than the general
body of the Whigs. Roebuck was not to be seen, having
met with defeat at Bath ; but, in spite of a similar defeat
in Middlesex, Joseph Hume, the vigilant and persistent
critic of the estimates, was in his usual place, having
already contrived to find a friendly refuge in Kilkenny.
Grote, who sat for the City of London, and who is remembered as the historian of Greece, if as a Radical politician
he is forgotten, was one of the group of philosophic
Radicals ; and another was Sir William Molesworth, a
young Cornish baronet, whose austerity in the matter of
political principle did not prevent him from being something of a dandy in his dress. Not far away were a
couple of friends of Disraeli's, Radicals of a different type
from Molesworth, but equally elaborate in their dress—
Edward Bulwer, the novelist, and ' honest Tom Dun-

combe,' a man of birth and fashion who was one of D'Orsay's chosen associates. Another friend of Disraeli's was a young patrician Radical of a more serious cast than Duncombe—Charles Villiers, already the persistent enemy of the Corn Laws, a pioneer in the cause of which he lived to be the Nestor.

To Sarah Disraeli.

Nov. 16.

DEAREST,

There is no news. I have just come from the House, where I went to be sworn. It was something like Quarter Sessions on a great scale.

The dinner to-day is merely a House dinner of 14—all our great men with the exception of Lord Ramsay[1] and myself, the only two new members. It has created some jealousy and surprise ; but W[yndham] L[ewis] is delighted, and says ' Peel has taken him by the hand in the most marked way.' . . .

D.[2]

November 21.

I tried to write you a line yesterday, as I was endeavouring to eat a sandwich, which I was not permitted to finish. Affairs are in a state of great excitement, and most interesting. All Sunday our members poured in, and at 4.30 the Carlton was full. Lyndhurst arrived rather unexpectedly on the Saturday night, and sent for me the following morning. I never saw him look so well, he really might have passed for five-and-forty, plump and rosy, and most gaily attired, and in the highest force and spirits. He was more than kind, and after paying a visit to Peel and the Duke, showed at the Carlton, where his appearance created great enthusiasm. Yesterday, after being obliged to go down to the House at eleven, to ensure a house for members to swear, I went to a great meeting at Peel's. There must have been 300 members. Peel addressed, full of spirit, and apparently eager for action. Thence again to the House, where we were summoned to the Lords at two o'clock. The rush was terrific ; Abercromby himself nearly thrown down and trampled upon, and his mace-bearer banging the members' heads with his gorgeous weapon, and cracking skulls with

---

[1] Afterwards Earl and Marquis of Dalhousie, the great Governor-General of India.

[2] Brit. Mus., Addit. MSS.

impunity. I was fortunate enough to escape, however, and also to ensure an entry. It was a magnificent spectacle. The Queen looked admirably, no feathers but a diamond tiara ; the peers in robes, the peeresses, and the sumptuous groups of courtiers rendered the affair most glittering and imposing. The Speech was intentionally vague, that no division might possibly occur. All was mystery until five o'clock. From the Lords I escaped, almost at the hazard of our lives, with Mahon,[1] who is now most cordial, and we at length succeeded in gaining the Carlton, having several times been obliged to call upon the police and military to protect us as we attempted to break the line, but the moment the magical words 'Member of Parliament' were uttered all the authorities came to our assistance, all gave way, and we passed everywhere. You never saw two such figures, our hats crushed and covered with mud, and the mobocracy envying us our privileges, calling out 'Jim Crow' as we stalked through the envious files.

I went down, after refitting at the Carlton, for about half an hour, during which I tried to scribble to you. The seat I succeeded in securing behind Peel I intend if possible to appropriate to myself. The House was so crowded later, that the galleries were all full of members ; many unable to obtain seats were sitting on the stairs and on chairs and benches behind the Speaker's chair. Lyndhurst and many peers were in their seats at the bar : the strangers' gallery of course crammed.

The address was moved by Lord Leveson,[2] a child apparently, in a rich diplomatic uniform, and seconded by Gibson Craig, a new member in a court dress. Leveson made a crammed speech like a schoolboy ; Gibson Craig, of whom the Whigs had hopes, rose, stared like a stuck pig, and said nothing ; his friends cheered, he stammered, all cheered, then there was a dead and awful pause, and then he sat down, and that was his performance. The address was then read, and Wakley[3] made a most Radical speech and amendment,[4] determined to bring affairs to a crisis. He was fluent, flippant, and vulgar ; a second-rate hustings orator. He was seconded by Molesworth, a most odious speaker, who wearied the House. . . . John Russell threw the Radicals over in a most matured and decided manner. It was a declaration evidently

[1] Afterwards 5th Earl Stanhope, the well-known historian and biographer of Pitt. As a grandson of Lord Carrington's he was a frequent visitor at Wycombe.
[2] Afterwards 2nd Earl Granville.
[3] Thomas Wakley, 1795-1862, medical reformer and founder of the *Lancet*.
[4] In favour of extension of the franchise.

the result of a Cabinet decision. The sensation was immense. Peel then rose and made one of the finest speeches I ever heard, most powerful and even brilliant. He broke the centre of the Government party for ever. The Radicals were mad. . . .

So, after all, there was a division on the Address in Queen Victoria's first Parliament—509 to 20. The division took an hour. I then left the House at ten o'clock, none of us having dined. The tumult and excitement great. I dined, or rather supped, at the Carlton with a large party off oysters, Guinness, and broiled bones, and got to bed at half-past twelve o'clock. Thus ended the most remarkable day hitherto of my life.[1]

[Dec. 5.]

DEAREST,

. . . Yesterday was rather amusing in the House. The Sheriffs of London, Sir Bob or Tom, and Sir Moses, and no mistake, appeared at the bar in full state to present, according to the privilege of the city of London, some petitions, after which they took their place under the gallery and listened to the debate,[2] which turned out to be the Jew question by a sidewind. Nobody looked at me, and I was not at all uncomfortable, but voted in the majority with the utmost *sangfroid*. . . .

D.[3]

Disraeli kept silent for something more than a fortnight, and then, on the evening of December 7, rose to deliver his maiden speech. The subject in debate touched the privilege of members, and was personal enough in its bearing to arouse a good deal of passion. The general election of the preceding summer had not seriously affected the numerical strength of parties, but the Melbourne Government, with its ordeal now behind it, and with a friendly Sovereign upon the throne, was in a

[1] *Letters*, pp. 117-120.
[2] On a Bill intended to relieve Quakers and Moravians from the obligation to take an oath before entering on municipal offices. Grote having moved that it should be an instruction to the Committee to extend the relief to persons of all religious denominations, the debate which followed was mainly directed to the question of Jewish disabilities ; but the leader of the House and the author of the Bill, though declaring themselves favourable to the principle of Jewish relief, argued against the attempt to introduce it into the present measure as impolitic, and Grote's instruction was defeated by a majority of sixteen.
[3] *Letters*, p. 120.

stronger position than before, though its position even
now was very far from strong.

The death of the King was a great blow to what had now
come to be generally styled the ' Conservative Cause.' It
was quite unexpected ; within a fortnight of his death, eminent
persons still believed that ' it was only the hay fever.' Had
His Majesty lived until after the then impending registration,
the Whigs would have been again dismissed. Nor is there
any doubt that, under these circumstances, the Conservative
Cause would have secured for the new ministers a Parliamentary majority.[1]

The spirits of the Tories had risen high during the
English elections ; but the Irish returns had robbed them
of their majority, and, exasperated at seeing their hopes
defeated in a second Parliament by O'Connell and his
' tail,' they opened a subscription for the promotion of
petitions in Irish constituencies represented by Repealers.
Burdett, among other English members of the House,
ostentatiously supported this subscription with his purse
and with his influence ; and Smith O'Brien, the same who
at a later day was to gain a luckless notoriety in another
field, and whose own seat was now in danger, brought
the matter before the House, complaining of Burdett's
conduct, and moving for a committee of inquiry. A
long debate ensued, in the course of which O'Connell
spoke, and was to have been answered by Lord Stanley ;
but while O'Connell was on his legs, Disraeli, it is said,[2]
went up to Stanley and obtained from him permission
to follow his old antagonist. With his un-English appearance, dandified dress, affected manner, and elaborated
style, Disraeli was hardly likely at the first attempt to
win the favour of the House of Commons, nor in that
jealous assembly would his outside reputation either as a
novelist or as a hustings orator do anything to help him.
In the ordinary course, however, he would have been
certain of a hearing ; but he had gone out of his way to
provoke the hostility of the Irish, on whom the traditions

of the House were least likely to impose restraint. 'We shall meet again at Philippi' had been his challenge to O'Connell, and by rising after O'Connell he had been careful to insure that the challenge should be remembered. He began with the usual appeal for the indulgence which the House was in the habit of allowing to those who for the first time solicited its attention. He then took up a point in the speech of 'the hon. and learned member for Dublin' (O'Connell); and when he described that speech as a 'rhetorical medley,' the House laughed, and it laughed again and louder when he alluded to some subscription, with which O'Connell himself had been connected, as 'a project of majestic mendicancy.' A hostile note soon began to be mingled with the laughter, but for a time the orator was able to proceed, and on the whole not without effect. Presently, however, the hostility became more marked, and he was constrained to renew his plea for indulgence :

I shall not trouble the House at any length. I do not affect to be insensible to the difficulty of my position, and I shall be very glad to receive indulgence even from the hon. members opposite. If, however, hon. gentlemen do not wish to hear me, I will sit down without a murmur.

For a minute or two there was comparative calm, but a declaration that since the Reform Bill 'the stain of boroughmongering had only assumed a deeper and darker hue,' and that intimidation was more highly organised than even under the old system, awoke the storm anew. 'Hisses, groans, hoots, catcalls, drumming with the feet, loud conversation, and imitation of animals,'[1] are among the noises recorded as coming from the Irish quarter of the House. Disraeli cannot have been much surprised, for he told his constituents later that he had been warned of the reception he would meet with, and that the warnings had only impelled him to face the ordeal the sooner. At all events he kept his temper. 'I wish,' he pleaded, 'I could induce the House to give

[1] Hitchman's *Life of Lord Beaconsfield*, I., p. 134.

me five minutes more ;' but the only response was uproar,
and when, to enforce his claims to a hearing, he tried to
put himself forward as virtually representative of the
new members of the House, he was rewarded with ' bursts
of laughter.' ' Now why smile ? Why envy me ?' was
his good-humoured retort. ' Why should not I, too, have
a tail, if it be only for a single night ?' And at this
sally we are told the laughter was long and general.
Henceforth the speech becomes almost unintelligible.
' I determined,' he explained to his constituents later,
' to be on my legs exactly the period I intended my
speech should occupy. I succeeded, sometimes in comparative calm, sometimes the cheers of friends joining
with the yelling of foes, sometimes in a scene of tumult
indescribable ; but I stood erect, and when I sat down I
sent them my defiance.' As he drew towards the close
he embarked on an elaborate period, which had no doubt
been prepared for use as a peroration, and which, beginning with a classical allusion to the ' amatory eclogue '
between ' the noble Tityrus of the Treasury Bench [Lord
John Russell] and the learned Daphne [? Daphnis] of
Liskeard [Charles Buller],' whose ' *amantium irœ* ' had
resulted, as he expected, in an ' *amoris integratio*,' ended
with a picture of ' the noble lord from his pedestal of
power wielding in one hand the keys of St. Peter and
waving with the other——': but the picture remained
unfinished, the conclusion of the sentence being lost
in shouts of laughter. ' Now, Mr. Speaker,' he proceeded, when his voice could be heard again, ' see
the philosophical prejudices of man. That image I
should have thought, when I was about to complete it,
might have been much admired. I would have cheered
it heartily if it had come from the lips of a political
opponent ; and I would gladly hear a cheer, even though
it should proceed from such a party.' The time he had
allotted himself had now expired. ' I hope I may thank
hon. gentlemen opposite for the sincerity of their expressions of approbation as well as disapprobation. I am not

at all surprised at the reception I have experienced. I
have begun several things many times, and I have often
succeeded at the last—though many had predicted that I
must fail, as they had done before me.' (Cries of 'Question, question !' and 'Hear, hear, hear !') And then, in
a voice which, by the testimony of every witness, rose
high above the clamour, and which one even describes as
'almost terrific': 'I sit down now, but the time will
come when you will hear me.'[1]

To Sarah Disraeli.
Dec. 8, 1837.

I made my maiden speech last night, rising very late after
O'Connell, but at the request of my party and the full sanction
of Sir Robert Peel. As I wish to give you an *exact* idea of
what occurred, I state at once that my *début* was a *failure*,
so far that I could not succeed in gaining an opportunity of
saying what I intended ; but the failure was not occasioned
by my breaking down or any incompetency on my part, but
from the physical powers of my adversaries. I can give you
no idea how bitter, how factious, how unfair they were. It
was like my first *début* at Aylesbury, and perhaps in that sense
may be auspicious of ultimate triumph in the same scene. I
fought through all with undaunted pluck and unruffled temper,
made occasionally good isolated hits when there was silence,
and finished with spirit when I found a formal display was
ineffectual. My party backed me well, and no one with more
zeal and kindness than Peel, cheering me repeatedly, which
is not his custom. The uproar was all organised by the Rads
and the Repealers. They formed a compact body near the
bar of the House and seemed determined to set me down, but
that they did not do. I have given you a most impartial
account, stated indeed against myself.

In the lobby at the division, Chandos, who was not near me
while speaking, came up and congratulated me. I replied
that I thought there was no cause for congratulations, and
muttered 'Failure !' 'No such thing !' said Chandos ; 'you
are quite wrong. I have just seen Peel, and I said to him,
"Now tell me exactly what you think of D." Peel replied,
"Some of my party were disappointed and talk of failure.
I say *just the reverse*. He did all that he could do under the

---

[1] For the concluding portion of the speech I have used the report in the
Mirror of Parliament, which is at once the fullest and the most intelligible.

circumstances. I say anything but failure ; he must make his way." '

The Government and their retainers behaved well. The Attorney-General, to whom I never spoke in my life, came up to me in the lobby and spoke to me with great cordiality. He said, ' Now, Mr. Disraeli, could you just tell me how you finished one sentence in your speech, we are anxious to know —" In one hand the keys of St. Peter, and in the other——" ?' ' In the other the cap of liberty, Sir John.' He smiled, and said, ' A good picture.' I replied, ' But your friends will not allow me to finish my pictures.' ' I assure you,' he said, ' there was the liveliest desire to hear you from us. It was a party at the bar, over whom we had no control ; but you have nothing to be afraid of.' Now I have told you all.

                                     Yours, D.—in very good spirits.[1]

Disraeli's many enemies in the press made the most, of course, of his ' failure,' though *The Times* went out of its way to soothe his wounded feelings by describing the speech as eloquent. We have independent testimony to the warmth of Peel's encouragement. ' Sir Robert Peel, who very rarely cheers any honourable gentleman, not even the most able and accomplished speaker of his own party, greeted Mr. Disraeli's speech with a prodigality of applause which must have been very trying to the worthy baronet's lungs. . . . He repeatedly turned round his head, and, looking the youthful orator in the face, cheered him in the most stentorian tones.'[2] Stanley, on the other hand, who rose immediately after Disraeli, and who, as there is reason to believe, was at this time deeply prejudiced against him, made no allusion whatever to the remarkable scene of which the House had just been witness.

                         From Lord Lyndhurst.

MY DEAR DISRAELI,

     Why have you not called upon me ? The scamps of Radicals were determined that you should not speak. I am sure you have the courage to have at them again. You are sure to succeed in spite of their bullying.

                                     Ever yours,
                                         LYNDHURST.

[1] *Letters*, pp. 120-122.   [2] Grant's *British Senate in 1838*, II., p. 334.

To Sarah Disraeli.

Monday [*Dec.* 11].

DEAREST,

I dined with Bulwer on Saturday, and, strange enough, met Sheil. I should have been very much surprised, had I not arrived first and been apprised. It thus arose : on Saturday, Bulwer walked into the Athenæum ; Sheil, who has just recovered from the gout, was lounging in an easy chair reading the newspaper ; around him was a knot of low Rads (we might guess them) abusing me and exulting in the discrimination of the House. Probably they thought they pleased Sheil. Bulwer drew near, but stood apart. Suddenly Sheil threw down the paper and said in his shrill voice, ' Now, gentlemen, I have heard all you have to say, and, what is more, I heard this same speech of Mr. Disraeli, and I tell you this : if ever the spirit of oratory was in a man, it is in that man. Nothing can prevent him from being one of the first speakers in the House of Commons (great confusion). Ay ! I know something about that place, I think, and I tell you what besides, that if there had not been this interruption, Mr. Disraeli might have made a failure ; I don't call this a failure, it is a crush. My *début* was a failure, because I was heard, but my reception was supercilious, his malignant. A *début* should be dull. The House will not allow a man to be a wit and an orator, unless they have the credit of finding it out. There it is.' You may conceive the sensation that this speech made : I heard of it yesterday, from Eaton, Winslow, and several other quarters. The crowd dispersed, but Bulwer drew near, and said to Sheil : ' D. dines with me to-day ; would you like to meet him ?' ' In spite of my gout,' said Sheil, ' I long to know him ; I long to tell him what I think.'

So we met : there were besides only D'Eyncourt,[1] always friendly to me, Mackinnon, a Tory, and one Quin[2] of the Danube. Sheil was most charming, and took an opportunity in conversation with me of disburthening his mind of the subject with which it was full. He insisted continually on his position that the clamorous reception was fortunate, ' for,' said he, ' if you had been listened to, what would have been the result ? You would have done what I did ; you would have made the best speech that you ever would have made : it would have been received frigidly, and you would have

---

[1] C. Tennyson D'Eyncourt, 1784-1861, Whig member for Lambeth, and Alfred Tennyson's uncle.

[2] No doubt Michael Joseph Quin, traveller and journalist, who a couple of years before had published a book entitled *A Steam Voyage down the Danube.*

despaired of yourself. I did. As it is, you have shown to the House that you have a fine organ, that you have an unlimited command of language, that you have courage, temper and readiness. Now get rid of your genius for a session. Speak often, for you must not show yourself cowed, but speak shortly. Be very quiet, try to be dull, only argue and reason imperfectly, for if you reason with precision, they will think you are trying to be witty. Astonish them by speaking on subjects of detail. Quote figures, dates, calculations. And in a short time the House will sigh for the wit and eloquence, which they all know are in you ; they will encourage you to pour them forth, and then you will have the ear of the House and be a favourite.'

I think that altogether this is as interesting a *rencontre* as I have ever experienced.

Yesterday I dined with Hope,[1] a sumptuous, but rather dull, party. Strangford and Cecil Forester,[2] Eaton, Beresford, Stanley of Cumberland, Baring, late of Yarmouth. On Saturday I dine with Peel, his first party.

Love,
D.

Sheil was unquestionably right. Disraeli had made the blunder of trying to take the House by storm without giving it time to become accustomed to the peculiarities of his manner, and only the hostility of the Radicals and O'Connellites had saved him from genuine failure. ' I am too far out of the world to know anything that's in it,' wrote his father, ' but I am always fearful that " theatrical graces " will not do for the English Commons. Whether any display of that nature you may have indulged in, I know not. Your own observation of what is about you must be your instructor.' The unfair turbulence of his enemies had not only averted ridicule, but had created a feeling in his favour ; and when, urged on, in his own phrase, by ' ambition, his constituents, and the hell of previous failure,'[3] he next addressed the House, the result was very different.

---

[1] Henry Hope of Deepdene, 1808-1862, eldest son of the author of *Anastasius*.

[2] Afterwards 3rd Lord Forester, 1807-1886.

[3] *Coningsby*, Bk. I. ch. 3.

To Sarah Disraeli.

Dec. 18, 1837.

Nothing daunted, and acting on the advice of Sheil (a strange Parliamentary mentor for me after all), I spoke again last night and with complete success.   It was on the Copyright Bill.   The House was not very full, but all the Cabinet Ministers and officials were there, and all our principal men. Talfourd,[1] who had already made a long speech (his style flowery, with a weak and mouthing utterance), proposed the Copyright Bill very briefly, having spoken on it last session. Bulwer followed him, and confined himself to the point of international copyright, which called up Poulett Thomson. Then Peel on the copyright of art ; and then I rose.

I was received with the utmost curiosity and attention. As there had been no great discussion I determined not to be tempted into a speech, which everyone expected of course I rose to make.   All I aimed at was to say something pointed and to the purpose.   My voice, in spite of our doings at Maidstone, was in perfect condition.   I suggested a clause to Talfourd, with the idea of which I had been furnished by Colburn. I noticed that the subject had already been done so much justice to on other occasions that I should not trouble the House, but I had been requested to support this Bill by many eminent persons interested in its success.   Thus far I was accompanied by continual ' hear, hears,' and I concluded thus : ' I am glad to hear from her Majesty's Government that the interests of literature have at length engaged their attention.   It has been the boast of the Whig party, and a boast not without foundation, that in many brilliant periods of our literary annals they have been the patrons of letters (' Hear, hear ' from John Russell & Co.).   As for myself, I trust that the age of literary patronage has passed (' Hear hear ' from leader of the Rads), and it will be honorable to the present Government if, under its auspices, it be succeeded by that of legislative protection.'   I sat down with a general cheer.

Talfourd, in reply, noticed all the remarks of the preceding members, and when he came to me said he should avail himself of ' the excellent suggestion of the honorable member for Maidstone, himself one of the greatest ornaments of our modern literature.'   Here Peel cheered loudly, and indeed throughout my remarks he backed me.   So on the whole

---

[1] Serjeant Talfourd, afterwards a Judge, but better known as the author of *Ion*.   His efforts ' in behalf of English literature and of those who devote themselves to the most precarious of all pursuits ' had just won for him the dedication of *Pickwick*.

there was glorification. Everybody congratulated me.
Colonel Lygon said, ' Well, you have got in your saddle again,
and now you may ride away.' Even Granville Somerset[1] said,
' I never heard a few sentences so admirably delivered. You
will allow me to say so, after having been twenty-five years in
Parliament.' But all agree that I managed in a few minutes
by my voice and manner to please everyone in the House. I
don't care about the meagre report, for I spoke to the House
and not to the public.

I have no time to tell you about Maidstone, except that
the banker gave me a banquet more splendid than many I
have had in this town, that we had the largest meeting on
record, and that I made a successful speech ; that Wyndham
Lewis is infinitely more warm than ever, and my constituents
far more enthusiastic, and it is my firm opinion that the next
time I rise in the House, which will be very soon in February,
I shall sit down amid loud cheers, for I really think, on the
whole, though I have not time now to give you the reasons,
that the effect of my *début*, and the circumstances that
attended it, will ultimately be favorable to my career. Next
to undoubted success the best thing is to make a great noise,
and the many articles that are daily written to announce my
failure only prove that I have not failed. One thing is
curious, that the opinion of the mass is immensely affected
by that of their leaders. I know a hundred little instances
daily, which show me that what Peel, and Sheil, and other
leading men have said, have already greatly influenced those
who are unable to form opinions for themselves.—Love to
all.

                                        D.[2]

One eloquent sentence in the speech at the Maidstone
banquet deserves to be rescued from oblivion : ' By the
Conservative Cause I mean the splendor of the Crown,
the lustre of the peerage, the privileges of the Commons,
the rights of the poor. I mean that harmonious union,
that magnificent concord of all interests, of all classes, on
which our national greatness and prosperity depends.'
' When I meet you again as my constituents,' he had
told the electors of Maidstone during the contest in July,
' not a person will look upon me without some degree of

[1] Lord Granville Somerset, 1792-1848, second son of the 6th Duke of
Beaufort.   He had held office in Peel's administration of 1834-35.
[2] *Letters*, pp. 125, 126.

satisfaction, perhaps some degree of pride.' His first
visit to them was paid under the shadow of his recent
failure, but his eloquence and spirit made it none the less
a triumph.

Parliament adjourned for Christmas under the shadow
cast by the news of the outbreak of rebellion in Canada,
and the holiday was shortened accordingly. Disraeli
spent it at Bradenham, busily plying his pen, one fruit
of his labours being a series of papers in *The Times* under
the title of ' Old England,' and with the signature ' Cœur
de Lion.' They are discourses on the familiar text, ' How
is the King's Government to be carried on ?'—' great
question of a great man, true hero-question '; or, ' How
is the Queen's Empire to be maintained ?'—Disraeli's
own variant on the Duke of Wellington's formula ; but,
save for an occasional indication that the writer had
been reading Carlyle, they are in no way remarkable.

To Mrs. Wyndham Lewis.

BRADENHAM,
Friday [Jan. 5, 1838].

MY DEAR MRS. WYNDHAM,

I was very sorry not to see you this morning, but very
imprudently I sat up late at night writing, which never does
for me. Slept little, and only towards morn, and woke
wretchedly shattered. I hope you have had not a very disagreeable journey to town, and found Wyndham well.

We miss you here all very much ; everything seems flat,
and everybody dull and dispirited, almost as dull and dispirited
as you think me.

Believe me,
Ever yours, with great regard,
DIS.

In the middle of January the House met again. Disraeli was no amateur politician seeking in public affairs
distraction for the intervals between more strenuous
amusements. He had devoted himself in all seriousness
to a political career, and politics henceforth were to be
the main business of his life. ' The greatest opportunity
that can be offered to an Englishman was now his—a

seat in the House of Commons ;'[1] and having won this
opportunity by much toil and effort, he was determined
to make the most of it. 'Let me tell you how to get on
in the House of Commons,' he said to a young member
twenty years later. 'When the House is sitting be
always in your place ; when it is not sitting read Hansard.'[2] We need not suppose that the author of this
maxim had submitted himself too literally to the terrible
discipline which it recommends, but he fulfilled the first
condition of Parliamentary success by throwing himself
with zeal into the life and work of the House. Luckily,
in these years of freedom from responsibility he found in
the House of Commons abundant time for writing letters.

To Sarah Disraeli.

Thursday, Jan. 18, 1838.

We have adjourned until Monday, after two nights of the
most feeble debates that can well be fancied. The frigid
genius of Canada pervaded our deliberations, and even Sir
Robert appeared to sink under it, for I never recollect him so
inefficient. I have no news to tell you, except that I shall go
and see Kean to-morrow with Mrs. W. L., provided she get a
good warm box.

Jan. 20.

Town is very dull ; everybody is frozen to death.
Brougham's speech[3] on Thursday was most clever, as good as
his old House of Commons harangues. Our peers mustered
thick, and seemed ' miching mallecho,' but the Duke of Wellington rose and spoilt all with his generosity and all that.
Great disgust in Tory ranks, even among the highest. Duke
supposed to be *passé*, and to like being buttered with Whig
laudation. . . .

I went to see young Kean last night, and the theatre was
full in spite of the frost, which thins all the other houses ; but
I will not criticise him, for one word describes all—mediocrity.
We went with the Horace Twisses ;[4] Lord Chesterfield's box,
a capital fire, our own tea, and really very amusing.

D.

[1] *Endymion*, ch. 52.
[2] *Lord Beaconsfield's Irish Policy*, by Sir J. Pope Hennessy.
[3] Debate on Canadian Rebellion.
[4] Horace Twiss, 1787-1849, lawyer, wit, politician, and journalist, nephew
of Mrs. Siddons and father-in-law of J. T. Delane.

LIBRARY OF HOUSE OF COMMONS,
Jan. 23.

To be impartial, which one should be when a man with brains is concerned, Roebuck[1] yesterday was not equal to the occasion. Sharp and waspish, he would have made a good petulant Opposition speech, but as the representative of a nation arraigning a Ministry of high crimes and misdemeanours, he was rather ridiculous : the subsequent debate was, on the whole, interesting. Sir G. Grey,[2] who had gained a reputation by the Canada revolt, contrived pretty well to lose it. Lord Francis Egerton spoke with all the effect which a man of considerable talent and highly cultivated mind, backed by the highest rank and 60,000*l.* per annum, would naturally command. He has a bad delivery, a good voice, but no management or modulation of it, and the most ungainly action conceivable ; nevertheless, on the whole impressive, and his style rich and somewhat ornate. Leader[3] ludicrously imitated Roebuck for more than an hour, and then the only feature was Pakington's[4] *début*, who sat next to me. His friends expected a great deal from him, and they announce that he quite fulfilled their expectations. He was confident, fluent, and commonplace, and made a good chairman of quarter sessions speech. ' It was the best speech that he ever will make,' said Sugden, ' and he has been practising it before the grand jury for the last twenty years.' However, I supported him very zealously, and he went to bed thinking he was an orator, and wrote to Mrs. Pakington, I've no doubt, to that effect.

[*Undated.*]

I went to a most *recherché* concert at Parnther's, where I found all the *élite* of town, and where the season commenced, as all agreed, very brilliantly. The Duke was there, looking very well in his garter, riband, and the golden fleece. There were indeed as many stars as in an Arabian story—

Ye stars, which are the poetry of dress![5]

I can scarcely tell you who was not there, for I saw Lans-

---

[1] He was heard at the bar as agent for the House of Assembly of Lower Canada against the second reading of the Canada Bill.
[2] Under-Secretary for the Colonies.
[3] A well-known Radical member.
[4] Afterwards as Sir John Pakington a Cabinet colleague of Disraeli's.
[5] ' It is pleasant,' says St. Barbe in *Endymion* (ch. 33), ' to talk to a man with a star.
      "Ye stars, which are the poetry of heaven,"
Byron wrote [*Childe Harold*, III. 88] ; a silly line ; he should have written,
      "Ye stars, which are the poetry of dress." '

downes, Salisburys, Stuart de Rothesay, Duke of Beaufort, Douro, Cantalupe, Fitzroy, Loftus, &c., and Mrs. W. L., who was very proud, evidently, of being there. But the most picturesque group was the Rothschilds, the widow still in mourning, two sons, some sisters, and, above all, the young bride,[1] or rather wife, from Frankfort, universally admired, tall, graceful, dark, and clear, picturesquely dressed, a robe of yellow silk, a hat and feathers, with a sort of *Sévigné* beneath of magnificent pearls ; quite a Murillo.

[*Undated.*]

I send you two good franks, the handwriting of two of the greatest ruffians in the House, and given to me by both of them when very drunk. They are ' Tailers,'[2] but have taken a sort of blackguard fancy to me, and very civil.[3]

Monday.

DEAREST,

We had a queer but amusing party at the Twisses. It was really given to Mr. and Mrs. Barnes ; the W. L.'s were got to meet them, and the rest were men—Lord Darlington, Lowther, G. Somerset, Lord Reay, H. Hardinge, Henry Baring, &c., and myself. The dinner was good for Twiss, and everything went off well ; Mrs. Barnes, who looked, as H. B. said, like a lady in a pantomime, very funny, surrounded by sons of dukes and privy councillors.

The weather was so bad, the streets being nearly half a foot deep in slough and snow, that I doubt whether I could have got to Salisbury House, short as was the distance, had not G. Somerset taken me. It was a most brilliant party, and the first time the world has been received there since the alterations which commenced since the old lady's death. Such a revolution ! There is not a vestige of the ancient interior ; even the staircase is entirely new and newly placed. There had been a grand dinner given previously to Lord and Lady[4] Lyndhurst—to meet the Duke, the Wharncliffes, Ellonborough, Pozzo di Borgos,[5] Francis Egertons, and other grandees. The assembly was most select. Lady Lyndhurst made a favourable impression, and afforded me an agreeable surprise. I was of course presented to her. . . . L. is in high spirits, but if he have not a son, I think he will sink under the disappointment. He talks of nothing else.

---

[1] Baroness Lionel de Rothschild.
[2] *I.e.*, O'Connellites.   [3] *Letters*, pp. 127-131.
[4] Lyndhurst's recently-married second wife, Georgiana, daughter of Lewis Goldsmith of Paris. She lived on into the twentieth century, surviving her husband nearly forty years.
[5] Count Pozzo di Borgo, the Corsican, famous as friend and enemy of Napoleon, was the Russian Ambassador in London.

Lady Salisbury, to whom I had never been introduced, received me with great cordiality, and talked to me a great deal. I find I owe the invitation to Lady Londonderry—at least, to her mention of me. I knew almost every man there. . . .

D.[1]

[*Undated.*]

On Saturday I dined with George Wombwell,[2] and met De L'Isle, Adolphus Fitzclarence, Auriol, and Hope. I drank a great deal too much wine, but a great deal less than my host, and his *fidus* Adolphus. I got away to the Salisburys, where there was a most brilliant and agreeable assembly.[3]

[*Undated.*]

I dined with the Powerscourts ; Lady P.[4] is without exception the most beautiful woman in London. The party was good, in some instances rather funny—the Murchisons and Mrs. Somerville,[5] Mahon, Redesdale,[6] and Bankes.[7] Murchison[8] a stiff geological prig, and his wife silent. Mrs. Somerville grown very old and not very easy, but Bankes was so very agreeable that I hardly ever was at a more pleasant meeting.

[*Undated.*]

The evening at the Salisburys last Saturday was very brilliant ; so many beautiful women, and among them the Princess of Capua. Her beauty is remarkable, added to in some degree by her gorgeous and fantastic dress. It was entirely of green velvet and gold ; her headdress of the same material, although in shape that of a contadina. Miss Burdett Coutts was also there, a very quiet and unpretending person ; not unlike her father, nevertheless. Lady Aldboro' made her first appearance for the season, and was very witty and amusing, and looked as fresh as ever. Lady Stanhope[9] is the very picture of Bob Smith, but I forgot you know her. . . . She has a very pretty daughter, Lady Wilhelmina.

[1] Brit. Mus., Addit. MSS.
[2] Said to be the original of Mr. Cassilis in *Coningsby*.
[3] Brit. Mus., Addit. MSS.
[4] She was a daughter of the 3rd Earl of Roden's, and in 1846 married as her second husband Disraeli's friend Castlereagh, afterwards 4th Marquis of Londonderry.
[5] The well-known scientific writer.
[6] The 2nd Lord Redesdale, raised to an earldom on Disraeli's recommendation in 1877.
[7] No doubt George Bankes, 1788-1856, the last of the Cursitor Barons of the Exchequer.
[8] The well-known geologist, afterwards Sir Roderick Murchison.
[9] A daughter of the 1st Lord Carrington's.

One of the prettiest and most interesting women I ever met, is Lady Powerscourt. I forgot to notice the Prince of Capua, a savage, dull-looking fellow covered with moustache, and stars. He is entirely ruled by his wife.

March 15.

I write to say I heard yesterday of the sudden death of my colleague. I have seen Mrs. Wyndham ; she is, of course, at present, extremely overwhelmed. She was sitting in the room with him when he died.[1]

On the day on which this last letter was written Disraeli spoke in a debate on a motion by Charles Villiers directed against the Corn Laws, and greatly distinguished himself.

To Sarah Disraeli.

Friday [March 16].

My Dearest,

You will hear with delight that last night, very unexpectedly, for I had given up all thought of speaking, and suffering naturally not a little both mentally and physically, I rose and made a most successful speech. Indeed, it was not merely a very good speech, but it was by far, and by all sides agreed, the very best speech of the evening, which it is always a great thing to achieve, as then nobody else is talked of.

I was so disturbed by deputations from Maidstone, rival candidates for the vacant post, the arrival of Jem, &c., &c., having been twice called out of the House to the Carlton, and having nearly lost my voice which I had been cooking with so much care for days, that at six o'clock, when I at last sat down in my place, I had quite given up all idea of speaking, but finding the House very thin, and getting more composed, I began to think I would take an opportunity of making a speech merely for the press. Even with this humble view, I was unfortunate ; thin as the House was, it seemed to consist only of speakers ; 12 or 14 fellows were on their legs at the same time, and Darby and Gally Knight, between whom I sat, were always up at the same time. In this state I went to our front and table bench, which was clear of all the great guns, who had gone to dinner, except Chandos, and told him my despair, and that I had given up the affair as a bad job. He recommended me to rise where I was, and boldly speak from the floor. Even here I could not catch the Speaker's eye, and time flew on, and the great guns one by one returned —Peel, Graham, Goulburn, Hardinge, Herries, &c., &c., and

[1] *Letters,* pp. 135, 137.

I was obliged to shift my plan and my place, till I at last had
none at all. About 10 o'clock, I think, when standing behind
the Speaker's chair, Hardinge beckoned to me, and I seated
myself between him and Graham. He wanted to speak about
moving the new writ for Maidstone. Having got a place, I
did not leave it, although I ought to have done so, having
answered his question, and I asked Graham whether he
would speak. He said No, and recommended me, but very
kindly, not to try, as he said the House was noisy, tired, and
uninterested, and wanted to divide. So I gave it up for ever,
but just as I rose to quit my seat, Clay, who was speaking, sat
down, and the Speaker, imagining that I was going to rise
to speak, called my name.

I was in for it, put my hat down, advanced to the table, and
dashed along. I got the House still in a minute, I was heard
with the greatest attention and good humor immediately,
succeeded in all my points, though of course I made a much
shorter speech than I would have done at an early hour and
a thin house,—and at length sat down amid loud cheers, and
really principally from the Government side. No one cheered
me more vehemently than Hobhouse, who was a little drunk :
Poulett Thomson paid great attention, and Cutlar Fergusson,[1]
who cheered very much also, came up to me in the lobby, and
spoke as warmly as you possibly can imagine. I had no
acquaintance with him, which I had with Parker of the
Treasury, a slight one, but he came up and shook hands with
me, and said, 'All our people agree it was one of the best
speeches ever made on the subject.'

Lord John said nothing, but sat with his arms folded, and
watched me very attentively. I thought he looked malignant,
and there was a smile on his face ; but I did him injustice, for
I walked home with Ossulston, who had only come down for
the division, and he said to me, 'I understand you have made
a most brilliant speech to-night ; I wish I had been down.' I
replied I supposed he had heard it from some friend. 'Oh,'
he answered, 'Johnny, I have only seen Johnny, and he says
it was the best thing he had heard for a long time ; a great
thing for one so scant of laudation.' . . .

As for our own people, Graham, Goulburn and Hardinge
and good old Herries shook hands with me immediately.
When I had regained my place, I was removed too far for
notice from Chandos and Sir Robert Peel, but I heard their
cheers. As for all the other congratulations I received, it is
impossible to enumerate them. In the lobby, all the squires
came up to shake hands with me, and thank me for the good

---

[1] The Judge Advocate General.

service. They were so grateful, and well they might be, for certainly they had nothing to say for themselves. I think Sugden was more pleased than anyone. I saw Chandos afterwards at the Carlton, where I received great congratulations from everybody. I need not say he triumphed. Even Harcourt tried to say something pleasant, and everybody appeared to sympathise, except Sir W. Y.,[1] who grinned much the same ghastly smile as he would at Aylesbury. All our party noticed the great courtesy of the Whigs and the other side generally to me. In fact, I think I have become very popular in the House ; I ascribe it to the smoking-room. . . .

Strange to say, I got Jem in the House, and missed him after my speech ; I hope he heard it. Chandos detected him early in the evening.

' Disraeli, is your brother here ?'

' Yes.'

' I thought so (smiling) ; no mistaking him.'

He asked me at the Carlton where he was. I said I had missed him. ' I suppose he has gone to *market*,' says Chandos.

I have scribbled all this nonsense in marvellous haste.

D.

From Sarah Disraeli.

[*March* 17, 1838.]

MY DEAREST,

We were grateful for your long despatch. Jem told us enough to make us desire to hear what you felt. Now that 400 have heard you, I seem to care for nothing. It was James's *début* in the House, so that we did not know how much to trust to him. He describes the rush into the House as prodigious when you began to speak, and then the profound silence, and then all the cheers. He heard many people speak of you, rejoicing in your speech and your reception ; and once before you spoke Castlereagh rushed in, saying. ' Has Disraeli been up ?' It seemed by his account of all the sensation produced that you were quite as great a man at Westminster as at Aylesbury. . . .

God bless you, dearest !

Yours affectionately,

S. D.

To Mrs. Wyndham Lewis.

Sunday [*March* 25].

I am at this moment off for Maidstone,—that Maidstone where we have been so happy ! They have sent for me sud-

---

[1] Sir William Young, one of the members for Bucks. Chandos and Harcourt were the others.

denly, and I must go ; with a dull spirit and a heavy heart, I
need not assure you.   I send you this line because you will
not hear from me for a day or two, but I hope on my return
my messenger will assure me that you are as well, not as we
could wish, but as we can hope.   God bless you, dear friend.

D.

BRADENHAM,
April 16.

Exmouth[1] and myself arrived here for dinner on Saturday,
and found them all well, but my father this morning is menaced
by a fit of gout ; at least, I hope so, and that it is nothing
worse, but he leads such an extraordinary life that he never
complains of the slightest ache, that I am not miserably
nervous.   There was one gleam of sunshine as we approached
Bradenham which welcomed us ; but otherwise the weather is
cold and gusty, and there is not the slightest evidence of
springlike vegetation.   I agree with Gally Knight, who told
me the other day that he was no admirer of Eastering.   At
Whitsun one has a better chance of sunbeams and blossom. . . .

While I have been writing this, the whole county has
become as white as a twelfth cake.   Jem, who is in the room,
with six or seven dogs, desires his love to Mrs. Wyndham,
and makes such a barking that I can scarcely write.

There is no news from this place, which of course is little
altered, though somewhat improved, particularly a new walk
thro' the woods devised and cut by Jem, and which you
will like very much.

All send their love to you from this roof.

Yours,
D.

April 19, 1838.

My father's health gives me the greatest possible uneasiness.
Although an eldest son, it seems to me that I could scarcely
survive his loss.   The first wish of my life has ever been that
after all his kindness to me, and all the anxiety which I have
cost him, he should live to see me settled and steady, and successful to his heart's content.   I cannot describe to you my
misery at the thought of losing him ; but he complains of his
head, and many other strange symptoms, and yesterday when
we were alone he nearly fell.

BRADENHAM HOUSE,
Sunday [*April* 22].

I shall be in town on Tuesday night, as it is expected that
Serjeant Talfourd's motion on Copyright will come on on
Wednesday, and I intend to speak on it. . . .

---

[1] Third Viscount, 1811-1876, grandson of the victor of Algiers, and a good
and loyal friend of Disraeli's to the end of his life.

I leave this place with great regret, even tho' the sun do not shine. After a week or so, one gets used to quiet habits, and feels, as I always do, the charm of domestic bliss. I experience a reluctance in once more entering the scene of strife and struggle, but after all, like the shower bath, it needs only a plunge. I never leave home without feeling as I did when I went to school, which is an odd though true thing for one to say who has been such a wanderer. A return, however, makes me just as nervous. I dread to detect the progress of time, and always anticipate misfortune. . . .

I send you an emblem of the spring-flowers without perfume. Farewell !

Yours,
D.

When Talfourd's Copyright Bill came up for second reading, Disraeli fulfilled his intention of joining in the debate.

To Sarah Disraeli.

[*April* 26.]

MY DEAREST,

I made a most brilliant and triumphant speech last night —unquestionably and agreed upon by all hands the crack speech of the night, and everyone who spoke after me, either for or against, addressed himself to me ; but of this you cannot judge by the reports. C. Wynn, in speaking of Southey, confirmed ' the statement in the eloquent speech of the hon. member for Maidstone.' Poor little Milnes plastered me with compliments, but his own speech was entirely smashed by the reporters. The Ministers tried not to make a House. We had a sharp run, and I think I may fairly claim carrying the measure ; at least Talfourd gave me credit for it, as I sent to the Carlton at 9.30, and got down a couple of members and absolutely converted Blakemore, if no others. . . .

The whole day has been passed in receiving compliments on my speech. Sir James Graham, who was in the House, was really most warm ; but of all this when we meet.

Love,
D.[1]

As the law then stood, copyright subsisted for twenty-eight years or the duration of the author's life, whichever period was the longer ; and Talfourd's Bill proposed to extend it to sixty years from the date of the author's

---

[1] Brit. Mus., Addit. MSS.

death. 'Literary men,' said Disraeli in the speech of which he wrote with so much complacency, 'exercise great power, often an irresistible power ; and I would ask whether it is wise for this House to debar from the right of property in their works the creators of opinion.' In spite of his persuasive eloquence, the second reading was only carried by 39 to 34, and the Bill perished in Committee.[1]

To Mrs. Wyndham Lewis. •

CARLTON,
Friday, April 27.

It is natural, after such severe trials as you have recently experienced, and such petty vexations as you are now forced to encounter, that you should give way to feelings of loneliness and sorrow. It is natural and inevitable ; but you must not *indulge* such sentiments, and you must endeavour not to brood over the past. The future for you may yet be full of happiness and hope. You are too young to feel that life has not yet a fresh spring of felicity in store. Although you have few near relations, they are such as are dear to you ; a mother whom you love, and a brother to whose return you look forward not only with affection, but with the charm and excitement of novelty. And I can assure you that you have in my family friends in the best and sincerest sense of the word, who have from their first acquaintance with you loved and appreciated you.

As for myself, I can truly say, that the severe afflictions which you have undergone, and the excellent, and to me unexpected, qualities with which you have met them, the talent, firmness and sweet temper, will always make me your faithful friend, and as far as my advice and assistance and society can contribute to your welfare or solace you under these severe trials, you may count upon them. For, as you well know, I am one of those persons who feel much more deeply than I ever express, and if ever I express feelings of regard to anyone, my memory assures me that it is never any fault of mine if they are not fervently cherished and if they do not endure.

I fear that you are at present in a miserable circle of narrow-minded people, incapable of any generous emotion and any

---

[1] Talfourd renewed his efforts in subsequent sessions, but had the misfortune to encounter the opposition of Macaulay ; and it was not till 1842 that the Act was passed which remained in force till 1911. The Act of 1911 grants copyright for a period of fifty years from the author's death.

genial sympathy ; but this is an infliction that will not last, and I recommend you by all means to command your temper and watch over your interests. . . .

Every paper in London, Radical, Whig, or Tory, has spoken of my speech in the highest terms of panegyric, except the wretched *Standard*, which, under the influence of that scoundrel Maginn,[1] always attacked me before I was in Parliament, and now always passes over my name in silence. . . . Mrs. Dawson[2] stopped the carriage in the street yesterday to congratulate me, and her manner was most hearty and, I think, sincere. . . .

I look forward now with great interest to your return. *Expedite* but do not *hasten* it. Be active, but do not be in a hurry, or you will have to return once more to that odious place and those odious persons whom I hope will speedily be banished from our memories.

And now God bless you, and believe me,

Ever your affectionate friend,

D.

May 5.

Town is very agreeable, the weather soft and warm ; and I suppose the fields and trees have put on their spring liveries these last few days, as well as the households of our fine people here.

Yesterday I dined with the Londonderrys *en famille*, and only met Lord[3] and Lady Hardwicke ; but it was most agreeable, for Lady Hardwicke is without exception the most dramatic singer I ever listened to ; her voice, too, is most sweet and powerful, and she is so unaffected that she actually sang without stopping for so long a time that it was near one when our *petite comité* broke up. I never met persons who seemed to enjoy life more, or who seemed fonder of each other, than the Hardwickes. I have known Lord H. for some time, and met him first at Smyrna when he was only Captain Yorke, and always liked him, he is so frank and gay. They asked me to dine with them to-morrow, but I am engaged to the Salisburys, which I regret.

All the world is talking of the grand festival which is to be given in Merchant Taylors' Hall by the Conservative members of Parliament to Sir Robert Peel. I am, of course, one of the hosts. It is to be one of the most magnificent and important gatherings ever witnessed. There is a gallery which

[1] See Vol. I., p. 69.
[2] A sister of Sir Robert Peel's and a great friend of Mrs. Wyndham Lewis's.
[3] The 4th Earl. His wife was a daughter of the 1st Lord Ravensworth.

will hold 70 ladies. Tickets to admit them were offered to Lady Peel, but she declined the dangerous honor, confident that the selection would create ill feeling : so the 70 ladies' tickets are to be balloted for by all the hosts. Every *grande dame* is mad to get a ticket. I know to whom I should venture to offer mine were she in London or could go, but I suppose, or rather feel, that is impossible.

The Chesterfields had the audacity to ask 5,000 guineas for the loan of their house to the Russian Ambassador Extraordinary,[1] and absolutely expected to get it. Lady Jersey asked 2,000. Lady Londonderry thought all this house-letting *infra dig.*, and had the spirit to write to the Empress, who had been most hospitable to herself and Lord L. when in Russia, and offered Holdernesse House and the whole establishment to the Grand Duke, who is coming over ; intending themselves to go into a hired house. The offer was declined by the Empress in a letter in English beautifully and correctly written, both in style and calligraphy, and in which she signs herself 'With reiterated love, your affectionate Alexandra.'

On the 19th Lord Chandos gives a grand banquet to the Duke of Wellington, Lord Lyndhurst, Lord and Lady Londonderry, Lord and Lady Jersey, Sir Robert and Lady Peel, Sir James and Lady Graham, and Lord Stanley. You will be rather surprised, I think—at least I was—that I should be invited to it : but Chandos is a good friend, and greatly triumphs in my success in the House.

I must cease at present all this gossip, which I thought would amuse you after your journey. Pray come to town cheerful and happy, and believe in a happy and brilliant future like

Your affectionate
D.

Sunday [*May* 20].

Your exquisite offering arrived just in time, and added by its opportune arrival to all the grace of the present. I assure you that with unaffected delight I felt that for the first time in public I wore *your chains*. I hope you are not ashamed of your slave.

I am sorry to say the Duke [of Wellington] continues so unwell that he could not join the party, which otherwise was very brilliant, and even gay. . . . The plate at Buckingham House is marvellous ; not merely costly, but rare, and the rooms are crammed with all possible curiosities and nicknacks, the spoils of our friend Emanuel, &c., for all which things Chandos has a passion. It is just the house to suit you.

---

[1] To the Coronation.

For guests we had the Londonderrys, Jerseys, Peels, Sir James and Lady Graham, Lyndhurst, Goulburn, Mahon, Sir H. Hardinge. All admired Lady Anna Grenville,[1] our host's only daughter, just presented.

I fear much the heavens do not smile on your Richmond expedition. I could only be consoled for not meeting to-day by the conviction that you were at least receiving pleasure, but Richmond on a rainy day is certainly not Paradise, though sometimes I have fancied it such when the sun was shining. . . .
Farewell! I am happy if you are.

Yours,
DIS.

For Disraeli, with his native love of pageantry and splendour, a rare opportunity was now drawing near. The Coronation of Queen Victoria was fixed for the end of June, and few in the thronging multitudes who were in London at the time can have felt a keener joy than he in the spectacles and festivities for which the ceremony gave occasion.

To Sarah Disraeli.

Monday [June 25].

MY DEAREST,
London is now very gay. The whole of the line of procession is nearly covered with galleries and raised seats; when these are clothed with carpets and colored hangings the effect will be superb. London teems with foreigners. There are full 200 (*on dit*) of distinction, attached to the different embassies, and lodged in every possible hotel from Mivart to Sablonière. Lord F. Egerton told me this morning that he had been paying a visit to a brace of Italian princes in the last-named crib on a third floor, and never in the dirtiest locanda of the Levant, Smyrna, or Alexandria, had he visited a more filthy and offensive scene; but they seemed to enjoy it, and are visible every night, with their brilliant uniforms and sparkling stars, as if their carriage at break of dawn were not changed into a pumpkin.

Your geranium gave me a flower to-day, and will give me a couple more. I have bought also a promising plant myself.
My love to all.

D.

[1] Afterwards Lady Anna Gore-Langton, mother of the 4th Earl Temple of Stowe.

[*Undated.*]

We had a very agreeable party at D'Orsay's yesterday. Zichy, who has cut out even Esterhazy, having two jackets, one of diamonds more brilliant than E.'s, and another which he wore at the Drawing-room yesterday of turquoises. This makes the greatest sensation of the two. He speaks English perfectly; is a great traveller, been to Nubia, all over Asia, and to Canada and the United States. Then there was the Duke of Ossuna, a young man, but a grandee of the highest grade. He is neither Carlist nor Christino, and does not mean to return to Spain until they have settled everything. Therefore they have confiscated his estates, but he has a large property in Italy, and also Belgium. He is a great dandy and looks like Philip II., but though the only living descendant of the Borgias, he has the reputation of being very amiable. When he was last at Paris he attended a representation of Victor Hugo's *Lucrezia Borgia*. She says in one of the scenes, ' Great crimes are in our blood.' All his friends looked at him with an expression of fear; 'but the blood has degenerated,' he said, ' for I have committed only weaknesses.' Then there was the real Prince Poniatowsky, also young and with a most brilliant star. Then came Kissiloffs and Strogonoffs, ' and other offs and ons,' and De Belancour, a very agreeable person. Lyndhurst, Gardner, Bulwer, and myself completed the party.

I must give up going to the coronation, as we go in state, and all the M.P.s *must* be in court dresses or uniforms. As I have withstood making a costume of this kind for other purposes, I will not make one now, and console myself by the conviction that to get up very early (eight o'clock), to sit dressed like a flunky in the Abbey for seven or eight hours, and to listen to a sermon by the Bishop of London, can be no great enjoyment.

Lyndhurst made a very successful speech the other night on Spain, and foreign politics are coming into fashion.

D.

June 29.

I went to the coronation after all. I did not get a dress till 2.30 on the morning of the ceremony, but it fitted me very well. It turned out that I had a very fine leg, which I never knew before ! The pageant within the Abbey was without exception the most splendid, various, and interesting affair at which I ever was present. To describe is of course useless. I had one of the best seats in the Abbey, indeed our House had the best of everything. I am very glad indeed that Ralph persuaded me to go, for it far exceeded my expectations. The Queen looked very well, and performed her part with great grace and completeness, which cannot in general be said of the other performers ; they were always in doubt as to what came next, and you saw the want of rehearsal. The Duke was loudly cheered when he made his homage. Melbourne looked very awkward and uncouth, with his coronet cocked over his nose, his robes under his feet, and holding the great sword of state like a butcher. . . . The Duchess of Sutherland [1] walked, or rather stalked, up the Abbey like Juno ; she was full of her situation. Lady Jersey [2] and Lady Londonderry blazed among the peeresses. [3]

[*July* 2.]

The beautiful lady [mentioned in a newspaper] was my friend the Countess Sablonouska, the beauty of the season. She did not sit with the foreign Ambassadors, but was led into the Abbey by a Russian nobleman to her seat among the fairest of the visitors opposite.

The Queen behaved with great grace and feeling about Lord Rolle : nothing could be more effective. She seemed for an instant to pause whether etiquette would allow her to rise from her throne, and then did so and held out her hand with infinite dignity and yet delicate sentiment.

Lyndhurst, as I think I told you, paid his homage with singular dignity, but committed the *faux pas* of not backing from the presence. Fanny [Lady Londonderry] looked an Empress. Her fête is put off on account of the Queen's ball to-night.

Exmouth paid his homage very well, but complained terribly of the weight of his robes and coronet, which were made for his grandfather at George IV.'s Coronation, and the old lord was a very tall, stout, burly man. I have got a gold medal given me as M.P., but I have presented it to Mrs. Wyndham.

O'Connell was in a Court dress and looked very well, and was deeply interested in everything, but was hooted greatly, *on dit*, by the mob. Hume, who would not put on Court attire, was prevented from sitting in our gallery, but was in the Abbey. I think I told you of Fector's [4] gorgeous suit ; it has been noticed in the papers. When we two got into his chariot, that cantankerous Norreys halloed out, ' *Make room for the Maidstone Sheriffs !*' Very good, I think, though rather annoying.

---

[1] The Mistress of the Robes.
[2] Sarah, eldest daughter of the 10th Earl of Westmorland by his wife the heiress of Robert Child the banker.
[3] *Letters*, pp. 138-140.　　　　[4] The new member for Maidstone.

Bulwer I did not see ; he certainly was not in the House. . . .

The procession was, I think, rather a failure : heavy, want of variety, and not enough music or troops. There are so few troops in the country, that they cannot get up a review in Hyde Park for Soult, and keep on the fair, they are so ashamed.

I saw Lord Ward after the ceremony, in a retiring room, drinking champagne out of a pewter pot, his coronet cocked aside, his robes disordered, and his arms akimbo, the very picture of Rochester.

Wednesday [July 4].

DEAREST SA,

. . . There was a very brilliant ball at the Salisburys' last night, all the remarkables and illustrious in whom London now abounds being there. I stayed till 2, but there were then no signs of separation, and the supper-room was just open. By-the-bye, the Countess Zavodouska, for I believe that is her name, appears quite the reigning beauty of the season, and moves surrounded by a crowd of glittering admirers. She did me the honour of remembering me, though not in Turkish costume, and told me she had read *Vivian Grey.*

Exmouth came up to Theodore Hook, full of indignation at the 31 Baronets in the night's Gazette. ' Thirty-one Baronets ! Here's a pretty game of the Whigs !' says he. ' They'll make a bloody hand of it, at any rate,' said Theodore.

The same wit and worthy was abusing the foreigners, and particularly Prince Poniatowsky, who, *on dit*, is anxious to turn the rich and pretty Mrs. Craven into a Princess. ' I suppose he can't show his face in his own land, the Radical scamp,' said T. H. Whereupon he was informed the Prince was no Rad, and had refused the crown of Poland. ' *Peut-être*,' replied Theodore. ' He may have refused a crown, but he looks very much now as if he would accept half a crown.'

The foreigners thought that Lord Rolle's tumble was a tenure by which he held his barony.

I hope you are all well, and I send you my love.

D.

Tuesday [July 11].

MY DEAREST,

Yesterday, the day being perfect, there was a splendid review in Hyde Park. I saw it admirably from Mrs. Wynd-ham's.[1] The Delawarrs, Rolles, Lawrence Peels, and Dawsons were there, but no one was allowed to be on the drawing-room floor, lest there should be an appearance of a party, except old Lord Rolle and myself to be his companion. Lord R. sat

---

[1] Her house was No. 1, Grosvenor Gate, now 29, Park Lane.

in the balcony with a footman each side of him, as is his custom. The Londonderrys after the review gave the most magnificent banquet at Holdernesse House conceivable. Nothing could be more *recherché*. There were only 150 asked, and all sat down. Fanny was faithful, and asked me, and I figure in the *Morning Post* accordingly. It was the finest thing of the season. Londonderry's regiment being reviewed, we had the band of the 10th playing on the staircase : the whole of the said staircase (a double one) being crowded with the most splendid orange-trees and Cape jessamines ; the Duke of Nemours, Soult, all the ' illustrious strangers,' the Duke and the very flower of fashion being assembled. The banquet was in the gallery of sculpture ; it was so magnificent that everybody lost their presence of mind. Sir James Graham said to me that he had never in his life seen anything so gorgeous. ' This is the *grand seigneur* indeed,' he added. I think it was the kindest thing possible of Fanny asking me, as it was not to be expected in any way. The splendor of the uniforms was remarkable.

Love,
D.[1]

A fortnight later we find him on the way to his constituents at Maidstone.

To Mrs. Wyndham Lewis.

ROCHESTER,
July 26.

Pressed as I am for time, wet, which is at least a novelty, hungry with no chance of my appetite being gratified, and about to make a speech of which I have not an idea ready, I send you this scrawl from a wretched pot-house, to tell you that you have not been the whole day a moment absent from my thoughts.

MAIDSTONE,
July 27.

I arrived here just a quarter of an hour before the meeting. Under the inspiration of a glass of brandy and water at Rochester, and the racket of the post-chaise, I contrived to collect some nonsense which turned into a capital speech ; but what I shall say at the dinner to-day I can't devise, having exhausted every possible topic of congratulation to our friends and of triumph over our foes. Let me avail myself of this moment, which I seize in a room full of bustle and chatter, to tell you how much I love you.

<hr>

[1] Brit. Mus., Addit. MSS.

To Sarah Disraeli.

[*July* 29.]

On Friday the Randalls gave a grand breakfast to the principal members of the party, which was well done, and 'equal to anything of the kind,' as they say.   But only conceive a grand *déjeuner* scarcely over at 3.30, and a grand dinner at 5.30 !   I took a walk into the country, as it was in vain to pay visits. We dined 107, more than the room could hold.   I had to make another speech ; never began a sentence with the slightest idea of its termination ; really in a funk, but never made a more successful one.   But to speak plainly, the two speeches cost me great efforts at the moment.   I never racked my brain so much, but it answered to the helm.

[*August.*]

The ball at Holdernesse House was a very brilliant affair. I was introduced to Lord Brougham by Lady William Powlett, and Sir Lytton[1] also made his appearance.   I spoke the other night after O'Connell, and with spirit and success.   I thought it as well that my voice should be heard at the end of the session, and especially on an Irish subject.   There were only eight Tories in the House, the subject having been brought on unexpectedly and without notice, and Brougham speaking in the Lords, which takes men away.   The Whig benches were tolerably full, as they had made a whip.[2]

This speech was a vigorous indictment of the Irish policy of the Government on the occasion of their abandoning an Irish Corporations Bill which the Lords had drastically amended.   It was characteristic of Disraeli that, having begun the session with a failure in speaking on an Irish subject immediately after O'Connell, he should have determined to bring it to a close by making a successful effort in a precisely similar situation.

[1] Bulwer, who had just been made a baronet.
[2] *Letters*, pp. 142, 143.

CHAPTER II.

MARRIAGE.

1838-1839.

Disraeli's thoughts were now again turned towards matrimony, and, as the reader has no doubt guessed, he was by this time fully satisfied that he had found the lady for his choice. The accident of his election for Maidstone had given to the 'pretty little woman,' the 'flirt,' and the 'rattle,' whose volubility had astonished him when he met her first at Bulwer's in 1832, a part among the principal actors in the drama of his life. Mrs. Wyndham Lewis, before marriage Mary Anne Evans, was born in 1792, the daughter of John Evans, a Lieutenant in the navy. Her father died on active service while she was still an infant, leaving his widow with two children in something less than affluence—a circumstance which has given rise to purely fanciful stories of a very humble origin for the future Lady Beaconsfield. In those days the navy, which was just about to enter on the period of its greatest achievements, offered a more open road to merit than perhaps any other English institution ; and Evans, joining as a lad, had had to make his way from the bottom of the service before winning his commission. But he appears to have come of a respectable farming stock in Devon,[1] and his wife, a Viney, belonged

[1] His parents lived at Brampford Speke, a village a few miles from Exeter, and there it is usually stated that Lady Beaconsfield was born ; but her birthplace would appear to have been Exeter itself, where in the register of baptisms for the parish of St. Sidwell there is the entry, under date Nov. 14, 1792 : ' Marianne, daughter of John and Eleanor Evans.'

to a family of good position and connexion in the West
of England. Beautiful though dowerless, their daughter
at twenty-three had won the hand of Wyndham Lewis,
a man of birth and fortune, who was then member for
Cardiff, and who at a later date became one of the two
members for Maidstone. The election of 1837 gave the
other seat to Disraeli, and Mrs. Lewis, as we have
seen,[1] at the very beginning of the closer acquaintance
which followed this event, divined the genius of her
husband's colleague, made him her ' Parliamentary *pro-
tégé*,' and prophesied his coming greatness ; while Disraeli in his turn rewarded her with a friendship that
was cordial from the first, and gradually became tinged
with a sort of mock devotion. The death of Wyndham
Lewis had of course changed their relations, and made
it necessary that they should be either more or less to
each other in future. Mrs. Lewis was now a widow, and
though she was already forty-five, twelve years older
than Disraeli, she was still by all accounts wonderfully
youthful for her years ; and, with this advantage in her
favour, there is no reason to believe that she varied in her
practice from the kindly race of women, or allowed her
suitor to suspect the real disparity in their ages. She
had been left with a house[2] in London and a good income[3]
for life, and the world has always assumed that in these
accessories is to be sought the explanation of that which
followed. But though Disraeli himself confessed, as we
shall see at a later stage, that when he first made his
advances he was prompted thereto by no romantic feelings, we shall find, nevertheless, good reasons for thinking
that the judgment of the world may stand in need of
revision.

[1] Vol. I., p. 376.
[2] No. 1, Grosvenor Gate, now 29, Park Lane. This, which more than
any other became Disraeli's house in London, alone remains unmarked by
tablet or inscription.
[3] At first, apparently, about £4,000 a year, and rather more later.

To Mrs. Wyndham Lewis.

Aug. 20, 1838.

The sun shines, and Bradenham looks beautiful ; most green and fresh, and to-day even bright. But you are not here. Come, and prithee quickly ; for though these people are kind and good, and as amusing as any other honest folk in the shires, their talk is insipid after all that bright play of fancy and affection which welcomes me daily with such vivacious sweetness.

Oct. 7.

I have not recovered from the stupefaction of yesterday. [when Mrs. Lewis had left after a long visit to Bradenham]. I have scarcely left my room, scarcely spoken to anyone. All is dull, silent, spiritless ; the charm is broken, the magic is fled !

All this may be inevitable, and I will believe it all may end well. But what future joy and prosperity, what fortune, even what fame, can compensate for this anguish ?

Oct. 9.

I have made up my mind to leave this place to-morrow, in order that I may have the delight of a day or two with your own sweet self. . . . I have not been out of the house since you left it, until this afternoon, having been in a state of apathy, a dull trance. This morning I rose pretty cheerful, was inspired by your letter, worked very well at the tragedy, recasting the great scene, greatly improving it, and writing a magnificent soliloquy. When the first act is complete you shall have it.

Love had driven him to poetry, as had happened once before. On the earlier occasion, to use a phrase[1] of his own, he had made an attempt ' to strike the long-mute strings of the epick lyre,' and with characteristic courage he now embarked on a still more risky venture—the composition of a great tragedy. Under the leadership of Macready there had been in recent years a marked revival of interest in serious drama. Talfourd's *Ion* had been produced in 1836, and had been followed at no long interval by Bulwer's *Lady of Lyons*. Disraeli was determined not to be behindhand, and set to work on *Alarcos*.

---

[1] In a letter to Lord Mahon.

To Sarah Disraeli.

[LONDON, *Oct.* 11.]

DEAREST,

. . . I understand that the trousseau of Julia Macdonald surpassed in fancy and splendor all late exhibitions, which, considering that her family collectively have not a sou, was surprising. She was married in a dress of white velvet with three flounces of point lace, and departed in a white silk costume with a trimming of birds of paradise feathers. But the most wonderful thing was D'Orsay's present to the bridegroom —a white silk waistcoat, *brodé* in gold, from Paris; the design by the Count, who was at the wedding. This surpassed anything ever seen. I shall call on him to-morrow. . . .

Sir Robert Peel very well and very courteous indeed. I chatted this morning an hour with Lyndhurst, who looks younger and brisker than ever—much. I never saw him so well. . . . Love.

D.[1]

. [LONDON, *Oct.* 13.]

DEAREST,

I called on D'Orsay yesterday, and found him very flourishing. He asked me to dine with him to-day to celebrate his birthday, but I was obliged, though with great regret, to docline. It is all lies about Macready, who goes on with the Theatre. . . .[2]

The Gibsons, George Wombwell, and Stapleton dined at Grosvenor Gate yesterday. There has been a row at Crockford's, and Ude dismissed. He told the committee he was worth £4,000 a year. Their new man is quite a failure, so I think the great artist may yet return from Elba. He told Wombwell that, in spite of his £4,000 a year, he was miserable in retirement ; that he sat all day with his hands before him doing nothing. Wombwell suggested the exercise of his art for the gratification of his own appetite. 'Bah !' he said, 'I have not been into my kitchen once : I hate the sight of my kitchen. I dine on roast mutton dressed by a cookmaid.' He shed tears, and said that he had only been twice in St. James's Street since his retirement, which was in September, and that he made it a rule never to walk on the same side as the Clubhouse. 'Ah, I love that Club, though they are *ingrats*. Do not be offended, Mr. W., if I do not take my hat off to you when we meet ; but I have made a vow that I will

---

[1] Brit. Mus., Addit. MSS.
[2] Covent Garden, where he was then playing *The Lady of Lyons.*

never take my hat off to a member of the Committee.' 'I shall always take my hat off to you, Mr. Ude.'

Love,

D.

To Mrs. Wyndham Lewis.

BRADENHAM,
Oct. 14.

This morning all the dahlias have disappeared, and the rigor of the night has been fatal to even sweeter things than they ; among them I grieve to say our favorite heliotrope. Tita is very blank about the vanishing of his favorites. I cannot say that I am happy, because that would not be true, but I exert myself to bear up against my sorrowful lot. My present feelings convince me of what I have ever believed, that there is no hell on earth like separated love.

Oct. 18.

I wrote your name in large characters and placed it before me. I remembered your parting injunctions. I poured all my spirit into my tragedy. The effort was great and painful, but as my brain warmed and my spirit rose, it was successful. I wrote all yesterday without ceasing. I did not go down to dinner, and never left my room till the evening. My imagination solaced me, for I poured into the fictitious scene my actual sensations, and the pages teem with passages which you will not read without emotion, for they came from my heart and they commemorate my love, my doubt, my misery. Your name was before me, the name of her who is my inspiration, my hope, perhaps my despair. . . .

I believe in [your promised visit] as men believe in the millennium. My faith is firm, but I cannot help sometimes reminding myself that my creed is in the impossible.

Oct. 19.

In health I am well ; which I ascribe to my ascetic diet, and the magic of cayenne, which has as completely removed all my nervous sensations of discomfort as Guinness did last year, so you have saved me twice. I rise early, and have worked yesterday and to-day from 9 to 2, breakfasting at 11. Beyond 2 I cannot write, and pass the day as well as I can ; reading a play, sauntering when it is genial as to-day, which was even balmy, and ever thinking of my sweet love. My progress has been great and brilliant ; you know I am not easily satisfied with my efforts, and not in the habit of speaking of my writings with much complacency. You may therefore credit there is some foundation when I tell you, that I think my present work will far exceed your expectations, and realise even my hopes. . . . I envy the gentlemen about you, but I am not jealous. When the eagle leaves you the vultures return. There ! that is sublime.

There is hardly a flower to be found, but I have sent you a few sweet-peas.

Oct. 23.

I write in good health and in good spirits. I prosper in my work. I am satisfied with what I have done. I look upon my creation and see that it is good. Health, my clear brain, and your fond love ;—and I feel that I can conquer the world.

Oct. 25.

Your letter recalls to me most fully, vividly, and painfully, the wretchedness of my situation, separated from my love, and what must be the inevitable result of our present life— fading emotion and final estrangement. I can write at no length to-day. The immortal gods, wherever and whatever they be, grant that the future may be different to what my prophetic soul paints it !

Oct. 29.

. . . I cannot reconcile Love and separation. My ideas of Love are the perpetual enjoyment of the society of the sweet being to whom I am devoted, the sharing of every thought and even every fancy, of every charm and every care. Perhaps I sigh for a state which never can be mine, which never existed. But there is nothing in my own heart that convinces me it is impossible, and if it be an illusion it is an illusion worthy of the gods. I wish to be with you, to live with you, never to be away from you—I care not where, in heaven or on earth, or in the waters under the earth. . . .

I would have written on Friday, but was really too unhappy. So I sauntered about thinking of you, and gleaned, for we can no longer gather, flowers which I sent to you, and which I amused myself by dexterously packing in franks ; for, to tell the truth, I spoiled more covers than one before I could stow them, which with the united aid of scissors and patience I at last contrived to succeed in. . . .

I thank you much for your political news, which is of great use to me, as I can make up a letter for Chandos, who complains of my no longer writing to him, and all that, but, alas ! I have nothing to say, nor, to tell the truth, do I care as of yore about politics. For love swalloweth up all things. . . .

I have lost all heart for my tragedy. I always aim in all I do at the highest. I see no use in writing tragedies unless they be as fine as Shakespeare's ; and as that is impossible to

attain, what am I to do ?   In Fame as well as Love, my motto
is ' All or Nothing,' because I prefer happy obscurity to
mediocre reputation.

Oct. 30.

The storm here was a hurricane. It broke our drawing-
room windows, peeled the lead off our roof, and tore up about
thirty trees, some valuable—ten young oaks in the coppice, the
only large elm we had, and the large laburnum at the end of
the terrace.   As for our orchards, there are cherry and apple
trees in all directions, as if the devil had been riding about on
a broomstick. . . .

I have heard nothing from Maidstone, and probably shall
not.   They seem to wish to saddle the money that is minus
on me, which of course is too ridiculous, so we shall quarrel.
We may as well do it at once, as they will doubtless throw me
over eventually.

Meanwhile he had contrived to provoke a quarrel with
the lawyers, antagonists more redoubtable than even
O'Connell, and won by his bearing not a little credit,
though in a sense he had to accept defeat and humiliation.   The by-election at Maidstone caused by the death
of Wyndham Lewis had been followed by a petition
against the successful Conservative candidate ; and in
opening the case for the petitioners, Charles Austin,[1] their
counsel, had made certain statements which seemed to
amount to a charge that Disraeli at the general election
had promised bribes to electors, and afterwards failed to
pay them.   The proceedings in the petition came to a
premature end through the respondent's resignation,[2]
and, finding himself thus deprived of the opportunity of
clearing himself before the committee of inquiry, Disraeli with characteristic impulsiveness sent a letter [3] to
the newspapers in which he repelled the charge with all
his customary emphasis, and, not content with this, proceeded, equally in his customary manner, to make a
vigorous counter-attack :

In opening the case of the petitioners against the return
of Mr. Fector for Maidstone on Friday last, Mr. Austin stated

---

[1] Macaulay's brilliant contemporary at Cambridge, and a younger brother
of John Austin, the jurist.

[2] He was at once re-elected.   [3] Dated June 5, 1838.

that ' Mr. Disraeli, at the general election, had entered into engagements with the electors of Maidstone, and made pecuniary promises to them, which he had left unfulfilled.'

I should have instantly noticed this assertion of the learned gentleman had not a friend, to whose opinion I was bound to defer, assured me that Mr. Austin, by the custom of his profession, was authorised to make any statement from his brief which he was prepared to substantiate, or to attempt to sub stantiate.

The inquiry into the last Maidstone election has now terminated, and I take the earliest opportunity of declaring, and in a manner the most unqualified and unequivocal, that the statement of the learned gentleman is utterly false. There is not the slightest shadow of a foundation for it. I myself never, either directly or indirectly, entered into any pecuniary engagements with, or made any pecuniary promises to, the electors of Maidstone, and therefore I cannot have broken any or left any unfulfilled. The whole expenses of the contest in question were defrayed by my lamented colleague, and I discharged to him my moiety of those expenses, as is well known to those who are entitled to any knowledge on the subject.

I am informed that it is quite useless, and even unreasonable, in me to expect from Mr. Austin any satisfaction for those impertinent calumnies, because Mr. Austin is a member of an honourable profession, the first principle of whose practice appears to be that they may say anything provided they be paid for it. The privilege of circulating falsehoods with impunity is delicately described as doing your duty towards your client, which appears to be a very different process to doing your duty towards your neighbour. This may be the usage of Mr. Austin's profession, and it may be the custom to society to submit to its practice ; but, for my part, it appears to me to be nothing better than a disgusting and intolerable tyranny, and I, for one, shall not bow to it in silence.

I therefore repeat that the statement of Mr. Austin was false, and, inasmuch as he never attempted to substantiate it, I conclude that it was, on his side, but the blustering artifice of a rhetorical hireling, availing himself of the vile licence of a loose-tongued lawyer, not only to make a statement which was false, but to make it with a consciousness of its falsehood.

His aim, it would appear, was to provoke a challenge. ' Anything,' he wrote to Mrs. Wyndham Lewis, ' is better than submitting to an insult. I am perfectly cool and perfectly prepared for him. But I fear there is no chivalry nowadays, and I dare say the fellow will not do what he ought.' His anticipations were realised, as the next letter shows :

To Mrs. Wyndham Lewis.

Mr. Austin does not fight, but applies to the Court of Queen's Bench. There is a great flutter among the lawyers, and there was a meeting, and the Attorney-General in the chair. I would have preferred a more expeditious and cheaper process of settling the business ; but at any rate it may save you some suffering, and this shall be my consolation. . . .

All my friends, and more than my friends, say that the letter was the best ever written, and that Austin is a poltroon to take the step he has adopted.

On the application of the Attorney-General, Lord Denman granted a rule nisi for a criminal information. Austin declared in his affidavit that his charges had been directed, not against Disraeli personally, but against the political party which had supported him, and when the matter came before the court Disraeli's counsel expressed his client's regret that he should have taken a step which would have been unnecessary if he had known the truth of the matter. The court, however, held that this apology was insufficient, and the rule was made absolute. Judgment on the criminal information was allowed to go by default, but when Disraeli appeared to receive sentence he addressed the court in a long speech in mitigation of punishment which is not the least famous or interesting of his efforts :

I will for a short time avail myself of the merciful permission of the Bench to offer some observations which, I think, may induce it to visit this misdemeanour in a spirit of leniency. I stand before the court confessedly guilty, not from any dislike to enter into an investigation of the circumstances which have induced me to commit this trespass, but because I have been advised that, whatever the moral effect might be, the legal effect could be but one—namely, a conviction. . . . It would be affectation in me to pretend that the (I will say, unfortunate) letter which has originated these proceedings was written for the atmosphere of Westminster Hall. . . . I

confess my feelings at that moment were considerably excited. I had lived to learn by experience that calumny once
circulated is more or less for ever current. . . . I found it
necessary to take a step which should cope with the calumny,
and which should be decisive. Two courses alone were open
to me. I might have gone down to my seat in the House of
Commons, and might have treated it as a breach of privilege.
I might have made the observations I afterwards wrote, and,
as your lordships know, I might have done so there with
impunity ; but I had a wish not to shield myself under my
privilege. Late at night I wrote this unfortunate letter, and
sent it instantly to all the newspapers. . . . I did not consider that the system of bribery spoken of by Mr. Austin
prevailed in any borough—certainly it did not in Maidstone.
. . . But . . . admitting there was such a system . . . I
must say the introduction of my name was most grievous and
most unwarranted. . . .

I regret what I have done. I not only feel regret, but great
mortification, for what I have done. I am sorry I should have
injured the feelings of any man who had not attempted to
injure me. I am sorry that through misconception I should
have said anything that could for a moment have annoyed
the mind of a gentleman of the highest honor and integrity.
I should myself be satisfied with that expression of deep
regret and mortification. But, my lords, from the manner
in which this declaration is couched, from several expressions
that have fallen at various times during these proceedings,
from the animus which has characterised them within and
without these walls, I cannot help fearing that I am brought
here by one of those fictions of law of which I have read, and
it is not so much for an offence against the law as an offence
against lawyers that I am now awaiting judgment. . . . My
lords, I am not desirous of vindicating the expressions used
in that letter in reference to the profession, any more than the
expressions used in reference to the individual. . . . I cannot
forget that from the Bar of England have sprung many of our
most illustrious statesmen, past and present ; . . . but I have
ever believed, I believe at this moment—I see no libel in
the expression of that belief, no want of taste, under the circumstances of the case, in expressing it even here—that there is
in the principles on which the practice of that Bar is based a
taint of arrogance; I will not say audacity, but of that reckless
spirit which is the necessary consequence of the possession and
the exercise of irresponsible power. . . .

I confess that I myself have imbibed an opinion that it is
the duty of a counsel to his client to assist him by all possible
means, just or unjust, and even to commit, if necessary, a

crime for his assistance or extrication. My lords, this may be an outrageous opinion ; but, my lords, it is not my own. Allow me to read a description of the duty of a counsel to a client, and by a great authority : ' An advocate, by the sacred duty which he owes his client, knows in the discharge of that office but one person in the world—that client and none other. To save that client by all expedient means, to protect that client at all hazards and costs to all others, and among others to himself, is the highest and most unquestioned of his duties ; and he must not regard the alarm, the suffering, the torment, the destruction, which he may bring upon any other. Nay, separating even the duties of a patriot from those of an advocate, and casting them, if need be, to the wind, he must go on, reckless of the consequences, if his fate it should unhappily be, to involve his country in confusion for his client's protection.' Here, my lords, is a sketch, and by a great master ; here, my lords, is the *rationale* of the duties of an advocate, and drawn up by a Lord Chancellor[1] ! . . .

My lords, I have done. I leave my case with confidence to your merciful consideration, briefly recapitulating the points on which I have attempted to place myself fairly before the Bench and the public. As to my offence against the law, I throw myself on your lordships' mercy ; as to my offence against the individual, I have made him that reparation which a gentleman should, under the circumstances, cheerfully offer, and with which a gentleman should, in my opinion, be cheerfully content. I make this, my lords, not to avoid the consequences of my conduct, for, right or wrong, good or bad, these consequences I am ever ready to encounter ; but because I am anxious to soothe the feelings which I have unjustly injured, and evince my respect to the suggestions of the Bench. But as to my offence against the Bar, I do with the utmost confidence appeal to your lordships, however you may disapprove of my opinions, however objectionable, however offensive, even however odious, they may be to you, that you will not permit me to be arraigned for one offence and punished for another. In a word, my lords, it is to the Bench I look with confidence to shield me from the vengeance of an irritated and powerful profession.[2]

Disraeli had submitted, but his submission was far from abject. In presence of the majesty of the law he had contrived, in fact, to repeat, though in more decorous language, the substance of the offending letter. The

---

[1] Brougham, in his speech in defence of Queen Caroline.
[2] From *The Times* of Nov. 23, 1838.

Attorney-General, however, accepted the rather dubious apology as 'ample,' and the court decided that it could with propriety pass over the offence unpunished. Denman was already involved in the dispute with the House of Commons which arose out of the case of Stockdale, the printer, and he and the other lawyers may have thought that it was more prudent not to provoke a second. They can hardly have believed that the honours really rested with them, and they were probably well aware that the sympathies of the lay world were wholly with their antagonist.

To Mrs. Wyndham Lewis.

LONDON,
Nov. 23.

I saw Lord Chandos to-day, passing through town to Avington, the Duke's seat in Hants. I have arranged to be with him at Xmas, which will exactly suit your plans. He was most kind, as he ever is, and warm about the speech and the 'pluck' (his own word) of the whole affair. He thinks to face lawyers is the boldest of achievements. But the most agreeable thing that happened to me was Lord Abinger[1] coming up, with whom I had a long conversation. His praise was great but discriminating. The quotation from Brougham he thought most apposite and admirable ; and he talked to me a great deal of the principles, so different from those then expressed, on which he always conducted his professional pursuits.

BRADENHAM,
Nov. 26.

I came down by a new engine called the North Star (on the Western Railroad), of enormous and unprecedented power. We were only 42 minutes reaching Maidenhead, which is at the rate of 36 miles an hour. It is the only satisfactory piece of railroad travelling I ever performed. By this means I got home by dinner-time, the bell sounding as I just touched the green.

I found them all very well, and my father very much delighted about the speech, which he thinks the best thing that has happened to me for a long time. I am glad to say the *Examiner* and *Spectator*, though Whig and Radical papers, gave the greatest encomiums for ' spirit and feeling,' especially the *Spectator*, which praised the whole affair very much. . . .

---

[1] The Lord Chief Baron.

I have not been out since my return, since I have not been sorry to have a little lazy quiet to calm my mind and collect my ideas. I pulled my papers out this morning, and warmed up a little, and hope that to-morrow will find me at my accustomed task !

Nov. 29.

I can tell you nothing, but that I love you, and, indeed, am so ill and stupid that I should not be surprised if you doubted it from this very weak expression. I have received a good many letters and papers from town about the speech, but that is now a stale affair. You will be glad to hear that all lawyers of all parties agree in its eulogium, and especially Follett,[1] who said at the Carlton more than I care to repeat But I know you like to hear of these things.

Dec. 2.

I have been in bed almost ever since I last wrote to you, but I trust I have now thrown off this attack [of influenza]. You know what a vile lowering disorder it is. . . . I try to think of my tragedy ; but I am convinced that to write a great tragedy is the *chef-d'œuvre* of literary skill; and that with the finest poetic genius, and even dramatic nature, one may fail. Of all compositions, it requires the utmost skill and practice, and profound conception. If mine ever appear, it shall be a masterpiece ; but that appearance is very doubtful. I have burnt more than I have written—that's a good sign at east.

Wednesday, Dec. 5.

I have been obliged to betake myself to my bed again. Although yesterday nearly bent double with the acuteness of this strange complaint which has now attacked me every year, more or less, since my return to England, I still hope to meet you on Friday.

Dec. 20.

Not five minutes after I left your dear presence, I met rather an adventure. A cortège of dandies and grooms riding up the lane to Bradenham, and, lo ! Count D'Orsay, Lord Albert Conyngham and Forester, about to call on me with an invitation from Lord Carrington to dine at Wycombe Abbey, where they were staying. They were resolved to pay their visit, so I drove on, begged the family to receive them as I could not, for the Aylesbury people were just entering the gates as I got on the green. So I could not join my guests for an hour, when I found them still here and well amused.

---

[1] Peel's Solicitor-General in 1834-35, and afterwards Attorney-General. He had appeared with the Attorney-General, Campbell, in the proceedings against Disraeli.

I had refused the invitation on the road, as I have not entered Wycombe Abbey for six years, and the present Lord Carrington, then Robert Smith, was my opponent on the hustings ; but I found Forester,[1] who is Lord Carrington's brother-in-law, had instructions to get me at all hazards ; so I was at length forced to consent to dine there to-day. Thus in a few hours has evaporated the feud of long years !

Dec. 22.

We had a most agreeable meeting at Lord Carrington's. I found there Lady Chesterfield, George and Mrs. Anson, the Albert Conynghams, Forester, the Crewes and D'Orsay ; all staying at the Abbey except myself. Our party was rather noisy, but very gay. I did not get home until past midnight, or rather near the chimes of one, and then with great difficulty, as I could scarcely resist their entreaties that I should remain and send for my toilette in the morning. At last I escaped, having made the greatest friends with all of them, and with half a promise, that when D'Orsay returns, who left on the next day, I would come and remain at the Abbey for two or three days.

I did not make them acquainted here with your passage through Wycombe as dexterously as you would have done yourself in my situation, not producing that dramatic suspense for which you are eminent ; but I did contrive at least that they should not obtain the information from any other person.

Dec. 23.

I shall not allow any feeling of false pride to prevent me from expressing my deep mortification at your strange and prolonged silence. I am not exacting in any of these lesser offices of the heart, because I prefer that at all times they should flow from the affections, and not be impelled by anything approaching to a sense of duty. . . . I also know that one of the arts of life is never to turn a pleasure into a bore, which correspondence immediately becomes as soon as it is considered a formal affair. . . . You told me once you required a year to study a character ; our year has nearly elapsed, and your meditations may have dissatisfied you with mine. What my feelings may be if I find that I am doomed ever to waste my affections, and that a blight is ever to fall on a heart which nature intended to be the shrine of sensibility, it matters not. At present I will believe that my fate is indissolubly bound up with yours, until your voice or your conduct assures me that all this time I have laboured under a miserable delusion.

[1] John George, 2nd Lord Forester, 1801-1874.

Dec. 26.

It is my joy and even my pride that we do not have many
lovers' quarrels ; truly they are not lovable things, and should
only be adopted by those whose flagging affections require
stimulus. Mine never do. Alas ! it is too much love that
makes me querulous, the suspense of affection and the pangs
of separation. . . . I do not intend to go again to the Abbey
—at least not to stay. I am gratified that the old feud has
ceased, but I don't think that such estrangements should be
succeeded by rapid intimacies. It is better to be sought than
to weary. D'Orsay comes here to-morrow night, shoots on
Friday, and is off on Saturday morning.

Saturday, Dec. 29.

I am entirely overwhelmed. Indeed, it has been one of
the most miserable weeks that I have ever passed ; and my
constitution, tried by the excitement and agitation of the
last six months, has quite given way. I have written to put
off all my engagements, and am lying on my sofa, so utterly
wretched that I cannot convey to you even a faint idea of
my prostration. And it is doubly painful, for I cannot bear
to complain, as I should have the house full of doctors, and,
alas ! they cannot minister to a mind diseased.

I have written to Lord Chandos to excuse my attendance
at the Bucks dinner and my visit to Stowe. Lord Carrington
came here on Thursday to ask D'Orsay, then expected, and
myself to come to him on Monday ; but I have declined, nor
shall I attend the Quarter Sessions. . . . D'Orsay arrived
on Thursday morning to breakfast. The day was fortunately
very fine, and he was amused out of doors with his gun ; he
left us this afternoon. It was useless for me to attempt to
conceal my feelings, and therefore I pleaded illness, which I
detest doing. I never saw him arrive with so much reluctance
or depart with so much satisfaction, and yet he is really, as
you well and truly say, a *friend*, and the best and kindest of
men. But what are friends, and what is all the goodness
and kindness in the world, if there is a cloud between you
and the being you adore ? . . . I am sure you never wish to
show your power over me, because I never wish to conceal it,
and, besides, you are above all that : but, indeed, this last
week is something too terrible to think of.

Dec. 30.

I am mad with love. My passion is frenzy. The prospect
of our immediate meeting overwhelms and entrances me. I
pass my nights and days in scenes of strange and fascinating
rapture. . . . Lose not a moment unnecessarily in coming.
I cannot wait. . . . I can scarcely believe in the joy of our

immediate meeting.   Will the time ever pass away until that
rapturous moment ?

Dec. 31.

The happiest of New Years ; and, indeed, I hope and believe
it will be the happiest of our lives.

Jan. 22, 1839.

'Tis twilight after a lovely day, but I have no dark thoughts.
All my motions are soft and glowing as the sky.   Sweetest
and dearest of women, our united loves shall flow like two
rivers ; as gentle and as clear. . . .   Bless you and bless and
bless you.

Jan. 23.

I love you, if possible, each day more truly and more ten-
derly.   All my hopes of happiness in life are centred in your
sweet affections, and I wish only to be the solace and glory of
your life.

Disraeli's conquest was, perhaps, not so easy as his
letters, taken by themselves, might lead us to believe.
In love, as in most things, beneath the placid surface he
was eager and impulsive.   She was by nature colder, and
she had also reached the age when passion waits upon
the judgment.   She was resolute, it would appear, that
there should be no open engagement till the conventional
year had elapsed from her first husband's death, and she
was, perhaps, not unmindful of those elusive feminine
arts by which the impetuous lover is at once baffled and
fascinated.   Matters came to a crisis about the time we
have now reached, and there is a strange letter from
Disraeli, found after Lady Beaconsfield's death carefully
disposed among her papers, which tells sufficiently the
story of their first and last serious quarrel.

To Mrs. Wyndham Lewis.

PARK STREET,
Thursday night, Feb. 7, 1839.

I would have endeavoured to have spoken to you of that
which it was necessary you should know, and I wished to have
spoken with the calmness which was natural to one humiliated
and distressed.   I succeeded so far as . . . to be desired to quit
your house for ever.   I have recourse therefore to this miserable method of communicating with you ; none can be more

imperfect, but I write as if it were the night before my
execution. . . .

I avow, when I first made my advances to you, I was
influenced by no romantic feelings. My father had long
wished me to marry ; my settling in life was the implied,
though not stipulated, condition of a disposition of his property, which would have been convenient to me. I myself,
about to commence a practical career, wished for the solace
of a home, and shrunk from all the torturing passions of intrigue. I was not blind to worldly advantages in such an
alliance, but I had already proved that my heart was not to
be purchased. I found you in sorrow, and that heart was
touched. I found you, as I thought, amiable, tender, and
yet acute and gifted with no ordinary mind,—one whom I
could look upon with pride as the partner of my life, who could
sympathise with all my projects and feelings, console me in
the moments of depression, share my hour of triumph, and
work with me for our honor and our happiness.

Now for your fortune : I write the sheer truth. That
fortune proved to be much less than I, or the world, imagined.
It was in fact, as far as I was concerned, a fortune which could
not benefit me in the slightest degree ; it was merely a jointure
not greater than your station required ; enough to maintain
your establishment and gratify your private tastes. To eat
and to sleep in that house, and nominally to call it mine—
these could be only objects for a penniless adventurer. Was
this an inducement for me to sacrifice my sweet liberty, and
that indefinite future which is one of the charms of existence ?
No ; when months ago I told you one day, that there was only
one link between us, I felt that my heart was inextricably
engaged to you, and but for that I would have terminated
our acquaintance. From that moment I devoted to you all
the passion of my being. Alas ! it has been poured upon the
sand ! . . .

By heavens, as far as worldly interests are concerned, your
alliance could not benefit me. All that society can offer is
at my command ; it is not the apparent possession of a jointure
that ever elevates position. I can live, as I live, without
disgrace, until the inevitable progress of events gives me that
independence which is all I require. I have entered into these
ungracious details because you reproached me with my interested views. No ; I would not condescend to be the minion
of a princess ; and not all the gold of Ophir should ever lead
me to the altar. Far different are the qualities which I require
in the sweet participator of my existence. My nature demands
that my life should be perpetual love.

Upon your general conduct to me, I make no comment. It

is now useless. I will not upbraid you. I will only blame myself. . . . But you have struck deep. You have done that which my enemies have yet failed to do : you have broken my spirit. From the highest to the humblest scene of my life, from the brilliant world of fame to my own domestic hearth, you have poisoned all. I have no place of refuge : home is odious, the world oppressive.

Triumph—I seek not to conceal my state. It is not sorrow, it is not wretchedness ; it is anguish, it is the *endurance* of that pang which is the passing characteristic of agony. All that can prostrate a man has fallen on my victim head. My heart outraged, my pride wounded, my honor nearly tainted. I know well that ere a few days can pass I shall be the scoff and jest of that world, to gain whose admiration has been the effort of my life. I have only one source of solace—the consciousness of self-respect. Will that uphold me ? A terrible problem that must quickly be solved.

Farewell. I will not affect to wish you happiness, for it is not in your nature to obtain it. For a few years you may flutter in some frivolous circle. But the time will come when you will sigh for any heart that could be fond, and despair of one that can be faithful. Then will be the penal hour of retribution : then you will think of me with remorse, admiration and despair ; then you will recall to your memory the passionate heart that you have forfeited, and the genius you have betrayed.

D.

Lovers at all times are apt to be histrionic, and it is their privilege that they can be histrionic without being insincere. This, if true of others, is true still more of a man like Disraeli, and of his sincerity in the present matter we have the devotion of a lifetime as convincing demonstration. The quarrel, of course, was speedily composed.

From Mrs. Wyndham Lewis.

For God's sake come to me. I am ill and almost distracted. I will answer all you wish. I never desired you to leave the house, or implied or thought a word about money. I received a most distressing letter, and you left me at the moment not knowing . . . I have not been a widow a year. I often feel the apparent impropriety of my present position. . . . I am devoted to you.

In later days she used laughingly to declare : ' Dizzy married me for my money, but if he had the chance again

he would marry me for love.' The world had made up
its mind that he had married her for her money, and it
was her knowledge of the truth that made it possible for
her to adopt the world's point of view. If her husband
sometimes did the same, it was characteristic of the man
to accept with easy acquiescence a theory which reduced
his conduct to a lower plane of motive than that of which
he was conscious.

Parliament met in February, and Disraeli has himself
depicted the situation in which Ministers found themselves at the beginning of the session :

> The balance of parties in the House of Commons, which
> had been virtually restored by Sir Robert Peel's dissolution of
> 1834, might be said to be formally and positively established
> by the dissolution of Parliament in the autumn of 1837,
> occasioned by the demise of the Crown. The Ministerial
> majority became almost nominal, while troubles from all
> quarters seemed to press simultaneously upon them : Canadian
> revolts, Chartist insurrections, Chinese squabbles, and mys-
> terious complications in Central Asia which threatened im-
> mediate hostilities with Persia, and even with one of the
> most powerful of European Empires. In addition to all this,
> the revenue continually declined, and every day the general
> prejudice became more intense against the Irish policy of the
> Ministry. The extreme popularity of the Sovereign, reflecting
> some lustre on her Ministers, had enabled them, though not
> without difficulty, to tide through the session of 1838 ; but
> when Parliament met in 1839 their prospects were dark, and
> it was known that there was a section of the extreme Liberals
> who would not be deeply mortified if the Government were
> overthrown.[1]

The great reforming impulse which had carried the
Whigs into power at the beginning of the decade was now
completely spent, and Whiggery, which was in fact a
survival from the conditions of a previous age, had lost
its vitality. As yet, however, there was nothing very
definite to take its place, and so the Whigs remained in
office, and Melbourne, the typical statesman of a time of
transition, easy alike in manner and in political principle,
remained Prime Minister. Of the duty which he dis-

[1] *Endymion*, ch. 55.

charged so well, and for which his name will live in history, the training of the young Queen for her memorable career as a constitutional Sovereign, he was perhaps himself not wholly conscious ; and as his Ministry staggered on from humiliation to defeat, and he rode through every difficulty with easy nonchalance, there were few who gave a thought to the service which all the while he was thus rendering to the nation.

To Sarah Disraeli.

[*February*, 1839.]

I went up with the Duke of Buckingham,[1] Praed, Fremantle, Christopher, Blackstone, and a host of Horwoods, Brickhills, &c., as a deputation to Lord Melbourne on the Corn Laws, which was very amusing. Melbourne, frank and rollicking, evidently in his heart a thorough Tory and agriculturist, rubbed his hands and laughed ; when the evil consequences insisted on, agreed to everything. ' And, my lord,' said some Horwood from Ely, ' will not the fundholder be endangered ?' ' Oh, of course,' said the Prime Minister.[2]

[*Feb.* 25.]

My Dearest,

Tommy[3] told me last night that he should bring the actresses on the stage again on Thursday night. I wish you would look into the books and let me know something about the matter. Is it ' ecclesiastical polity ' or is it a puritanic innovation ? If the latter, I would justify my vote.

How was it in James the First's time and Eliza's ? Is the arrangement alluded to in the Book of Sports ? Payne Collier[4]—what says he ? Or the other Collier ?[5] Find out what you can—that is to say, if you be well and have no head-ache—and let me have it on Thursday morning. This will give you a couple of days' research.

I dined at Sir Robert's on Saturday, and came late, having mistaken the hour. I found some 25 gentlemen grubbing in solemn silence. I threw a shot over the table and set them going, and in time they became even noisy. Peel, I think,

---

[1] Disraeli's friend Lord Chandos, who had succeeded on the death of his father, the 1st Duke, at the beginning of the year.

[2] *Letters*, p. 146.

[3] Duncombe, who had a motion for the abolition of certain restriction on theatrical entertainments in Lent, which were then enforced by the Lord Chamberlain in the City of Westminster.

[4] Shakespearian critic.

[5] No doubt Jeremy Collier, the famous Non-juror, who led the movement for the purification of the stage at the end of the seventeenth century.

was quite pleased that I broke the awful stillness, as he talked
to me a good deal, though we were far removed ; he sitting
in the middle of the table. I had Sir Robert Inglis[1] on my
right hand, whose mind I somewhat opened. He requested
permission to ask after my father, and inquired whether he
was at Bradenham.

The dinner was curiously sumptuous. There was really
' every delicacy of the season ' ; and the second course of
dried salmon, olives, caviare, woodcock pie, foie gras, and
every combination of cured herring, &c., was really remarkable. The drawing-room and picture-gallery were lit up, and
the effect was truly fine. . . .

Love,
D.

Friday [*Mar.* 1.]

MY DEAREST,

We dined yesterday at Scrope's,[2] and met the Poulett
Scropes, who are staying with him, the Murchisons, Sir Charles
and Lady Morgan, and Lord Sudeley : the house magnificent
and the contrast remarkable to the bare walls and Ionic
meagreness of my last visit. Rooms crimson, with green silk
curtains : spectral colors ; fine pictures, marqueterie chairs
and some splendid cabinets : good dinner and silver-gilt plate.
Paired off to half-past 10 anticipating debate on Mexico.
Found Mexico put off and Tommy about to jump up : never
heard a more entertaining debate. Duncombe's drollery
inimitable. Though I had not intended to speak—I had not
even your note in my pocket—it animated me, and though
full-figged (in costume), I rose with several men at the same
time ; but the House called for me, and I spoke with great
effect and amid loud cheering and laughter. Supposed to
have settled the question, which, to the disgust of Government,
was carried by a majority of 20. Never saw Johnny in a
greater rage ; he sent for Alfred Paget, who was going to vote
for us, and insisted that he should not. . . .

Love,
D.

---

[1] A well-known Tory of the old school, member for Oxford University,
where he had ousted Peel on the Catholic question in 1829.

[2] William Scrope of Castle Combe. There was some family connexion
between the Scropes and the Vineys, in which Disraeli after his marriage
took considerable pride. In his last year of office as Prime Minister he
endorsed a letter from a member of the Scrope family putting forward a
claim to a dormant peerage : ' Mr. Scrope was a relation of Lady Beaconsfield, and I am much interested in his case. His blood is the best in England.
I don't wish to alter the laws of the country even for the Scropes, but I
wish justice to be done.' Poulett Scrope was a younger brother of Poulett
Thomson's, and had married William Scrope's daughter and sole heiress.

On this and on many other occasions in these early sessions, Disraeli acted with the Radicals against the bulk of his own party. A week later, on the second reading of the Ministry's now annual Bill[1] for the reform of Irish corporations, he found himself again in a different lobby from his leaders. Peel and Stanley had accepted the Government policy in principle, but Disraeli was one of a small minority, composed mainly of Irish Tories and extreme English supporters of the Protestant supremacy, who persisted in opposing the Bill. He was careful, however, to dissociate himself in motive from the bulk of his allies. Disclaiming religious bigotry, he argued against the measure on the ground of its tendency to weaken the central government in Ireland. ' In England, where society was strong,' he said, ' they tolerated a weak government; but in Ireland, where society was weak, the policy should be to have the government strong."[2] The significance of the Irish question cannot be exhausted in a formula, but in that single sentence there is more of wisdom and enlightenment than in many thousands of the dreary pages of Irish debate that are buried in the volumes of Hansard.

To Sarah Disraeli.

March 9.

My last speech was very successful, the best *coup* I have yet made. And it was no easy task, for I spoke against the Government, the great mass of the Conservative party, and even took a different view from the small minority itself. I was listened to in silence and the utmost attention. Peel especially complimented me, sore as he was at the Conservative schism, and said, ' Disraeli, you took the only proper line of opposition to the bill '; and Hardinge, a sharp critic, said I had entirely got the ear of the House, and overcome everything.

[April.]

The game is in Peel's hands ; but he evidently has resolved that the Ministers shall resign and not be turned out. The Radicals clamour against him for not permitting them to assist him. However, all is bustle, and 500 members at

---

[1] See Vol. I., p. 328.   [2] Hansard, March 8, 1839.

prayers, in order to secure places. This is just one of those
occasions in old days when I used to feel so mortified at not
being an M.P. *Assisting*, as the French say, at such a ' crisis,'
has considerable fascination, and all must feel it though they
can't and won't confess. One cannot walk down Parliament
Street under such circumstances without some degree of
exultation.[1]

Ministers did not wait for actual defeat. Early in May,
in a full House, their majority sank to five in an important
division, and Melbourne at once resigned.

To Mrs. Wyndham Lewis.

Wednesday [*May* 8].

The Queen sent for the Duke of Wellington this morning at
12, and about 2 she sent by his advice for Peel, who passed
in his carriage down Pall Mall, to the Palace, opposite the
Carlton. He was in *full* dress, which is etiquette on these
occasions. About 4 he left the Queen and went to the Duke
of Wellington. Nothing at 6 o'clock had transpired except
that Peel had expressed his readiness to take office.

GEORGE STREET,
2 *o'clock* [*May* 10].

A messenger post-haste reached me as I was just turning the
corner of Park Street to you, desiring me to come on here
[Lord Lyndhurst's] instantly.

Peel is out and given up the Government already in consequence of Whig intrigues about the household. I have not
the slightest doubt that her Majesty will be obliged to surrender. I am writing something which Lord L. thinks may
be of service to them and myself.

CARLTON,
[*May* 12].

I have finished a letter to the Queen, and am now copying it,
very exhausted. . . . There are all sorts of rumors, and the
most credited are very unfavorable, viz*t*, a Radical Government and a dissolution : but I hope they are Sunday lies.

' This,' writes Disraeli in *Endymion*,[2] ' was the famous
Bedchamber Plot, in which the Conservative leaders, as
is now generally admitted, were decidedly in error, and
which terminated in the return of the Whigs to office.'
Even in *Coningsby* and *Sybil*, written not many years

---

[1] *Letters*, pp. 149, 150.   [2] Ch. 58.

after the event, he had come to the opinion that Peel had
made a blunder : ' It was unfortunate that one who, if
any, should have occupied the proud and national position
of the leader of the Tory party, the chief of the people,
and the champion of the throne, should have commenced
his career as Minister under Victoria by an unseemly
contrariety to the personal wishes of the Queen.'[1] At
the moment, however, like a good party man, Disraeli
defended his leader, and in his letter, which appeared in
The Times[2] over the signature of ' Lælius,' he lectured
the young Queen on the dangers of her resolution to
retain as her companions the wives and sisters of her
outgoing Ministers :

Your Majesty has confidence in the strength of your own
character. You are convinced that the line of demarcation
between public duty and private affection is broad and deep.
On all that concerns the State, you are assured that your lips
and your heart will be for ever closed to the circle in which
you pass your life. Be it so. I humbly presume to give
your Majesty credit for all the exalted virtues which become
a throne. But where, then, are the joys of companionship ?
The Royal brow is clouded, but the Royal lip must never
explain its care. The Queen is anxious, but the Lady in Waiting must not share her restlessness or soothe her disquietude.

Madam, it cannot be. You are a queen ; but you are a
human being and a woman. The irrepressible sigh will burst
forth some day, and you will meet a glance more interesting
because there is a captivating struggle to suppress its sympathy. Wearied with public cares, crossed, as necessarily
you must sometimes be, the peevish exclamation will have
its way, and you yourself will be startled at its ready echo.
The line once passed, progress is quick : fascinating sympathy,
long-suppressed indignation, promised succour ; the tear, the
tattle, the innuendo, the direct falsehood ; in a moment they
will convince you you are a victim, and that they have heroes
in wait to rescue their Sovereign. Then come the Palace conspiracy and the backstairs intrigue. You will find yourself
with the rapidity of enchantment the centre and the puppet
of a camarilla, and Victoria, in the eyes of that Europe which
once bowed to her, and in the hearts of those Englishmen who
once yielded to her their devotion, will be reduced to the level
of Madrid and Lisbon.

[1] *Sybil*, Bk. IV. ch. 14.   [2] Of May 13, 1839.

In another letter which ' Lælius ' addressed to Melbourne a fortnight later there is a character of Peel which deserves to be rescued from the oblivion of a newspaper file :

Let me consider the character and position of a political leader whom, to use only the admissions of his adversaries, I may describe as a man unrivalled for Parliamentary talents, of unimpeached integrity, of unsullied personal conduct, of considerable knowledge, both scholastic and civil, and of an estate ample and unencumbered—one of long official practice, of greater political experience ; of that happy age when the vigor of manhood is not impaired, and when men have attained as much experience as, without over-refining action, is compatible with practical wisdom ; when an elevated and thoughtful ambition is, not eager, yet prepared, for power, free from both the restlessness of youth and the discontent of declining age—epochs that alike deem life too short for delay.   Add to this a temperament essentially national, and a habit of life pleasing to the manners and prejudices of his countrymen, with many of the virtues of the English character and some of its peculiarities ; confident, rather than sanguine ; guided by principles, yet not despising expedients ; fearful to commit himself, yet never shrinking from responsibility ; proud, yet free from vanity, and reserved rather from disposition than from an ungenerous prudence ; most courageous when in peril ; most cautious in prosperity.   It is difficult to estimate the characters of our contemporaries, but this I believe, though a slight, to be not an incorrect, sketch of that of Sir Robert Peel.[1]

To Sarah Disraeli.

[*Undated.*]

Dined *en famille* with the Duke of Buckingham, to eat venison ; a regular Bucks party.   Sir East and a widow daughter, enthusiastically blue, and boring Chandos about my genius, who seemed quite puzzled and proud at having an author for his friend.   I believe Lady Anna has not been allowed to read the tragedy [*Alarcos*], therefore she hopes it will be acted.   She is great fun.

[*June.*]

Douro's[2] marriage has taken place : a great concourse and much cheering in the streets, and would have been in the church had not the Dean of Carlisle with apostolic *naïveté* preliminarily warned the audience.   The church crowded ; three

---

[1] *The Times*, May 28, 1839.   [2] Afterwards 2nd Duke of Wellington.

or four ladies in pulpit ; pews engaged weeks before. I have
not seen the lady, but, according to Douro, she weighs
11 stone 5 lbs. I hear a beautiful face, and came out last
year. They were married before twelve, and at four o'clock
he was riding in the park.

I was at Madame Montefiore, *née* De Rothschild, as she
says at court : a most magnificent concert. Two royal princes
(Sussex and Cambridge) and the Duke of Wellington gartered
and fleeced. Grisi and Persiani sang a duet, and the supper
very splendid. The weather is at length charming, and I
think you must really look after my summer costume. . . .

Social London is rather dull, in contradistinction to political
London ; indeed no one thinks of anything but politics. I
send you a very good thing in the shape of Theodore Hook's
epitaph on Lord de Ros—' Here lies Henry, 17th Baron de
Ros, in joyful expectation of the last Trump.' I am reading
the Indian papers,[1] which are the most amusing thing I have
met with since the *Arabian Nights*.

June 23.

I didn't get home till half-past five on Friday morning,
and had only time yesterday before post to receive the congratulations of my friends, which came thick as the leaves of
Vallombrosa. How strange that nearly in despair at the end
of the session I should have made by universal consent the
best speech on our side on the most important party question.
After listening to Ewart as long as he replied or attempted to
reply, which was about ten minutes or so, I thought the
moment he began to repeat by rote I might retire, and I went
to the Carlton. The rumor of my success had preceded me.
Canterbury was very warm ; he has always taken an interest
in my Parliamentary career. It was Charles Buller who
told him it was one of the best speeches. I had touched up
Charley a little, though with courtesy. He is erroneously
represented in the papers as not being in the House, whereas
the ' laugh ' which you may observe in the report was occasioned by his taking off his hat and making me a bow. Two
of my old foes, Lord Lincoln and Lord Ashley, tendered me
their congratulations with extended hands. As for *Alarcos*,
Colburn, on the strength of the speech I suppose, advertises
it this morning as ' Mr. Disraeli's Tragedy.'

D.[2]

Nothing, as a rule, can surpass in dulness the dead
political speeches even of famous men, but these early

---

[1] The papers setting forth the antecedents of the first Afghan War, which
was then in progress.
[2] *Letters*, pp. 151-153.

efforts of Disraeli's have often a quality which preserves their freshness after the lapse of two generations. His speech on this last occasion, which occupies nearly two columns of *The Times*,[1] is an excellent case in point. The subject in debate was Lord John Russell's scheme for the foundation of a central Education Board, with an endowment of £30,000 a year—the grain of seed which has grown into our present vast system of national education. Churchmen were jealous of the scheme as conceived in the interest of the Dissenters, and Gladstone had taken the high line of ' objecting to any infringement whatever of the principle on which the Established Church was founded—that of confining the primary support of the state to one particular denomination.' Disraeli also opposed the measure, but was content with lower ground. ' He was an advocate for national education, but it did not follow that he should also be an advocate for State education.' China and Persia in the East, Austria, ' the China of Europe,'[2] and Prussia, with its paternal government, were the countries with highly developed systems of state education. Paternal government and state education, in fact, went hand in hand together. ' It had been discovered that the best way to insure implicit obedience was to commence tyranny in the nursery.'

The same system which tyrannised in the nursery under the pretence of education would . . . immure old age within hated walls, under the specious plea of affording relief. It was always the state, and never society—it was always machinery, never sympathy. By their system of state education all would be thrown into the same mint, and all would come out with the same impress and superscription. They might make money, they might make railroads ; but when the age of passion came, when those interests were in motion, and those feelings stirring, which would shake society to its centre, then . . . they would see whether the people had received the same sort of education which had been advocated and supported by William of Wykeham. . . . No ; other

---

[1] Of June 21, 1839.
[2] The phrase reappears in *Coningsby*, Bk. VI. ch. 3.

principles had actuated the men of former days, and let them
look abroad on England and witness the result.   Where would
they find a country more elevated in the social scale ? where
a people more distinguished for all that was excellent in the
human character ?   The time would come, if they persisted in
their present course, when they would find that they had
revolutionised the English character ; and when that was
effected, then they could no longer expect English achievements.

Incidentally he protested against an attempt which had
been made to raise the cry of ' No Popery !'   Nor did he
share the apprehensions of members on his own side, that
the proposed system of education might lead to national
infidelity. By a united effort of the sectarians the
national Church might be overthrown, but the penalty,
as in the time of the Commonwealth, would be the wild-
ness of fanaticism, the fury and violence of contending
sects, not the general spread of ' miserable, cold, and
restless infidelity.'   And when the moment of anarchy
was past, and the people of England sought a return to
peace, they would not plunge into infidelity, ' which was
abhorrent to their nature, and at variance with all the
better feelings of the human heart '; but they would revert
to the Church of their fathers, or perhaps seek refuge in
that other Church which ' had the advantage of being
able to appeal to unrivalled antiquity, and also strongly
to the feelings and imaginations of men '—the Church of
Rome.

To Mrs. Wyndham Lewis.

July 8.

Lord Fitzgerald[1] asked me to dinner on Tuesday, which I
have refused, as I hope to be in the House of Commons ; it is
said that he is the most difficult man to dine with in London,
and I therefore tell it you as a specimen of the Parliamentary
barometer ; for he is one who considers success in debate as
the great object of existence.

[1] The Mr. Vesey Fitzgerald whose appointment as President of the
Board of Trade in the Wellington Ministry in 1829 led to the Clare election
and the triumph of O'Connell.

To Sarah Disraeli.

July 8.

I dined at Greenwich with the Duke of Buckingham on Saturday. A large party embarked at Whitehall in a steamer, but I went by land with Lyndhurst. A sumptuous banquet, and Brougham made nearly fifty speeches full of comic humor and fierce slashing of Whigs ; declared it was impossible to turn them out of power, to Chandos's blank despair, because they were not *in* power, to Chandos's chuckling relief. Lyndhurst was also capital. I dined with him yesterday to meet Webster,[1] who is, I believe, considered a very refined and *spirituel* Yankee, but seemed to me a complete Brother Jonathan—a remarkable twang, as ' *ty*rannical ' and all that ; he also goes to the *levéé*. A fine brow, lofty, broad, and beetled deep-set eyes, and swarthy complexion. He is said when warmed to be their greatest orator. Strangford was there, very airy and sparkling ; all the rest Americans and principally relatives.[2]

Saturday [July 13].

My dearest Sa,

I made a most capital speech on Chartism last night, of which *The Times* gives a fair and accurate report. The *Morning Herald* has taken up the speech and written a leader on it, and calls it ' a speech of very considerable talent.' It was made under every disadvantage, for the Tories, supposing Chartism would only be a squabble between the Whigs and Radicals, were all away, while the Ministerial benches were crowded—all the Ministers, all the Whigs, and all the Radicals. Peel, however, was in the House, having come down on the Penny Postage. It was a very damaging and disagreeable speech to the Government, and they didn't like it. . . .

Powerscourt has invited *us* to pass our autumn in Ireland : he raves about *Alarcos*, and literally knows it by heart. He declares 'tis the finest tragedy that ever was written. Milnes,[3] the poet, is astonished that I didn't give it Macready, as ' it would have made his fortune.'

Strange that I never yet wrote anything that was more talked of in society, and yet it has never been noticed by the scribbling critics.

My love to all.

D.[4]

---

[1] The American statesman.   [2] *Letters*, p. 153.
[3] Richard Monckton Milnes, afterwards Lord Houghton, 1809-1885.
[4] Brit. Mus., Addit. MSS.

There is some reason to believe that Disraeli had, in fact, submitted his play to Macready, who was then at the height of his fame, and that he only resorted to publication when he had failed to get it accepted for production on the stage. The play as published was dedicated to Lord Francis Egerton, himself a poet, as ' an attempt to contribute to the revival of English tragedy,' and in this dedication Disraeli traced its origin, as he had previously traced the origin of the *Revolutionary Epick*, to his Mediterranean journey, though, having learnt something in the meantime, he entered the lists against Shakespeare with more diffidence than he had shown in his earlier challenge to Milton.[1]

Do you remember the ballad of ' the Count Alarcos and the Infanta Solisa ' ? . . . Years have flown away since, rambling in the Sierras of Andalusia beneath the clear light of a Spanish moon, and freshened by the sea-breeze that had wandered up a river from the coast, I first listened to the chaunt of that strange and terrible tale.

It seemed to me rife with all the materials of the tragic drama ; and I planned, as I rode along, the scenes and characters of which it appeared to me susceptible.

That was the season of life when the heart is quick with emotion, and the brain with creative fire ; when the eye is haunted with beautiful sights, and the ear with sweet sounds ; when we live in reveries of magnificent performance, and the future seems only a perennial flow of poetic invention.

Dreams of fantastic youth ! Amid the stern realities of existence I have unexpectedly achieved a long-lost purpose.

Strange and terrible the tale is indeed, as anyone who has read Lockhart's rendering of the ballad will be able to recall—too strange and terrible for success on the stage,

[1] As in the *Epick* we find a certain far-off mimicry of Milton, so in *Alarcos* there is a certain far-off mimicry of Shakespeare :

> ' Thou art too young to die,
> And yet may be too happy. Moody youth
> Toys in its talk with the dark thought of death,
> As if to die were but to change a robe.
> It is their present refuge from all cares
> And each disaster. When the sere has touched
> Their flowing locks, they prattle less of death,
> Perchance think more of it.'
>
> Act III., Scene ii.

or even to give pleasure in a literary play. Disraeli's tragedy, as might be expected, shows sufficient literary workmanship to redeem it from contempt. There is a certain weird impressiveness in the development of the plot, and a certain measure of skill in the conduct of the dialogue. But horror is piled on horror till the reader has supped too full; and though *Alarcos* may have been talked about at the time of its publication, it has never since found many admirers. While Disraeli was Prime Minister in 1868, an adaptation was produced at Astley's Theatre Royal. It ran for five weeks, ' with the loudest demonstrations of applause from delighted audiences,' as the courtly manager wrote to the author at the close, but, unfortunately, as he had to add, with heavy losses to himself as the penalty of his enterprise.

To Sarah Disraeli.

[*July* 26.]

I went down to Rosebank to a *petit bal* given by the Londonderrys, after a dinner to the Duchess of Cambridge on her birthday. The place itself is but a beautiful cottage, but there is a grand conservatory more than sixty feet long, lofty and broad in proportion, and, adorned with festoons of flowers, formed a charming ball-room, and I met a great many of my friends. In reality, the brilliant moon, the lamplit gardens, the terraces, the river, the music, the sylvan ball-room, and the bright revellers, made a scene like a festa in one of George Sand's novels.

[*Aug.* 16.]

I dined at Burdett's yesterday. Dinner at seven o'clock precisely ; everything stately and old-fashioned, but agreeable. The house charming ; the dining-room looking into delightful gardens, with much old timber, beyond St. James's Park. I got away by 9.30, and went down to the House, which I found dozing in committee, but I made a speech. Unfortunately, as generally happens on long committee nights, there was scarcely a reporter in the gallery. I analysed all the evidence of the constabulary report. It made great effect, quoting all the pages and names without any document. The complete command of the House I now have is remarkable, and nothing can describe to you the mute silence which immediately ensued as I rose, broken only by members hurrying to their places to listen.

On Monday I was more than four hours at Lord Palmerston's
private residence on business of no slight importance. Prince
Esterhazy, who came into the dining-room whilst I was waiting,
said, ' I have come to introduce myself to Mr. Disraeli. I
have long wished to know you ; I read your speeches with
admiration.'[1]

The business with Palmerston seems to have had reference to some member of the consular or diplomatic service
who had been recalled by the Foreign Office, and had
asked Disraeli to take up his case.

From Lord Palmerston.

STANHOPE STREET,
Aug. 15, 1839.

MY DEAR SIR,
I am very much obliged to you for your note of the 12th,
and for the patient attention which you gave to the long statement I was obliged to make to you ; and I can assure you I
am very sensible to the great candour and fairness with
which you have dealt with the matter which formed the
subject of our conversation.
My dear sir,
Yours faithfully,
PALMERSTON.

Parliament was prorogued on August 27, and next day
Disraeli was married to Mrs. Wyndham Lewis at St.
George's, Hanover Square. ' I feel,' he had written to
her not long before, ' that there never was an instance
where a basis of more entire and permanent felicity
offered itself to two human beings. I look forward to the
day of our union as that epoch in my life which will seal
my career : for whatever occurs afterwards will, I am
sure, never shake my soul, as I shall always have the
refuge of your sweet heart in sorrow or disappointment,
and your quick and accurate sense to guide me in prosperity and triumph.' Many have gone to the altar with
high hopes like these, but few have seen them come to
such complete fruition. It was in some respects a
strange alliance. In a curious document which survives,

[1] *Letters,* pp. 155, 156.

Mrs. Disraeli analyses her husband's character and her own, and tabulates their opposing qualities so as to emphasise the contrast :

Very calm.	Very effervescent.
Manners grave and almost sad.	Gay and happy-looking when speaking.
Never irritable.	Very irritable.
Bad-humoured.	Good-humoured.
Warm in love, but cold in friendship.	Cold in love, but warm in friendship.
Very patient.	No patience.
Very studious.	Very idle.
Very generous.	Only generous to those she loves.
Often says what he does not think.	Never says anything she does not think.
It is impossible to find out who he likes or dislikes from his manner. He does not show his feelings.	Her manner is quite different, and to those she likes she shows her feelings.
No vanity.	Much vanity.
Conceited.	No conceit.
No self-love.	Much self-love.
He is seldom amused.	Everything amuses her.
He is a genius.	She is a dunce.
He is to be depended on to a certain degree.	She is not to be depended on.
His whole soul is devoted to politics and ambition.	She has no ambition and hates politics.

' He is a genius, she is a dunce ': there, naïvely stated, we have a fundamental difference which might have been expected to exclude lasting sympathy. If we add to her own testimony the testimony of those who knew her, we see in Mrs. Disraeli a woman vain, pleasure-loving, and effervescent, to the casual observer a little shallow and irresponsible, outspoken to the point of tactlessness, but of an exuberant kindness of heart which covered a multitude of defects ; of little mental cultivation, and in the things on which society largely bases its judgments— dress, furniture, and manners—of a certain oddity of taste which naturally grew more marked as the years went on, and made her a bizarre and unconventional figure. But, fortunately, Disraeli was bizarre enough himself to be blind or indifferent to many of her peculiarities ; and if his wife had little care for the things of the mind, she was very far from being a ' dunce ' in the proper meaning of the word, as the tabulated characters set forth above, with the penetration shown on one side and the self-knowledge on the other, would alone suffice to prove. The ' quick and accurate sense ' of which her husband wrote was something more than a phrase. She had not only in liberal measure the gift of feminine intuition, but the rarer gift of judgment ; and in the lesser business of life, in which Disraeli himself was helpless, she had practical ability of no mean order. Marriage did not end his financial embarrassments, but it relieved him of their severest pressure, and it gave him at last a fixed home in London, and a companion who could shelter him from most of the sordid detail that he always found so distasteful. If there were nothing more to be said, these things alone would suffice to explain the ' gratitude ' on which he once laid stress, according to a well-known story, as the keynote of his affection.

But there is something more to be said. Commonplace in intellect his wife may have been, but there was a strain of heroism in her character which, if her lot had been different, might have remained unrevealed, or at least unrecorded, but which, aided by the good fortune or the happy inspiration of her marriage to a man of genius, has won for her a place in the company of women whose names are held in honour. ' There was no care which she could not mitigate, and no difficulty which she could not face. She was the most cheerful and the most courageous woman I ever knew.' Such was her husband's tribute when, after more than thirty years, death came to part them. She may have had no ambition and have hated politics, as she tells us, but she knew how to devote herself with perfect singleness of purpose to her husband's career ; while her faith in his coming greatness, her confidence in his power of surmounting every obstacle, her

buoyant courage in the hour of trial, and her invincible
constancy in misfortune, approached the sublime. And
she had her reward. Disraeli always found it hard to
persuade the world of his sincerity, even when he was
most sincere, but his bitterest enemies never ventured
to cast a doubt on the sincerity of his devotion to his
wife. Shortly before her death she told a woman friend
that ' her life had been a long scene of happiness, owing
to his love and kindness.' Her own testimony is supported both by the testimony of all who knew them and
by the testimony of the records, which is in this case, as
it chances, hardly less convincing : for every scrap of
paper that had once, for good or evil, been touched by
' dear Dizzy's ' pen, and fell into the hands of his wife,
became from that moment sacred, and was hoarded
among her treasures ; with the result that we are able to
catch illuminating glimpses of their intimate life such as
would otherwise have been impossible. Throughout the
thirty years and more for which their union lasted, not
even the shadow of a passing cloud seems ever to have
rested on their mutual affection. When Disraeli wrote
the glowing sentence, ' My nature demands that my life
should be perpetual love,' he pitched his ideal high, but
not higher than the actual truth which was realised in his
marriage.

The honeymoon was spent partly at Tunbridge Wells,
and later in a Continental tour which carried them as far
as Munich.

To Sarah Disraeli.

TUNBRIDGE WELLS,
Sept. 4.

We have had unceasing rain, and have therefore not left
our rooms, which we find very agreeable, except to drive to
Bayham[1] amid squalls, and an excursion to Penshurst yesterday amidst showers. De L'Isle was out shooting, but we saw
the children, whom we found quite charming. . . . I have
only been on the Pantiles once, and have met Lord Monteagle,[2]

---

[1] Lord Camden's.
[2] Mr. Spring Rice had just been succeeded as Chancellor of the Exchequer
by Mr. Francis Baring, and had gone to the Upper House as Lord Monteagle.

Mrs Disraeli.
1840.
from a picture by A.E. Chalon. R.A. at Hughenden.

with whom I am very good friends, notwithstanding our skirmishing. There is scarcely anybody here that we know, or care to know.

BADEN-BADEN,
Sept. 19.

This is the most picturesque, agreeable, lounging sort of place you can imagine. A bright little river winding about green hills, with a white sparkling town of some dozen palaces called hotels, and some lodging-houses, like the side scenes of a melodrama, and an old ruined castle or two on woody heights. I don't think we shall stay more than a week. Mary Anne says it is not much better than Cheltenham—public dinners, balls, promenades, pumps, music and gambling.

MUNICH,
Oct. 2.

We travelled from Baden to Stuttgart, through the Black Forest for two days—a region of uninterrupted interest, most savage and picturesque, though rich from its vegetation and occasional valleys of pasture. . . . Stuttgart a very handsome town of the Turin school, modern but improving ; but the Grecian villa of the king in the park is charming, and most tastefully furnished. We fell upon great *fêtes*, which pleased us much. The king, surrounded by a brilliant court, sat in a pavilion in the midst of a beautiful mead, which was enclosed by tiers of covered seats, and distributed prizes to the Wurtemberg peasants for oxen, horses, &c. 'Twas much finer than the tournament. More than 20,000 persons I should think present ; the peasantry in rich and bright dresses, dark velvets with many large silver buttons, vivid vests, and three-cornered cocked hats. It was fine to see a family leading a bull crowned with roses, rams worthy of the antique garlanded for altars. After this races, which were not very good, though the passion of the king is for horses, and his stables are, I believe, the finest in Europe. The whole scene was very patriarchal, though her Majesty came in half-a-dozen blue carriages with scarlet liveries. The king rode a fine barb, followed by grooms, &c., in scarlet.

We visited the studio of Dannecker, and I insisted on seeing the artist, whom I found a hale old man, more than eighty, but with a disorder in his throat which prevents him from speaking. He was much affected by our wishing to see him, and when we drove off opened the window of his room, waved his hand, and managed to say, ' Viva, viva !'

I have read enough of Hallam to make me thirst for literary history in detail. . . . I don't think his English literature his strongest point. He is very meagre and unjust—on Sir

Thomas Browne for instance. Compare Hallam with Cole-
ridge hereon. He never notices the extraordinary imagination
of B. In general, I see in Hallam a dash of German affectation
in his style, which he has imbibed of late years. My paper is
full.

Thousand loves to all.
D.

MUNICH,
Oct. 14.

After a fortnight's residence in this city, I find it difficult to
convey to you an idea of it. Since Pericles no one has done
so much for the arts as the King of Bavaria. Galleries of
painting and sculpture, Grecian temples, Gothic and Byzan-
tine churches, obelisks of bronze, equestrian statues of brass,
theatres and arcades painted in fresco, are but some of the
features of splendor and tasteful invention which on every
side solicit the eye, and which I can only allude to. . . . We
have seen the king several times, tall, meagre, and German—a
poet, which accounts for Munich, for a poet on a throne can
realise his dreams.[1]

HÔTEL DE L'EUROPE, RUE RIVOLI, PARIS,
Nov. 4.

We arrived here on Saturday very well ; and your very welcome letters reached me instantly. October until the last
two days presented to us a cloudless sky, which rendered our
travelling from Munich to Frankfort very agreeable. We
visited Ratisbon, a very ancient Gothic city. Walhalla, a
height on the Danube, crowned with a Grecian temple larger
than the Parthenon, but of beauty not less eminent, raised to
the genius of Germany by the King of Bavaria ; Nuremberg,
a city which retains all its olden character, the Pompeii of the
middle ages, and Wurtzburg-on-the-Maine, once the capital
of a princely prelate who sojourned in a much nobler palace
than our sovereigns. So to Frankfort, where after a few days
we crossed the Rhine, having travelled in our tour by the
waters not only of that river, but of the Neckar, the Danube,
and the Maine : the four principal rivers of Germany. The
Neckar and the Maine are charming, though not as famous
as the Rhine, nor offering at one point such an aggregate
of beauties as are clustered together between Bingen and
Coblentz. The famous Danube is but an uncouth stream ;
its bed is far too considerable for its volume, so that it presents
a shallow, shoaly look, with vast patches of sand and shingle
in the midst of its course.

---

[1] Disraeli contributed a short paper on Munich to the *Book of Beauty*
for 1840.

Henry Bulwer, who is now a great man, called on us on Sunday.

PARIS,
Nov. 22.

I hope to reach England in a week, and shall be very glad to find myself there again. The political horizon is cloudy and disturbed, but the serious illness of the Duke of Wellington, which has just reached our Embassy, may yet assist the Whigs on their last legs. I always hold that no one is ever missed, but he is so great a man that the world will perhaps fancy his loss irreparable. . . . We have been very gay in Paris and our friends very kind to us, having been invited to the Embassy, Canterburys, Sheridans, &c. . . . Mary Anne is particularly well, and in her new costumes looks like Madame de Pompadour, who is at present the model of Paris—at least in dress. . . . Paris is very much changed since my first visit ; there are *trottoirs* in every street, and in the most ordinary corners you find shops which Regent Street cannot equal. But their efforts in the higher arts, of which they talk so much, will not pass muster after Munich. We hope to meet my father quite himself again.

D.

His father, in their absence, had been attacked by an affection of the eyes from which he never recovered, and which ended in total blindness.

To Sarah Disraeli.

GROSVENOR GATE
[Undated].

Your letter would have made me very happy had it brought more satisfactory tidings of my father. I had persuaded myself from your account that the enfeebled vision merely arose from bodily health, sedentary habits, &c. We are very uneasy and unhappy about him, and we would take great care of him if he would come up for advice. Everything is very flat, and we live in the midst of perpetual fog, and shall be glad when business will let us find ourselves at Bradenham.

Dec. 18.

Alexander has just left us ; he seems to think with skill and care my father ought to recover his sight. There is no news otherwise, except my father thinks me looking very well, which makes me fear he is really blind, as this is the first time in his life he ever thought so. Last week we dined *en famille* with Mrs. Montefiore to meet Antony Rothschild, who is to marry one of the Montefiores, Charlotte. There were Rothschilds, Montefiores, Alberts, and Disraelis—not a Christian name, but Mary Anne bears it like a philosopher.

D'Orsay sent on his horse to Wycombe Abbey, as Bob Smith has none ' worth riding,' but he could not get out of the house the whole time he was there, even to pay you a visit. It was so foggy he was obliged to give it up. They had a roaring, robustious, romping party, of which he gave very amusing details. Playing hide-and-seek, they got into the roof, and Albert Conyngham fell through the ceiling of one of the rooms—an immense long leg dangling out. Carrington came to look at it with his eye-glass, but took it very good-humoredly. Great regrets on his part that I was not at Bradenham.[1]

[1] *Letters,* pp. 156-164.

CHAPTER III.

The Condition of England.

1839–1841.

That 'most capital speech on Chartism' in the last weeks of the session of 1839, of which we have already heard something, calls for more attention. It is remarkable in itself as a contribution to the study of the ' condition of England question,' which had long been in Disraeli's thoughts, and which a few years later was to provide him with a subject for the deepest of his novels ; and it stands out among the speeches of his first years in Parliament as the boldest proclamation to his leaders and to the world at large that he had by no means abandoned the position he had taken up in the early stages of his political career, and that he still desired to see a regenerated Toryism resting on the broad basis of faith in the people.

Chartism was the direct descendant of the older Radical movement with which Disraeli had been in sympathy at the time of his first incursions into the domain of practical politics. Since the passage of the Reform Act, Radicalism had changed its character, and an entirely new school—the so-called ' philosophic ' Radicals—had gained the ascendancy. With these, the orthodox upholders of the Benthamite tradition—men like Grote or Molesworth in Parliament, or the Mills outside—Disraeli had never anything in common. But when he entered the House of Commons there were still a few Radical members of the older or philanthropic type—men, for instance, like Fielden and Wakley—who inherited the

traditions, half Radical and half Tory, of Cobbett and
Burdett, and were inspired, not by abstract theories, but
by natural sympathy with the people and an active interest in their welfare. With these and their like Disraeli soon established friendly relations, possibly at first
through Bulwer and Duncombe, who were Radicals themselves, and as wits and dandies were already his friends ;
and friendly relations led in due course, on certain subjects of common interest, to a working alliance.

The philosophic school was essentially middle-class in
its genius and ideals, but English Radicalism in its origin
had been essentially popular and democratic. It had begun
in the closing decades of the eighteenth century as a movement for electoral reform, its earliest demands anticipating
the five points of the Chartists—annual Parliaments, manhood suffrage, vote by ballot, payment of members, and
abolition of the property qualification for a seat in the
House of Commons. The movement languished during
the Napoleonic wars, but renewed its vigour after the
peace, with Burdett as its leader and spokesman in the
House of Commons, and the counties as the main source
of its Parliamentary strength, but drawing also much
support from the manufacturing towns, which had been
brought into existence by the industrial revolution of the
preceding half-century. This revolution—the greatest
of its kind in the history of the world—had introduced
two new and disturbing factors into the old social order.
On the one hand it had created a large and wealthy class
of manufacturing capitalists, who regarded with jealous
eyes the monopoly of political power that was now in the
hands of the territorial aristocracy ; and on the other it
had congregated in the great towns of England a multitude of workers—men, women, and children—the misery
of whose lives was a disgrace to the nation. It was from
this suffering multitude that the movement which
ended in the first Reform Act drew most of its strength.
Ostensibly, political enfranchisement had been the object
of the agitation, but the deep sense of grievance which

was the real motive power had been far more social
than political in its origin.

The revolution, when accomplished, proved, however,
to be political far more than social in its significance and
results. The workers by whose aid the middle classes
had won their way into the citadel of power found themselves shut out. In abolishing the rotten boroughs, the
Whigs had taken occasion to make the borough franchise
less popular than before ; and if there was still a popular
element in the electorate for the counties, it owed its
preservation to the efforts of the Tories. The Reform
Bill, in fact, as Disraeli had been quick to see, was an
essentially class measure. Indirectly, no doubt, as he
remarks in *Sybil*, it tended in the long-run to further the
cause of social amelioration. ' It set men a-thinking ; it
enlarged the horizon of political experience ; . . . and
insensibly it created and prepared a popular intelligence,'
to which the statesman could appeal for the redress of
social evils. The people gained ultimately from the clash
between the ideals and ambitions of the aristocracy and
those of the middle class ; but at first it seemed to them
that they had only changed masters, and in many ways
for the worse, their new rulers being less sympathetic
than the old, and having certainly far less of the instinct
of public duty. From the beginning the new House of
Commons gave very little thought to the condition of
the multitude. During the period of Whig rule many
great and memorable measures were passed into law,
but in the domain of social and economic reform the
achievement of the thirties is not to be compared with
what had been accomplished in the unreformed Parliament during the preceding decade under the guidance
of Tory statesmen like Huskisson and Canning and
Robinson and Peel. The ten-pound householders, who
to their everlasting honour put an end at once to West
Indian slavery, had no eyes for the slavery, hardly less
real, that was close to their own doors. Class interest
blinded the rich manufacturers to the foundations of

human misery on which their wealth was raised, and the
dominant philosophy of the hour was ready with convenient formulæ to provide a sanction for their indifference. Disraeli, writing in *Sybil* in 1845, thus summed the
matter up :

If a spirit of rapacious covetousness, desecrating all the
humanities of life, has been the besetting sin of England for
the last century and a half, since the passing of the Reform
Act the altar of Mammon has blazed with triple worship.
To acquire, to accumulate, to plunder each other by virtue of
philosophic phrases, to propose a Utopia to consist only of
Wealth and Toil, this has been the breathless business of enfranchised England for the last twelve years, until we are
startled from our voracious strife by the wail of intolerable
serfage.[1]

The two achievements of the new Parliament in the
sphere of social legislation were a Factory Act to limit
the labour of children, passed in 1833, and the famous
new Poor Law of 1834. The Factory Act was the outcome of a movement which had been begun in the unreformed Parliament by the Tory Michael Sadler, a man
whose fame ought to be greater than it is, and continued
after the Reform Act by another Tory, Lord Ashley,
when Sadler had been rejected by the new middle-class
electorate in the great industrial town of Leeds in favour
of the very genius of triumphant Whiggery, Macaulay.
Unhappily, Ashley's efforts, like those of Sadler before
him, were to a great extent frustrated by the thinly-
veiled hostility of the Whig Ministry on the one
hand, and the fierce and open opposition of the manufacturing capitalists and their allies, the philosophic
Radicals, on the other ; and in the result the provisions
of the Act of 1833 were but a meagre and grudging concession to the crying needs of the case. The Poor Law
of 1834 was an even more characteristic expression of the
spirit of the new political order, both in its good points
and in its bad. In the last decades of the eighteenth
century and during the Napoleonic wars a change had

[1] *Sybil*, Bk. I. ch 5.

been in progress in English agriculture analogous to that which had substituted the capitalist manufacturers for the small masters in industry.   Hitherto, the farmers had been on much the same social level as the labourers among whom they lived ; now, while the less fortunate sank to the condition of their labourers, the more fortunate formed themselves into a wholly separate class, and a class that, as long as the war lasted, remained highly prosperous.   At the same time the position of the labourers changed rapidly for the worse, their relation to their employers, somewhat as in the case of the workers in the towns, though of course less completely, becoming, in Carlyle's phrase, an affair of cash nexus.   As the conditions of their life grew harder, the rural justices, who were charged with the administration of the Poor Law, began in a spirit of compassion the demoralising practice of supplementing wages out of the rates, and in the bad times of the war, when bread was at famine prices, this practice was extended, till in the Southern counties especially the great mass of the labouring poor had been converted into paupers.

For this state of things the Poor Law Amendment Act of 1834 was intended to provide a remedy.   It put an end to great abuses, and the Spartan rigour with which it was administered may in the long-run have been salutary, but the future gain was purchased at the price of much immediate suffering.   The transition to the new system was conducted with the ruthless logic of men possessed by a theory, and the first effect, undoubtedly, was greatly to increase the misery of the poor.   ' If paupers are made miserable,' said Carlyle grimly, ' paupers will needs decline in multitude.   It is a secret known to all rat-catchers.'   ' That this Poor Law Amendment Act,' he added, ' should be, as we sometimes hear it named, the chief glory of a Reformed Cabinet, betokens, one would imagine, rather a scarcity of glory there.' [1]   In its passage through the House of Commons the Bill had been

[1] *Chartism*, ch. 3.

supported, not only by the philosophic Radicals and the main body of the Whigs, but also by Peel, who in such matters, indeed, was a more faithful exponent of middle-class ideals than the Whig leaders themselves. It had been bitterly opposed, however, by the small band of Tories and philanthropic Radicals, through whose exertions the Factory Act had been carried in the previous year; and when in 1837, the year after the new Poor Law had come into force, a period of bad harvests and bad trade began, the distress that resulted led to a formidable agitation for the repeal of the measure.

With this agitation Disraeli was in active sympathy from the very beginning. He had been well aware, indeed, that the administration of the old law called for reform; and, as he indicated in one[1] of the speeches of his first year in politics, he would have endeavoured to reform it by bringing the Poor Laws ' back to the system of 1795 '—that is, to the old Elizabethan system before it had been perverted under the stress of the war. But he heartily disliked the Act of 1834, not only because it treated the pauper as a criminal, but also because it abolished the old parochial constitution, and violated, as he thought, in its centralising tendency the traditional principles of English self-government. As has been seen,[2] he fulminated against the new system during his contest at Maidstone, like many other candidates in the elections of that year; but, as both the front benches were opposed to the agitation, few of those who reached the House retained their interest in the matter, and it was ' quietly and good-naturedly hinted ' to Disraeli, as he afterwards related,[3] that if he wished to advance in public life he had better keep his opinions on the new Poor Law to himself. This hint, however, failed to deflect him from his course, and early in his first session, when ' an inconvenient and most unaccommodating Radical '[4] brought forward a motion for the immediate repeal of the Act,

[1] Vol. I., p. 220.
[2] *Ibid.*, p. 373.
[3] Speech at Shrewsbury, Aug. 27, 1844.
[4] Fielden.

he was one of a minority of thirteen Tories and philanthropic Radicals who voted in its favour against the
forces of the Government and the Opposition combined.
This crushing defeat checked for the moment the progress
of the agitation, but it was not sufficient, as we shall see,
to bring it to an end.

If the bad harvests which began in 1837 brought deeper
misery to the agricultural poor, the bad trade by which
they were accompanied made the condition of the industrial workers, if possible, even worse. The descriptions in *Sybil* of the rural town of Marney help us to
realise the sufferings of the one, the pictures of life in
Mowbray and the mining district near it the sufferings
of the other. It was under such conditions that Chartism
had its rise. Misery turned the thoughts of the working
classes once more to their invidious exclusion from
political rights, and, recalling the old Radical programme
from oblivion, they embodied its five points in a document which became famous as the People's Charter.
Great mass meetings were held in the North during
the autumn and winter of 1838, and when Parliament
met for the session of 1839 a National Convention of
Chartist delegates, which was called by its own constituency the People's Parliament, met in London at the
same time. The Convention devoted its energy to preparing a monster petition in favour of the Charter ; and
when, after some delay caused by the intervention of the
Bedchamber crisis, the time for its presentation came,
this petition, Disraeli tells us, ' was carried down to Westminster on a triumphal car, accompanied by all the delegates in solemn procession. It was necessary to construct
a machine in order to introduce the large bulk of parch-
ment, signed by a million and a half of persons, into the
House of Commons, and thus supported its vast form
remained on the floor of the House during the discussion.
The House, after a debate which was not deemed by the
people commensurate with the importance of the occasion, decided on rejecting the prayer of the petition, and

from that moment the party in the Convention who advocated a recourse to physical force in order to obtain their purpose was in the ascendant.'[1]

In the debate,[2] which as a matter of fact took place a month after the solemn procession, on a motion that the House should resolve itself into committee to consider the petition, Disraeli, who, as his letters show, had anticipated the occasion, and carefully prepared himself, spoke immediately after the leader of the House. He had learnt a good deal since the days when he himself believed in political mechanism as a remedy for social evils, so he began by admitting the fallacy by which, as Russell had insisted, the petition was pervaded—that political rights would necessarily insure social happiness. But though they might reject the remedy suggested by the Chartists, they ought none the less, he argued, to try and cure the disease. The nature of the disease was not clearly understood. The Chartist movement could not be explained as the work of professional agitators or as the outcome of mere sedition. Neither could it be wholly explained as the result of the new Poor Law, though he believed there was an intimate connexion between the two. Both Charter and new Poor Law, with many other evils, he would trace to the same origin—the Reform Act and the constitution which the Reform Act had established. The old constitution had an intelligible principle ; the present had none. 'Great duties could alone confer great station,' and while the old constitution imposed great public duties on the small class to which it entrusted political power, our new ruling class was not bound up with the great mass of the people by the performance of social duties, and had attained political station without the conditions which should be annexed to its possession. Having thus gained power without responsibility, our new rulers naturally were anxious to save themselves trouble and expense ; hence on the one hand the cry for cheap government, and their eagerness on the other

[1] *Sybil*, Bk. V. ch. 1.   [2] July 12, 1839.

to transfer to a centralised Government the social duties
which they ought to have accepted as the necessary
accompaniment of their new political privileges.   Hence,
for instance, the new Poor Law, which taught the desti-
tute not to look for relief to their neighbours, but to a
distant Government stipendiary.   It would be said,
indeed, that the Opposition were responsible in some
degree for the enactment of the new Poor Law, and he
admitted the fact ; but he also regretted it, and—here,
we may fancy, with a fugitive glance at Peel—he thought
their consenting to such a Bill was a very great blunder.
The Tory party would yet rue the day they did so, for
they had acted contrary to principle—the principle of
opposing everything like centralised government, and
favouring in every way the distribution of power.

The noble lord (John Russell), who was tolerant of the
advanced demands of his Radical supporters, treated the
Charter with derision because it was not compatible with
the retention of political power by the class which he
had created ; but if he thought that in this country a
monarchy of the middle classes could be permanently
established he would be indulging a great delusion—a
delusion which, if persisted in, must shake our institutions and endanger the throne.   Such a system was
foreign to the character of the English people.   In the
speeches of the Chartist leaders there was to be found
the greatest hostility to government by the middle
classes.   They made no attack on the aristocracy, none
on the Corn Laws ; but they attacked the new constituency, that peculiar constituency which was the basis
of the noble lord's government.   The whole subject, he
was aware, was distasteful to both the great parties in
the House.   He regretted the fact.   He was not ashamed
to say, however much he disapproved of the Charter, he
sympathised with the Chartists.   They formed a great
body of his countrymen, and no one could doubt they
laboured under great grievances.   This must always be
considered a very remarkable social movement.   It was

a social insurrection, and if they treated it as a mere temporary ebullition they would be grievously mistaken.

Having thus made his protest against the indifference with which the petition was treated on both sides of the House, Disraeli voted in the majority by which the motion was rejected. Charles Egremont, in *Sybil*, spoke on the same occasion, and a conversation in the novel well reflects the bewilderment which Disraeli's speech must have caused to Peel as he listened, or to any others who took the trouble to think of it at all :

' It was a very remarkable speech of Egremont,' said the grey-headed gentleman. ' I wonder what he wants.'

' I think he must be going to turn Radical,' said the Warwickshire peer.

' Why, the whole speech was against Radicalism,' said Mr. Egerton.

' Ah, then he is going to turn Whig, I suppose.'

' He is ultra anti-Whig,' said Egerton.

' Then what the deuce is he ?' said Mr. Berners.

' Not a Conservative certainly, for Lady St. Julians does nothing but abuse him.'

' I suppose he is crotchety,' suggested the Warwickshire noble.

' That speech of Egremont was the most really democratic speech that I ever read,' said the grey-headed gentleman. . . .

' What does he mean by obtaining the results of the Charter without the intervention of its machinery ?' inquired Lord Loraine, a mild, middle-aged, lounging, languid man, who passed his life in crossing from Brooks' to Boodle's, and from Boodle's to Brooks', and testing the comparative intelligence of these two celebrated bodies. . . .

' I took him to mean—indeed, it was the gist of the speech— that, if you wished for a time to retain your political power, you could only effect your purpose by securing for the people greater social felicity.'

' Well, that is sheer Radicalism,' said the Warwickshire peer ; ' pretending that the people can be better off than they are is Radicalism, and nothing else.'[1]

Before the debate took place the Convention had been transferred to Birmingham, and there, three days later, there was a riot so fierce that the Duke of Wellington

[1] *Sybil*, Bk. V. ch. 1.

sought a parallel for the scene of devastation in his recollections of the Peninsula. But when Russell, as Home
Secretary, asked the House of Commons to authorise an
advance to the Birmingham Corporation for the establishment of a police force, Disraeli opposed, insisting that
inquiry into the insurrectionary spirit should precede the
grant of extraordinary powers, and in a House of 150
he had the courage to enter the lobby as one of a minority
of three[1] against the resolution. Next day, on the first
reading of a Bill for the institution of a local constabulary, he accused Lord John of declaring war against Birmingham, and levying 5,000 troops against his former
allies. His speech on this occasion drew a severe reproof
from the Chancellor of the Exchequer,[2] and an Under-
Secretary[3] had the temerity to denounce him as ' an
advocate of riot and confusion.' Disraeli in his rejoinder
gave them both a taste of his quality :

I have heard some comments made upon me by the Chancellor of the Exchequer and an Under-Secretary of State
which I do not choose to pass unnoticed. Indeed, from a
Chancellor of the Exchequer to an Under-Secretary of State
is a descent from the sublime to the ridiculous, though the
sublime is on this occasion rather ridiculous, and the ridiculous
rather trashy. How he became Chancellor of the Exchequer,
and how the Government to which he belongs became a
Government, it would be difficult to tell. Like flies in amber,
' One wonders how the devil they got there.'[4]

At a later stage of the same Bill, Disraeli scored a palpable hit at the expense of Lord John Russell, who had
ascribed the disturbances in the country to Oastler,[5] a
well-known Tory Chartist, and to the agitation against
the Poor Law, in which Oastler had been a leader.
' Far be it from me,' said Disraeli, ' to cope with the
noble lord in endeavouring to trace the pedigree of

---

[1] Fielden and Wakley were the others, the tellers being Leader and
Duncombe.
[2] Spring Rice.
[3] Fox Maule, afterwards Lord Panmure and 11th Earl of Dalhousie.
[4] It is to this incident that Disraeli alludes in his letter on p. 70.
[5] Richard Oastler, 1789-1861, known as the ' Factory King,' Sadler's
friend and chief ally in his crusade against the abuses of the factory system.

sedition, but I confess I feel disposed to trace it to a higher source than Mr. Oastler. . . . There was a time, as you are all aware, after the Reform Bill had passed this House, when we were told 200,000 men were to march from Birmingham to assist the decision of the other House of Parliament. That was before Mr. Oastler. . . . The noble lord regards the Chartists as if they were the first body of men who had appealed to physical force. He talks as if the hon. and learned member for Dublin had never appealed to a petition signed by 50,000 fighting men.'[1] Peel in the next session took the same line of argument, and followed it with great effect.

Rioting in the towns and rick-burning in the country continued during the recess, and at Newport in Wales there was positive insurrection. When Parliament met in January, a vote of want of confidence was moved from the Opposition benches, and the Ministry formally charged with responsibility for these disorders.

To Sarah Disraeli.

HOUSE OF COMMONS,
Friday [Jan. 31, 1840].

MY DEAREST,
This is a hurried sketch of our debate. Sir Yarde[2] was very bad, but not much less effective than Acland last year in a similar position ; but more stupid, the difference being Sir Tom only stuttered, Sir John stuck. Sir George Grey made a dashing House of Commons speech which I should have liked to have answered, but as he concluded about 8, and I had not dined, it was impossible. I had no intention of speaking the first night, and am very sorry I did, for, although I said some good things and was very well received, I was debarred by circumstances from making the speech I had intended. The fact is the Government put up Gisborne, who is sometimes a most rakehelly rhetorician, and produces great effects in a crowded house, but uncertain. There was and had been for some time a general rumor that he was to make a great display, and when he got up Fremantle came to me and asked me to reply to him. He began very well, but after some little time regularly broke down, was

---

[1] *The Times,* Aug. 10, 1839.
[2] Sir John Yarde-Buller, afterwards Lord Churston.

A.E.Chalon. R.A. &c. 1840.

Benjamin Disraeli.
1840.
from a picture by A.E.Chalon.R.A at Hughenden.

silent for some moments, sent for oranges, coughed, stuck
again and again and again, and finally, pleading 'some
physical inability' which had suddenly deprived him of his
voice, sunk overwhelmed with his own exposure. We thought
he was drunk, but the Whigs say the fault was he was not,
and that when he is tipsy and is not prepared he is very good.
I found, however, I had a lame bird to kill, or rather a dying
one : and though I made a somewhat brilliant guerilla operation, there was not that solid tactical movement that I had
originally contemplated.

The next night we had it all our own way, Howick making
the most extraordinary announcement[1] which you have read
and alone justifies the debate. Graham very rigorous and
malignant, and Macaulay[2] plunging into the most irretrievable
slough of failure you can possibly conceive ; nothing could be
worse—manner, matter, and spirit, ludicrously elaborate and
perfectly inappropriate. The Speaker with difficulty preserved order, and it was clear to everyone that in future
Macaulay will no longer command the House, on such an
occasion, and to such a personage, of course, always lenient.

Yesterday we again had it all our own way, Stanley being
very effective. The debate is with us, but the division[3]—
though Arthur Lennox has rallied to the Tories—will, I apprehend, be very seedy.

Vale.

D.

Disraeli in his speech resumed towards the Chartists
his attitude of the previous session. ' I am not ashamed
or afraid to say that I wish more sympathy had been
shown on both sides towards the Chartists. . . . I am
not ashamed to say that I sympathise with millions of
my fellow-subjects.' Guerilla operation as the speech
may have been, it contains one passage that became
famous—a characteristic fling at Lord John Russell :

The time will come when Chartists will discover that in a
country so aristocratic as England even treason, to be successful, must be patrician. They will discover that great truth,
and when they find some desperate noble to lead them they

---

[1] In explanation of his withdrawal from the Ministry at the beginning
of the recess.

[2] ' That unfortunate speech on Buller's motion in 1840 ; one of the few
unlucky things in a lucky life,' was Macaulay's own verdict many years
later (Trevelyan's *Life*, ch. 8).

[3] The Government had a majority of 21 in a House of nearly 600 members.

may, perhaps, achieve greater results. Where Wat Tyler
failed, Henry Bolingbroke changed a dynasty, and although
Jack Straw was hanged, a Lord John Straw may become a
Secretary of State.

In the course of the session Disraeli had the courage
to help his Radical friends in attempts to secure remission of what he regarded, and not without reason, as the
excessive punishment inflicted on some of the Chartist
leaders,[1] voting on one occasion in a minority of five ;
denouncing the Whig Government as harsher in its practice than even the Star Chamber ; asking ' how it happened that the same thing obtained impunity in Ireland
under the name of agitation, which in England was
punished under the name of sedition ;' and making a
characteristic appeal to the Tory members around him
not to forget that they were the natural leaders of the
people. ' Yes, I repeat,' he added, in response to cries
of protest from the Whig side of the House, ' the aristocracy are the natural leaders of the people, for the
aristocracy and the labouring population form the nation.'[2]

His conduct in these matters drew an approving letter
from a notable popular leader, Charles Attwood,[3] of Newcastle, to which Disraeli sent an interesting reply :

To Charles Attwood.

GROSVENOR GATE,
June 7, 1840.

. . . I am honored by your approbation of my public conduct.
I entirely agree with you, that an union between the Conservative party and the Radical masses offers the only
means by which we can preserve the Empire. Their interests
are identical ; united they form the nation ; and their division
has only permitted a miserable minority, under the specious
name of the People, to assail all rights of property and person.
Since I first entered public life, now eight years ago, I have
worked for no other object and no other end than to aid the

[1] Six years later (March 11, 1846), when he had won a great position in
the House of Commons, he spoke and voted again in favour of a motion
with the same object in view, and was again in a minority.

[2] Hansard, July 10, 1840.

[3] Founder of the Northern Political Unions, which played a great part
in the Reform Bill agitation, and brother of Thomas Attwood, the member
for Birmingham, Cobbett's ' King Tom.'

formation of a national party. And when I recollect the
difficulties with which this proposition struggles, and the
contests and misrepresentations which I have personally
experienced in advocating its adoption, you may understand
the extreme satisfaction with which I have witnessed the
recent progress of events, and now learn, on your unquestionable authority, that in Northumberland, long the sacred refuge
of Saxon liberty, a considerable party, founded on the union
in question, is at present in process of formation and of rapid
growth.

None but those devoid of the sense and spirit of Englishmen
can be blind to the perils that are impending over our country.
Our Empire is assailed in every quarter ; while a domestic
oligarchy, under the guise of Liberalism, is denationalising
England. Hitherto we have been preserved from the effects
of the folly of modern legislation by the wisdom of our ancient
manners. The national character may yet save the Empire.
The national character is more important than the Great
Charter or trial by jury. Notwithstanding the efforts of the
Whigs to sap its power, I still have confidence in its energy.

Meanwhile, in spite of his sometimes aggressive independence, Disraeli had succeeded in winning the approbation of a leader whose approbation was never lightly
given. In the first days of the session of 1840 Peel
invited him to attend what would now be called a ' shadow
Cabinet '—a conference of the principal members of the
Conservative Opposition, sixteen in all, of whom, as Mrs.
Disraeli proudly records, ' Dizzy was the only one who
had not been in office.' On the very day that he received
this signal proof of confidence he reasserted his independence by a brilliant incursion into debate in opposition
to his leader, and by voting against him in the division
that followed. The House of Commons had become
involved in the famous affair of Stockdale, and was now,
at the instance of both the front benches, about to
commit the Sheriffs of London to the custody of the
Serjeant-at-Arms for executing orders of the Court of
Queen's Bench which were represented as a breach of
privilege. An overzealous legal member, in the course
of the debate, was foolish enough to enlarge on the
tyranny of the courts in the time of Charles I., and Dis-

raeli, who was well read in the history of that period, replied at once in a speech ' of great eloquence and vigour,' as the newspapers described it, in which he gave a vivid account of the tyranny of Parliament in the same troubled age, and showed that the tyranny of the courts was nothing in comparison. He ended with a declaration which has not lost its significance, that there was a difference between the law of Parliament and the law of the House of Commons, and that ' he for one would never consent to see the country subjected to the law of the latter.'

To Sarah Disraeli.

[*Jan.* 19, 1840.]

Peel congratulated me very warmly on my marriage. . . . Yesterday I gave my first male dinner-party. Everything went off capitally ; Lyndhurst, Strangford, Powerscourt, Ossulston, D'Orsay, Sir R Grant, and Sir L. Bulwer, &c. . . . I have been introduced at last formally to the Duke of Wellington at Lyndhurst's ; he accorded me a most gracious and friendly reception, and looked right hearty. The Queen is to be married February 10.

5.30 [*Jan.* 23].

Since Tuesday I have done nothing but receive congratulations about my speech. . . . Lord Fitzgerald just told me that since the good old days of Canning he had never heard so brilliant a reply. . . . Hogg says it was not only a good speech : it was something better, an effective. The curious thing is that *The Times*, which gives an admirable report of what I said, gives a most inefficient impression of the effect produced. I never heard more continued cheering : the house very full, about half-past 10 when I sat down, a prime hour and every man of distinction there. I never spoke better even in Bucks. It is in vain to give you any account of all the compliments, all the congratulations, the shaking of hands, &c., which occurred in the lobby during the division, but time and this damned post prevent all communication. . . . From Sir Robert Peel downwards there is but one opinion of my great success. Eliot very warm indeed.

I have been to see the sheriffs in prison. They really think themselves martyrs. I told them they would ' live in history,' and they answered, ' No doubt of it.'

Burn this egotistical trash.   Love,

D.

[Undated.]

Eastell, who dined with me yesterday, had just come up from old Lord Sidmouth at Richmond. The fine old gentleman, now 85, takes the most lively interest in the question, and, strange for an old Speaker, is on the side of law. He was in raptures with my speech.

Feb. 12.

The Duke of Bucks has dined with me ; he was really quite gay and seemed delighted with everything, which with him is very rare, as society bores him. I have asked sixty M.P.'s to dine with me, and forty have come. I shall now rest upon my oars. We are in great confusion with Stockdale. He bore his examination with great coolness, without being audacious, and unbroken presence of mind. The sheriffs and under-sheriffs have been under examination, but the House only gets deeper in the mire, and I think the result is that they must commit the sheriffs, which will occasion a riot, and eventually the judges, which will cause a rebellion. If Follett had not misled Peel originally, the Whigs would have been crushed.

[Feb. 18.]

MY DEAREST,

I went up yesterday with our House,[1] very strong in numbers and very brilliant in costume ; but it was generally agreed that I am never to wear any other but a Court costume, being, according to Ossulston, a very Charles II.

The peers preceding our procession by only half an hour, the golden carriages of the Lord Chancellor and the Speaker were almost blended in the same crowd, and the quantity of carriages and personages of note, to say nothing of courtiers, gentlemen-at-arms, and beefeaters, was very fine. All our men were costumed, but Scholefield and Muntz, and a few Rads, including, to my surprise, O'Connell, *en bourgeois*. The Speaker, with John Russell on his right and Peel on his left, both in the Windsor dress, marched up to the throne in good style ; we followed somewhat tumultuously. The Queen looked well : the Prince on her left in high military fig very handsome, and the presence was altogether effective. Always having heard the Palace abused, I was rather agreeably surprised : the hall is low, but the staircase is not ineffective ; the antechamber, a green drawing-room, in which we were assembled for half an hour, leads at once to the Throne room. After the Bavarian palaces, all this is nothing, but I was amused, for the scene was busy and brilliant.

My love to all.

D.

---

[1] To congratulate the Queen on her marriage.

BRIGHTON,
April 20.

We have found this place pleasant enough, the weather being very fine. I have eaten a great many shrimps, which are the only things that have reminded me I am on the margin of the ocean ; for it has been a dead calm the whole week, and I have not seen a wave or heard the break of the tide. There are a good many birds of passage here, like ourselves. I had a long stroll with the Speaker,[1] who is the most amiable of men and not one of the least agreeable, fresh as a child and enjoying his holidays.

June 1.

After all, poor Lady Cork did not die of old age ; she was arranging her plants in a new fashion and caught cold. On Saturday at Hope's I sat next to Rogers, and he made one or two efforts at conversation which I did not encourage ; but after the second course (Rogers having eaten an immense dinner), both of us in despair of our neighbours, we could no longer refrain from falling into talk, and it ended by a close alliance, the details and consequences of which are so amusing that I must reserve them for our visit.

All the world has been this morning to Exeter Hall to see Prince Albert in the chair. Peel moved one of the resolutions, and produced a great effect on his Highness.

Friday, June 12.

The political world is convulsive : the Government, by extraordinary efforts and pledging themselves that if in a minority they would resign, having induced Howick and all the malcontents, rats, and shufflers to return to their allegiance, came to pitched battle again last night, and were, to our surprise as much as their own consternation, ignobly defeated. After this occurred a scene which only can be compared to Donnybrook fair. O'Connell insanely savage, the floor covered with members in tumultuous groups, Stratford Canning pale as a spectre, with outstretched and arraigning arm, hooting, cheering, groaning, and exclamations from unknown voices in the senatorial crowd. Maidstone in full dress, fresh from the Clarendon, re-enacting the part of the English Marcellus, and Norreys with a catcall.

To-day the Houses went up to the Queen with congratulations on her escape.[2] I didn't go.

On Wednesday the Lyndhursts, Ingestres, Ernest Bruces, Hoggs, Lords Munster, Claud Hamilton, Walpole, Gardner, Follett, and the Duchess Dowager of Richmond, dined with

---

[1] Shaw-Lefevre, afterwards Viscount Eversley.
[2] From the attempt on her life by the madman Oxford.

us : very brilliant and successful, and Mary Anne much pleased, particularly as she is going to-night to the musical ball, and afterwards to Lady Lyndhurst's supper, which is revived and is to be very grand.

July 14.

Last night I massacred Dr. Bowring.[1] . . . I answered the Chancellor of the Exchequer, and was replied to by the President of the Board of Trade, who, however, had nothing to say for himself, and was obliged to take refuge in mere assertions. My facts flabbergasted him, as well as Bowring's champion, Hume, who was ludicrously floored. His speech is not in the least reported, but convulsed the House when he said the ' hon. and *learned* member for Maidstone ' had taken him by surprise, quoting authors he had never read, &c. &c. Peel most gallantly came to the rescue of his ' hon. friend the member for Maidstone,' and gave me immense *kudos.*

Aug. 7.

Yesterday Louis Napoleon, who last year at Bulwer's nearly drowned us by his bad rowing, upset himself at Boulogne. Never was anything so rash and crude to all appearances as this ' invasion,' for he was joined by no one. A fine house in Carlton Gardens, his Arabian horses, and excellent cook was hardly worse than his present situation.

In a note of later years Disraeli recounts at length the incident at Bulwer's :

Bulwer, who then lived at Craven Cottage, gave a breakfast party there. We arrived late, and all the guests had gone up the Thames in a steamer. Walking on the Terrace, quite alone, two gentlemen who had arrived still later came up to us. These were Prince Louis Napoleon and Persigny. My wife explained to the Prince why the assembly was so scant. Upon which the Prince said : ' We will get a boat, and I will row you down to meet them.'

There was a boat and boatman lingering about, whom we hailed from the Terrace. The Prince took the oars, and for a little time we went on very well. At last, to escape the swell of a steamer that was approaching, the Prince contrived to row into a mudbank in the middle of the river, and there we stuck. Nothing could get us off. I was amused by the

[1] A well-known Benthamite who had been employed by Government to make commercial investigations abroad, as the Opposition alleged, from motives of political jobbery, and at a greatly excessive remuneration. He was afterwards, as Sir John Bowring, Plenipotentiary in China, and became famous in connexion with the Arrow affair in 1856-57.

manner in which my wife, who was alarmed especially, and not without cause, from the fear of other steamboats which caused a great swell on the water, rated the Prince : ' You should not undertake things which you cannot accomplish. You are always, sir, too adventurous,' &c. &c. &c. I remained silent. At length the boatman, who had come to the rescue, got us off, and we arrived again at Craven Cottage just as Bulwer's company appeared in the distance. Nothing could be more good-natured than the Prince, and I could not have borne the scolding better myself. We often used to smile over this adventure ; and many years after (I think 1856) my wife sat next to the Emperor at dinner at the Tuileries, and as he was chatty, and often adverted to the past, she ventured to remind His Majesty of the story, which he said he quite remembered. The Empress, who overheard them, said : ' Just like him.'

To Sarah Disraeli.

WOOLBEDING,
Sept. 7.

We are staying a few days with the Maxses. There is no one here except Tom Duncombe ; but, as you know, the place is very beautiful, a paradise of flowers and conservatories, fountains and vases, in the greenest valley with the prettiest river in the world. This was a former temple of Whiggery. Charles Fox's statue and portrait may be seen in every nook and every chamber, a sort of rural Brooks's.

[Undated.]

Walpole[1] went to dine yesterday with the Miss Berrys, who now live at Richmond ; the party consisting of Miss Montague, Guizot, and Pollington—very *recherché* and ' Strawberry Hillish.' The old ladies a little in love with the Horace Walpole of the nineteenth century, who, by the bye, is more elegant, fantastical, and interesting than ever, and talks of changing his name, retiring to Parma or Cremona, or some city equally decayed and unvisited. Venice too vulgar, with Monckton Milnes writing sonnets in every gondola, and making every bridge ' a bridge of sighs.' I breakfasted with him to-day, and he really was divine. I never met anything like him—such a stream of humor, fancy, philosophy, and quotation, in every language. When last in Egypt he met Botta, who talked of me much.

Peace, peace is the order of the day, and French funds have risen 5 per cent. in one day. The Princess Augusta still lives, but everybody else in London seems dead.

---

[1] Afterwards 4th Earl of Orford.

Throughout the autumn England and France were hovering on the verge of war, for this was the memorable year of the expulsion of Mehemet Ali's Egyptians from Syria, Palmerston's greatest triumph in his career as a Foreign Minister. With due reserve of judgment as to the intrinsic wisdom of the Minister's policy, Disraeli has celebrated the achievement in a glowing passage of *Tancred :*

When we consider the position of the Minister at home, not only deserted by Parliament, but abandoned by his party and even forsaken by his colleagues ; the military occupation of Syria by the Egyptians ; the rabid demonstrations of France ; that an accident of time or space, the delay of a month or the gathering of a storm, might alone have baffled all his combinations ; it is difficult to fix upon a page in the history of this country which records a superior instance of moral intrepidity. The bold conception and the brilliant performance were worthy of Chatham ; but the domestic difficulties with which Lord Palmerston had to struggle place the exploit far beyond the happiest achievement of the elder Pitt.[1]

To Sarah Disraeli.

Oct. 15.

The King of Holland has abdicated, and Beyrout, after a bombardment of nine hours, has been taken by the English. The Cabinet have decided on 'carrying out' the treaty of July to the letter, with only four dissentients. *On dit* that even Lord Holland, that old Gallomaniac, ratted to Palmerston, who is quite triumphant. Great panic exists here, and even the knowing ones, who from their confidence in Louis Philippe have all along been sanguine of peace, look very pale and blue. Alas ! that a Bourbon dynasty, even of Orleans, should absolutely depend for its existence on a Guizot or a Thiers, a *professeur* and a *rédacteur.* My domestic ministry, which is as troublesome as the French, is provisionally formed.

Oct. 22.

Lord Holland was found dead in his bed this morning. This, though not considered as yet a very significant event, is in my eyes not unimportant. It breaks up an old clique of pure Whiggery, and the death of a single Minister, by causing Cabinet reconstruction, is always of some weight. . . . We have had a delightful visit to Deepdene. In the midst of romantic grounds and picturesque park Hope has built,

---

[1] *Tancred,* Bk. III. ch. 6.

or rather is still building, a perfect Italian palace, full of
balconies adorned with busts. On the front a terraced
garden, and within a hall of tesselated pavement of mosaics,
which is to hold his choicest marbles. We found there Mr.
and Mrs. Adrian Hope, and Harness,[1] now grown an oldish
gentleman, but still juvenile in spirits, and even ready to act
charades and spout poetry. Mrs. Adrian is French, a child
of nature—never heard of Sir R. Peel. She is the daughter
of the famous General Rapp.

Nov. 21.

There is no doubt that Acre has fallen, and therefore the
matter is settled. What was the poor Pacha to do against
all Europe ? He has been infamously misled by that rascal
Thiers, a thorough representative of the *gaminerie* of Paris.
In the meantime, the Liberals are infinitely disgusted with
Palmerston's triumph, and quarrel among themselves in much
the same fashion as Monsieur Thiers. . . .

We intend spending Christmas at Deepdene, and from
thence to Bradenham. We had the Lyndhursts and Tanker-
villes, with Cis Forester and Hope, to dinner the other day,
when we had a perfect *Spanish pudding*. Lyndhurst recognised his old Bradenham friend. Tankerville's French cook,
he tells me to-day, has been trying his ' 'prentice hand ' at
it, but a fiasco. He says he finds a French cook can never
execute out of his school, and Cis wants the receipt for the
mess, but Mary Anne won't give it.

DEEPDENE,
Dec. 26.

We arrived here a week ago, with our host and Adrian
Hopes. Then came Mr. Mitchell, very amusing ; Baron
and Baroness de Cetto, Walpole, Lord de L'Isle, Sir A. Grant,
and Lord and Lady Ernest Bruce ; two days after came
Baron Gersdorf, Sir Hume Campbell ; and these formed our
Christmas party, with the addition of the delectable Mr.
Hayward. . . . Our party very merry and agreeable, and we
have had many Christmas gambols, charades, and ghosts ;
and our princely host made all the ladies a Christmas box ;
to Mary Anne two beautiful specimens of Dresden china, a
little gentleman in cocked hat and full dress, and a most
charming little lady covered with lace. A thousand loves,
and good wishes for a real happy Christmas and New Year.
God grant it may turn out so for all of us.

D.[2]

---

[1] Doubtless William Harness, 1790-1869, divine and author, schoolfellow
and friend of Byron, and at this time incumbent of Regent Square Chapel.
[2] *Letters*, pp. 176-180.

Peel's clumsy management of the crisis of 1839 had renewed the Whig lease of office for a longer term than he or anyone else expected. The popularity of the young Queen had waned after the Bedchamber affair, and had not been increased by her German marriage ; but it had been revived in full force by the attempt on her life in the summer of 1840, and the Ministry of which her popularity was the mainstay profited accordingly. The triumph of Palmerston's foreign policy in the autumn of that year had brought them great prestige ; and if discontent was still rife, disorder at least had been checked, and the Chartists dragooned into a sombre inactivity. It was small wonder if for a moment in that winter of 1840 many Whigs believed that the long downward movement had at last been arrested, and that their party was in the fair way of recovering its authority.

But, as Mr. Tadpole observed with much originality at the Carlton, they were dancing on a volcano. It was December, and the harvest was not yet all got in, the spring corn had never grown, and the wheat was rusty ; there was, he well knew, another deficiency in the revenue to be counted by millions ; wise men shook their heads and said the trade was leaving the country, and it was rumored that the whole population of Paisley lived on the rates.[1]

It was the fourth time in succession that the harvest had failed, and there was no sign of trade recovering its activity. Population had increased immensely since the end of the great war, and wages had been steadily falling ; but up to a certain point there had been compensation for the fall in their higher purchasing power, and even the price of food had, in spite of the Corn Laws, on the whole been trending downward. During the twenty years before the accession of the Queen the wretchedness of the people had been due to low wages rather than to dear food ; but the long period of high prices, combined with exceptionally bad employment since the opening of her reign, had made the position intolerable, and some great measure of social

[1] *Endymion*, ch. 65.

renovation was clearly required. The Whigs appeared to be helpless ; Disraeli's friends, the Chartists, had come forward with their remedy, but it had been contemptuously rejected, and discontent, debarred from one mode of expression, was seeking another channel.

It was now that the agitation, hitherto fitful, for the repeal of the Corn Laws began to gather power, and that the great question which was to transform the whole of English politics came to the forefront. The Corn Laws were so long the gage of party battle, and they raise issues with regard to which party feeling is still so vehement, that it is by no means easy to thread a way through the controversial tangle in which they are involved. Anyone who tries will find himself at once in a bewildering atmosphere of legend and exaggeration, of half-truths masquerading as indefeasible principles, and rival theories appropriating such facts as fit them, while ignoring the rest. When he realises, as he soon will, the infinite complexity of the social and economic organism which is the field of investigation, and the enormous difficulty of segregating the effects of any given cause in the multitudinous play of social and economic forces ; when he tries, for instance, to distinguish between the influence on prices of tariff legislation in the first half of the last century and what in all probability was the far more potent influence of currency conditions during the same period ; when he sees how easily even the best-established principles may be thwarted or obscured in their operation by counteracting agencies, and the readiness with which figures can without falsification be selected to prove any given thesis, he will be apt, if he set forth without partisan purpose, to take refuge in a sort of economic agnosticism. He will learn at all events not to trust the confident dogmatism of either school of partisans, and perhaps to suspect that the question of high tariff or low in its strictly economic bearing is a good deal less important than either believes ; and when he has also come to see how the economic question proper involved in the controversy was overshadowed from the first by great political issues, he will not think more lightly of the difficulties in the way of retrospective judgment.

The Corn Laws were a natural development of the great mercantile system the foundations of which had been laid by Burleigh in the reign of Elizabeth, and which, built up gradually during the storms of the seventeenth century, was sedulously maintained by the Whig aristocracy that governed England in the eighteenth. Whatever its practical defects or the theoretical fallacies by which it was sometimes defended, this system had the merit of setting before itself a single definite aim, which it pursued with steadfast purpose, and which gave it unity and coherence. Its aim was political power, and, if it sometimes erred in its choice of measures, it chose them with more enlightenment, as is now generally recognised, than critics in the first reaction which led to its overthrow were disposed to admit ; and certainly during its sway of two centuries or more England rose to an astonishing height of prosperity and greatness. The system extended its reach over the whole field of economic activity, not only commerce and industry, but agriculture also. Up to near the end of the eighteenth century England exported corn, and for nearly a hundred years from the time of the Revolution production had been encouraged by a bounty on export, which it is claimed, and it would seem with justice, helped to steady prices as between years of scarcity and abundance. Then came a period of transition, when imports were sometimes necessary, and for nearly twenty years, under an Act of 1773, there was comparative free trade. By the time of the French Revolution the home supply had become permanently deficient, and in 1791 there was a reversion to the old policy of encouraging home production, now, however, by the method of a duty on imports intended to exclude foreign supplies when the home price fell below a certain standard ; but under the abnormal conditions of the revolutionary wars this and subsequent legislation remained practically a dead letter. Prices soon rose to the point at which corn could have been imported at a merely nominal duty ; but foreign supplies were not available, and in spite of all efforts to increase the home production, wheat continued to rise till in 1812 it actually reached the level of 155s. the quarter. With this result, of which the depreciated currency seems to have been the principal cause, the Corn Laws had nothing to do. Whatever the intention of their framers, up to 1815 they had in practice hardly affected the price of corn or bread ; yet it was probably the recollection of those terrible famine years more than any subsequent experience that made the name of Corn Law stink in the nostrils of the people.

The famine prices of the war had, of course, brought advantage to landlords and farmers, in spite of the burden of the rates under the old Poor Law, which grew with their profits ; but on the restoration of peace the whole structure of English agriculture seemed to be threatened with collapse, and the assistance of the legislature was accordingly invoked. It was natural enough, and in harmony with the whole spirit of the mercantile system, that something should be done to help the greatest national interest through a difficult transition ; but the Corn Law of 1815 exceeded all bounds, altogether prohibiting the import of foreign wheat when the home price fell below 80s. a quarter.[1] Fortunately, its injustice was frustrated by its ineptitude, and the attempt to maintain prices at the 80s. level was an absolute failure. Encouraged by the security, real or apparent, which the law gave to the corn-grower, the home production rapidly increased ; and when the resumption of cash payments had led to a general decline in prices, wheat fell in a few years to a level below the average of the generation that followed the complete repeal of the Corn Laws.

[1] By an interesting provision wheat was admitted from Canada at 67s. a quarter.

The result was an inquiry into agricultural distress, and an attempt in 1822 to bring the law more nearly into unison with the facts by a reduction of the price at which importation began to 70s. a quarter. The failure to control prices was again, however, complete. When the Corn Laws became an object of party attack, there was much exaggeration of the evils they had caused. As late as 1840 Peel was able to show that the average amount of duty levied on all the wheat imported under these laws did not exceed 5s. 3d. a quarter. But in one respect their mischief could hardly be exaggerated. By depriving the country of the steadying effect of moderate importation, the Acts of 1815 and 1822 seriously increased the fluctuation of prices, and the Act of 1828, which eventually took their place, only made matters worse. This Act, which was passed by the Wellington Ministry, and which was the Act that remained in force till Peel took the matter in hand in his second administration, employed the complicated mechanism of a sliding scale of duties, the duty being nominal at 73s., and rising to a maximum of 23s. 8d. inversely as the price fell to 64s. It was obviously now the interest of the importers to hold back corn till prices had reached their zenith, and the fluctuations in consequence were more violent than ever.

Moreover, by 1828 the moral justification for a Corn Law so stringent had largely disappeared. The earlier legislation had been an addition to a general code which gave a fairly balanced protection to all economic interests. But the country had been outgrowing the old mercantile system, and Huskisson had reconstructed it, during his memorable term of office as President of the Board of Trade from 1823 to 1827, to suit the new conditions. He by no means, indeed, discarded the traditional principle of regulating trade in the interest of maritime power and economic equilibrium, but he swept away a multitude of antiquated restrictions originally devised in the interest of commerce, and abolished or reduced an immense number of duties for the protection of industries now

strong enough to stand alone. Though Huskisson is said
to have been the inventor of the sliding scale, it is certain
that he would not have applied it as it was applied in the
Act of 1828 ; and it is unfortunate that he was not allowed
or encouraged to deal with the Corn Laws in the same
liberal spirit which he had brought to his reforms affect-
ing industry and commerce. The question was left for
settlement to Wellington's ill-starred Ministry, and they
entirely forgot that Huskisson's reforms had made the
position accorded to agriculture appear special and invidious, so that the Corn Laws henceforth wore the aspect
of a class measure.

In a sense the new Poor Law of 1834, by diminishing
the burden of the rates, which under the old system had
weighed so heavily on the land, tended also to deprive
the Corn Laws of their moral justification.   Otherwise
during the period of Whig rule in the thirties the position
remained unaltered.   The Whigs were protectionists by
the tradition of their party, and they suffered at this
time from complete incapacity in all matters of public
economy and finance. The Act of 1828, as completely as
its predecessors, failed to maintain prices at the level
that was aimed at ; and under it production so rapidly
developed that, according to an estimate of Peel's on the
eve of its supersession, nearly 90 per cent. of the wheat
consumed by the nation was, in spite of the great increase
of the population to be fed, still grown at home even in
a bad year.   In 1835, after a series of good harvests, the
average price of wheat was actually less than 40s. the
quarter, and as long as bread was cheap there was no
practical grievance and little agitation. But when the
bad harvests which began in 1837 forced up the price of
corn, the question rapidly ripened. An Anti-Corn-Law
Association was founded in Manchester in 1838, and by
the energy of Richard Cobden was speedily developed into
the organisation which became famous as the Anti-Corn-
Law League. As one bad harvest succeeded another,
and trade continuously sank into deeper stagnation, the

League became more active in its campaign of agitation, and the results were soon visible. The Corn Laws had been an open question in the Melbourne Cabinet, though the Prime Minister himself was a violent protectionist ; but whereas in 1837 only three Ministers had voted in the free trade minority, in 1839 no fewer than ten voted with Villiers on his now annual motion. After that year, as Chartism for a time fades into the background, the League is at the centre of the political situation.

The movement identified with the name of Cobden was not bounded in its scope by the question of the Corn Laws, and Cobden's triumph, when it came, meant far more than the triumph of a particular set of economic principles. The Corn Laws had become the symbol of the political predominance of the landed aristocracy—a predominance which had been rudely shaken, but by no means overthrown, by the passage of the Reform Act. It is a commonplace of history that some time is required for the disclosure of the full consequences of a political revolution, the traditions of the old order retaining their power long after the change in the political arrangements which gave them vitality. In our own days, for instance, we often hear it remarked that it is only now becoming possible to discern the real significance of the great extensions of the franchise in the last generation. It was the same in the case of the Reform Act of 1832. Nominally that Act established the middle classes in power ; in practice, in the Whig Governments that ruled England during the thirties, the aristocratic tradition remained all-powerful. The great bulk of their supporters were Whigs rather than Radicals, and the Radicals themselves were divided and impotent. Benthamism, indeed, which may be regarded in a sense as the middle-class philosophy, was already a great influence as a spirit in the air pervading political thought and informing legislation ; but it was only when it had been transformed into what the Germans call ' Manchesterismus ' that it attained its full potency in Parliament and party. Its professional exponents in the Parliaments of the thirties, the philosophic Radicals, were pedants without power of appealing to men in the mass ; and it was not till the genius of Cobden had taken control of the Radical movement, and given it a definite aim and fresh acceleration, that it became really effective. In Cobden, in fact, the middle classes found themselves. By his victory in the struggle that raged around the Corn Laws he dealt a staggering blow to the power of the aristocracy, and thus completed the work begun by the Reformers in 1832.

His agitation from the first was so essentially middle-class that it was regarded with deep distrust by the populace and their leaders, who remembered the great betrayal of ten years before ; and from the Chartists especially, who beneath the clamour for cheap bread suspected a middle-class design for the reduction of wages, the League encountered violent opposition. If the agricultural interest and their friends the Tories had known how to place themselves at the head of the masses from whom the Chartists drew their strength, if Peel had possessed a tithe of Disraeli's political insight or popular sympathies, Cobden's agitation might have perished ingloriously, and the whole subsequent history of England have been different. But Cobden was helped from the beginning by the fact that the leader of the forces opposed to him was at heart on the side of the middle classes himself, and had no political ideal, aristocratic or democratic, fundamentally different from Cobden's own. ' There,' said Wellington of Peel, ' is a gentleman who never sees the end of a campaign.' Peel was trying to substitute for the Toryism of the past something which was almost a contradiction in terms—a middle-class Toryism. His Toryism was better than Eldon's in that it was in motion ; but he moved, not according to principles or towards a goal of his own choice, but by a series of retreats before the pressure of the enemy, and this could only end, as it did, in his facing about and adopting the

enemy's line of march. Peel made no attempt to probe
the grievances of the Chartists or devise a medicine for
their ills. He was content to encourage the Whigs in
their policy of repression, and to leave the suffering multitude without guidance or hope. And as a result Cobden
was enabled to enlist their sympathy to a great extent
on the side of his agitation, and, as had happened once
before, to use popular forces for advancing the power of
the middle classes at the expense of the aristocracy.

Cobden was the real author of the middle-class Liberalism which dominated England for more than a generation, and the tradition of which is still so powerful; or if
there is anyone to dispute with Cobden the credit of its
authorship, it is Peel himself. As the note of the old
Whig order, Disraeli would have said, was oligarchic
selfishness, so the note of the new Liberal order was a
vague cosmopolitanism—both inconsistent, though in
opposite ways, with truly national principles. With
hostility to the Corn Laws and hostility to the landed
gentry there was associated in Cobden's mind a certain
hostility to the national idea of which the landed gentry
were the especial custodians. During the long peace the
national idea had gradually been growing dim, the very
strength of our position among the nations of Europe
tending to obscure it, and the cosmopolitan principles of
which Cobden's mind was full met with a good deal of
acceptance. He was to find, indeed, later, when he had
overthrown the landed gentry and broken the Tory party,
that the national idea was still stronger than he had
imagined. The middle classes, when they had fairly
entered on their long lease of power, chose Palmerston
as their leader, and marched contentedly under his
guidance into the Crimean War, forgetful of the reign
of peace of which Cobden had been dreaming. In
another direction, however, Cobden's influence was more
effective. If to the national idea he was cold, he hated
the imperial idea with a sincere and deadly hatred, and
he succeeded in giving to the Liberal party, which he did

so much to shape, an anti-imperial bias that almost
destroyed the Empire.

Party in this country is rigorous in its divisions, and
party would have us believe that the English world was
then divided into protectionists who upheld the worst
abuses of the Corn Laws, and free traders who adopted the
cosmopolitan views of Cobden. Disraeli was in neither
camp. He could appreciate the genius of the ' inspired
bagman with his calico millennium,' to quote Carlyle's
description of Cobden, but he never, like Peel, fell under
his sway, and neither was he ever ruled by the fanatics
of protection. He was one of the few people of that
generation to grasp firmly the truth which has hardly
even now found any wide acceptance—that protection
and free trade were made for man, and not man for
either of them. Free trade, as he maintained, was an
expedient, not a principle, and that was the keynote of
nearly all his speeches. From the first he was resolute
in looking at the question as a whole and in its concrete
relations, and in refusing to be drawn aside into abstract
lines of argument ; in studying it in the light of history ;
and in fixing his eyes above all on its political significance.
' Reduce the burdens that so heavily press upon the
farmer,' he said as early as 1832,[1] ' and then reduce his
protection in the same ratio. That is the way to have
cheap bread . . . without destroying the interest which
is the basis of all sound social happiness.' Apart from
the effective cry of cheaper bread for the people, there
were two main arguments, not wholly congruous, employed by the opponents of the Corn Laws—one, that the
high cost of living for which they were responsible made
it impossible for our manufacturers to compete with the
foreigner ; the other, that the free admission of corn from
abroad would enable foreign countries to buy our manufactures. The argument from the cost of living was that
which chiefly weighed with the bulk of the manufacturers,
and was strongly urged by Villiers in the session of 1838.

[1] Vol. I., p. 220.

The answer, as Gladstone on the opposite benches and the Chartists outside Parliament were equally quick to see, was ' Thank you. We quite understand. Your object is to get down the wages of your workpeople.'[1] In his speech[2] on this occasion Disraeli denied the premiss that the Corn Laws had any appreciable effect in raising the cost of manufacture, and he then proceeded to lay bare the political motive that underlay the whole agitation :

Whose interest was it to have the Corn Laws repealed ? It was the interest solely of the manufacturing capitalist, who had contrived to raise a large party in favor of that repeal by the specious pretext that it would lead to a reduction of rents, and by obtaining the co-operation of a section in this country who were hostile to a political system based on the preponderance of the landed interest.

Two years later, probably through the now rising influence of Cobden, who was always guarded in his language as to the effect the abolition of the Corn Laws would have on the cost of living, Villiers laid the stress on the argument drawn from an abstract theory of exchange : ' Repeal the Corn Laws, and you will create new markets for our manufactures, and England will become the workshop of the world.' Disraeli spoke again, protesting against the matter being considered and decided as a mere abstract question of political economy. The whole Cobden theory was founded on a curious belief in the total absence of competition between nations as a whole combined with the most strenuous competition between the individuals that compose them ; and Disraeli showed the danger of a one-sided development of the industry of the country, and the economic dependence that it must inevitably imply, and pointed to the fate of Holland as a warning against the belief that ' the industry of foreign nations was to be regulated by a mere devotion to our interests and necessities.' Tillage, the Dutch had said in the seventeenth century, was to them of no

---

[1] Morley's *Gladstone*, I., p. 249.   [2] *V. supra*, ch. 1.

account, for ' Europe was their farm,' and that expression would be an appropriate pendant to the formula
that Britain should be the workshop of the world.   Such
' arrogant aspirations ' were based, he was certain, ' on
profound ignorance of human nature ; and however we
might modify our own tariff, the industry of other nations
would ramify into various courses, and would establish
opposing interests in the same community.'[1]   In the same
interesting speech he showed how Prussia, which at the
Congress of Vienna had only five million subjects, had by
' the machinery of commercial union conquered Germany
in peace,' quoting from the paper in which the whole
plan of union was ' laid down by Stein, the celebrated
Prussian Minister.'   ' If Prussia had conquered by the
arms of her generals, the acquisition could not have been
more complete.'   Somewhat later[2] in the same session,
in a debate on foreign policy, he showed again that he
was studying the actual circumstances of foreign trade ;
tracing in detail the effect of Palmerston's rule at the
Foreign Office, and arriving at the conclusion that
' during the last nine years the commerce of England
had received greater injury than in any other like period
under any other Minister.'

Though the Whigs were already doomed when the
session of 1841 began, the end was slow in coming.
Humiliation the Ministry cheerfully accepted, and re-
verses they ignored ; and after what he called their sixth
defeat of the session Disraeli wrote to Lady Blessington :
' Their feebleness is of so vigorous a character that I
doubt not they will still totter on.'   As is usual on such
occasions, impatient Tories thought that their leaders
were remiss in not dealing the final blow, and Wellington
especially was suspected of unwillingness to see a change
of Government.   Disraeli set forth ' the state of the case '
in a letter to the Duke which appeared in The Times[3]
over the signature of ' Atticus.'   ' Atticus is a great hit,'

---

[1] The Times, April 2, 1840.   [2] July 22, 1840.
[3] March 11, 1841.

he wrote to his sister, and the letter certainly marks
a notable advance in style on his earlier journalistic
efforts. Beginning with the assumption that it was the
Duke who was keeping the Whigs in office, the writer
dismisses at once the explanation given by some, that,
' satisfied by the celebrity of an unrivalled career, his
Grace is indisposed to enter the arena of political responsibility.'

This idea of retiring on a certain quantity of fame, as some
men retire on a certain quantity of money, has the twang
of mediocrity. It is generally the refuge of those whose
distinction has been more owing to chance than their own
conceptions. . . . But original and creative spirits are
true to the law of their organisation. An octogenarian Doge
of Venice scaled the walls of Constantinople ; Marius had completed his seventieth year when he defeated the elder Pompey
and quelled the most powerful of aristocracies ; white hairs
shaded the bold brain of Julius II. when he planned the
expulsion of the barbarians from Italy ; and the great King of
Prussia had approached his grand climacteric when he par-
titioned Poland. In surveying your Grace's career of half
a century, I cannot perceive any very obtrusive indications
of moderation in your purposes, though abundant evidence of
forbearance in your conduct. Celebrated for caution, I should
rather select as your characteristic a happy audacity. No
one has performed bolder deeds in a more scrupulous manner ;
and plans, which, in their initial notion, have assumed even
the features of rashness, have always succeeded from the
wariness of your details. . . . Your physical aspect is in
complete harmony with your spiritual constitution. In the
classic contour of your countenance, at the first glance, we
recognise only deep thoughtfulness and serene repose ; but
the moment it lights up into active expression, command
breathes in every feature ; each glance, each tone, indicates
the intuitive mind impervious to argument, and we trace
without difficulty the aquiline supremacy of the Cæsars.

No ; if the Duke is reconciled to the continuance in
office of the existing administration, it is not because he
shrinks from action ; it is rather from an opinion that,
checked by his power, they can do no harm, and that in
the enjoyment of place they will not care to project it.
An erroneous opinion, as ' Atticus ' thinks, for there is

no little danger, as he proceeds to show, in ' a state of affairs which accustoms the great body of the people to associate the idea of regular government with that of revolutionary doctrines ':

As long as public credit is to be maintained, or the national honor vindicated, a tax to be raised, or an armament equipped—in a word, as long as anything is to be done—a successful appeal is made to the loyal support of the Conservative party ; but the moment that party evinces any ambition to possess itself of the forms as well as the spirit of power . . . some abstract declaration as to the nature of ecclesiastical property, or the exercise of the political franchise, is pompously announced ; the capacity of an administrative body is made to depend upon the Parliamentary assertion of some unfeasible principle ; and by the assistance of the revolutionary majority it is demonstrated that the Conservative party are disqualified for the conduct of public business. . . . These ingenious manœuvres are described in Ministerial rhetoric as the assertion of a great principle.

A Parliamentary policy ' that permits the Whigs simultaneously to carry on the Government by a Conservative majority and to carry on the revolution by a Radical one ' cannot be wise. Refined political tactics may mystify the popular mind. A nation perplexed, like a puzzled man, will blunder, and the blunder of a people may prove the catastrophe of an Empire.

The great difficulty of the Whigs was the financial situation, and on the Budget of the year the crisis finally came. Bad harvests and bad trade, aided by the business incapacity of the Government and by an adventurous foreign policy, had brought the finances of the country into serious disorder, deficit following deficit till the total reached millions. The Whigs in desperation sought an exit from their difficulties in a tentative advance towards the principles of free trade. ' "Lord Roehampton thinks that something must be done about the Corn Laws," murmured Berengaria one day to Endymion, rather crestfallen ; " but they will try sugar and timber first. I think it all nonsense, but nonsense is sometimes necessary." This was the first warning of that famous

Budget of 1841 which led to such vast consequences, and which, directly or indirectly, gave such a new form and colour to English politics.'[1]   The Budget scheme included a reduction of the duties on foreign sugar and timber, and the substitution of a fixed duty of a shilling the bushel on corn for the existing sliding scale.   But the country had come to the conclusion that Peel was the one man who could deal with the situation, and this simultaneous attack on three great protected interests by a weak and tottering Ministry precipitated the end.   The reduction of the sugar duty favoured slave-grown sugar, and on this the Opposition concentrated their attack.   The ground was well chosen for combining with the protectionists the uncompromising anti-slavery men on the Ministerial benches, and after a debate of eight nights the Government were defeated by a majority of thirty-six.

To Sarah Disraeli.

May 15.

I spoke with great effect last night in the House, the best speech on our side ; it even drew ' iron tears down Pluto's cheek,' *alias*, applause and words of praise from Peel.   A full House about half-past nine o'clock, and all the Ministers there. . . .   The times are terribly agitating, and I can give you no clue to what may happen.

May 20.

The debate on Tuesday was powerful and exciting.   I dined with the Guests, but regained my post behind Sir Robert by ten o'clock, a few minutes before he rose.   He spoke for three and a quarter hours, equally divided between commerce, finance, and the conduct of the Government ; the latter division very happy and powerful.   I think it will end in dissolution.[2]

The Ministry, however, had no false pride, and after their defeat they neither dissolved nor resigned, but only proposed to revert to the old schedule of sugar duties, and to proceed to the development of the rest of their scheme.   Peel, however, moved a formal vote of want of confidence, and carried it by a majority of one ; but

[1] *Endymion*, ch. 65.   [2] *Letters*, p. 181.

even then, instead of resigning, Ministers decided to ask
for a dissolution of Parliament, and this the Queen
granted, though five years later she had come to the
opinion that she had ' made a mistake.'[1]   In his letter
to the Duke of Wellington, Disraeli had declared that
' our domestic history for the last ten years had been a
visible and violent attempt to govern this country in
spite of its Parliament.'   In the final debate he enlarged
on the same familiar theme.

The House of Commons affected some astonishment that
the Government, being in a minority, did not resign. . . .
The House of Commons, proud of its new-fangled position as
a reformed house, had allowed the Ministers to stigmatise a
vote of the House of Lords as the whisper of a faction ; but
the poisoned chalice was now returned to their own lips, and
they who had treated the House of Lords with insult now
treated the House of Commons with contempt.   Had they
supported the House of Lords when it was insulted, they
would not now be in the situation they occupied. . . .   This
was not the first time they were in that situation ; the consequence of Whig policy had been seen before this, when, being
strong in the Lords, they assailed and insulted the House of
Commons, and changed its existence from a triennial to a
septennial duration.   Throughout their whole history one
thing was always apparent—a systematic course of assault
upon the Parliamentary institutions of the country.   The
Ministers remained in power in spite of the House of Commons,
and in spite of the House of Lords.[2]

[1] See her letter to Lord John Russell of July 16, 1846, in the *Letters of
Queen Victoria.*
[2] *The Times*, May 28, 1841.

CHAPTER IV.

A POLITICAL ECONOMY PARLIAMENT.

1841–1843.

A couple of years earlier Disraeli had broken with his constituents at Maidstone. The dispute apparently arose out of some question of money, but its merits are obscure; though it is easy to understand that, having, when he became their member, had a rich man behind him, he did not find it easy to satisfy the requirements of an exigent constituency when left to his own resources. Turned adrift from Maidstone, he had received, through the good offices of his friend Lord Forester, a requisition to stand for Shrewsbury, and thither accordingly he hastened when the campaign began. He was accompanied by his wife, who played a great part in the election and won immense popularity. On the question of the day, Disraeli said in his address that, believing that the interests of the agriculturist, the manufacturer, and the merchant, were the same, he would ' resist the sacrifice of any of these great classes to the fancied advantage of the others.' In his speech on the hustings he told his hearers that there were three great objects which he had always set before him for his guidance in public life—the maintenance of the constitution, the interests of the poor, and the liberties of the people. After a short but bitter contest he was returned by a substantial majority a few votes behind the other Conservative candidate, who had been longer in the field.

113

To Sarah Disraeli.

CARLTON CLUB,
July 7.

Here I am again, having been only five days out of Parliament! We had a sharp contest, but never for a moment doubtful. They did against me, and said against me, and wrote against me all they could find or invent; but I licked them, and the result is that we now know the worst; and I really think that their assaults in the long run did me good, and will do me good. After the chairing, which was gorgeous and fatiguing, after quaffing the triumphal cup at forty different spots in Salop—a dinner and a speech—we went and stayed till Monday at Loton Park, Sir Baldwin Leighton's, one of the most charming old English halls, and filled with a family in their way as perfect. A complete old English gentleman, whom I first met at Stamboul, a most agreeable wife, the finest amateur artist I know, and children lovelier than the dawn. . . .

Are there any strawberries left, or will there be in a week? We mean to run down by rail to see you.

Thousand loves,
D.

In the course of this election, it is worthy of note, Disraeli's well-known crest, the Castle of Castile, with the now famous motto, *Forti nihil difficile*,[1] made what would seem to be its first appearance, emblazoned on a Tory banner. All his fortitude and courage were needed during the contest. As the letter to his sister shows, he had to face personal attacks more than usually envenomed, and they were directed on this occasion to the really vulnerable point of his financial position. When he was first announced as candidate, an anonymous placard[2] appeared accusing him of seeking a place in Parliament to avoid bankruptcy or a prison, and setting forth a list of judgments for sums amounting in all to £22,000 which had been recorded against him within the previous three years. In an address to the electors, Dis-

---

[1] All is easy to the brave; or, as a hostile paper preferred to translate it, 'The impudence of some men sticks at nothing.'

[2] The charges of this placard were subsequently adopted by one Yardley, a barrister, and, according to the local papers, the quarrel became so hot that Yardley sent a challenge, and he and Disraeli were summoned before the Mayor and bound over to keep the peace.

raeli declared that the statement of the placard was
·'utterly false,' and that there was not a single shilling
in the list of judgments which had not been completely
satisfied ;[1] explained that the judgments of recent date
had been entered up by him as collateral security for a
'noble friend,' who had subsequently relieved him of all
liability ; and ended with the protest : ' I should not have
solicited your suffrages had I not been in possession of
that ample independence which renders the attainment
of any office in the state, except as the recognition of
public service, to me a matter of complete indifference.'

As a matter of fact, marriage had by no means put an
end to Disraeli's financial embarrassments. To his wife,
from whom he appears to have had few or no secrets in
any other matter, he seems at first to have adopted, with
regard to his debts, the same policy of half-confidence
that he had pursued towards his father. 'Very unwell
from these damned affairs,' he writes, a year after his
marriage, to Pyne, his solicitor ; and a little later : 'A writ
delivered in my absence to my lady and other circumstances have produced a terrible domestic crisis.' Pyne
about this time seems to have fallen into decay, with the
dire result that Disraeli was obliged, as he complained,
'to attend personally to his affairs,' and personal attention seems only to have made him an easier prey than
ever to the rapacity of usurers. We find him, for example,
borrowing money at 40 per cent. to meet a bill of D'Orsay's[2]
for which he had become responsible. His liabilities
were now more than £20,000, and by his peculiar financial
methods they tended constantly to grow. 'I cannot
understand,' wrote his wife on the occasion of one of his
customary 'operations,' 'why only £5,000 is wanted.'
Probably, if the truth were known, neither could her husband. For every statement in his address in reply to

---

[1] To his solicitors he had written : ' On looking over the list I see nothing
but settled affairs, but there are some names which were not personally
settled by me. I take it for granted they are all right.'
[2] D'Orsay was most probably the 'noble friend' who is alluded to in the
Shrewsbury letter.

the placard there appears to have been at least a formal justification, but it must be confessed that in its general effect it was hardly such as to give the good people of Shrewsbury an accurate view of the financial position of their candidate.

The elections everywhere went against the Whigs, but the Ministry met Parliament, and only resigned after an amendment to the Address had been carried against them by a majority of over ninety. In the debate on this amendment Disraeli spoke again, the burden of his speech being a criticism of the Government for remaining in office after the vote of want of confidence passed in the previous Parliament, and after it had become clear that the country was confirming the judgment of Parliament in the elections. Graham and Stanley, we are told,[1] showed their disapproval of this novel constitutional doctrine by a negative shake of the head, and it was left to Disraeli himself, more than a quarter of a century later, to create the precedent of resigning in anticipation of the verdict of a new and hostile House of Commons. Seeing clearly that, though the country had refused to entrust the task to the Whigs, the entire fiscal system stood in need of revision, he also attacked at once, as he was to attack often again, the assumption that the Whigs had a monopoly in commercial, as indeed in all other reform—an assumption which was then comparatively novel. 'Why, the progress of commercial reform,' he exclaimed, with much truth, 'was only arrested by the Reform Act.' The tariff, in his opinion, ought long before this to have engaged the attention of the Government, and must sooner or later be the subject of legislation. The nation had, indeed, declined to allow a Ministry which was 'rickety and staggering' to attempt the reconstruction of the commercial system of the country, but it had shown no lack of sympathy with the enterprise itself.

1 *Lord Broughton's Recollections*, VI., p. 40.

To Sarah Disraeli.

Aug. 25.

The speech was successful.   Bernal[1] made a *brioche*, which
I was delighted at, as he malignantly attacked me, and his
manner was most flippant and audacious.   After the first
minute he commenced, ' Gentlemen,' as if on the hustings—
cries of order.   ' Well, I suppose you are gentlemen '—cries
of disgust.   After this he five times made the same blunder,
in fact lost his head.

Saturday [Aug. 28].

I suppose that the Editor of the *Herald*, when the Queen
sends for him to form a Government, intends to leave Lyndhurst out, which is distressing.   It is some consolation that
he has made me Paymaster of the Forces, which is agreeable.
As for all these editorial figments and newspaper *on dits*, they
are manufactured for country cousins.   Peel *never opens his
mouth*, and very properly ; until he is entrusted with the task
of forming a Government, it would be the height of arrogant
impertinence in him to appoint any of his colleagues. . . .
We are frightened out of our wits about the harvest, but
as the glass has been gradually rising for some days I do not
despair.   If the sun ever shine again we shall get down to
Bradenham, I hope, but about Monday I shall be able to write
more definitely.[2]

The fatal division had been taken the night before this
letter was written, and on Monday, August 30, Peel went
to Windsor and kissed hands as Prime Minister.   His
Cabinet was soon completed, with Lyndhurst as Lord
Chancellor ; Graham, Aberdeen, and Stanley, Home,
Foreign, and Colonial Secretaries ; and the Duke of
Wellington leader in the Lords, without the burden of
office.   By the end of the week most of the subordinate
offices in the Ministry had been filled, but day followed
day and no messenger or message came to Grosvenor
Gate, and on the Sunday, in despair, Disraeli wrote to
the Prime Minister :

---

[1] Ralph Bernal, afterwards Bernal Osborne, Whig member for
Wycombe.
[2] Brit. Mus., Addit. MSS.

To Sir Robert Peel.

GROSVENOR GATE,
Sept. 5, 1841.

DEAR SIR ROBERT,

I have shrunk from obtruding myself upon you at this moment, and should have continued to do so if there were anyone on whom I could rely to express my feelings.

I am not going to trouble you with claims similar to those with which you must be wearied. I will not say that I have fought since 1834 four contests for your party, that I have expended great sums, have exerted my intelligence to the utmost for the propagation of your policy, and have that position in life which can command a costly seat.

But there is one peculiarity in my case on which I cannot be silent. I have had to struggle against a storm of political hate and malice which few men ever experienced, from the moment, at the instigation of a member of your Cabinet, I enrolled myself under your banner, and I have only been sustained under these trials by the conviction that the day would come when the foremost man of this country would publicly testify that he had some respect for my ability and my character.

I confess to be unrecognised at this moment by you appears to me to be overwhelming, and I appeal to your own heart—to that justice and that magnanimity which I feel are your characteristics—to save me from an intolerable humiliation.

Believe me, dear Sir Robert,
Your faithful servant,
B. DISRAELI.

Mrs. Disraeli, who, as has been seen, was an intimate friend of Peel's sister, had written the night before without her husband's knowledge :

Mrs. Disraeli to Sir Robert Peel.

GROSVENOR GATE,
Saturday night.

DEAR SIR ROBERT PEEL,

I beg you not to be angry with me for my intrusion, but I am overwhelmed with anxiety. My husband's political career is for ever crushed, if you do not appreciate him.

Mr. Disraeli's exertions are not unknown to you, but there is much he has done that you cannot be aware of, though they have had no other aim but to do you honour, no wish for recompense but your approbation.

He has gone farther than most to make your opponents his

personal enemies. He has stood four most expensive elections since 1834, and gained seats from Whigs in two, and I pledge myself as far as one seat, that it shall always be at your command.

Literature he has abandoned for politics. Do not destroy all his hopes, and make him feel his life has been a mistake.

May I venture to name my own humble but enthusiastic exertions in times gone by for the party, or rather for your own splendid self ? They will tell you at Maidstone that more than £40,000 was spent through my influence only.

Be pleased not to answer this, as I do not wish any human being to know I have written to you this humble petition.

> I am now, as ever, dear Sir Robert,
> Your most faithful servant,
> MARY ANNE DISRAELI.[1]

Peel replied to Disraeli :

From Sir Robert Peel.

WHITEHALL,
Sept. 7, 1841.

MY DEAR SIR,

I must in the first place observe that no member of the Cabinet which I have formed ever received from me the slightest authority to make to you the communication to which you refer.

Had I been consulted by that person, I should have at once declined to authorise a communication which would have been altogether at variance with the principle on which I have uniformly acted in respect to political engagements, and by adhering to which I have left myself at entire liberty to reconcile—as far as my limited means allow—justice to individual claims with the efficient conduct of the public service.

I know not who is the member of the Cabinet to whom you allude, and cannot but think he acted very imprudently. But quite independently of this consideration, I should have been very happy had it been in my power to avail myself of your offer of service ; and your letter is one of the many I receive which too forcibly impress upon me how painful and invidious is the duty which I have been compelled to undertake. I am only supported in it by the consciousness that my desire has been to do justice.

---

[1] Thirty-six years later the wheel had come full circle, and, oddly enough, Peel's daughter-in-law wrote to Lord Beaconsfield to inform him that her husband was 'most anxious to serve' him in the event of any change in his Government leading to a vacancy.

I trust also that, when candidates for Parliamentary office calmly reflect on my position, and the appointments I have made—when they review the names of those previously connected with me in public life whom I have been absolutely compelled to exclude, the claims founded on acceptance of office in 1834 with the almost hopeless prospects of that day, the claims, too, founded on new party combinations—I trust they will then understand how perfectly insufficient are the means at my disposal to meet the wishes that are conveyed to me by men whose co-operation I should be proud to have, and whose qualifications and pretensions for office I do not contest.

Believe me, my dear sir,

Very faithfully yours,

ROBERT PEEL.

This reply drew a second letter from Disraeli :

To Sir Robert Peel.

GROSVENOR GATE,

Sept. 8, 1841.

DEAR SIR ROBERT,

Justice requires that I should state that you have entirely misconceived my meaning, in supposing that I intended even to intimate that a promise of official promotion had ever been made to me, at any time, by any member of your Cabinet.

I have ever been aware that it was not in the power of any member of your Cabinet to fulfil such engagements, had he made them : permit me to add that it is utterly alien from my nature to bargain and stipulate on such subjects. Parliamentary office should be the recognition of party service and Parliamentary ability, and as such only was it to me an object of ambition.

It appears to me that you have mistaken an allusion to my confidence in your sympathy for a reference to a pledge received from a third person. If such a pledge had been given me by yourself, and not redeemed, I should have taken refuge in silence. Not to be appreciated may be a mortification : to be baulked of a promised reward is only a vulgar accident of life, to be borne without a murmur.

Your faithful servant,

B. DISRAELI.

There for the present the matter remained at rest. Offers of service and requests for ' recognition ' when a Ministry is in the making are far more common than the outside world realises, and there was nothing that was discreditable either in the fact or in the mode of Disraeli's application.   His rejoinder to Peel's reply is not without dignity, while that reply itself smacks of the debater, reading into Disraeli's letter an interpretation which it will not bear, and expatiating on this in order to cover embarrassment.   Peel's tone, in fact, betrays a certain consciousness that his omission of Disraeli stood in need of explanation.   For one habitually so cold and ungracious in his manner, he had shown in Disraeli an interest that was exceptional ; had honoured him more than once with marks of appreciation, and had gone out of his way to take him into his counsels.   In his first Parliament, Disraeli, though ready enough, as we have seen, to assert his independence when opportunity offered, had yielded for the most part a submission to his leader that was sometimes even ostentatious ; and the leader in his turn had betrayed no resentment at his follower's occasional guerilla operations.   Only a few weeks before the correspondence just set forth, Peel had sent a friendly acknowledgment of a letter in which Disraeli announced his victory at Shrewsbury.   Moreover, notwithstanding Peel's proverbial lack of foresight, he could hardly, with his intimate knowledge and long experience of the House of Commons, have been blind to the possibility that a Disraeli estranged might mean trouble in the future.   Why, then, did he ignore him in the formation of his Ministry ?

The fact is, it is almost certain that Peel really wanted to give Disraeli office.   Apart from traditions that have been handed down to this effect, there is one definite statement.   In 1854 an article appeared in a newspaper[1] which had been founded by Disraeli himself, defending him against the attacks of a more than usually malevolent ' biography ' that had just made its appearance.   This article was written, as Disraeli's papers show, by his friend George Smythe, who was also a friend of Peel's, had held office under Peel in 1846, when Disraeli's re-

[1] *The Press*, Jan. 7, 1854.

bellion was at its height, and sat with him in the House
of Commons till his death in 1850 ; and it contains this
statement : 'The common opinion that Peel did not
appreciate Disraeli is a mistake. The present writer is
aware that Sir Robert wished to offer office to Mr. Disraeli in 1841. This was prevented by the political parasites by whom it was the weakness of the great Minister
to be surrounded, and we owe to this circumstance those
immortal sketches of the Rigbys, the Tadpoles, and the
Tapers, which Beaumarchais never surpassed.' The suggestion here appears to be that Peel was turned from his
purpose by the Crokers and Bonhams, and men of that
type and standing ; but there is a story[1] which seems to
provide a more probable explanation, that Stanley was
the real cause of Peel's change of mind. It has been
mentioned before that Stanley was at this time deeply
prejudiced against Disraeli—through misapprehension
of the facts of an incident ten years earlier, in which a
member of his family and Disraeli had been involved,
but in which Disraeli's part appears to have been wholly
creditable ; and, according to the story, when Peel suggested Disraeli as eligible for office, Stanley declared, in
his usual vehement way, that 'if that scoundrel were
taken in he would not remain himself.'[2] If this be the
true account, we may imagine Peel's reflections not many
years later when he saw Stanley and Disraeli in league
against his influence.

From Sarah Disraeli to Mrs. Disraeli.

[*September.*]

I suffer much for your and dear Dis' disappointment, but
we must not despair. After all, it is not half so bad as losing
an election. We have, I hope, a long future before us, and
changes may occur every day. Our *Examiner* has missed

---

[1] Deriving from the late Lord Houghton.

[2] Smythe's article speaks, though in another connexion, of Stanley's
prejudice against Disraeli in earlier years as having been 'notorious in the
House of Commons ' ; but if Stanley really intervened in 1841, it was
obviously impossible in 1854 to make allusion to the fact in an article for a
paper controlled by Disraeli.

this morning, so that we do not know the latest appointments ; but up to the latest, except Gladstone, there is not
one single untitled or unaristocratic individual.

For Disraeli and his wife a visit to Normandy, where
we find them established in the old town of Caen, helped
to fill the interval between the brief autumn session and
the entrance of the new Parliament on its real labours in
February. The new Ministers meanwhile were preparing to grapple with the difficult problems of tariff and
finance bequeathed to them by their predecessors. If the
Parliament, as Lady Montfort says in *Endymion*, was ' a
political economy Parliament,' Peel's, as Cobden said,
was ' peculiarly a politico-economical intellect.'[1] Peel had
supported Huskisson in his commercial reforms nearly
twenty years before, and Robinson, who had then been
Chancellor of the Exchequer, was now, as Ripon, in
Huskisson's former office of President of the Board of
Trade. As leader of the Opposition, Peel had shown all
the wariness of an old Parliamentarian, and his hands
were in consequence comparatively free for the task now
before him. To his freedom there was, indeed, only one
limitation. He could modify the Corn Laws ; but by the
last debates of the old Parliament, by the circumstances
of the general election, and by explicit declarations of
his own,[2] and of his followers,[3] he and his Ministry were
deeply committed to the maintenance of the principle of
protection to agriculture.

Peel's general plan for restoring order to public finance
was based on the same idea as that of the Whigs—the
reduction of duties with a view to promoting consumption, and so increasing revenue. But his plan was de-

---

[1] Morley's *Cobden*, I., p. 237.
[2] Take, for instance, his speech of August 27, 1841, immediately before
the division that dislodged the Melbourne Ministry : ' We both acknowledge
the principle of protection to agriculture. The first Finance Minister of
the Crown, being asked if this measure of a fixed duty was a tax or a protection, answered : " It is a protection." We start, then, from the same point.'
[3] Gladstone, for example, said, in seeking re-election at Newark : ' There
were two points on which the British farmer might rely, the first of which
was that adequate protection would be given to him, while the second was
that protection would be given to him by means of the sliding scale.'

veloped with less precipitancy and a more secure sense of power, and as he now had behind him the elections, which the Whigs when they produced their Budget still had before them, he was able to adopt the bold expedient which Huskisson had suggested, of an income-tax to meet immediate needs of revenue till remissions should have time to tell on consumption. He began with the Corn Laws. In his scheme for their reconstruction he clung tenaciously to the unlucky device of the sliding scale ; but he reduced the rates of duty, and he substituted for the old plan of continuous variation inversely with the price a system of variation by a series of leaps from one resting-place to another, in the hope that the merchants might thus have less motive for withholding corn from import in the expectation of higher prices, and to the injury of the consumer and the revenue alike. The scheme gave satisfaction neither to the extreme free traders nor to the agricultural interest, and the Duke of Buckingham, who was in the Cabinet as Lord Privy Seal, carried his dissent to the point of resignation.

To Sarah Disraeli.

[*February,* 1842.]

A thunderbolt in a summer sky could not have produced a greater sensation than the resignation of the Duke of Bucks. All is confusion. I had a long conversation with him the other day. ' He has only one course—to be honest.' I am sorry to say I hear he has taken the Garter. . . . Peel seems to have pleased no party, but I suppose the necessity of things will force his measure through.

Disraeli does not appear to have been wholly in love himself with the plan adopted by Peel, and it is possible that he thought then, as he had evidently come to think when at the end of his life he surveyed the situation retrospectively in *Endymion,* that a moderate fixed duty such as the Whigs had proposed would have been the best working arrangement. But whatever his doubts, he kept them to himself. The legend that the neglect of his pretensions to office in 1841 drove him at once into

opposition to Peel is so firmly established that to many
the facts will come as a surprise. For two whole sessions
he gave his support to Peel's Government and its principal measures — a support, moreover, that was not
grudging nor even mechanical, but active and intelligent ;
and another year was to elapse before he embarked on
anything that could be regarded as deliberate and
systematic opposition. Attempts were made from the
first to lure him into rebellion, but he steadfastly resisted
them, though on the new Corn Law, at all events, something of the kind appears to have been expected. 'I am
obliged,' he tells his wife, who was detained at Bradenham
for some weeks by an illness of her mother's, 'to be very
careful about pairing, as Mrs. Dawson, Bonham and Co.
are full of good-natured rumors.' 'I saw Mrs. Dawson,'
he writes another day. 'She was most friendly and particularly disagreeable.'

To Mrs. Disraeli.

Feb. 25.

You cannot conceive how solitary I feel : utterly isolated.
Before the change of Government, political party was a tie
among men, but now it is only a tie among men who are in
office. The supporter of administration, who is not in place
and power himself, is a solitary animal. He has neither hope
nor fear.

Feb. 26.

Last night Sir Robert Peel carried his [corn] resolutions by
an immense majority—far beyond anticipation. Sir Richard
Vyvyan, Mr. Blackstone, and Lord Ossulston (who is a great
malcontent) rose, and left the house together, determined
no more to support Peel. The general rumor was that I had
done the same, and several men expressed their surprise,
when they saw me in the lobby ; I believe these rumors
have been intentionally circulated, but the fact is I have had
a thorough understanding with Fremantle[1] throughout—or
at least for the last week—and I am sure the Government
themselves had, or rather have not now, the slightest doubt
of my supporting them. However, my presence at the late
divisions has been most politic and necessary.

---

[1] Sir Thomas Fremantle, 1798-1890, afterwards 1st Lord Cottesloe, at
this time chief Government Whip.

Disraeli in the meantime had found a subject of his own. In the course of his commercial studies he had been impressed with the inefficiency of our consular establishment, which was then, in the words of Peel, too often a retreat for such as were ' disqualified for public situations.' Disraeli doubtless felt impelled, after his recent rebuff, to make a demonstration ; and here, he may have thought, was a subject which would serve, bristling as it was with detail, to win him credit as a practical man who could be solid as well as brilliant. So he put down a motion for the blending of the consular with the diplomatic body, and prepared an elaborate speech.

To Mrs. Disraeli.

Feb. 21.

I went through my whole speech this morning without a reference to a single paper, so completely am I master of all its details. It took me three hours, an awful period ; but I fear I cannot retrench it, at least materially. The details are so numerous, so varied, and so rich. I am full of confidence as to its effect in the House, but I am very doubtful as to the opportunity being speedily offered.

Feb. 22.

You were prepared for my disappointment in not bringing forward my motion to-night, but the infernal debate[1] drags its slow length along. . . . George Smythe [2] made a most elaborate speech ; very Radical indeed, and unprincipled as his little agreeable self, but too elaborate—his manner affected and his tone artificial, and pronunciation too ; but still ability though puerile.

Monday [*March* 7].

Yesterday Lord Claud Hamilton called on me, to ask to second my motion. It was just the thing I wanted, as being stepson to Lord Aberdeen, the Secretary of State for Foreign Affairs, it gives, as George Smythe says, an official character to the affair. . . . I feel a calm confidence, and I think I cannot fail of making some impression. . . .

Wynne [a prominent constituent from Shrewsbury] called on me this morning, and, though I was at home to no one, James had the sense to admit him. He had called previously on Tomline [the other member for Shrewsbury]

---

[1] On the corn resolutions.
[2] George Sydney Smythe, 1818-1857, afterwards 7th Viscount Strangford.

and asked if he were at home.   The servant hesitated, finally
took in Wynne's card, and brought out word that Mr. Tomline
was not at home.   Conceive the rage of Wynne !   It is something awful, solemnly severe and unappeasable ; the last
visit on Mr. Tomline, he says.   I heaped coals on the fire
without appearing to do so ; told Wynne that I was at home
to no one to-day and the reason, but there was a standing
order always in his exception ; asked him to dinner, which he
refused, as he was engaged, but very charmed ; and finally
gave him an order for the House on Tuesday if in town.   He
left me as devoted to us as was he deadly to Tomline.   I
could not help laughing, remembering Tomline's last visit
to me : the tables fairly turned.

Yesterday, after a hard morning's work, I went out for a
little air, found Maxse at our door, and walked with him for
about an hour in the Park.   He was very kind, and I hoped
to have got some small talk for you, as he is a gossip and a
lounger, but there is nothing stirring.   Croker is one of the
five executors of Lord Hertford, but the will is not yet
open. . . .

I will now give you my blessing, as well as send you my
love deep and dear.   The more we are separated the more I
cling to you. . . .   'Tis your approbation and delight for
which I am now laboring, and unless I had that stimulus I
don't think I could go on.

Wednesday [*March* 9].

The affair last night realised all my hopes ; the success was
complete and brilliant.   I rose at five o'clock to one of the
most disagreeable audiences that ever welcomed a speaker.
Everybody seemed to affect not to be aware of my existence,
and there was a general buzz and chatter.   Nevertheless, not
losing my head, I proceeded without hesitation for ten
minutes, though when I recollected what I had to travel
through, and the vast variety of detail which I had per-
spicuously to place before the House, I more than once
despaired of accomplishing my purpose.

In about ten minutes affairs began to mend ; when a quarter
of an hour had elapsed there was generally an attentive
audience ; and from that time until near half-past seven,
when I sat down, having been up about two hours and twenty
minutes, I can say without the slightest exaggeration, that not
only you might have heard a pin fall in the House, but there
was not an individual, without a single exception, who did not
listen to every sentence with the most marked interest, and
even excitement.   The moment I finished, Peel, giving
me a cheer, got up and went to dinner upstairs. . . .   Henry

Baillie, Dicky Hodgson, and Lord John Manners,[1] and several others came in turn and sat by me, after I had sat down, to give me the general impression of the House, that it was not only, by a thousand degrees, the best speech I had ever made, but one of the best that was ever made. The enthusiasm of young Smythe extraordinary ; he and several others particularly mentioned my manner, perfectly changed and different to what it used to be—' Exactly as you talk at the Carlton or at your own table,' he said, ' particularly my voice, not the least stilted, but the elocution distinct, the manner easy, a little nonchalant, and always tinged with sarcasm.'

Now for the other side. [Milner] Gibson came to me to say that they all agreed on their side that it was the most amusing speech they ever listened to, and carried them on completely ; Tom Duncombe, that it was one of the best statements he ever heard, and if I had followed it up by a loose, indefinite resolution I might have made a very strong division. But what think you of the mighty *Mister Cobden* coming up to me to offer me his thanks for the great public service I had done, &c. ?

I put Palmerston on his mettle. He made one of his usual dashing, reckless speeches, which men who have been Secretaries of State can venture to do in a scrape and backed by a party ; but there was a general feeling on all sides of the House that he had not succeeded in shaking the minutest detail of one of my facts. He spoke with great pains, and with as much effort as if he were answering Peel. I made a most happy reply to his insinuation as to my being disappointed about office, or rather his sarcastic hopes that I might obtain it. What I said was literally this : ' I must in the first place return my thanks to the noble Lord for his warm aspirations for my political preferment. Coming from such a quarter, I consider them auspicious. The noble Viscount is a consummate master of the subject, and if to assist my advancement he will only impart to me the secret of his own unprecedented rise, and by what means he has contrived to enjoy power under seven successive administrations, I shall at least have gained a valuable result by this discussion.' Graham cheered this most vehemently.

After the debate congratulations came thick. Dudley Stuart embraced me at Crockford's, and declared, before Chesterfield and a crowd of dandies, that my speech was one of the most effective he had ever listened to. Even Jemmy Macdonald told me he heard ' I had had a hell of a flare-up.'

[1] Baillie (1803-1885, afterwards Right Hon. H. J. Baillie) was member for Inverness, Hodgson for Berwick, and Manners (1818-1906, afterwards 7th Duke of Rutland) Gladstone's colleague at Newark.

I walked from the House with Henry Baillie, who told me in his cold, quiet way : 'Upon my soul, I am not sure it was not the best speech I ever heard.' All young England, the new members, &c., were deeply interested. . . .

But I think what I am going to tell you is the most gratifying and remarkable. Sidney Herbert just now came down to sit by me, and said : 'I don't know whether it is a fair question, but might I ask where you got that mass of extraordinary information which you gave last night ?' I replied : 'From study and observation and inquiry, from no particular source.' He observed : 'I think it a most remarkable display ; it is thought so.'

I am going to dine with the Baillies to-day—House of Commons dinner—only George Smythe, and come down afterwards. There are odd rumors that a section of the Tories will declare against Peel to-night, on the second reading of his [Corn] Bill. On Friday comes on the Budget—a very important week ; but the news from India[1] fills everyone with alarm.

March 10.

. . . Last night Lord Eliot said to me : 'Well, you are one of the few who have broken lances with Palmerston and rode away in triumph.' He said it would have made an admirable party motion a year ago, and would have thrown the Government into a minority. . . .

At supper at Crockford's, H. Twiss, sitting next to me, between his mighty mouthfuls, at length saturninely turned round, and said suddenly and without any preliminary observations : 'I am not sure whether your retort on Palmerston in reply last night was not the completest case of having a man on the hip that I ever remember in Parliament.' . . .

Now for one or two good things—genuine, for I heard them myself. George Beresford, coming into the House, said to Augustus O'Brien,[2] who was standing at the Bar : 'How did Beresford Hope speak ? He's my cousin.' 'My dear fellow,' said O'Brien, 'if he were your own brother, he could not have spoken worse.'

Monckton Milnes said to George Smythe, with his queer face of solemn deprecation and conceit, speaking of the same oratorical effort : 'Why don't you interfere to prevent him speaking, Smythe ?' 'Why, I don't interfere to prevent you speaking, Milnes !' was the retort, and even Milnes' impudence was floored.

[1] Of the murder of Sir William Macnaghten, the British Envoy in Cabul, and the destruction of Elphinstone's force in the retreat to Jellalabad.

[2] Afterwards Augustus Stafford, 1809-1857.

March 11.

I already find myself without effort the leader of a party, chiefly of the youth and new members. Lord John Manners came to me about a motion which he wanted me to bring forward, and he would ' second it like Claud Hamilton.' Henry Baillie the same about Afghanistan. I find my position changed.

March 12.

Letters on the consular business every day. Peel alluded to the subject in the House of Commons last night, and many suggestions as to future motions. But at present the Budget engrosses all minds, and I was very fortunate in having gained my opportunity. The Income Tax, or rather the Property and Income Tax, is a thunderbolt ; but Peel can do anything at this moment.

Sunday [*March* 13].

I am not particularly anxious to be in town at this moment, political affairs are very confused ; and Vyvyan, since the consular speech, always ' whispering in my ear.' Yesterday he came with a formal proposition—viz., to oppose the further progress of the Corn Bill to-morrow in consequence of Peel's financial statement. He intends to do it himself, and begged me to speak—' in the same tone, exactly the same tone as the other night, that's the thing. You have got the ear of the House.' I declined interfering, said I hated speaking, &c. &c., must watch events, &c. But as old Talleyrand, when he did not clearly see his way, always took to his bed, so I think it would be as well for me if, in consequence of a cause which, thank God, no longer exists, domestic anxiety were to take me into the country—rather suddenly. . . .

I have agreed to dine at Gore House to-day, Lady B[lessington] having asked me every day. But I dislike going there, D'Orsay being in high spirits, quite unchanged, but Lady B. very altered—silent, subdued, and broken. She told me another year would kill her, and complained bitterly that, after having fought against so much prejudice, and made a sort of position, with her two nieces about her, and not owing a shilling in the world, she is perhaps to see it all shattered and scattered to the winds. I think it is horrid. But perhaps it may end better than she anticipates.

Monday [*March* 14].

Hertford's will is still the subject of endless tales. It appears now that by a codicil, revoking former legacies to them, he left £25,000 apiece to his valet and Croker. This is a fact. He had left his star[1] of the Order of the Garter, in costly brilliants, with a long panegyric to Peel, as the saviour of his country and all that, and the legacy was afterwards revoked. I suppose his ghost smelt the Income Tax. . . . The Zichy has £150,000 because she saved Lord Hertford from being poisoned by her mother. . . . The new Lord cut off his mustachios on his accession, saying : ' There never was a Marquis of Hertford with mustachios.'

March 15.

On Thursday for certain I shall be with my beloved. . . . I trust this is our last separation ; indeed, I believe it, and it has only taught us to love each other, if possible, more and more. . . .

Will you believe it?—Dr. Bowring [2] has just been to ask me what I think of the quarantine question, and whether I will speak on his motion to-night and support him if I approve of it. I know nothing of the question, and don't mean to stay at the House ; but I told him, touched by his imperturbable good temper, that I was entirely of his opinion on the subject, and paid him a general compliment.

I kept from the House [yesterday], because Vyvyan, as I was informed, was going to attack Peel, and oppose the progress of the Corn Bill. He was in the House armed with many papers ; but the spirit did not move him. I believe there is to be a grand row on Friday, but I shall steal off the morning before, and all the better, as affairs political are very queer. . . .

This morning and yesterday at breakfast I placed the bouquet of violets on my table (you know how fond I am of flowers on my breakfast-table), and fancied it was a very apt representative of yourself.

Every morning I have kept a sort of diary of affairs and thoughts in French, which I write now with great ease and some elegance.

The speech on the consular motion was largely an attack on Palmerston's administration during his long reign at the Foreign Office, and in the course of this and the following session Disraeli returned persistently to the same congenial theme. The line of inquiry on which he was now embarked—a study of foreign policy in its

[1] This star was presented by Sir Richard Wallace to Lord Beaconsfield when he received the Garter on his return from the Congress of Berlin in 1878.
[2] See p. 93. Disraeli had returned to the attack in his speech on the consular motion.

bearing on our foreign trade—had for him two attractions. It provided him with opportunities for attacking the Whigs, and it enabled him to escape from the dull and unenlightening detail of economic discussion into a more spacious atmosphere, where his vision had wider range. Whatever the starting-point of debate, Disraeli soon contrived to rise into the region of foreign affairs. He deeply disliked the income-tax, but when the Bill came up for second reading, instead of blaming the Minister, he ingeniously connected the tax with the disasters in Afghanistan, of which all minds were full, and which, as all knew, were a heritage from the policy of the Whigs. The war on the Indian frontier had compelled the Prime Minister to take the 'bold but sagacious step' of introducing an account of the finances of our Indian Empire into the annual Budget statement. Vigorous action had been needed to avert bankruptcy in India and cope with great deficiencies both there and in England, and he believed that the income-tax, though it was 'a tax of a most odious and inquisitorial character,' was absolutely necessary. He complained on this occasion that Parliament had never been consulted with regard to the war, and a couple of months later he seconded his friend Baillie in a motion for papers, which led to an animated debate.[1] To avoid the appearance of hostility to the Government in office, Disraeli aimed his attack directly at Palmerston. The foreign policy of the noble lord 'seemed to lie in an alternation of fatal inertness and more terrible energy'; it was a 'constant transition from a state of collapse to one of convulsion'; it was 'a system which commenced with the neglect of our duties, and terminated by a violation of the rights of other nations.' The late Ministers of the Crown had 'proclaimed war without reason, and prosecuted it without responsibility.' He was not alarmed by a single disaster; he was not afraid of our losing India through internal intrigue or foreign invasion; but if ever India were lost,

[1] June 23, 1842.

it would be lost by financial causes, by draining its resources to maintain wars such as that in which we were then engaged. Members had not been vigilant in the business of India, but perhaps, now that this war had led to a tax which, in the words of Bacon, came home to men's business and bosoms, they would cease to be indifferent. This speech, which is remarkable for the knowledge and grasp it shows of the Indian situation, made an impression in the House, and provoked Palmerston to a reply which was, however, deft rather than conclusive.

When Peel unfolded[1] his plan for the simplification of the tariff, Disraeli reminded the House that the real pedigree of free trade was other than the Whigs believed, and that the Minister's conduct was entirely in harmony with the traditions of his party. If they would read and digest the speeches of Lord Shelburne, ' the most remarkable man of his age,' they would find that in the science of political economy they were far behind many of the great statesmen who flourished at the end of the previous century. The principles of free trade had been developed —and not by Whigs—fifty years before. It was Mr. Pitt[2] who first promulgated them in 1787 as a system of reciprocity, while Fox and the other famous Whigs of that day came forward as the champions of the old system of restriction. Nor had the party which originally brought free trade principles into notice been false to those principles, as he showed in greater detail in a speech[3] later in the session. The settlement of 1815 was indeed an anti - commercial settlement, but Lord Liverpool had soon seen that it was impossible to continue on the basis then adopted. From 1820 to 1830

[1] May 10, 1842.
[2] Disraeli was on other occasions in the habit of carrying back the pedigree to Bolingbroke and the Treaty of Utrecht. If he was to begin with the later statesman, he might have taken as his starting-point Pitt's Commercial Propositions of 1785 for establishing free trade between Great Britain and Ireland, which were opposed by the Whig leaders, Burke, alas ! included, with a display of faction and unenlightenment that surpassed even their performance on the French commercial treaty of 1787.
[3] July 21, 1842.

the history of this country was a history of commercial progress. The true principles of commerce were applied in Parliament, and while the home Government was carrying its great measures of renovation, their Foreign Minister was calling new markets into existence. Then the Whigs came into office, and from 1831 to 1841 not a single step was taken to advance the commercial principles of Pitt and Shelburne and Lord Liverpool and Huskisson. Nay, more, during this period our Foreign Minister was pursuing a system of anti-commercial diplomacy. No fewer than five commercial treaties with European States had been lost by his misconduct, and our Eastern markets, which on many accounts were the most valuable we possessed, had been harassed and disturbed. But now that the Prime Minister had in one class of his measures recurred to the policy which had been so beneficial in the past, he hoped that he would apply that policy as a whole. His Corn and Customs Bills were the legitimate continuation of a movement that had been arrested, and he was certain that he also felt the importance of treaties of commerce with the great communities of Europe, and that he was deeply sensible of the bearing of our foreign policy on our foreign trade.[1]

To Sarah Disraeli.

HOUSE OF COMMONS,
April 7.

I write to give you the earliest intelligence that the Shrewsbury petition is withdrawn. This great *coup*, almost, in the present state of affairs, as great as my return, was effected in the most accidental and happy manner by my agent, Bailey of Gloucester, without any interference and barely knowledge of either of the great parties. On his own responsibility he paired off Shrewsbury against Gloucester. Under circumstances of extreme difficulty which must be reserved for narrative, I never knew a happier instance of daring energy and address combined. He left town on Tuesday by mail,

---

[1] This last speech, according to *The Times*, to which it gave the text for a series of articles on ' Foreign Policy and Foreign Trade,' ' obtained considerable notice '; and that not only ' for its intrinsic merits,' but because ' it struck upon a chord to which the public mind was attuned.'

and I was called out of the House eight o'clock yesterday (Wednesday), and found him. I expressed my surprise, perhaps my regret, that he had not departed, when, to my astonishment, I found that in the four-and-twenty hours he had been to Gloucester, Shrewsbury, and returned. It was like the story of the rise of Wolsey.

The committees work so ill under the new system that I really despaired sometimes of keeping my seat, and was convinced that the Shrewsbury people would proceed. But the Gloucester Whigs prevailed upon them to sacrifice themselves for the extrication of their neighbors.

GROSVENOR GATE,
Saturday morning [April 23].

The horses are at the door, and we are going with the living Horace Walpole to visit for the last time Strawberry Hill. Last night, after going to the City, I fired a most effective shot in the debate[1]—cheered by Peel and all the Ministers, loudly by Hardinge, who said to me in the lobby : ' You made an admirable speech, Di.' I observed I was sensible of his support, &c. Replied, taking my arm : ' You know what I said to you years ago—you would become "one of the clearest and most forcible speakers in the House." '

Sir J. Graham came up to me, and said : ' Never was a party pinned more effectively ; the pin was pushed in to the middle, and to the very head.' Just at this moment, when he was unbuttoning his heart, a thick-headed Alderman forced himself upon us and spoilt all.[2]

CARLTON,
Aug. 11.

MY DEAR SA,

This delicious weather makes one sigh for country air ; but we are still prisoners.

Last night Peel made the most effective speech by very far I ever heard from him. He crushed Palmerston,[3] who on the last night, like an excited player, lost on one dashing stake all his hard-won winnings of the last month. I was in the leash to speak, but the effect of Peel's speech was so overwhelming that all the Whigs (Vernon Smith, Charley Buller, Hawes, &c.) took refuge in silence, and Cobden, seizing the opportunity, attempted to an impatient and excited House to foist off his intended speech of the night before, and turned the whole course of the debate, or rather burked it, being followed by Hume, Ewart, and Co. in an American corn vein.

---

[1] On the income-tax. [2] Brit. Mus., Addit. MSS.
[3] Palmerston, on a motion for papers, had made a general attack on the policy of the Government.

Palmerston looked overwhelmed, but was infinitely mortified by the turn of the debate, which rendered his position still more ludicrous — most ludicrous, however, when Philip Howard, the butt of the House, and who pours forth endless *niaiseries*, rose to vindicate ' his noble friend,' which he did with agonising detail, till Peel went away, the House nearly emptied, and Palmerston, bound to remain, refrained even from replying, for which he had prepared.

By-the-by he quoted me very courteously at his commencement, and, indeed, ' went off ' with me, which produced an effect in the House.

Fremantle asked me, after Peel's speech, to reply to any man of note who rose on the opposite benches.

I sigh for news from Bradenham. Your vegetable cargoes are most welcome.

A thousand loves,
D.

The session of 1843, like that of the previous year, was marked by recurrent motions on commercial depression and distress in the country ; and in his speeches on these motions, which were of course only a pretext for attacks on the Corn Laws, Disraeli's line of argument was always the same. Commercial depression was a complex phenomenon. Its origin could be found in no single cause, and it was ridiculous to pretend to cure it by any single or sudden remedy. Certainly no measures, however liberal, of ours would induce foreign Powers to ameliorate at once their present commercial policy. ' A species of Berlin decrees, more stringent even than those of Napoleon, were silently but surely spreading over the Continent against us ; and it required far more than the mere repeal of the Corn Laws to effect a reciprocal liberalisation of European commercial relations.'[1] Of one[2] of these speeches a not over-friendly witness, Lord Morley, has testified that 'it is remarkable to this day for its large and comprehensive survey of the whole field of our foreign commerce, and for its discernment of the channels in which it would expand.'[3] This particular speech, hardly more remarkable than others in their kind, was made in the debate on a motion of

[1] July 1, 1842, from *The Times* report.   [2] Feb. 14, 1843.
[3] *Life of Cobden*, II., p. 336.

Lord Howick's which is memorable for the dramatic scene between Peel and Cobden. Disraeli had spent the winter in Paris, and it was his first deliverance after his return. Following his usual line of argument, he protested against a policy that would apply a single remedy to our commerce in all its branches without regard to varying circumstances. He thought our markets could fairly be divided under three general heads—our European markets, the markets of the East, and the markets of the New World. Our European markets must be regulated by commercial treaties. He believed, for instance, there was a majority in the present French Chamber friendly to a treaty of commerce, and it was in the power of the House of Commons whenever it chose to come to a right understanding with the people of France. If this were done, the session need not end without the conclusion of such a treaty. Having dealt with other treaties of commerce which had been the subject of negotiations, though they had not been carried out, he came to the East. There we addressed ourselves to a very ancient state of society, and our trading intercourse must be conducted on the ancient principles of commerce. If we acted in Europe by negotiation, we could only penetrate the East by enterprise ; and though no immediate or vast impulse to our trade could be expected, we had a right to look for an increase in the three great Eastern markets—in the Levant, in India, and in China. In the New World, again, we encountered a third set of conditions, and commerce with that region, by the nature of the case, must be an affair of speculation—' rapid profits, shattering losses, unnatural expansion, paralysing collapse.' It was not our tariff, not our Corn Laws, that induced the present stagnation in our New World trade ; but its causes were transitory, and there and elsewhere he believed the breeze of prosperity in its own good time would come. He thought it wisest to wait for it—indeed, he saw no other remedy.

I would give an ample trial of the measures of the Government introduced last year.   I supported those measures, not from any blind submission to the Minister who introduced them, but because I approve of the principle on which the commercial system of the right hon. gentleman is founded. The principle of his tariff is a fair protection to native industry —a principle, in my opinion, perfectly consistent with a large and liberal commercial intercourse.   As regards the present Corn Law we know as yet but little.   I am not prepared to stand or fall by the details of that measure, nor am I, for one, surprised that the right hon. gentleman declines to do so. With respect to that law, I will reserve to myself the most unbounded licence.   I will not rest my character for political consistency on a fixed duty or a sliding scale.   But I will support that system which, to use the expression of the noble lord [John Russell], maintains the preponderance of the landed interest.   I believe that preponderance to be essential to the welfare of the country ; I attribute to that preponderance the stability of our institutions ; I uphold that preponderance, not for the advantage of a class, but for the benefit of the nation. . . .   I will venture to remind the House of the words of a great prince, appropriate to the occasion, for they were not only the words of a great prince, but also of a great merchant—I mean that Doge of Venice who, looking out from the windows of his Adriatic palace on the commerce of the world anchored in the lagoons beneath, exclaimed : ' This Venice without *terra firma* is an eagle with one wing.'   I wish to see our national prosperity upheld alike by a skilful agriculture and by an extended commerce.[1]

The reform of the tariff in the previous year had been intended to prepare the way for the policy of reciprocal arrangements with the other states of Europe which Disraeli advocated so zealously ; but this policy made little progress, and on April 25 the impatient free traders called for a further remission of duties without waiting for the commercial treaties which were to provide the opportunity.   Disraeli in the debate tried to defend a Ministry whose principles were now in a state of rapid flux, and which, consequently, no longer found it easy to defend itself.   He quoted ' the work of Dr. List,'[2] then little known in England, but now canonised as the Bible

[1] Hansard, Feb. 14, 1843.
[2] *The National System of Political Economy.*

of modern protection. He reminded the free traders
that the Governments of Europe had often other objects
than the wealth of nations in view in their commercial
arrangements ; that political considerations were always
present to their minds ; and that they sometimes maintained manufactures at a loss ' as the elements of future
strength.' Until those Governments had accepted ' our
high notions of political economy,' we were certain to
have difficulties. The motion meant 'that they should fight
against hostile tariffs with free imports,' and he believed
that would be a policy of the most disastrous kind.   Free
trade, which had originally meant a large and liberal
intercourse, in contradistinction to the old colonial system,
now appeared to mean, in the mouths of gentlemen
opposite, an absence of all restrictions ; but surely there
was some analogy between civil and commercial freedom,
and a man was not the less free from being subject to
certain regulations.   Was it not the natural course to
adopt the happy medium always followed by practical
men — the principle of reciprocity ?   The free traders,
of whose school the total neglect of circumstances was
a peculiar characteristic, ignored the fact that powerful
interests had grown up in other countries as a consequence
of our commercial system, to enforce and advocate our
views ; and in a commercial negotiation the Minister of
England had elements of strength denied to any other
country.   If we acted with decision we must attain our
end, and he thought we could not do better than adhere
to a method which, even if it failed to-day, might always
succeed to-morrow.

In this and other speeches Disraeli chivalrously came
to the rescue of his ' right hon. friend, the Vice-President
of the Board of Trade '—that is to say, Gladstone, whose
reputation among the Conservatives on the question of
protection had, to use his own expression, already ' oozed
away.'[1] Both in Parliament and in the country confidence

---

[1] Morley's *Life of Gladstone*, I., p. 262.

in the Ministry was beginning to be shaken,[1] and Disraeli thought it necessary to go down to Shrewsbury and justify to his constituents the support he had given them. This task he accomplished in a speech that is full of interest, and is as clear an exposition, both of his own point of view in the controversies of the hour, and of enlightened Tory sentiment throughout the party struggle which has lasted ever since, as any he ever delivered. He had voted, he said, for the Corn Bill and the revision of the tariff because he believed them to be measures that were wise and expedient. The principle of these measures was ' protection to native industry, avowed, acknowledged, and only limited because the Minister desired that that protection should be practical . . . such as should compensate for enormous taxation, and should not allow the energies of the country to merge and moulder into a spirit of monopoly.' He was not himself an enemy to free trade according to his idea of free trade. He had never supported either prohibitions or monopoly, or made native industry the stalking-horse by which to shield abuses. ' But my idea of free trade is this : that you cannot have free trade unless the person you deal with is as liberal as yourself. If I saw a prize-fighter encountering a galley-slave in irons, I should consider the combat equally as fair as to make England fight hostile tariffs with free imports.' He believed that Sir Robert Peel had adopted opinions which were just and right, and that he was anxious to support the native industry of the country ; but every Government was entitled, as long as it adhered to principle, to an ample allowance for circumstances, and Sir Robert Peel, though he would be their Minister, was not the man to be their tool. What he had done so far had been for the public advantage.

You should not part with him for what he has done ; neither should you part with him because you think he will

---

[1] In Shrewsbury itself the leading Conservative paper was openly denouncing them.

do a certain act which I believe that he will not. If I find
the Government seceding really from their pledges and
opinions—if I find them, for instance, throwing over that
landed interest that brought them into power—my vote will
be recorded against them. I do not come down to Shrewsbury
to make a holiday speech and say this. I have said this at
Westminster, sitting at the back of Sir Robert Peel, alone, and
without flinching, and I say it again here.[1]

I never will commit myself on this great question to petty
economical details ; I will not pledge myself to miserable
questions of 6d. in 7s. 6d. or 8s. of duties about corn ; I do
not care whether your corn sells for this sum or that, or
whether it is under a sliding scale or a fixed duty ; but what I
want, and what I wish to secure, and what, as far as my
energies go, I will secure, is the preponderance of the landed
interest. Gentlemen, when I talk of the preponderance of
the landed interest, do not for a moment suppose that I mean
merely the preponderance of ' squires of high degree.' My
thought wanders farther than a lordly tower or a baronial
hall. I am looking in that phrase . . . to the population of
our innumerable villages, to the crowds in our rural towns :
I mean that estate of the poor which, in my opinion, has been
already dangerously tampered with ; I mean the great estate
of the Church, which has before this time secured our liberty,
and may, for aught I know, still secure our civilisation ; I
mean also by the landed interest that great judicial fabric,
that great building up of our laws and manners, which is, in
fact, the ancient polity of the realm.

They had all heard how Mr. Cobden, who was a very
eminent person, had spoken in a very memorable speech
of the barbarous relics of the feudal system. If there
were any relics of the feudal system remaining, he regretted that there were not more. What was the fundamental principle of that system ? That the tenure of all
property should be the performance of its duties—' the
noblest principle that was ever conceived by sage or ever
practised by patriot.'

When I hear a political economist, or an Anti-Corn-Law
Leaguer, or some conceited Liberal reviewer, come forward
and tell us, as a grand discovery of modern science . . . that
' Property has its duties as well as its rights,'[2] my answer is

---

[1] This passage, which, from its bearing on Disraeli's subsequent action,
is of great biographical interest, is omitted in Mr. Kebbel's reprint.
[2] This famous aphorism had been promulgated in Ireland by the great
administrator, Thomas Drummond, five years before.

that that is but a feeble plagiarism of the very principle of
that feudal system which you are always reviling. Let me
next tell those gentlemen who are so fond of telling us that
property has its duties as well as its rights, that labour also
has its rights as well as its duties ; and when I see masses of
property raised in this country which do not recognise that
principle ; . . . when I hear of all this misery and all this
suffering ; when I know that evidence exists in our Parliament
of a state of demoralisation in the once happy population of
this land which is not equalled in the most barbarous countries
—I cannot help suspecting that this has arisen because
property has been permitted to be created and held without
the performance of its duties.

If the Anti-Corn-Law League succeeded, how long
would the present law of inheritance in land survive the
whole change of their agricultural policy ? And if they
recurred to the Continental principle of parcelling out
estates, how long could they maintain the political system
of the country ? Some would say, ' Let it go '; but his
answer to that would be, ' If it goes it is a revolution, a
great, a destructive revolution ; and it is not my taste
to live in an age of destructive revolution.' England had
been made by the preponderance of the landed interest.
We should never have been able to conquer the greatest
military genius the world had ever seen, and to hurl him
from his throne, if we had not had a territorial aristocracy
to give stability to our constitution. Without that preponderance of the landowner he did not see why Great
Britain, probably very contented and very prosperous,
should have been a greater Power than Denmark or
Sweden ; and he, for one, would not be the citizen of a
third-class State if he could be the citizen of a first-class
Empire. Nor did they, who had all the memories of an
historical past, want, he was sure, ' to be turned into
a sort of spinning-jenny, machine kind of nation.'

He knew, indeed, there was a deterioration of society
in the present day which was not to be seen only in the
lower classes of the country ; that the nobility and gentry
of the land, who had vindicated our rights, defended our
liberties, and founded our greatest colonies, were deficient

in those high qualities which they had always hitherto exhibited. But he had still some confidence in the national character of Englishmen. This country had experienced great vicissitudes in the past, and we had even had revolutions on a very great scale. The King, the Church, and the constitution, had all been swept away; yet the nation eventually had returned to itself.

Shall I tell you how it was that the nation returned to itself, and Old England after the deluge was seen rising above the waters? This was the reason—because during all that fearful revolution you never changed the tenure of your landed property. That I think, gentlemen, proves my case; and if we have baffled a wit like Oliver Cromwell, let us not be staggered even before Mr. Cobden! The acres remained; the estates remained. The generations changed: the Puritan father died, and the Cavalier son came into his place, and, backed by that power and influence, the nation reverted to the ancient principles of the realm. And this, gentlemen, is the reason why you have seen an outcry raised against your Corn Laws. Your Corn Laws are merely the outwork of a great system fixed and established upon your territorial property, and the only object the Leaguers have in making themselves masters of the outwork is that they may easily overcome the citadel.[1]

Over and over again in the course of this speech we find Disraeli declaring his personal belief that, notwithstanding the new Corn Law and the revision of the tariff, measures only intended for the correction of abuses, Peel remained faithful to the principle of protection. In this belief, as we now know, Disraeli was mistaken. Four days after the speech was delivered, Peel told Gladstone, whom he was taking into his Cabinet as President of the Board of Trade, ' that in future he questioned whether he could undertake the defence of the Corn Laws on principle'; and, in his record of the conversation made on the day it took place, the new President intimates that Peel's ' words were addressed to a sympathising hearer.'[2] It is not a mere coincidence that the Shrewsbury speech

[1] This speech is reported at length in the *Shropshire Conservative* for May 13, 1843.
[2] Morley's *Gladstone*, I., p. 260.

was Disraeli's last attempt at a whole-hearted defence of Peel's administration. He had promised his constituents that if he found the Government throwing the landed interest over his vote would be given against them, and before the month was out he had occasion to fulfil his pledge. The Government had committed themselves to a scheme for reducing to a nominal amount the duty on corn from Canada, and under the conditions then prevailing a capital result would be the indirect admission of corn from the United States at the low fixed duty of 4s. the quarter. At this aspect of the measure the agricultural interest, already suspicious and uneasy, took serious alarm; though Stanley, who, as Colonial Secretary, was immediately responsible, and who, as the future was to show, was a sincere believer in protection, tried hard to convince them that the effects in practice would be small. When he next saw his constituents, Disraeli, after reminding them of the pledge he had given at the time of his previous visit, explained the circumstances in which it had come up for fulfilment.

Upon my arrival in London, the first information I received on entering the lobby of the House of Commons was that the Government had determined to force through the Canadian Corn Bill. . . . I had not the moral courage nor the immoral audacity to say one thing to my constituents, and within 24 hours[1] vote diametrically opposite. . . . At that time there was a most powerful party arrayed against the Government, and how easy it would have been for me to have made a violent and damaging speech against them, and have influenced the passions of those friends who were then in opposition ! Such a course of action on my part would have told with double effect, because I had defended the Ministry on their two previous measures ; but I had no wish to do so, and I only recorded my silent suffrage against them.[2]

The Government carried their Bill, but in the teeth of opposition from many of their supporters and at no small cost to their popularity and prestige.

[1] The interval was short, but the ' 24 hours ' is a piece of Disraelian rhetoric, and is not to be taken literally.

[2] Speech at Shrewsbury, August 28, 1844.

To Sarah Disraeli.

GROSVENOR GATE,
May 12.

We left Shrewsbury after breakfast, and arrived at home for dinner. For the provinces I think my speech was a great effect. Nothing could equal the enthusiasm of my auditors or be stronger than my position there. . . . We did not arrive at Shrewsbury till ten at night, by which we lost a triumphant entrance, the streets having been filled with the expectation of our immediate arrival from six to eight o'clock ; guns on the English bridge ready to be fired and frighten our horses, and deputations at the column. After the dinner we went to the Bachelors' Ball, which was very gay and well attended. Mary Anne, who never looked so well (in white with a dark wreath of velvet flowers twined with diamonds), was the grand lady of the evening, and led out to supper by the Lord Mayor. The next day we went to the races ; saw Retriever win the Tankerville—an excellent race—and shook hands with a great many of our friends. Lord Newport [1] was our travelling companion up to town, and very agreeable ; a shrewd, tall, fair, unaffected, very young man. I was at the House last night and received many compliments about my speech and Shrewsbury campaign. I spoke at Shrewsbury, they tell me, an hour and twenty minutes, but it did not seem long. M. A. was in the gallery, and got even more cheering than I did. . . . Tell my mother we feasted on her chickens. Her slippers were much admired at Shrewsbury.

---

[1] Afterwards 3rd Earl of Bradford, 1819-1898.

CHAPTER V.

A WINTER IN PARIS.

1841–1843.

'This,' said Lady Montfort one day to Endymion, 'is a political economy Parliament, both sides alike thinking of the price of corn and all that. Finance and commerce are everybody's subjects, and are most convenient to make speeches about for men who cannot speak French and who have had no education. Real politics are the possession and distribution of power. I want to see you give your mind to foreign affairs. . . . But foreign affairs are not to be mastered by mere reading. Bookworms do not make Chancellors of State. You must become acquainted with the great actors in the great scene. There is nothing like personal knowledge of the individuals who control the high affairs. . . . What I think you ought to do is to take advantage of this interval before the meeting of Parliament, and go to Paris. Paris is now the capital of diplomacy.'[1] Disraeli himself profited by this sage advice, and shortly after the prorogation of 1842 we find him and his wife established in the Rue de Rivoli.

To Sarah Disraeli.

HÔTEL DE L'EUROPE, RUE RIVOLI,
Oct. 14.

. . . We have for the last ten days or so had the most beautiful weather here, which will, they say, last during the month : our rooms, looking to the gardens of the Tuileries, so warm

[1] *Endymion,* ch. 71.

that we sit with the windows open, the glass 70 in the shade.
Mary Anne has entirely recovered, and I think I never saw
her looking so well. We have found agreeable acquaintance
in the de Gramont family. The Duchess Count D'Orsay's
sister, and like him in petticoats. She receives three times
a week, and the few people in Paris may be found in her little
house in the Faubourg St. Honoré, crammed with pretty
furniture, old cabinets, and pictures of the de Gramonts.
The Duc as well as his spouse extremely good-looking, and
brother of Lady Tankerville, who we also find here and who
is very kind to us. She is staying with Marshal Sebastiani,
who married her sister, recently dead. The Duc, when Duc
de Guiche, was an officer in our 10th Hussars, in the days of
Lord Worcester, Pembroke, and George Wombwell. One of
his three sons, the Vicomte de Gramont, is with them, and
their two daughters, on the point of coming out, and the
first considered very pretty, and celebrated in the novels of
Eugène Sue, the only *littérateur* admitted into fashionable
society here ; the rest are savages. We see these Mlles.
de Gramont in the evening, where they are trying their
wings, previous to a formal *début*, and kiss their mother at
ten o'clock and go to bed.

Of English here are the Adrian Hopes, who arrived from
Normandy yesterday ; Henry Hope, who has been here as long
as ourselves ; George Smythe, Cochrane,[1] Lord Pembroke,
Antony de Rothschilds, Mrs. Montefiore. Antony succeeds
the Duke of Orleans[2] in his patronage of the turf, and gives
costly cups to the course, which his horses always win.
Through Goldsmith[3] I have made the acquaintance of
Mauguin,[4] whom I see much of and like, and Odilon-Barrot,
the leader of the Opposition, called on me yesterday. Thiers
is in the country, as well as almost every other leading man,
but they will soon cluster in. He frequents the *salon* of the
Duchess, and seems in favor with the Carlists ; here also I
shall find Berryer.[5] Goldsmith gave us a grand banquet and
good company—the Swedish and Spanish Ministers, the
U. S. for Foreign Affairs, Mauguin, and other diplomats.
They all talked at the same time, shouted, and gesticulated,
the noise Neapolitan, and the *salle à manger* being very small,
and there being fourteen *bougies* alight on the table, independent
of several side-lamps, the effect was overwhelming. Mary

---

[1] Alexander Baillie Cochrane, 1816-1890, afterwards 1st Lord Lamington.
[2] Louis Philippe's eldest son, who had been killed in a carriage accident
in the previous July.
[3] The father of Lady Lyndhurst.
[4] A well-known lawyer and politician.
[5] A leading Legitimist politician.

Anne and myself have taken advantage of the fine weather
to visit several places which I had never seen—Père la Chaise
and all that—and yesterday we made with Smythe a charming
pilgrimage to the Luxembourg. . . . Smythe and Cochrane
dined with us yesterday. We have a *cuisinière bourgeoise*, very
pretty. Mary Anne begs you net to have any stays made
till she comes home, as she can give you valuable information
thereon. . . We meet at the de Gramonts, Princes de
Beaufremont, Counts de Chambellan, Duchesses de Marmier.
What names ! But where are the territories ? There are
only 100 men in France who have ten thousand per ann.
Henry Hope and De Rothschild could buy them all.

Nov. 9.

Our English friends have nearly all departed, and the
serious illness of the Duc de Gramont has put a stop to the
pleasant *réunions* at their house. We have dined with Lord
and Lady Cowley : a very pleasant dinner. . . . The ambassador is very like the Duke, but much taller. Lady Cowley
has the most polished yet natural manners, very well-informed
and rather clever. Paris is very empty of notables, though
some few are stealing in. The season will be late and sombre,
owing to the death of the Prince Royal, and the non-conse-
quent autumn meeting of the Chambers, which will not
now reassemble till the middle of January. We have passed
an evening at Madame Baudrand's, the wife of the general
and aide-de-camp of the King, and friend. She is an Englishwoman, and young enough to be his daughter. We also met
her friend, Miss Tennyson d'Eyncourt, who remembered
dining with me seven or eight years ago at Bulwer's. Many
Frenchmen have English wives—Madame Lamartine, Odilon-
Barrot, and De Tocqueville.

Nov. 22.

MY DEAR SA,
. . . I have seen a good many persons since I wrote last. I
think I was then on the eve of paying a visit to Thiers, whom
I found in a very handsome house, and in his cabinet, or
sanctum, a long gallery room, full of works of art ; at the
end his desks and tables covered with materials, maps and
books and papers for the life of Napoleon, or rather the history
of the Consulate and Empire. I stayed with him two hours :
a very little man, but well proportioned, not dwarfish, with
a face full of intelligence and an eye full of fire. Madame
Thiers receiving every evening, Mary Anne and myself paid
our respects to her a few nights after. We met there Mignet,[1]
Count Walewski, the son of Napoleon, whom we knew before,

[1] A well-known historian.

and others. Thiers paid M. A. the greatest courtesy and attended her to her carriage. Madame Thiers pretty : her mother, Madame Dorne, there. I believe the house, which is very handsome, belongs to Monsieur Dorne, the father-in-law.

Next day to the Sorbonne, where I paid a visit to the celebrated Cousin, late Minister of Instruction and now Dean of the University : great power of elocution ; he delivered me a lecture which lasted an hour and a half, very perspicuous and precise, dogmatic but not a pedant. I have seen also the great Dupin,[1] who is rich and lives in a very handsome hotel ; his brother Charles—a pair of zanies ; and I also made a visit to the prince of journalists, M. Bertin de Vaux, an ox who lives in a fat pasture manured by others. He dwells in a fine hotel, and lives like a noble ; indeed, few have such a rich estate as the *Journal des Débats*.

Yesterday, however, was my most distinguished visit ; like a skilful general, I kept my great gun for the last. On Sunday night I received a letter from the royal aide-de-camp in service to inform me that the King would receive me in a private audience at St. Cloud on the morrow at half-past eleven. I was with his Majesty nearly two hours alone ; the conversation solely political, but of the most unreserved and interesting kind. He was frank, courteous, and kind. In taking my leave, which of course I could not do until he arose, he said he hoped my visit to St. Cloud had made as favorable an impression on me as mine had on him ; that he hoped to see me in the evenings at the palace, when he should have the pleasure of presenting me to the Queen. There is no court of any kind at this moment, and therefore M. A. cannot be presented, and we hear that the poor Queen is still dreadfully depressed. After my audience had concluded, General Baudrand, whom I rejoined in the ante-chamber, took me over the palace. But I cannot now attempt to give you the faintest idea of its splendor and beauty. The pages, courtiers, equerries were all in the deepest mourning. I went in my usual morning costume. I ought to tell you that while, previous to the audience, I was sitting in the chamber of the aide-de-camp, one of the courtiers brought me from the King, by his Majesty's express order, a despatch just received, and which he had not himself read, containing the news of the conquest of Cabul[2] and the release

[1] President of the Chamber from 1832 to 1840.

[2] 'You will be surprised to hear,' wrote his sister from Bradenham, in reply to this letter, ' that it was our first account of the conquest of Cabul, our papers having miscarried, as they always do when there is anything of importance ; so that we owed as much as you did to the courteousness of his most Christian Majesty.'

of the prisoners.   His Majesty said afterwards he was
happy that our meeting took place on a day which had
brought such good news for England.

Be very particular and minute in your information about
my father's eyes.   Scarcely a day passes without some inquiry
being made after him here, especially by the *hommes-de-lettres*.
His works are universally known here, and Buchon,[1] Sainte-
Beuve, Bertin de Vaux, Philarète Chasles,[2] &c., are familiar
with every page he has written.

Ever affectionately yours,

D.

Disraeli had sought his audience through General
Baudrand, with whom he had become intimate, in order
' to lay before his Majesty some facts respecting the
state of parties and the disposition of power in our Parliament, which if properly appreciated might exercise an
important and immediate influence on the lasting policy
of the two countries.'   Palmerston, who in 1830 had
begun his rule at the Foreign Office by an attitude so
friendly to the new monarchy in France as to provoke
Disraeli's ire in his *Gallomania* tract, had, when his rule
came to an end in 1841, left a France profoundly irritated
by his policy in the Levant ; but Aberdeen and Guizot,
the Foreign Ministers of the two countries, were now
endeavouring to restore friendlier relations, and Disraeli,
who had travelled far since the days of the *Gallomania*,
was anxious to make his contribution to this desirable
result.   Through General Baudrand he submitted to the
King a long memorandum,[3] in which, with a courtly
compliment to ' the genius of a great Prince, eminently
fertile in resource and strengthened by an unprecedented
experience of life,' he suggested a course of action in the
English Parliament and Press likely, in the writer's
opinion, to lead to the speedy restoration of ' a genuine
and hearty alliance ' between the two countries.   Louis
Philippe, who well knew that an understanding with
England was almost essential to the existence of his

[1] Historical scholar.
[2] A literary critic like Sainte-Beuve, though of less celebrity.
[3] For the full text see Appendix.

throne and dynasty, was impressed by the memorandum ; and whatever may have been the political results of the audience that followed, the impression was maintained. Thenceforward the King was prodigal of marks of his favour, and he continued to regard Disraeli as a friend to the hapless end of his own career.

Dec. 2, 1842.

My dear Sa,
   . . . I don't think when I wrote to you last that I had made a visit to Augustin Thierry, or rather a pilgrimage. He is only forty-five, but paralysed to his centre, and quite blind ; but he entirely retains his faculties, and even with the aid of amanuenses continues his composition, and even researches. He sent many messages to my father, whose name is very familiar with all the *literati* of Paris. T. is married, and his wife very worthy and devoted, but she takes the words out of his mouth a little too much. After this I called for M. A., and made a visit together to Madame Thiers (the evening of course, when all visits are paid in Paris), and then I made my *début* at the Comtesse de Castellane, a charming woman of the highest fashion, and who smiles on M. Molé—a *grand seigneur*, and once Prime Minister. I was presented to her by Henry Bulwer, and have since presented M. A. to her.
On Tuesday I dined with the Minister for Foreign Affairs, his first dinner for the season, and given only to the great personages ; even the Cabinet Ministers only appeared at the soirée. The guests were the English Ambassador, the Austrian Ambassador (Count Apponyi), the Prussian Minister, the Duke Decazes, Grand Referendary of France, Count de Chabot, Baron Alexander Humboldt, General Sebastiani, Governor of Paris, Baron Regnier, the Chancellor of France, Rothschild and myself, and Colonel Fox. Guizot, his mother, very old, his sister-in-law, who heads his establishment, and his private secretary, made up the party. All was sumptuous, servants in rich liveries and guests with every ribbon of the rainbow. Sat between Sebastiani and Rothschild, whom I met for the first time, and whom I found a happy mixture of the French dandy and the orange-boy. He spoke to me without ceremony, with ' I believe you know my nephew ?' On Wednesday, after making a preliminary visit to Madame Castellane to present Mary Anne, we went to a grand rout at the British Embassy, where we saw every diplomatic character in Paris, including the fat Nuncio of the Pope, and the Greek Minister, Odelli, in native costume, many of the high French and shoals of the low English.

Returning home, I found a note from General Baudrand, saying that at St. Cloud in the morning the King had said : ' Mr. Disraeli has never been at St. Cloud in the evening. I wish to present him to the Queen.' Accordingly last night I was obliged to go off, and arrived at St. Cloud about nine. The palace, situate on a hill and brilliantly illuminated, had a fine effect. I passed for the first time in my life an evening in the domesticity of a Court. When I arrived the Royal family were still in the apartments of the Duchess of Orleans : a few courtiers and one or two visitors, my friend Count Arnim, the Prussian Minister, loitering in the saloons, and three ladies sitting at a table working. In about a quarter of an hour the Court was announced, and his Majesty entered with the Queen, followed by Madame Adelaide, the Princesse Clementine, the Duke and Duchess of Nemours, and some attendants. We formed a distant circle. The Queen and the ladies, all in deep mourning, seated themselves around a large round table, working. Ices were handed, and the King commenced speaking a few words to each.

He was extremely gracious when he observed me, and, after saying a few words expressing his pleasure that I had arrived, called to a courtier to present me to the Queen. Her Majesty asked me six questions, to which I replied. She is tall and sad, with white hair ; a dignified and graceful phantom. Then I was presented to Madame Adelaide, who is very like her brother. In the course of the evening the King conversed with me a considerable time. I am a favorite with him, and doubtless owe to his good word my grand dinner with M. Guizot, who told me that the King had observed to him, ' he had had a most interesting conversation with me.' I hope to hear good news of all, to whom a thousand loves. M. A. is very well indeed, and sends many kind loves and messages.

D.

Dec. 21.

Many thanks for your 'happy returns' received this morning. ... We have attended a meeting of the Académie Française for the reception of a new member, the celebrated Baron Pasquier, Chancellor of France, who made a long eulogium on Frayssinous, the late Bishop of Hermopolis, and was replied to by the president of the day, M. Mignet, in a speech of considerable ability. The grand hall of the institute was crowded, all the genius and fashion of Paris present. My ticket was given me by Comte Molé, Mary Anne's by M. Guizot. Afterwards I dined at a grand party at the Luxembourg, with the Grand Referendary of the Chamber of Peers, the celebrated Duc Decazes, and sat next to his Duchess, a daughter of St.-Aulaire,

the French Ambassador at our Court. In the evening there
was a very choice reception at Madame de Castellane's to
celebrate the election of Pasquier ; the hero of the day was
there himself, and many celebrities. I was introduced among
others to Barante, now a Baron and an Ambassador and
President of the Society of French History, of which I have
been elected a member. . . .

On Saturday last I received a command to dine at the
Tuileries on the following Monday at six o'clock. I was
ushered, through a suite of about twenty illuminated rooms,
to the chamber of reception, where I formed one of the circle,
and where I found seated the Queen of Sardinia, at present a
guest, and her ladies. Soon after the Court entered and went
round the grand circle. I was the only stranger, though
there were sixty guests. Dinner was immediately announced,
the King leading out the Queen of Sardinia, and there were
so many ladies that an Italian princess, duchess, or countess
fell to my share. We dined in the gallery of Diana, one of
the *chefs-d'œuvre* of Louis XVI., and one of the most splendid
apartments perhaps in the world. . . . In the evening the
King personally showed the Tuileries to the Queen of Sardinia,
and the first lady in waiting, the Marquise de Dolomieu,
invited me, and so did the King, to join the party, *only eight*.
It is rare to make the tour of a palace with a King for the
cicerone. In the evening there was a reception of a few
individuals, but I should have withdrawn had not the King
addressed me and maintained a conversation with me of great
length. He walked into an adjoining room, and motioned
me to seat myself on the same sofa. While we conversed the
chamberlain occasionally entered and announced guests.
' S. A. le Prince de Ligne,' the new Ambassador of Belgium.
' J'arrive,' responded his Majesty very impatiently, but he
never moved. At last even Majesty was obliged to move,
but he signified his wish that I should attend the palace in
the evenings. . . .

You must understand that I am the *only* stranger who has
been received at Court. It causes a great sensation here.
There is no Court at present, on account of the death of
the Duke of Orleans ; and the Ailesburys, Stanhopes, and
Russian princes cannot obtain a reception. The King speaks
of me to many with great *kudos*.

It was not only his first taste of the joys of a Court that
Disraeli found exhilarating. Social artist as he was, he
delighted in the brilliant society of Paris, in its freedom
from snobbishness, its homage to intellect, its graceful

ease. In *Coningsby*, which was written in the course of
the following year, we can see some of the results of his
present observations.

Nothing strikes me more in this brilliant city than the
tone of its society, so much higher than our own. What an
absence of petty personalities ! How much conversation,
and how little gossip ! Yet nowhere is there less pedantry.
Here all women are as agreeable as is the remarkable privilege
in London of some half-dozen. Men, too, and great men,
develop their minds. A great man in England, on the contrary, is generally the dullest dog in company ![1]

Or, again :

What is more consummate than the manner in which a
French lady receives her guests ? She unites graceful repose
and unaffected dignity with the most amiable regard for
others. She sees everyone ; she speaks to everyone ; she sees
them at the right moment ; she says the right thing ; it is
utterly impossible to detect any difference in the position of
her guests by the spirit in which she welcomes them. There
is, indeed, throughout every circle of Parisian society, from
the *château* to the *cabaret*, a sincere homage to intellect ; and
this without any maudlin sentiment. None sooner than the
Parisians can draw the line between factitious notoriety and
honest fame ; or sooner distinguish between the counterfeit
celebrity and the standard reputation. In England we too
often alternate between a supercilious neglect of genius and a
rhapsodical pursuit of quacks.[2]

Or take the description of the Duchesse de G[ra-
mon]t's receptions, where

It seemed that every woman was pretty, every man a wit.
Sure you were to find yourself surrounded by celebrities, and
men were welcomed there if they were clever before they were
famous, which showed it was a house that regarded intellect,
and did not seek merely to gratify its vanity by being surrounded by the distinguished.[3]

In some notes written by Disraeli about twenty years
later there are sundry reminiscences of this visit to Paris,
and another which he paid in the winter of 1845 :

[1] *Coningsby*, Bk. V. ch. 8.   [2] Bk. V. ch. 7.
[3] Bk. VI. ch. 1.

When I was in Paris in 1842, the Court was slowly recovering from the death of the Duke of Orleans. The King, however, was full of confidence in himself and in his dynasty. He dwelt on the resemblance of the position of William III. of England and himself. He had this additional advantage—children. I had my first audience with King Louis Philippe at St. Cloud at the end of the autumn. The audience was long and not formal. It was the only time in my experience in which the King did not engross the conversation, and few foreigners have enjoyed a greater intimacy with that sovereign than myself. I have been in the habit of remaining after the evening receptions at the Tuileries, and sitting with him in his cabinet until a very late hour, he himself dismissing me by a private way, as all the royal household had retired. In these conversations, or rather communications, he seemed to conceal from me nothing. Sometimes he would speak only of his early life, his strange adventures, escapes, hardships, and necessities. The last time I was alone with him in 1846 he had indulged in this vein, and in reply to an observation which I had made I remember well his saying : ' Ah, Mr. Disraeli, mine has been a life of great vicissitude !' He would always speak English with me. He had a complete command of our language, even of its slang (*argot*). Perhaps it might be said that his English was a little American.

In 1842 the King was entirely master—his own chief Minister in fact. He was fond of affairs, and jealous of the interference or aspirations of his sons. The King had a conviction that he thoroughly understood Frenchmen, and knew how to manage them. He despised his people. More than once, when I had made a suggestion, he would remark : ' Ah, I have to deal with a very different people from you.' And then a peculiar grimace of contempt and dislike. ' The way to manage these people is to give them their head, and then know when to pull them up.'

In the King's time there never was a dinner given at the Tuileries—no matter how stately ; I have seen it in the Gallery of Diana with a hundred guests—without a huge smoking ham being placed, at a certain time, before the King. Upon this he operated like a conjurer. The rapidity and precision with which he carved it was a marvellous feat : the slices were vast, but wafer-thin. It was his great delight to carve this ham, and indeed it was a wonderful performance. He told me one day that he had learnt the trick from a waiter at Bucklersbury, where he used to dine once at an eating-house for 9d. per head.

One day he called out to an honest Englishman that he

was going to send him a slice of ham, and the honest English-man—some consul, if I recollect right, who had been kind to the King in America in the days of his adversity—not used to Courts, replied that he would rather not take any. The King drew up and said : ' I did not ask you whether you would take any ; I said I would send you some.' A little trait, but characteristic of the dash of the *grand seigneur*, which I often observed latent in L. Philippe, though from his peculiar temperament and his adventurous life of strange vicissitude he was peculiarly deficient in dignity. . . .

General Baudrand, Governor of the Comte de Paris, and entirely devoted to the House of Orleans, a man who had risen from the ranks, I believe, but a natural nobleman, a man of the highest moral tone as well as social breeding, doing every justice to the King, to whom he was attached, often concluded his confidential observations by saying : ' What the King wants is *dignity* '—' Ce que le roi manque, c'est la dignité.' Baudrand, without stiffness, for he was genial, had as great a share of dignity as I ever met.

King Louis Philippe sent Baudrand on his accession to the Duke of Wellington to explain everything and obtain an immediate recognition. Baudrand's account of his interview with the Duke very interesting. Wellington was not so grieved about the ' three glorious days ' as some suppose. The elder branch, in their anxiety to become popular, were going very wrong, and were about to attack the Rhine. The Duke accepted the election of the House of Orleans as a pledge for constitutional and moderate government. Baudrand was exactly the envoy the Duke would appreciate—a distin-guished soldier, with a simplicity like his own.

King Louis Philippe vindicated to me one day his refusal in 1830 of the [office of] Lieutenant-General of the Kingdom during the minority of the Duc of Bordeaux (Henri V.). He said he would have preferred leaving France. He said if the Duc had died during the regency nothing would have pre-vented [him from] being looked upon as a criminal. ' The Duc of Bordeaux would never have had a bellyache without my being denounced throughout the world as a poisoner.'

At Paris in 1842-43, Guizot Minister, but not supposed to be very strong. His strength increased with the strength of Peel, and Madame Lieven consolidated the alliance between Guizot and Lord Aberdeen. His rivals were Thiers, who had been Minister and was leader of the Opposition, and Comte Molé, descendant of the Grande Barbe, and inheriting not merely his name, but the honors and estates of the family ; for Molé had been a minor in the days of the emigration, remained in France under wise guardians, and preserved the

whole of his estates, which during his lifetime the Code
Napoléon, almost as bad as the emigration, could not diminish.
Molé was a *grand seigneur*, of the highest breeding ; courtly,
finished, dignified if necessary, but easy and simple. Excellent talents, very general information, a complete political
culture, and not a mean orator when under pressure. He
was supposed to lean to the Russian Alliance, though I believe
this was only a newspaper theory. I was on terms of great
intimacy with him, and he spoke freely to me of his views as
regards England. He was short in stature, like his rivals
Guizot and Thiers. His countenance was dark, with regular
features of the Jewish cast, and he was supposed to inherit
his physiognomy from a famous Hebrew heiress, who married
into his family. He lived in the Hôtel Molé in good state,
and entertained as became his rank—the only personage in
Paris who gave great dinners except the Ministers and high
functionaries and Rothschilds.

Affairs were changed in 1846. Guizot was rooted in power,
and had persuaded the King that he was the Richelieu of a
Louis XIV. Thiers, who had a considerable following in
1842-43, the remains of his position in 1839 of first Minister,
was greatly sunk, had reverted to literature, and was very
disaffected. The Hôtel Molé had been pulled down, and
the Comte lived in a new one in the modish quarter of F. St.
Honoré. His chance seemed quite to have vanished.

Guizot's manner had no charm ; it was indeed repulsive.
Not exactly pedantic, but professional, hard, dogmatic,
arrogant. His countenance very fine ; a brow of beaming
intellect, and a wondrous flashing eye. His general countenance often reminded me of Roubiliac's bust of Pope. Thiers
looked and chattered like a little journalist ; a monkey, but
wonderfully sharp and self-complacent and clever.

Thiers said to me one morning, as we were walking together
in the Champs Elysées : ' As for French politics, they are
simple. I am forty-seven, M. Guizot is fifty-seven, and Comte
Molé is sixty-seven.[1]

To Sarah Disraeli.

PARIS,
Jan. 16, 1843.

The uncertainty of our movements and the great pressure
of business and pleasure have daily made me delay writing.
Our life goes on the same, only more bustling. I have been
a great deal at Court ; had the honor of drinking tea with

---

[1] As a statement of fact this remark could not, either in 1842 or 1845,
have been literally accurate, but literal accuracy in such matters was never
the foible of either Thiers or his reporter.

the Queen and Madame Adelaide alone, and one evening
was sent for to the King's cabinet. I am in personal as well
as political favor there. We had tickets from the household
to witness the opening of the Chambers and to hear the
King's speech, which was extremely interesting. The splendid staff of a hundred general officers and the marshals
of France, in their gorgeous uniforms, seated on one bench,
very fine. We have been also to the Chamber of Peers,
worthy of the Roman Senate ; to the Luxembourg, to a
concert given by the Duchess Decazes, and we were the only
English there.

One of our most amusing parties was a strictly French
dinner, to which we were invited by the Odilon-Barrots. A
capital dinner, and surrounded by names long familiar to me—
Lamartine, Tocqueville, Gustave de Beaumont [1] ; the first
tall and distinguished in appearance, all intelligent. In the
evening a *soirée*, in which all the Opposition figured. By-the-
by, the Turkish Ambassador dined at Barrot's ; I happened
to praise some dish which I remembered eating in Turkey ;
and on Sunday his cook brought one as an offering to Mary
Anne. Reschid Pacha is his name, a great celebrity. I went
by invitation one evening to talk Eastern politics and smoke
a chibouque, which he offered me, brilliant with diamonds.
He told me then that since we last met he had been recalled,
' a simple *rappel*.' He knew not whether he was to be dis-
graced, or to be made Prime Minister ; but I suspect the latter
will be his destiny.

Another day we went to an assembly at the Hôtel de
Ville, given by the wife of the Prefect of the Seine—costly
beyond description, in the style of the Renaissance ; and
after it, where do you think we went at half-past twelve
at night, M. and Madame Adolphe Barrot, ourselves, and
Odilon ? To the masqued ball at the Opera. They had an
admirable box, the scene indescribable. Between three and
four thousand *devils* dancing and masquerading beyond
fancy. A thorough carnival ; the *salle* of the Grand Opera
formed into one immense Belshazzar's hall with a hundred
streaming lustres. The grand galoppe, five hundred figures
whirling like a witches' sabbath, truly infernal. The contrast, too, between the bright fantastic scene below and the
boxes filled with ladies in black dominoes and masks, very
striking, and made the scene altogether Eblisian. Fancy me
walking about in such a dissolute devilry, with Odilon-
Barrot of all men in the world, who, though an excellent
fellow, is as severe as a *vieux parlementaire* of the time of the

---

[1] De Tocqueville's colleague in his memorable mission to America in 1831.

Fronde.   I have omitted much more than I have told ; but you must manage to pay your visit to town immediately after our arrival.

CARLTON,
Saturday [Feb. 4].

I can give you no news from this ; all at present uncertain and unsatisfactory.   Peel feeble and frigid, I think, and general grumbling.

Our latter days at Paris were some of our most brilliant : the principal features, the ball at the English Embassy ; 1,000 folks and orange-trees springing from the supper-table ; my farewell audience with his Majesty ; a grand dinner at Molé's[1] ; I sat between Humboldt and Tocqueville, and was surrounded with celebrities—Mignet, Victor Hugo, Cousin, &c.   But above all spectacles was the ball at Baron Solomon de Rothschild's—an hotel in decoration surpassing all the palaces of Munich ; a greater retinue of servants and liveries more gorgeous than the Tuileries, and pineapples plentiful as blackberries.

The taste of this unrivalled palace is equal to the splendor and richness of its decorations.   The company all the *élite* of Paris.   You must obtain from M. A. when you see her an account of this unrivalled fête.

I saw Hahnemann at Paris, very hale and active, and eighty-eight !

The influence of his stay in Paris and of his conversations with Louis Philippe is clearly visible in Disraeli's conduct in the new session of Parliament.   Not only, as we have seen, did he urge the Government to conclude, if possible, a commercial treaty with France : he returned with fresh zest to his attacks on the Palmerston system in foreign affairs, and supported Peel and Aberdeen in their resolution to pursue a less provocative policy.   ' I have at last,' he writes to his sister when the session was a month old, ' made a great speech at a late hour, in a full house, and sat down amid general cheering.'   The

---

[1] ' I dined at Comte Molé's,' is the reminiscence of the sixties, ' and sate next to Alexander Humboldt at dinner.   He was then a very old man, though he lived ten [really sixteen] years more.   But he had none of the infirmities of age, being vivacious and both communicative and sympathising.   I am ashamed to recall so little when the effect was so pleasing.   Victor Hugo sate opposite to me ; a handsome man, not then more than forty, and looking younger.'

subject was the Afghan War, the occasion a motion by
Roebuck for a select committee of inquiry ; and Disraeli's speech[1] in its general tone was a curious anticipation of speeches to be made against himself a generation
later. Before the trouble began we had, he argued, a
perfect boundary ; but anticipating, as we thought, a
movement by Russia, we had invaded Afghanistan, and
so courted disaster. Russia, he admitted, was menacing,
but only by virtue of her geographical position. Her
policy was not offensive. Our late Foreign Minister had
been the real aggressor, sending secret agents to the
shores of the Black Sea to intrigue against Russia, who
naturally had replied by sending similar agents into
Central Asia. This speech he followed up by voting, as
often before, in a minority mainly Radical, against both
the front benches ; but when, only a week later, the
Opposition forces were mobilised officially for an attack
on Lord Ellenborough, the Indian Governor-General, who
had brought discredit on a policy that seems in essence
to have been statesman-like, by his theatrical proclamation on the recovery of the gates of Somnath, he voted
with the Government. Before the end of the month he
was helping them again on a question of foreign policy.
Palmerston made an attack on the treaty which Lord
Ashburton had just negotiated in Washington for the
settlement of the Maine boundary and other outstanding
differences between Great Britain and the United States,
and Disraeli defended it in a speech[2] in which he showed
more knowledge of the facts of a very intricate question
than Palmerston, or even Peel, who had the Foreign
Office to guide him.[3]

By Disraeli's friends in Paris, where Palmerston was
detested, these speeches, of course, were read with no
little satisfaction.

[1] March 1, 1843. [2] March 22, 1843.
[3] So I am assured by an authority who has made a special study of the
subject.

From General Baudrand.

PARIS,
1 *Avril.*

J'ai vu sans étonnement, mais avec une véritable satisfaction, la décision avec laquelle vous avez abordé la lutte avec lord Palmerston.   Sortir vainqueur du combat contre un athlète aussi redoutable est un glorieux triomphe parlementaire.   Cet avantage ne peut manquer d'agrandir votre influence et fortifier votre crédit parmi vos amis politiques. Je vous en fais mon sincère compliment, et je suis chargé de vous en faire un autre, non moins sincère que le mien, de la part d'un personnage, dont l'approbation ne peut manquer de vous flatter et de vous donner une vive satisfaction.   Le succès de votre attaque contre la politique hostile et agressive de lord Palmerston, et l'appui que vous avez donné aux intentions pacifiques et éclairées et conformes aux véritables interêts de l'Angleterre de l'homme recommendable maintenant placé à la tête de votre gouvernement, justifient la confiance que le roi a montrée dans la loyauté de vos sentiments et la fermeté de vos convictions.

CHAPTER VI.

YOUNG ENGLAND.

1843–1844.

On the Tory side in the Parliament of 1841 there was a little group of young men who had been educated together at Eton and Cambridge, and who were united not only by the memory of their school and college friendship, but by a common stock of ideas on questions of Church and state. Their leading spirit was George Smythe,[1] whom we have already encountered, ' a man,' as Disraeli described him long after his death, ' of brilliant gifts, of dazzling wit, infinite culture, and fascinating manners ;'[2] though from lack of serious purpose he was to disappoint his friends, and, in the words in which one[3] of them summed up his career, to prove ' a splendid failure.' Smythe, as is well known, was the original of the hero in *Coningsby ;* but the figure there presented is less true to life than a portrait in *Endymion,* where he reappears as Waldershare.

Waldershare was one of those vivid and brilliant organisations which exercise a peculiarly attractive influence on youth. He had been the hero of the debating club at Cambridge, and many believed in consequence that he must become Prime Minister. He was witty and fanciful, and, though capricious and bad-tempered, could flatter and caress. At Cambridge he had introduced the new Oxford heresy. . . . Waldershare prayed and fasted, and swore by Laud and Strafford. He took, however, a more eminent degree at

[1] See p. 126. [2] General Preface to the Novels, 1870.
[3] Lord Lyttelton.

Paris than at his original Alma Mater, and becoming passionately addicted to French literature, his views respecting both
Church and state became modified — at least, in private.
His entrance into English society had been highly successful,
and as he had a due share of vanity, and was by no means
free from worldliness, he had enjoyed and pursued his
triumphs.   But his versatile nature, which required not only
constant, but novel excitement, became palled even with
the society of duchesses. . . .   Waldershare was profligate,
but sentimental ; unprincipled, but romantic ; the child of
whim, and the slave of an imagination so freakish and de-
ceptive that it was always impossible to foretell his course.
He was alike capable of sacrificing all his feelings to worldly
considerations, or of forfeiting the world for a visionary
caprice.[1]

' My morbid, keenly analytic, introspective, Jean-
Jacques-like temper ' is a phrase in a letter he wrote to
Disraeli in the last year of his short life ; and again, ' I
once heard that you had said of me " that I was the
only man who had never bored you." '

Chief among the youths who were Smythe's chosen
companions, and who felt the spell of his brilliant mind
and fascinating personality, was Lord John Manners,
second son of the Duke of Rutland—a man inferior to
Smythe in intellectual gifts, but of a loyalty, purity,
and kindliness of nature, that amounted almost to genius.
He appears as Lord Henry Sydney in *Coningsby* and
Tancred, and some of the charm of the original character
is caught in the portrait. Another member of the coterie
who had found his way into the House of Commons was
Alexander Baillie Cochrane, a young Scottish laird who
appears in *Coningsby* as Buckhurst, ' the fiery and
generous Buckhurst.'

It is not easy now to discriminate between the ideas
which the little group had brought from Cambridge and
those which they acquired later when they came under
the influence of Disraeli's riper mind.   Like most of the
generous youth of the nineteenth century, they were in
the first place romantics—in eager sympathy with the

---

[1] *Endymion*, ch. 22.

protest against a utilitarian age to which romanticism
was committed in all its manifestations. From the foremost spirits of the time, Newman, Carlyle, and the others,
who with their several voices were bearing similar
testimony, they had learnt to deplore the excessive
worship of mere wealth and machinery that prevailed to
the neglect of all the higher interests of man. Nurtured
politically in the romantic school of Scott, they were of
course Tories from the first, and their Toryism never lost
a certain Jacobite flavour. As in the case of Scott
himself, acceptance of the reigning family did not prevent
them from cherishing Stuart traditions ; and one of the
cardinal articles of their political faith was that monarchy,
as Smythe put it, was a principle rather than an instrument, one of their primary aims the restoration of
dignity and influence to the Throne. On his very first
appearance as an active politician, Smythe had found an
opportunity of proclaiming these opinions with dramatic
effect. He came forward as a candidate for a vacant
seat at Canterbury shortly before the dissolution of 1841,
and at a time when the Tories were at the height of
their irritation over the repeated postponement of their
hopes of office since the Bedchamber incident two years
before. Attributing the happier fortunes of their rivals,
the Whigs, to the favour of the Palace, heated Tory
partisans were displaying their resentment openly, or
at most under the cover of a barely decent cloak of
loyalty ; but the boy fresh from Cambridge had the
courage to reprove their folly and set them the right
example. He embodied in his first speech a glowing
eulogy of the young Queen, and so taking the wind out
of the sails of his opponents won the election.

By a sure instinct the young Cambridge men had
turned their backs on the degenerate Toryism of privilege
and immobility, and sought their inspiration in the
enlightened principles and practice of the younger Pitt
and Canning. In undergraduate days they had seemed
to see in Peel the heir to the traditions of these their

George Smythe, Viscount Strangford.
from a picture by R. Buckner at Hughenden.

favourite statesmen, and had watched with enthusiasm the steady growth of his influence. But Peel was a practical politician with no romantic tendencies, and the views of his young admirers were not to be bounded by the Tamworth manifesto. They desired for the Church a position of greater independence than the Erastian spirit of the eighteenth century had been willing to sanction, or than Peel himself, we may surmise, would have been disposed to concede. Like all true romantics, they had an antipathy to the middle class, which was Peel's political idol ; they dreaded its growing influence, and hoped to provide a counterpoise by reawaking the sense of duty in the nobility and gentry, and restoring them to their rightful place as leaders and protectors of the people. With the people at large their sympathy was real and active. They had that faith in the lower orders which the Tory party had lost, and the courage to believe that it might be possible to redeem them from the misery and serfdom into which they had fallen. Their minds were fertile in ideas, some of them too picturesque, perhaps, to be practical, but all of them noble and disinterested, for bringing back joy to the sombre and monotonous lives of the labouring poor, and renewing the harmony between classes that had been one of the characteristics of the ' Merrie England ' of the past. The paternity of these ideas is to be traced especially to Manners :

An indefinite yet strong sympathy with the peasantry of the realm had been one of the characteristic sensibilities of Lord Henry [Sydney] at Eton. Yet a schoolboy, he had busied himself with their pastimes and the details of their cottage economy. As he advanced in life the horizon of his views expanded with his intelligence and his experience ; and . . . on the very threshold of his career, he devoted his time and thought, labour and life, to one vast and noble purpose, the elevation of the condition of the great body of the people.[1]

Disraeli had known Smythe before they were brought together in Parliament, and through Smythe in due

[1] *Coningsby*, Bk. IX. ch. 1.

course he came to know the others. Between him and the little group there appears from the first to have been a mutual attraction. Disraeli was now nearing forty ; but, as we see in his novels, an instinctive love of youth was one of his marked characteristics, and it became more rather than less marked as his own years went by. He could sympathise with the ardour and enthusiasm of the young, admire their generous impulses and tolerate their foibles ; and he was altogether free from that insidious form of envy which often causes older men, even though they be themselves quite unconscious of the feeling, to watch with a certain annoyance the progress of the rising generation. Early in the session of 1842 Smythe and his friends began to rally round him. 'I already find myself without effort the leader of a party chiefly of the youth and new members,' he wrote on one occasion, as we have seen, to his wife. For ten years he had been preaching the political truth that was in him to an inattentive public and an indifferent House of Commons, and had only succeeded in adding to his reputation of political adventurer the reputation of political visionary, which was still more damaging. Now at last he had found an audience whose minds were prepared and who listened to him gladly. More than a century earlier his hero Bolingbroke had written to one of ' the Boys ' who were then arrayed against Walpole : ' I expect little from the principal actors which tread the stage at present : I turn my eyes from the generation that is going off to the generation that is coming on.' Disraeli, who liked to think of himself as the inheritor of Bolingbroke's mission, turned, doubtless, to the young Cambridge men in much the same spirit.

Presently he or Smythe conceived the idea of a closer association than was implied in mere friendship without formal ties. It happened that Smythe and Cochrane were in Paris in the autumn of 1842, and there, as we saw, they dined with Disraeli one evening in October. A letter written by Smythe a week later from London, and addressed, according to his habit, to 'Disraeli the Younger, M.P.,'[1] sets forth the sequel.

From the Hon. George Smythe.

Oct. 20, 1842.

DEAR DIZ,

I have fulfilled your instructions and written to John Manners and H. Baillie.[2] The first I have told that we are to sit together and vote as the majority shall decide, and that any overture involving office ought to be communicated to the esoteric council of ourselves. To the Celt I have been more guarded and reserved, having only proposed that we should sit together in the hope that association might engender party. Have you attended to my suggestion and seen much of Cochrane? It cost me three hours' walking over the Place Vendôme after your dinner to reconcile him anew to our plan. He was all abroad—angry, jealous because you had talked to me more than to him. He said you did not appreciate him, that you had known me longer, but that him you did not understand. . . .

Pray lay me at the little feet of Madame, and believe me, dear Diz,

Yours affectionately,
G. SYDNEY SMYTHE.

Disraeli's immediate design is made sufficiently clear by the memorandum which he submitted to the King of the French.[3] In the Ministerial majority of ninety there were already, as he explained, between forty and fifty agricultural malcontents : 'It is obvious, therefore, that another section of Conservative members full of youth and energy, and constant in their seats, must exercise an irresistible control over the tone of the Minister. Sympathising in general with his domestic policy, they may dictate the character of his foreign, especially if they appeal to a conviction which, at the bottom of Sir R. Peel's heart, responds to their own.' Such a party, he added, could easily be found ; in fact, ' a party of the youth of England, influenced by the noblest views

---

[1] On the ground, as he explained, that ' one does not write "Shakespeare, Esq." '

[2] Baillie was a man of Disraeli's own age, who had recently married a relative of Smythe's.

[3] See Appendix.

and partaking in nothing of a parliamentary intrigue,'
was at the moment only waiting for a leader. This
appears, however, to have been an unduly sanguine
view. While Disraeli was writing in Paris, Smythe was
reporting from London the outcome of his first efforts,
Henry Baillie 'is afraid the paucity of our members
would provoke the same ridicule now proper to Vyvyan.'
Manners, from another Scotsman, 'gets this for answer :
"Should you be able to concoct any scheme for the
conduct in Parliament of the thirty or forty members
you mention, it might prove of essential service." The
thirty or forty members he mentions ! It must be
John Falstaff not John Manners who wrote to him ;
but clear it is that the two Scots dread our proximity.'
Disraeli had been counting on aid from *The Times*, where,
though his friend Barnes was now dead, and had been
succeeded by Delane in the editorial chair, the proprietor,
John Walter, who was in the present Parliament, was
expected to be friendly. Hostility to the new Poor
Law was still a bond of sympathy between him and
Disraeli, and his eldest son and heir, John Walter the
third, who was now assisting him in the management
of the paper, had been a member of the Smythe and
Manners set at Eton ; but in spite of these advantages
Smythe foresaw difficulties.

As a matter of fact, no party, numbering few or many,
bound by formal pledges such as Smythe had suggested
to Manners, and voting consistently together, seems ever
to have been formed ; but in the course of the session
of 1843 the little group of friends, Smythe, Manners,
and Cochrane, succeeded in winning recognition as a
definite coterie, and came to be known in the House by
the name of Young England. Whether this name[1] was
a heritage from Cambridge days, or, as one of[2] Disraeli's

[1] We have seen (p. 129) Disraeli using it early in the Peel Parliament as
a general description of the new members on the Tory side of the House.
Monckton Milnes appears (*Life*, I., p. 239) to have invented it at an earlier
date as a title for some clique or movement of his own ; but no connexion
is traceable between this and the later usage.
[2] At Bingley, Oct. 11, 1844.

speeches would seem to imply, was given at first in derision, and afterwards adopted by the coterie itself, is not quite clear. Smythe had once suggested, with characteristic wit and flippancy, that the new party they were projecting should be called the 'Diz-Union.' Smythe, indeed, from the first appears to have meant mischief—probably as much from a freakish love of mischief as with any serious purpose—and there is nothing to indicate that he was encouraged by Disraeli in any designs he may have harboured of hostility to the Government. The enthusiasm which the three friends had once felt for Peel as an enlightened Tory leader had not long survived their entry into Parliament, and daily experience of the Minister's repellent manners, ponderous commonplaces in debate, and opportunist policy; but Cochrane has left it on record that, because 'they were not supposed to adopt a factious line,'the members of Young England sat, not below the gangway, but immediately behind the Ministerial front bench.[1] Here, as we know, Disraeli also had his place; and he was clearly the guiding spirit of the movement from the first, though he seems to have remained ostensibly aloof till the three friends by their own efforts had won a certain recognition.

Faith in the genius of Toryism; a conviction of the possibility of restoring it to vigour by a recurrence to its historic traditions, and a reconstruction of the party on a popular basis; a desire to maintain and strengthen the influence of the upper orders combined with a readiness to trust the masses of the people and a genuine interest in their well-being; above all, dislike of the Whigs, and of the middle-class Liberalism in which Whiggery was merging—these things Disraeli and his younger friends had in common. It was, naturally, the riper man who gave shape and definition to the vague ideas and aspirations of the boys fresh from Cambridge; but if he taught them a great deal, they also taught him

[1] Lord Lamington's *In the Days of the Dandies*, p. 174.

something. When Disraeli was a youth, romanticism
had been flowing in the revolutionary channel prepared
for it by Byron ; it was now flowing strongly in the
channel of reaction. That memorable revolt against the
domination of liberalism in politics and religion, which
had issued from Oxford early in the thirties, and taken
thence its name, had soon won a footing in the sister University. One of the earliest workers in this mission-field
was Frederick Faber, and among the friends whom he was
in the habit of visiting at Cambridge were the under-
graduates Smythe and Manners.[1] He is said to have
made their acquaintance while they were on a reading
tour in the Lake country ; and he, at all events, it was
who brought them under the sway of the ideas that were
now becoming so potent in the Church. ' Waldershare
prayed and fasted and swore by Laud and Strafford.'
If with Smythe the religious exercises were only a passing
affectation, the influence of Laud and Strafford over
him and his companions was in other respects enduring.
The Oxford movement gave a seventeenth-century colour
to their political ideals. They had already carried their
political researches into the preceding generation, and found
in Pitt and Canning the model Tory statesmen ; Disraeli
had travelled farther, and drawn inspiration from the age
and writings of Bolingbroke ; but now the young Cambridge men boldly went behind the glorious Revolution
sacred to the Whigs, and sought the fountain-head of
Toryism in the reign of Charles I. In the matter of the
Church the Oxford movement completed their emancipation from the thraldom of Erastian ideas ; in the matter
of the Crown it transmuted their sentimental Jacobitism
into a reasoned political theory and a serious political
purpose ; and working through them it produced parallel
effects in the mind of Disraeli. If he never wholly
sympathised with their views respecting the Church, he
speedily assimilated what was novel in their teaching
with regard to the monarchy.

[1] *Life of Father Faber,* p. 7. Faber appears in *Sybil* as Aubrey St. Lys.

In the *Vindication*, as we saw,[1] he had accepted the
Revolution as wholesome and necessary, and had begun
at a subsequent date his attempt to reconstruct our
political history on a plan of his own, in sharp opposition
to the dominant Whig theory ; in *Sybil* we shall find a
new point of view, and not only the Revolution, but even
the Reformation, treated with scant respect. The change
is probably to be ascribed in no small degree to the
influence of Smythe and Manners and their tractarian
ideas, as also is the change of judgment on the Bedchamber affair which has been noted as taking place
between the time of that crisis and the writing of *Coningsby*. In his earlier speeches and in the *Vindication*,
Disraeli had shown a clear perception of the part the
Sovereign had played, and might usefully play again,
as the protector of the people from oligarchic ambition ;
and he had even borrowed the comparison frequent in
earlier writers between the shackled monarchs of the
Revolution and the doges of Venice ; but it was only
now that he began to appraise at their full worth the
possibilities of the throne as a democratic institution,
to see that it was an imperative duty to guard it from
the encroachments of the jealous middle classes, and
to dream of an eventual restoration of its prestige. It is
not fanciful to believe that through the indirect agency
of Faber and Young England the Oxford movement
helped to shape the policy of Queen Victoria and her
favourite Prime Minister a generation later.

'To change back the oligarchy into a generous aristocracy round a real throne ; to infuse life and vigor into
the Church, as the trainer of the nation . . . ; to establish
a commercial code on the principles successfully negotiated
by Lord Bolingbroke at Utrecht, and which, though
baffled at the time by a Whig Parliament, were subsequently and triumphantly vindicated by his political
pupil and heir, Mr. Pitt ; to govern Ireland according to
the policy of Charles I., and not of Oliver Cromwell ; to

[1] Vol. I., p. 316.

emancipate the political constituency of 1832 from its
sectarian bondage and contracted sympathies ; to elevate
the physical as well as the moral condition of the people,
by establishing that labour required regulation as much
as property ; and all this rather by the use of ancient
forms and the restoration of the past than by political
revolutions founded on abstract ideas '—there, con-
veniently set forth in a retrospective survey,[1] and with
very little colouring from the experience of a later time,
is the task, as conceived by Disraeli and Young England,
that lay before the Tory party. We shall find their
conception of the Tory ideal expounded at greater length
in *Coningsby* and *Sybil*, but this may stand for the present
as an adequate summary of their political aims when
the process of mutual education was complete.

Across St. George's Channel the movement, which
came to be known by the name of Young Ireland, had
now begun its career, and, appropriately enough, it was
in an Irish debate that Young England first succeeded
in arresting attention. Ireland was again in the political
foreground, and to govern her ' according to the policy
of Charles I., and not of Oliver Cromwell,' was one of
the cardinal maxims of Young England politics.
O'Connell's agitation for the repeal of the Union had
slumbered during the years when he was maintaining
the Whigs in office, and had seemed to receive its death-
blow when his followers were reduced to a handful in
the General Election of 1841 ; but the problem of Irish
government was very far from being solved, and after
a year of profound peace the agitation was renewed with
fresh spirit and enthusiasm. That movement of conscious effort after national unity and independence, the
results of which were to be so memorable in European
history, was just beginning to gather force, and the
agitation in Ireland now took from it a colour. In the
autumn of 1842 a few young Irishmen of genius founded
the *Nation*, and by their inspiring appeals to national

---

[1] General Preface to the Novels, 1870.

sentiment contrived to produce a transient and delusive
semblance of union between the contending creeds and
classes of a sorely distracted country. As the session
of 1843 advanced, the movement began to attract attention in Parliament, and Smythe and Manners—the one
having family connexions with Ireland, and the other,
as on one occasion he reminded the House, being grandson of a popular Tory Lord Lieutenant—crossed the
Channel to see for themselves. They returned little
satisfied with the policy of the Government, which, as
far as it had then been disclosed, was limited to the
well-worn expedient of an Arms Bill—in accordance with
the tradition that English Governments should atone for
their neglect and inaction in periods of calm weather
by a resort to spasmodic violence when storms broke
out afresh. Graham, who, as Home Secretary, was
the Cabinet Minister responsible, had even been foolish
enough to declare, in a speech on the Arms Bill, that
' conciliation in Ireland had been carried to its utmost
limit '; and the Duke of Wellington, it was well known,
thought that this limit had already been transgressed.

Ireland was now, as Disraeli wrote to his sister, ' the
only thought and word,' and in July there was a debate
which lasted many nights, on a resolution of Smith
O'Brien's asking for inquiry with a view to the redress of grievances. Cochrane, Manners, and Smythe all
three spoke, and all gave free expression to the discontent they felt. Manners held up the administration of
Strafford as an example to be followed, and announced
that, as he did not think the question of confidence was
involved, he would vote for the motion. Smythe told
the Ministry that they ought to govern Ireland in the
spirit of Mr. Pitt, who would not have come down with
an Arms Bill and an Arms Bill alone ; and he also took
occasion to express his regret that Catholic Emancipation
had been carried by Peel rather than by Canning—by an
enemy rather than by a friend—and that so the healing
effects of that measure had been lost. Peel was strangely

maladroit in his handling of a situation the difficulties of
which, if a little tact had been applied, need hardly have
been formidable. With equal lack of good temper and
good sense he recommended Smythe to vote against the
Government, telling him that this would be a more manly
course than to lend them a hollow and seeming support ;
and it is not surprising to find that the triumvirate[1] all
three took him at his word, and voted in the minority
for O'Brien's motion. Well might Peel's pupil and
admirer, Gladstone, say that his chief ' was not skilful in
the management of personal and sectional dilemmas.'[2]

In a subsequent debate Smythe flung out the taunt,
which was greeted with loud cheers from both sides of
the house, that different language had been heard when
majorities were counted by units instead of by hundreds.
Others had noted a change in Peel's demeanour towards
his supporters since his establishment in office with overwhelming strength ;[3] but his arrogance towards Young
England is the less easy to understand, as the prestige
of his Ministry was now at its lowest ebb. Ireland, if
their chief, was by no means their only difficulty. Distress and discontent were still rife in Great Britian.
The agricultural interest was in a state of extreme irritation over what it regarded as a fresh attack on its position
in the concessions just granted to American corn. The
disasters in Afghanistan, for which the responsibility of
the present Ministers was really slight, had nevertheless
brought them odium ; and when the turn of fortune
came, Lord Ellenborough, their Governor - General, so
managed that the odium was converted into ridicule.
To a nation that had grown accustomed to Palmerston's
boisterous methods, Aberdeen's foreign policy seemed
lacking in spirit, and it did nothing to diminish the
unpopularity of the Government. A letter of Macaulay's,
written less than a fortnight after the Irish debate, gives

[1] Disraeli was absent.   [2] Morley's *Gladstone*, I., p. 253.
[3] See, for instance, some bitter remarks of Lord Ashley's in Hodder's
Life of Shaftesbury, ch. 9.

a picture of the situation as it presented itself to a keen
observer on the front Opposition bench.

As to politics, the Ministers are in a most unenviable situation ; and, as far as I can see, all the chances are against
them.   The immense name of the Duke, though now only
a ' magni nominis umbra,' is of great service to them.   His
assertion, unsupported by reasons, saved Lord Ellenborough.
. . . . But he is 74, and in constitution more than 74.   His
death will be a terrible blow to these people.   I see no reason
to believe that the Irish agitation will subside of itself, or that
the death of O'Connell would quiet it.   On the contrary, I
much fear that his death would be the signal for an explosion.
The aspect of foreign politics is gloomy.   The finances are
in disorder.   Trade is in distress.   Legislation stands still.
The Tories are broken up into three or more factions, which
hate each other more than they hate the Whigs—the faction
which stands by Peel, the faction which is represented by
Vyvyan and the *Morning Post*, and the faction of Smythe
and Cochrane.   I should not be surprised if, before the end
of the next session, the Ministry were to fall from mere
rottenness.[1]

Hitherto Disraeli, though he had voted against the
Government on the Canadian corn question, had uttered
no word in criticism of their policy, but when the Irish
Arms Bill came up for its third reading in August he took
the side of Young England in a speech which shows signs
of careful preparation.   Ireland being in the foreground,
he had, in accordance with his habit, been studying
Irish history, a thing that English statesmen have very
rarely done.   'Irish policy is Irish history,' he said in
the House of Commons a quarter of a century later,[2]
' and I have no faith in any statesman who attempts to
remedy the evils of Ireland who is either ignorant of the
past or who will not deign to learn from it.'   He began
on the present occasion by urging that, as the Minister
since his accession to office had thrown over the Irish

---

[1] Macaulay to Napier, July 22, 1843 : Trevelyan's *Life*, ch. 9.   It would
appear, from a letter of General Baudrand's, that Disraeli himself had
written a month earlier to his friends in Paris that the Ministry was in
danger.
[2] March 16, 1868.

policy which he had advocated while in opposition, his
supporters were now free from all bonds of party on
this particular subject.   An hon. member on his own
side (Smythe) had put forward opinions which had
excited some surprise, but which he had defended as the
old and legitimate Tory doctrines.   The defence was at
once historically true and politically just.   He could
find no grounds in history for the common assumption
that hostility to the Irish people was a characteristic of
Tory policy.   The policy of Charles I. had been based
on conciliation of the Roman Catholics of Ireland, and
at no later period, when the Tories had been preponderant,
had their policy been different ; whereas the Whigs,
when they held the command of the Government for
the long period of seventy years in the eighteenth century,
had been consistently hostile to the Irish Roman Catholics.
At a time like the present, when those who had been their
leaders no longer led, and they found themselves sinking
into a faction without principles, it was their duty to
recur to the traditions of the party; and he thought there
was nothing more strange than that the gentlemen of
England, who were the descendants of the Cavaliers,
should be advocates for governing Ireland on the principles of the Roundheads.

Ministers had announced almost with ostentation that
they intended to do nothing, and this paralysis of policy
appeared to be caused by dissensions in the Cabinet.
' The leader of the Government in another House[1] was
chalking " No Popery " on the walls, while the leader
of the Government in that House told them that he,
for himself, cared nothing about Protestant or Papist.'
When he found systems so inconsistent, resulting only
in imbecility, he had a right to suppose that there were
dissensions in the Cabinet, and he believed that they
would destroy this or any other Cabinet which did not
address itself to the question of Irish government in
a very different spirit.   It was perfectly clear that if

[1] The Duke of Wellington.

they abolished the Protestant Church to-morrow and
established the Roman Catholic, or chose any isolated
remedies one after the other, they would produce no
improvement in the condition of Ireland. It had arrived
at that pitch which required a great man to have recourse
to great remedial measures. They must reorganise and
reconstruct, not only the government, but even the
social state of the country.

With regard to the present measures he had little
to say :

There are some measures which to introduce is disgraceful,
and which to oppose is degrading. I have given no vote on
this Bill one way or the other, and I shall continue that
course, being perfectly persuaded of its futility. Believing
that Ireland is governed in a manner which conduces only
to the injury of both countries ; that the principles declared
by Ministers are not capable of relieving us from the difficult
position in which we are placed ; believing that the old principles of the party with which I am connected are quite
competent, if pursued, to do that, I hope the time will come
when a party framed on true principles will do justice to
Ireland, not by satisfying agitators, not by adopting in despair
the first quack remedy that is offered from either side of the
House, but by really penetrating into the mystery of this
great misgovernment, so as to bring about a state of society
which will be advantageous both to England and Ireland,
and which will put an end to a state of things that is the
bane of England and the opprobrium of Europe.

The insubordination of Smythe and his friends had
attracted little notice, but this speech of Disraeli's was
a more serious matter, and evoked a great deal of comment. The Whig press of course made the most of the
opportunity. Disraeli spoke from his usual place just
behind Peel and Graham, and one malicious journalist
describes with graphic detail the behaviour of the two
Ministers during the performance. The Prime Minister,
he tells us, endeavoured to ' palliate the effects of the
castigation by industriously rubbing his nose ; while the
Home Secretary, edging occasionally round, would look
up in the face of the orator with that sort of uneasy smile

by which one sometimes tries to convey the idea of being not only perfectly at ease, but exceedingly amused.'[1] Smythe rose later and resumed his attack on Peel, sheltering himself under the plea that when persons were substituted for principles personality became a duty;[2] and angrily declaring that, talk as they might of the intolerance of the Roman Catholics, their intolerance could be matched on the benches below. Peel when he rose could find nothing better in the way of reply than a sneer at Disraeli's 'new-born zeal' for Ireland; a regret that he could not see in the hon. member himself the man who was to realise his vision of the great statesman with a comprehensive policy; and a renewal of his former invitation to Smythe to vote against the Government.

Disraeli, we may suppose, was not the less willing to criticise the Government, as he was now convinced that Peel had ceased to be conciliatory in his demeanour towards himself. In the course of the present Parliament he had asked half a dozen questions, most of them on matters of current foreign policy; and one seems to detect in the Minister's replies, even as they appear in the dry record of Hansard, a certain needless curtness or hint of disapproval. No offence may have been intended, for Peel's manners even in Parliament, where he was most at his ease, were notoriously ungracious, and he was not skilful in those blandishments of 'my honourable friend' by which a tactful leader knows how to soften the asperity of a refusal of information to an inquisitive supporter. On a recent occasion his discourtesy to Disraeli, whether intentional or not, had been more apparent than usual. An insurrection in Servia had led to the usual difficulties between Russia and the

---

[1] *Morning Chronicle,* August 11, 1843.

[2] ' I came in with others,' he said in a speech to his constituents a few years later (July 6, 1847), ' full of hot thoughts and ardent speculations, and we sat by men who . . . had but one rule, . . . the will of the sole Minister. When persons were thus substituted for principles, personalities became a duty with those who wished to substitute principles for persons.'

Porte ; and Disraeli, already anxious, as he showed in his remarks, about ' the integrity of the Turkish Empire,' and with his anxiety possibly quickened by communications from the King of the French,[1] who had no love for Russia, pressed the Minister as to his policy. He received a rebuff, and did not forget it. A few days[2] after the speech on the Irish Arms Bill, Palmerston opened a debate on the situation in the East, and Disraeli, rising after Peel, criticised severely the inaction of the Government. It was a strange termination of his campaign against Palmerston, and he made the occasion memorable, not only by the support he gave to his former antagonist, but by aiming a personal shot, the first of many, at Peel. ' I remember,' he remarked, ' some time since to have made an inquiry of the right hon. gentleman with respect to the interference of Russia in Servia, an inquiry couched, I believe, in Parliamentary language, and made with all that respect which I feel for the right hon. gentleman, and to which the right hon. gentleman replied with all that explicitness of which he is a master, and all that courtesy which he reserves only for his supporters.' The great Minister was regarded by many of his supporters as schoolboys regard a severe head-master, and as he was well known to have a weakness for the applause of his opponents—a weakness which seems incident to Parliamentary leadership — one can imagine the secret joy with which the sarcasm was hailed on the benches behind him.

In the light of Disraeli's later career the matter of this speech has an interest of its own. The real question, he said, was whether England would maintain the independence and integrity of the Ottoman Empire. He wished to guard himself from being supposed to hold fanatical opinions as to Russian designs. He believed these designs to be perfectly legitimate. He saw much

[1] During Disraeli's stay in Paris, Louis Philippe had lamented 'l'insouciance avec laquelle l'Autriche et l'Angleterre laissaient tomber l'Empire Ottoman sous le bon vouloir de la Russie.'

[2] On Aug. 15.

to respect in Russia ; he respected her nationality, he
respected her intelligence, he respected her power. We,
too, had nationality and power ; but we were deficient
in that intelligence, especially with regard to the East,
for which Russia was eminent. The great question of
foreign policy was simpler than statesmen were inclined
to admit. If they looked at the map, they would see
that the two strongest positions in the world were the
Sound and the Dardanelles, and as long as these positions
were held as at present the balance of power was
safe. But Russia was approaching them gradually,
regularly, sometimes even rapidly, and if she obtained
possession of one the balance of power would be disturbed, while if both fell under her authority universal
empire would be threatened. Our true policy was,
therefore, by diplomatic action to maintain Turkey in
a state to hold the Dardanelles. Turkey indeed was
prostrate ; but what ground was there for the assumption
that her regeneration was hopeless ? If she had lost her
finest provinces, so had England little more than half a
century back ; if her capital had been occupied, that was
a calamity that had befallen every State in Europe with
the exception of England. Her resources were still
unequalled, and it was the diplomacy of Europe during
the last twenty years that had reduced her to her present
condition. Once more he imputed no blame to Russia,
who was pursuing her own interest by legitimate means.
She had a fixed, deep policy founded on ample knowledge ; we opposed to it a policy uncertain and superficial, and founded in ignorance, a policy that at the
present moment had made us the laughing-stock of
Europe.

As a matter of fact, Aberdeen's diplomacy at this time,
and his complaisance to the Tsar Nicholas when he
visited England in the following year, did not a little
to foster the ambitions that led to the Crimean War ;
but the House of Commons was less occupied with the
intrinsic value of Disraeli's criticism than with the fact

that he should have had the temerity to criticise at all.
Peel's position in the Conservative party had so long been
commanding, and his authority so long unquestioned, that
any display of independence was a matter for astonishment;
and this speech of Disraeli's, coming after his attack on
the Irish policy of the Government, made no small impression. An incident that followed showed the temper
that prevailed on the Ministerial benches. Lord Sandon,
a prominent supporter of Peel's, rose and rebuked Disraeli's presumption, absurdly accusing him of having
heaped 'the grossest terms of contumely and opprobrium' upon Her Majesty's Ministers, whom he affected
to support. When challenged to cite the terms of opprobrium, Sandon was unable to recall the exact words he
had in mind, and his extravagance was reproved by
speaker after speaker in the subsequent debate, including
men as little prejudiced in favour of Disraeli as Hume
and Palmerston himself. Disraeli, as we shall see, suspected that the attack had been inspired by the Government, and *The Times* would appear to have shared
his suspicion, for in its comments on the incident it
condemned such attempts to 'cow and bully' private
members as fatal to the principle of free and fair debate,
and reminded the Minister that it was not for the public
benefit, or really for his own, however much for his convenience, that he should be above all question from his
own side of the House. Peel declared afterwards that
he was innocent in the matter, and Sandon's attack was
probably spontaneous; but whether he received encouragement from the front bench or not, a letter from
Graham to Croker, written a week later, leaves us in
no doubt as to the feelings towards Disraeli that were
harboured in that quarter :

With respect to Young England, the puppets are moved
by Disraeli, who is the ablest man among them : I consider
him unprincipled and disappointed, and in despair he has
tried the effect of bullying. I think with you that they will
return to the crib after prancing, capering, and snorting ;

but a crack or two of the whip well applied may hasten and insure their return. Disraeli alone is mischievous ; and with him I have no desire to keep terms. It would be better for the party if he were driven into the ranks of our open enemies.[1]

The general spirit of this letter may help us to understand why the eminent man who wrote it was so little loved by his contemporaries, and in the light of the disposition towards Disraeli which it reveals subsequent events become a good deal less surprising.

To Sarah Disraeli.

CARLTON CLUB,
Monday [July 17].

London, that a little while ago seemed so dull that the shopkeepers were in despair, is suddenly favored by the most animated season, for which the Cockneys are indebted to the King of Hanover, now the most popular man in town— for the first time in his life. Grand *fêtes* every day, and apparently interminable. We have had and are to have our fair share.

On Thursday the Duchess of Buckingham after a banquet held an assembly which was extremely brilliant and well arranged. The Duke had gotten the band of the Life Guards in the galleries of his grand staircase, which is of the Italian style and mounts to the roof of his house, and the effect was stirring. Every guest welcomed with a martial flourish. The Duchess of Gloucester and the Grand-Duke of Mecklenburg and his intended father-in-law were there as well as his Majesty. There were six Dukes : Wellington, Cleveland, Marlboro', Argyll, Buccleuch, and Buckingham. Four of these Knights of the Garter, while two others appeared in the shapes of Salisbury and Jersey, to say nothing of the royal Knights. Richmond himself wore two immense diamond stars—the Grand Cross of the Guelph, in honor of his Guelphic guest, as well as that of the Garter—but persists in wearing the garter itself on pantaloons !

On Friday Lady Lyndhurst had a select reception after a royal dinner. We formed a Court circle, and the King went round. I was presented by the Lord Chancellor in a flowery harangue, and received gracious compliments from His Majesty. He even shook hands with me. The second King who has shaken hands with me in six months !

---

[1] *Croker Papers,* III., p. 9.

Lady Peel has asked us to a grand rout and royal reception on the 21st, and the St. Aulaires to a ball [at the French Embassy], which is to be the most magnificent ever given in London, on the 27th.

On the 22nd Sir Edward Bulwer gives a grand *déjeuner* at Craven Cottage : and we are engaged to dinner on the same day to the Antony de Rothschilds, but as our host and hostess are going to the breakfast as well as ourselves, I trust we shall none of us get away till night, and so escape the dinner.

HOUSE OF COMMONS,
Friday [*July* 21].

Yesterday we were at a most delightful *fête*, Gunnersbury, Madame de Rothschild *mère*. A most beautiful park and a villa worthy of an Italian Prince, though decorated with a taste and splendor which a French financier in the olden times could alone have rivalled.

The bright morning unfortunately ended in a dingy afternoon, which threw us much on the resources of indoor nature, notwithstanding the military bands, and beautiful grounds, temples and illuminated walks. However, we had a cheering concert, a banquet of illimitable delicacies, and, at the end, a ball. All the world of grandeur present : Ernest I., the Cambridges, Duchess of Gloucester. We were much gratified : and I got well waited on by our old friend Amy, who brought me some capital turtle, which otherwise I should have missed.

[*Undated.*]

We returned from Deepdene this morning, after a most agreeable visit, with beautiful weather. One night I sat next to Mrs. Evelyn of Wotton, a widow ; her son, the present squire, there also ; a young Oxonian and full of Young England. We are going to Manchester and Liverpool—a rapid visit which I must make—and after a respite of forty-eight hours for business we should like to come to Bradenham for as long as you will have us. I am writing [*Coningsby*], and want a workroom ; therefore, if it does not inconvenience anybody, let me have my old writing-room next to your room. The journals daily descant on the ' new party ' that has arisen to give a new color to modern politics, &c.'

In a letter to a friend, Mrs. Disraeli recounts in detail their movements during the recess.

Nov. 24.

After passing a few days with Sir E. and Lady Sugden, we went to our friend Mr. Hope, and remained all September

with him at the beautiful Deepdene.   On our return we went
to Manchester, Liverpool, and Chester.   At the former place
we were much fêted.   There was a grand literary meeting
at the Free Trade Hall : they sent a deputation to Dis suggest-
ing his presence ; he declined, and they sent a deputation of
ladies, which, you know, he could not refuse ; so he went, and
made a fine speech for them—all said by far the finest—
literary not political.

At the Manchester meeting Charles Dickens was in
the chair.   Disraeli in his speech, after a graceful allusion
to another of the speakers as 'his hon. friend Mr.
Cobden,' denounced as vulgar and superficial the prejudice 'which associated with commerce and manufacture
an inability to sympathise with the fair inventions of
art or the poetic creations of the human intellect,' and
held up before the people of Manchester the stimulating
examples of the great merchants of Venice, who were
the patrons of Titian and Tintoretto ; the merchant
family of the Medici, who made Florence the home of
genius ; and the manufacturers of Flanders, who dwelt
in such cities as Bruges, Ghent, and Mechlin.[1] The
chairman described the speech as 'very brilliant and
eloquent,' and the admiring wife of the orator does
not seem to have exaggerated in her report of its
success.

Parliament met in February, and its meeting supplied
the occasion for an interesting correspondence between
Disraeli and Peel.   Disraeli would appear to have had
little or no suspicion of the manner in which his speeches
of the previous summer were resented, or of the strength
of the prejudice against him in the Ministry.   He had
even during the recess been simple enough to write to
Graham, of all men, and ask him to bestow some office
on one of his brothers.   Having returned what he called
'a civil but flat refusal,' Graham informed the Prime
Minister of this 'impudent' application, and the answer
sent by Peel is worth reproducing :

[1] *Manchester Guardian*, Oct. 7, 1843.

Dec. 22, 1843.

I am very glad that Mr. Disraeli has asked for an office for his brother. It is a good thing when such a man puts his shabbiness on record. He asked me for office himself, and I was not surprised that being refused he became independent and a patriot. But to ask favours after his conduct last session is too bad. However, it is a bridle in his mouth![1]

This letter of Peel's, taken in connexion with Graham's avowed wish to drive Disraeli into open hostility, will help us to interpret the following correspondence :

To Sir Robert Peel.

GROSVENOR GATE, PARK LANE,
Feb. 4, 1844.

DEAR SIR ROBERT,

I was quite unaware until Friday night, when I was very generally apprised of it, that the circumstance of my not having received the usual circular from yourself to attend Parliament was intentional.

The procedure admits, of course, of only one inference.

As a mere fact, the circumstance must be unimportant both to you and to myself. For you, in the present state of parties—which will probably last our generation—a solitary vote must be a matter of indifference ; and for me, our relations, never much cultivated, had for some time merged in the mere not displeasing consciousness of a political connexion with an individual eminent for his abilities, his virtues, and his station.

As a matter of feeling, however, I think it right that a public tie, formed in the hour of political adversity, which has endured many years, and which has been maintained on my side by some exertions, should not terminate without this clear understanding of the circumstances under which it has closed.

I am informed that I am to seek the reasons of its disruption in my Parliamentary conduct during the last session.

On looking over the books, I perceive that there were four occasions on which I ventured to take a principal part in debate.

On the first I vindicated your commercial policy on grounds then novel in discussion, but which I believed conducive to your interest and your honor ; and the justness

---

[1] Parker's *Peel*, III., p. 425.

and accuracy of which, though never noticed by yourself or
any of your colleagues, were on a subsequent occasion distinctly and formally acknowledged by the leader of the
Opposition.

In the second instance I spoke on a treaty of a difficult
and delicate nature, against which the Opposition urged no
insignificant charges, and to assist you to defend which I
was aware you would not be likely to find much efficacious
support on your own side. I have reason to believe that my
efforts on this occasion were not wholly uninfluential on
opinion ; although, certainly, I never learned this from any
member of her Majesty's Government.

At the very end of the session there were two other
occasions on which I spoke, and against isolated points of
the policy of the Government—I mean with respect to Ireland
and the Turkish Empire. Although an indiscreet individual,
apparently premonished, did in the last instance conceive
a charge against me of treating the Government with
' systematic contumely,' he was utterly unable to substantiate, scarcely equal to state, the imputation ; and the
full miscarriage was generally admitted. I can recall no
expression in those remarks more critical than others which
have been made on other subjects, as on your agricultural
policy, for example, by several of the supporters of your
general system. Those remarks may indeed have been deficient in that hearty good-will which should be our spontaneous sentiment to our political chief, and which I have
generally accorded to you in no niggard spirit ; but pardon
me if I now observe, with frankness, but with great respect,
that you might have found some reason for this, if you had
cared to do so, in the want of courtesy in debate which I
have had the frequent mortification of experiencing from
you since your accession to power. Nor have I had the
consolation of believing this fanciful on my part, since
it has long been a subject of notice on both sides of the
House.

Under these circumstances, stated without passion, and
viewed, I am sure, without acrimony, I am bound to say
that I look upon the fact of not having received your
summons, coupled with the ostentatious manner in which
it has been bruited about, as a painful personal procedure,
which the past by no means authorised.

I have the honor to remain,

Your faithful servant,

B. DISRAELI.

From Sir Robert Peel.

WHITEHALL,
Feb. 6, 1844.

MY DEAR SIR,

Although the omission on my part to request your attendance at the meeting of Parliament was not an accidental or inadvertent omission, it certainly was not the result of any feeling of personal irritation or ill-will on account of observations made by you in the House of Commons.

I hope I have not a good memory for expressions used in debate which cause surprise or pain at the moment, and it would be quite unsuitable to the spirit in which your letter is written, and in which it is received, were I, after the lapse of several months, to refresh my recollection of such expressions, if such were used.

My reason for not sending you the usual circular was an honest doubt whether I was entitled to send it—whether towards the close of the last session of Parliament you had not expressed opinions as to the conduct of the Government in respect to more than one important branch of public policy, foreign and domestic, which precluded me, in justice both to you and to myself, from proffering personally an earnest request for your attendance.

If you will refer to the debate on the Irish Arms Bill, and to that on Servia, and recall to your recollection the general tenor of your observations on the conduct of the Government, you will, I think, admit that my doubt was not an unreasonable one.

It gives me, however, great satisfaction to infer from your letter—as I trust I am justified in inferring—that my impressions were mistaken and my scruples unnecessary.[1]

I will not conclude without noticing two or three points adverted to in your letter.

I am unconscious of having on any occasion treated you with the want of that respect and courtesy which I readily admit are justly your due. If I did so, the act was wholly unintentional on my part.

Any comments that were made on expressions used by you towards the Government were, so far as is consistent with my knowledge, altogether spontaneous on the part of the member from whom they proceeded. They were at any rate not made at my instigation or suggestion, direct or indirect.

---

[1] Peel's curious readiness to place the worst construction on the criticisms of a supporter is shown again a few months later in the case of Lord Ashley, who sent him a private remonstrance against the action of the Government in the matter of the sugar duties, and was answered in a letter regretting the withdrawal of his confidence and support (Parker, III., p. 153).

Lastly, I cannot call to mind that I have mentioned to a single person—excepting to the one or two to whom the mention was absolutely unavoidable—that I had omitted to address to you a request for your attendance. Nothing could be farther from my wishes or feelings than that there should be any ostentatious notice of the omission.

    I have the honour to be, my dear sir,

Faithfully yours,
ROBERT PEEL.

We may doubt whether Disraeli, though he had not, like us, the advantage of knowing Peel's real sentiments, was led far astray by this very plausible letter ; but, as it was conciliatory in tone, he seized the first opportunity of showing that he himself had no desire for an open breach. Ireland was still in the political foreground. The success of the Irish executive in securing the abandonment of the Clontarf meeting in October had averted the danger of immediate revolution ; but the Government were now involved in the tangle of the O'Connell trial, and soon after the House met the leader of the Opposition moved what was tantamount to a formal vote of censure on their Irish administration. The debate lasted nine nights, and Disraeli at the close voted with the Government, leading his three friends, Smythe, Manners, and Cochrane, into the same lobby. He explained his position in a speech on the fourth night, which not only had a great immediate success, but is of interest to this day as one of the most remarkable pronouncements on the Irish question ever heard in Parliament. He showed once more that he had been reading Irish history,[1] resuming, with his habitual continuity of thought, every thread of argument in his Irish speech of the previous session ; and though he obviously wished to be friendly to Peel, he repeated every offending phrase he had used on that occasion, as if determined to prove that his criticisms had not been prompted by any feeling

---

[1] 'He is the only English Prime Minister,' says an Irish writer, with this speech in his mind, ' who has appealed to historic incidents that touch the hearts of the Irish people ' (*Lord Beaconsfield's Irish Policy*, by Sir John Pope Hennessy, p. 11).

of pique, and that, anxious as he might be for peace with
the Government, he was not prepared to purchase it
by the sacrifice of opinions deliberately formed.

He began with a picture, rose-coloured, perhaps, of
the happy condition of Ireland during the administration of Strafford, when a system of perfect civil and
political equality had reconciled the Roman Catholics
under a King, a Viceroy, and an established Church all
Protestant. The troubles that followed were all to be
traced to Puritanism—to Puritanism, and not to Protestantism. It was Puritanism that was responsible for
the confiscations[1] and the penal laws ; it was Puritanism
that had fostered the spirit of exclusion which had so
long prevailed ; it was a Puritanic spirit that had destroyed the influence of the Church of Ireland. For
these things the Tories had no responsibility, and he was
anxious to see them rescued from the untenable position
they were now supposed to occupy, that it was one of the
heirlooms of their party to look with jealousy on Ireland.

He had said the year before that for the settlement of
the Irish question two things were necessary—to put
down the turbulence by which Ireland was convulsed,
and to recognise and remove its causes. They had put
down the turbulence, and were beginning to talk of the
necessity of inquiring into its causes. If he asked what
was their remedy, he might again, perhaps, subject himself
to the imputation of new-born zeal ; but zeal was a
quality so rare in that house, and he feared in that age
and country, that he was not overwhelmed by such an
imputation. As a matter of fact, his views as to the
government of Ireland were the same as they had always
been, and he had explained them on the only fitting
occasion[2] that had presented itself—in a debate on the
subject of municipal corporations, at the close of which

---

[1] It is to be feared that this is only true because Puritanism triumphed,
and so secured the opportunity. Strafford's own record in the matter of
confiscations is very far from clean.

[2] See p. 57.

he had voted against the counsel of his leader. He had argued in that debate against the fallacy that justice to Ireland implied an identity between Irish and English institutions.

I then asked the House whether those forced establishments, those mimetic corporations, those grand juries, those imitative benches of English magistrates, could be expected to produce beneficial results, and I ventured to lay down as a principle that the government of Ireland should be on a system the reverse of England, and should be centralised ; that we should have a strong executive and an impartial administration. I beg distinctly to say that I have never changed my principles on Irish policy or in any other respect. I say this without reservation—at no time, at no place, under no circumstances, have I ever professed any other principles than those I now maintain. They are Tory principles, the natural principles of the democracy of England. . . . Let us forget two centuries of political conduct for which Toryism is not responsible ; let us recur to the benignant policy of Charles I. ; then we may settle Ireland with honor to ourselves, with kindness to the people, and with safety to the realm.

If anyone came forward with a comprehensive plan for the solution of the Irish problem, he would support it at any sacrifice—yea, even though he should afterwards have to retire from Parliament.

But I confess I have no apprehension of that. I have the honour to represent the oldest Tory constituency in the country, and I have already succeeded in weeding from their minds some most inveterate Whig prejudices. Last year, for example, when I was told that I had lost my seat because I had supported the right hon. gentleman's tariff, I went down to see my friends in the country, and explained the history of England to them (great cheering and laughter) ; and I can assure the House that after that they took the most enlightened views upon the subject, and were proud to recur to old Tory principles of commerce.

He could not understand the new morality of the House of Commons, which shrank from what was desirable because of difficulties and prejudices. Why, in

1832 it was thought that nothing could be more difficult
than to reconstruct the Conservative party ; but the
right hon. gentleman set to work like a man, and it
was done, and done well.

There were prejudices to be removed in that case, too—
the prejudices of very eminent personages ; but that also
was done with time and resolution ; and there sits the
right hon. baronet at this moment with a Secretary of
State on each side of him, whose prejudices he has succeeded
most effectually in removing. (Loud cheers and laughter
from every part of the house, in which Sir Robert Peel, sitting
between Lord Stanley and Sir James Graham, could not
refrain from joining.) ... I do not think it is more difficult to
reconstruct the social system of Ireland than to reconstruct
a party destroyed by a revolution ; nor do I think it a more
arduous task to remove the prejudices of those who think
little than of those who think a great deal. All the right
hon. baronet will have to do will be what public men do
not seem to think they have the power of doing—to create
public opinion instead of following it ; to lead the public
instead of always lagging after and watching others.

With regard to the immediate question, he could not
vote for the noble lord (John Russell), because he offered
nothing more than her Majesty's Ministers. They
offered a great deal for them ; the noble lord offered little,
though he offered it in a great way. That was not what
he wanted.

I want to see a public man come forward and say what
the Irish question is. One says it is a physical question ;
another, a spiritual. Now it is the absence of the aristocracy,
then the absence of railroads. It is the Pope one day,
potatoes the next. Consider Ireland as you would any other
country similarly situated, in your closets. You will see a
teeming population which, with reference to the cultivated
soil, is denser to the square mile than that of China ; created
solely by agriculture, with none of those sources of wealth
which develop with civilisation ; and sustained, consequently,
upon the lowest conceivable diet, so that in case of failure
they have no other means of subsistence upon which they
can fall back That dense population in extreme distress
inhabits an island where there is an Established Church
which is not their Church (loud cheers from the Opposition),

and a territorial aristocracy the richest of whom live in distant capitals. Thus you have a starving population, an absentee aristocracy, and an alien Church, and in addition the weakest executive in the world. That is the Irish question.

Anyone reading of such a country would say the remedy was revolution, but here the connexion with England made revolution impossible. What, then, was the duty of an English Minister ? To effect by his policy all those changes which a revolution would effect by force.

The moment you have a strong executive, a just administration, and ecclesiastical equality, you will have order in Ireland, and the improvement of the physical condition of the people will follow—not very rapidly, perhaps ; you must not flatter yourselves that it will. But what are fifty years, even, in the history of a nation ? and I will say, if these recommendations are adopted, that fifty years hence the men who shall succeed the present generation in Parliament will find the people of Ireland a contented and thriving peasantry. . . . I look to no foreign, no illegitimate influences for bringing about that result—not to the passions of the Irish people, not to the machinations of their demagogues, not to the intrigues of distant nations, but to a power far more influential, far more benignant, a power more recently risen in the world, not yet sufficiently recognised (' What, Young England ?')—no, not Young England, but a power which Young England respects —that irresistible law of our modern civilisation which has decreed that the system which cannot bear discussion is doomed.[1]

In the subsequent debate Peel took occasion to make graceful mention of ' the very able speech of the hon. member for Shrewsbury—a speech not the less to be admired because it departed from the ordinary routine of Parliamentary eloquence and touched on more comprehensive and general views ' ; and Macaulay was moved by Disraeli's attack on the Puritans, in his ' very ingenious speech,' to a learned disquisition, which is still worth reading, on the historical causes of Irish discontent. A note in Disraeli's hand, with the date Sunday night, February 18, 1844, and the inscription, ' Written at Mary

[1] *The Times*, Feb. 17, 1844.

Anne's command after dinner,' records some other contemporary comments :

Bernal met Smythe, and said, ' Disraeli's speech was the
greatest thing I ever heard.' Smythe said, ' I don't think
so, for I have heard Disraeli make as great.' Bernal replies,
' I tell you what it is : if he was a Lord Tom Noddy, that
man would revolutionise the nation.' Smythe is all for Tom-
Noddyism.

  *   *   *   *   *   *

On Saturday morning a breakfast at Milnes's ; Lord John
Manners, Chevalier Bunsen, Hallam, and others. Nothing
(Lord J. tells it) spoken of but my speech. Hallam much
taunted that the Whigs were only Puritans. Defended the
Whigs very much, &c.

  *   *   *   *   *   *

Serjeant Murphy told Eaton that it was the most brilliant
speech he ever heard—nothing but epigrams. According to
Smythe, ' he did not know how any sentence would end or
what would come next.'

  *   *   *   *   *   *

Lord Mahon followed me into a corner with outstretched
hand to congratulate me on a speech with which he could
not on many points agree, but which was unquestionably
one of the ablest ever delivered. His panegyric was unqualified.

  *   *   *   *   *   *

Sterling had read all the debates, and there was only one
speech of a man of genius. His criticism in detail very interesting. The bit about the Secretaries immortal.

The speech became famous during the Disestablishment
debates a quarter of a century later. ' A more closely
woven tissue of argument and observation,' said Gladstone on one occasion, praising it for his own purposes,
' has seldom been heard in the debates of this House.'
The phrases about the ' alien Church ' were of course
turned against their author ; but when reminded of them,
Disraeli nonchalantly replied that at the time he made
the speech nobody seemed to listen. ' It may have been
expressed with the heedless rhetoric which I suppose is
the appanage of all who sit below the gangway, but in

my historical conscience the sentiment of that speech
was right.'[1]

Sarah Disraeli to Mrs. Disraeli.

[*February.*]

Dis must, I think, now be *quite satisfied :* the best speech he
has made, and, what is more, the most applauded, is in his
own original vein. Are not Young England proud of their
leader ?

April 10.

I went yesterday to Turville. . . . I never saw Milord
[Lyndhurst] more blooming : he looked as young and as well
as Chalon's picture. We did not see much of him, as he was
full of work and not dressed ; but when he did appear, he
said a great deal in a little time. Almost his first inquiry
was after Dis. ' And so he is going to turn us out,' he said :
' I am told he is not exactly one of Young England, but their
mentor and guide.' The speech about Ireland was mentioned
—' And a very good speech it was,' he added : whereupon
I said, ' So it pleased Sir Robert Peel to say.'

Aided by such speeches, Young England during this
session steadily grew in influence. It retained, indeed,
its original character as a group of personal friends with
a common stock of ideas, and did not aspire to become
a party formally organised and equipped with definite
principles. ' Living much together, without combination we acted together,'[2] was Disraeli's own account of
the matter many years later. The house at Grosvenor
Gate was their rallying-point in London. In the country
they met at the Deepdene, whose owner, Henry Hope,
though no longer in Parliament, had from the first been
a zealous supporter of the movement ; sometimes at
Bearwood, the country-house of the Walters, whose
sympathies had been secured, and with them, if not the
support, the benevolent interest of *The Times*. In the
House of Commons the movement gained several new
adherents, who often reinforced the original group of
friends. Of these the most notable were Augustus

---

[1] Hansard, March 16, 1868.
[2] General Preface to the Novels, 1870.

Stafford O'Brien, a master of epigram, who was popular
on both sides of the House; and William Busfield Ferrand,[1]
a Yorkshire squire with 'a Dantonesque appearance,'
who denounced in a stentorian voice, and with an embarrassing knowledge of his subject, the crimes of the
manufacturers and the woes of their employees.
Monckton Milnes fluttered uneasily around the group,
hesitating to commit himself. Outside the House they
numbered among their friends, in addition to Hope and
Faber, Ambrose Lisle Phillips,[2] a well-known Roman
Catholic, the Eustace Lyle of *Coningsby*. The social
popularity of Smythe and other members caused Young
England to be an object of some interest to society, and
a dialogue between a couple of dandies[3] in *Coningsby*
gives us, we may suppose, a very fair conception of the
intelligence with which society made its comments.

'Buckhurst [said Mr. Melton] swears by Henry Sydney,
a younger son of the Duke, and young Coningsby; a sort of
new set; new ideas and all that sort of thing. . . . When
they were staying with the Everinghams at Easter they were
full of it. Coningsby had just returned from his travels,
and they were quite on the *qui vive*. Lady Everingham is one
of their set. I don't know what it is exactly; but I think
we shall hear more of it.'
'A sort of animal magnetism, or unknown tongues, I take
it from your description,' said his companion.
'Well, I don't know what it is,' said Mr. Melton; 'but it has
got hold of all the young fellows who have just come out. . . .
I had some idea of giving my mind to it, they made such a
fuss about it at Everingham; but it requires a devilish deal
of history, I believe, and all that sort of thing.'
'Ah! that's a bore,' said his companion. 'It is difficult
to turn to with a new thing when you are not in the habit of
it. I never could manage charades.'
Mr. Ormsby, passing by, stopped. . . .
'Here's a new thing that Melton has been telling me of,
that all the world is going to believe in,' said Mr. Cassilis;
'something patronised by Lady Everingham. . . . Young

---

[1] 1809-1889.   [2] 1809-1878.
[3] Mr. Melton and Mr. Cassilis, representing Disraeli's friends James Macdonald and George Wombwell.

Coningsby brought it from abroad ; didn't you say so,
Jemmy ?'
  ' No, no, my dear fellow ; it is not at all that sort of thing.'
  ' But they say it requires a deuced deal of history,' con-
tinued Mr. Cassilis. ' One must brush up one's Goldsmith.
Canterton used to be the fellow for history at White's. He
was always boring one with William the Conqueror, Julius
Cæsar, and all that sort of thing.'[1]

But *Coningsby* itself, to which we now come, did far
more than the social successes of its hero, or even the
speeches of its author, brilliant as they were, to awaken
interest in Young England.

[1] *Coningsby*, Bk. VIII. ch. 1.

CHAPTER VII.

Coningsby.

1844.

English literature owes a debt of gratitude to Peel—or to Stanley, if to Stanley it is more appropriately due; their exclusion of Disraeli from office in 1841 led to *Coningsby* and *Sybil* and the creation of the political novel. Except for *Alarcos* and a few political pieces, Disraeli's pen had been idle since his election to the House of Commons; but he now conceived the idea of applying the methods of fiction to his new world of experience, and began to write again. It was Henry Hope, he tells us,[1] who first urged him to treat in a literary form the political ideas which they were in the habit of discussing; but it was only after reflection, as he elsewhere[2] records, that he chose the form of fiction as that ' which, in the temper of the times, offered the best chance of influencing opinion.' This appears to have been at the Deepdene in the autumn of 1843, and a novel was there and then begun, and continued during the winter at Bradenham and elsewhere.

To Lord John Manners.

BRADENHAM,
Nov. 29, 1843.

My dear Lord John,

. . . I get on to my satisfaction : but authors are not the best critics of their own productions : I am more anxious

---

[1] General Preface to the Novels, 1870.
[2] Preface to the Fifth Edition of *Coningsby*, 1849.

197

about your opinion than my own. The sustained labor is,
however, very painful : and I am daily more convinced that
there is no toil like literature. However once in, etc. It is too
late to moralise. I want to clear the deck if I can by the end
of January, for action and speculation will never blend. . . .

Ever yours,

D.

Coningsby was, in fact, itself an attempt to make action
and speculation blend.

The main purpose of its writer was to vindicate the just
claims of the Tory party to be the popular political confederation of the country ; a purpose which he had more or less
pursued from a very early period of life. The occasion was
favorable to the attempt. The youthful mind of England
had just recovered from the inebriation of the great Conservative triumph of 1841, and was beginning to inquire what, after
all, they had conquered to preserve. It was opportune,
therefore, to show that Toryism was not a phrase, but a fact,
and that our political institutions were the embodiment of our
popular necessities. This the writer endeavored to do without prejudice, and to treat of events and characters of which
he had some personal experience, not altogether without the
impartiality of the future.[1]

' *Coningsby* wants little but a greater absence of
purpose,' says one [2] of its best critics, ' to be a first-rate
novel. If Mr. Disraeli had confined himself to the
merely artistic point of view, he might have drawn a
picture of political society worthy of comparison with
Vanity Fair.' Here, perhaps, mingled with a certain
amount of truth, there is some of the sophistry of ' art
for art's sake,' the same spirit of paradox that made the
critic wish that ' Disraeli could have stuck to his novels
without rising to be Prime Minister.' If Disraeli had
been a mere politician, and nothing besides, he could
never, of course, have written his political novels ; but one
wonders whether the mere artist who was not also something besides, who was not, in fact, himself an interested
man of action, could have penetrated like Disraeli to the

---

[1] Preface to the Fifth Edition.   [2] Sir Leslie Stephen.

Henry Hope.

from a picture in the possession of Mr Adrian Hope.

inmost soul of politics, or painted a picture of political society worthy of comparison with *Coningsby.*

The novel was published in May, 1844, its full title being ' Coningsby ;[1] or, The New Generation,' and Disraeli on the title-page describing himself as M.P. and author of *Contarini Fleming.* 'Conceived and partly executed amid the glades and galleries of the Deepdene,' it appeared with a dedication to Henry Hope, the friend to whom its inception was due, and whom Disraeli described in the single pregnant sentence written after his death : ' He was learned and accomplished, possessed a penetrating judgment and an inflexible will.' The book issued from the office of Disraeli's old publisher Colburn, and the profits were divided equally between publisher and author, the author's share on 3,000 copies being about £1,000. The success was great and immediate, and Disraeli told his sister that it had exceeded all his hopes. The first edition of 1,000 copies went off in a fortnight. ' Three considerable editions were sold in this country in three months ; it was largely circulated throughout the Continent of Europe, and within a very brief period more than 50,000 copies were required in the United States of America.'[2]

The popularity of *Coningsby* has proved to be lasting, and it is still more read than any of Disraeli's works, with the possible exception of *Lothair.* Its success was helped, no doubt, at first by the fact that it was regarded as the manifesto of Young England, which had been making a considerable noise ; and still more by the fact that it contained many references, some of them caustic, to living statesmen by name, many figures that were intended to be accepted as portraits, and many others for which the keymakers, with more or less plausibility, were able to suggest originals of whom the author had never dreamt.

---

[1] Coningsby was the name of a well-known public man of the age of Queen Anne ; and it is worth noting as a coincidence, if nothing more, that Carlyle's John Sterling, who died shortly after the appearance of Disraeli's book, had published a forgotten novel called *Arthur Coningsby* in 1833.
[2] Preface to the Fifth Edition.

But the main reason both for the immediate success and the enduring fame of the novel is rather to be sought in its own genuine merits as a first and happiest effort in the new form of art which its author had invented.

'I have seen Hope,' Disraeli wrote in a hurried note to his wife one day in the week after publication ; 'he only says he is enchanted, but will say nothing more till he has finished and taken in the whole : Cochrane raving : Manners full of wild rapture.' Let Smythe speak for himself :

From the Hon. George Smythe.

Thursday night.

DEAR DIZ,

I have just finished it. What can I say, or write, or think ? I am so dazzled, bewildered, tipsy with admiration the most passionate and wild !

I never read anything, thought of anything, felt anything, believed in anything, before.

Thank God I have a faith at last ! 'The blessing of all the prophets be with you,' is the prayer of a disciple more enthusiastically devoted than any they ever counted.

Yours ever most affectionately,

G. S. SMYTHE.

'I stop one minute,' wrote his sister from Bradenham, 'to tell you that we are fascinated and delighted beyond expression. . . . Papa says the man who has made the finest speech of the session has written the best book that ever was written.' 'Even you and Dis's family,' said his old friend Lady Blessington in a letter to Mrs. Disraeli, 'take not a livelier pleasure or a greater pride than I in the brilliant success of *Coningsby*.' 'I have read *Coningsby*—who has not ?' wrote another old friend, the Lord Chancellor, Lyndhurst ; 'full of wit and talent and splendid pictures.' 'Everybody here, from the Princess of Prussia downwards,' wrote Monckton Milnes from Berlin towards the close of the year, 'is reading and talking *Coningsby*.'

The underlying story of the novel is slight, just enough to link together the politics and history, and

to serve as an excuse for the introduction of the scenes
of social and political life, and the long procession
of figures, social and political, that marches across the
stage. Harry Coningsby, the ostensible hero, who, as
has been seen, stands for Smythe, is the grandson of the
Marquis of Monmouth, a younger son's child and a solitary
orphan, to whom ' the sweet sedulousness of a mother's
love or a sister's mystical affection ' has never been
known. The story opens in the year 1832, when as a
boy of fourteen he is summoned to London from Eton
to have his first interview with his formidable grandfather,
whom the crisis of the Reform Bill has brought over to
England from his usual residence abroad. Lord Monmouth, who is presented as a nobleman of vast wealth,
great political influence, rare sagacity, unbending will,
intense selfishness, and licentious habits, is intended to
reproduce that famous voluptuary, the third Marquis
of Hertford,[1] who was also the original of Thackeray's
Marquis of Steyne ; and in the first chapter we make
acquaintance with the Right Hon. Nicholas Rigby, who
as political adviser and confidential man of business holds
to Lord Monmouth much the same relation that John
Wilson Croker held to Lord Hertford. Rigby is the type
of the clever and resourceful, but base and shallow,
parasite ; ' bold, acute, and voluble, with no thought but
a great deal of desultory information ' ; ' fruitful in small
expedients, and never happier than when devising shifts
for great men's scrapes ' ; at once obsequious to his
superiors and tyrannical to his inferiors ; a persistent
intriguer, ' confided in by everybody, trusted by none ' ;
an adept in subterranean journalism, and the author of
many slashing articles in a Tory review ' written in a
style apparently modelled on the briefs of those sharp
attorneys who weary advocates with their clever commonplace, teasing with obvious comment and torturing with
inevitable inference.' ' In most of the transactions of
life there is some portion which no one cares to accom-

[1] 1777-1842. See p. 130.

plish, and which everybody wishes to be achieved. This
was always the portion of Mr. Rigby. . . . Notwithstanding his splendid livery and the airs he gave himself in the
servants' hall, his real business in life had ever been to do
the dirty work.'

Rigby has had charge of Coningsby during his patron's
absence abroad, but Lord Monmouth, until now indifferent
to his grandson, is attracted when he sees him, and henceforth gives him a place in his ambitious calculations. In
the first book we have a picture remarkable alike for
its truthfulness [1] and charm of the boy's life at Eton.
Coningsby is already the centre of a group, his greatest
friends being Lord Henry Sydney and Sir Charles Buckhurst, representing, as we have seen, Manners and Cochrane ;
and a third, Oswald Millbank, a manufacturer's son, who,
as far as he is intended to suggest a real person, stands for
John Walter, [2] the heir-apparent of the ruling dynasty
of *The Times*. Through Millbank, Coningsby discovers,
when his interest in politics begins to awaken, that they
mean something more than an hereditary struggle between
Tory nobles, like his grandfather, and the Whig nobles
of whom he hears from his Whig friend Lord Vere. He
becomes aware for the first time of the existence of a
great class distinct from the nobility, but rivalling it in

[1] Disraeli seems to have taken what for him was unusual pains to make
this picture faithful ; and he had some assistance from an Eton master, the
Rev. W. G. Cookesley, who is mentioned by name in the novel, and who had,
in fact, been Smythe's tutor. It is curious, however, to find that Lord
Lyttelton (4th Baron, 1817-1876), who appears in the novel as ' the calm
and sagacious Vere,' and who wrote as ' a faithful Etonian ' to the author
that ' the main features were given with admirable fidelity and life,' was
able to fill a quarto sheet with critical comments ' on very minute matters '—
his ' grave doubts,' for instance, whether the boys ever in practice had a
goose for breakfast.

[2] 1818-1894. In an unauthorised key to Coningsby that appeared in the
year of its publication, it was absurdly stated that Gladstone was the original
of Oswald Millbank, and the statement has often been repeated, a certain
resemblance, real or fancied, giving it plausibility. The resemblance, if any,
was purely accidental. Disraeli in 1844 had no reason for feeling any
particular interest in Gladstone, and certainly none for working him into his
Young England scheme by transferring him to an Eton generation nearly
ten years later than his own. Walter, on the other hand, was in close
relations with Young England, had been a contemporary and friend of Smythe
and Manners at Eton, and, like Millbank, had gone to Oxford when they
went to Cambridge.

wealth, and determined to acquire power ; and in Millbank's crude opinions caught up from his father he finds materials for thought and a stimulus to a mind already predisposed to political inquiry.

Presently we come to the crisis caused by the King's dismissal of Melbourne in 1834, and we have a picture, cynical but amusing, and drawn by a master hand, of the aspect of politics that is most visible at such a time. Two days after Peel's audience of the King, Mr. Ormsby,[1] celebrated for his political dinners, gave one to a numerous party, and we are allowed to catch some fragments of the conversation of his assembling guests.

' Do you hear anything ?' said a great noble who wanted something in the general scramble, but what he knew not ; only he had a vague feeling he ought to have something having made such great sacrifices.

' There is a report that Clifford is to be Secretary to the Board of Control,' said Mr. Earwig, whose whole soul was in this subaltern arrangement, of which the Minister of course had not even thought ; ' but I cannot trace it to any authority.'

' I wonder who will be their Master of the Horse,' said the great noble, loving gossip though he despised the gossiper.

' Clifford has done nothing for the party,' said Mr. Earwig.

' I dare say Rambrooke will have the Buckhounds,' said the great noble, musingly.

' Your Lordship has not heard Clifford's name mentioned ?' continued Mr. Earwig.

' I should think they had not come to that sort of thing,' said the great noble, with ill-disguised contempt. ' The first thing after the Cabinet is formed is the Household : the things you talk of are done last ;' and he turned upon his heel, and met the imperturbable countenance and clear sarcastic eye of Lord Eskdale.[2]

' You have not heard anything ?' asked the great noble of his brother patrician.

' Yes, a great deal since I have been in this room ; but unfortunately it is all untrue.'

' There is a report that Rambrooke is to have the Buckhounds ; but I cannot trace it to any authority.'

' Pooh !' said Lord Eskdale.

[1] John Irving (d. 1853), a well-known Crœsus of the day, member for Co. Antrim.
[2] Said to be a lifelike picture of the 2nd Earl of Lonsdale, 1787-1872.

' I don't see that Rambrooke should have the Buckhounds
any more than anybody else. What sacrifices has he made ?'
    ' Past sacrifices are nothing,' said Lord Eskdale. ' Present
sacrifices are the thing we want : men who will sacrifice their
principles, and join us.'
    ' You have not heard Rambrooke's name mentioned ?'
    ' When a Minister has no Cabinet, and only one hundred
and forty supporters in the House of Commons, he has something else to think of than places at Court,' said Lord Eskdale,
as he slowly turned away.

Among Mr. Ormsby's guests were Tadpole and Taper,
two political parasites of the type we should now call
' wire-pullers,' members of the class of statesmen ' who
believe the country must be saved if they receive twelve
hundred a year.'

It is a peculiar class, that ; £1,200 per annum, paid quarterly,
is their idea of political science and human nature. To receive
£1,200 per annum is government ; to try to receive £1,200 per
annum is opposition ; to wish to receive £1,200 per annum is
ambition. If a man wants to get into Parliament, and does
not want to get £1,200 per annum, they look upon him as daft ;
as a benighted being. They stare in each other's face, and
ask, ' What can * * * * * want to get into Parliament for ?'
They have no conception that public reputation is a motive
power, and with many men the greatest.

Tadpole and Taper, who were great personal friends,
and neither of whom ' ever despaired of the Commonwealth,' withdrew after dinner to a distant sofa for a
confidential talk.

    ' And what do you put our numbers at now ?' inquired Mr.
Taper.
    ' Would you take fifty-five for our majority ?' rejoined Mr.
Tadpole.
    ' It is not so much the tail they have, as the excuse their
junction will be for the moderate, sensible men to come over,'
said Taper. ' Our friend Sir Everard for example, it would
settle him.'
    ' He is a solemn impostor,' rejoined Mr. Tadpole ; ' but he
is a baronet and a county member, and very much looked up
to by the Wesleyans. The other men, I know, have refused
him a peerage.'
    ' And we might hold out judicious hopes,' said Taper.

'No one can do that better than you,' said Tadpole. 'I am apt to say too much about those things.'

'I make it a rule never to open my mouth on such subjects,' said Taper. 'A nod or a wink will speak volumes. An affectionate pressure of the hand will sometimes do a great deal; and I have promised many a peerage without committing myself, by an ingenious habit of deference which cannot be mistaken by the future noble.'

.   .   .   .

'Ah! Tadpole,' said Mr. Taper, getting a little maudlin; 'I often think, if the time should ever come, when you and I should be joint Secretaries of the Treasury!'

'We shall see, we shall see. All we have to do is to get into Parliament, work well together, and keep other men down.'

'We will do our best,' said Taper. 'A dissolution you hold inevitable?'

'How are you and I to get into Parliament if there be not one? We must make it inevitable. I tell you what, Taper, the lists must prove a dissolution inevitable. You understand me? If the present Parliament goes on, where shall we be? We shall have new men cropping up every session.'

'True, terribly true,' said Mr. Taper. 'That we should ever live to see a Tory government again! We have reason to be very thankful.'

'Hush!' said Mr. Tadpole. 'The time has gone by for Tory governments; what the country requires is a sound Conservative government.'

'A sound Conservative government,' said Taper, musingly. 'I understand: Tory men and Whig measures.'

The dramatic struggle between parties during the period of Peel's short administration raised to the highest pitch the enthusiasm of Eton for Conservative principles; but when the enthusiasm had subsided, Coningsby and his friends began to ask the question what Conservative principles meant. The final answer was only to shape itself in Coningsby's mind after several years of thought and study at Cambridge; but before he left Eton he had attained to an earnest though rather vague conviction that the present state of feeling, both in politics and religion, was very far from healthy, that for the prevailing latitudinarianism of belief something deep, fervent, and definite would have to be substituted, and that the priests of the new faith must be sought in the ranks of the New Generation. With his mind in this condition, he is ready to profit by an adventure that befalls him in the interval between his leaving Eton and beginning residence at Cambridge. On his way to pay a visit to his friend Henry Sydney at his ducal home Beaumanoir, he meets a stranger in a forest inn, one of those men, sometimes encountered, 'whose phrases are oracles, who condense in a sentence the events of life,' and who are able to utter 'words that make us think for ever.' The description of the forest, breathing Disraeli's sympathy with nature in the aspects in which she appealed to him most, of the storm which drove the travellers for refuge to the inn, and of the colloquy that then followed, make what is perhaps the best chapter in the book.

Coningsby had never met or read of anyone like this chance companion. His sentences were so short, his language so racy, his voice rang so clear, his elocution was so complete. On all subjects his mind seemed to be instructed, and his opinions formed. He flung out a result in a few words ; he solved with a phrase some deep problem that men muse over for years. He said many things that were strange, yet they immediately appeared to be true. Then, without the slightest air of pretension or parade, he seemed to know everybody as well as everything. Monarchs, statesmen, authors, adventurers, of all descriptions and of all climes, if their names occurred in the conversation, ho described them in an epigrammatic sentence, or revealed their precise position, character, calibre, by a curt dramatic trait. All this, too, without any excitement of manner ; on the contrary, with repose amounting almost to nonchalance. If his address had any fault in it, it was rather a deficiency of earnestness. A slight spirit of mockery played over his speech even when you deemed him most serious ; you were startled by his sudden transitions from profound thought to poignant sarcasm. A very singular freedom from passion and prejudice on every topic on which they treated, might be some compensation for this want of earnestness, perhaps was its consequence.

The stranger teaches Coningsby to have faith in the divine influence of individual character and in the power of the creative mind, dispensing with experience, to achieve greatness in youth. Almost everything that is great has, he asserts, been done by youth. For life, indeed, in general 'there is but one decree : Youth is a blunder ; Manhood a struggle ; Old Age a regret.' But though youth itself is not genius, genius when young is divine. Why, the greatest captains of ancient and modern times both conquered Italy at five-and-twenty ; Gaston de Foix at Ravenna and Condé at Rocroy were only twenty-two ; Innocent III. and Leo X. were both Popes at thirty-seven ; Ignatius Loyola and John Wesley both worked with young brains ; Pascal, the greatest of Frenchmen, Raphael, and Byron, all died at thirty-seven ; Richelieu at thirty-one was Secretary of State ; Pitt and Bolingbroke were both Ministers before other men left off cricket. The history of heroes, in fact, is the history of youth, and the way to be a hero is to believe in the heroic ; but when Coningsby remarks that the stranger's own actions should in that case be heroic, he receives the reply : 'Action is not for me ; I am of that faith that the Apostles professed before they followed their Master.'

At Beaumanoir we have a picture of high life at its best —grace, beauty, and refinement, dignity and repose, charity and a strong sense of social and public duty. Here we make acquaintance with the daughters of the house, Lady Theresa Sydney and her married sister Lady Everingham, one of those fascinating women of society whom we find in Disraeli's novels—light, airy, ultra-feminine, with wit, spirit, and breeding, and a spice of delicious mockery.

Lady Everingham thoroughly understood the art of conversation, which, indeed, consists of the exercise of two fine qualities. You must originate, and you must sympathise ; you must possess at the same time the habit of communicating and the habit of listening. The union is rather rare, but irresistible. Lady Everingham was not a celebrated beauty, but she was something infinitely more delightful, a captivating woman. There were combined in her, qualities not commonly met together, great vivacity of mind with great grace of manner. Her words sparkled and her movements charmed.

Among the incidents of Coningsby's visit is an expedition to St. Geneviève,[1] the neighbouring home of Eustace Lyle,[2] a young and wealthy Roman Catholic, in whom we see again Disraeli's feeling for the 'ancient faith.' The Roman Catholic Church attracted him not only as it has attracted so many others, by an appeal to his romantic instincts, but also, it would appear, in its political aspect, as the thing most opposed to Whiggery. Eustace Lyle, though his father had been galled by political exclusion into allying himself with the Whig party, has not forgotten that it was the fall of the Papacy in England that founded the Whig aristocracy; but when he looks about for an alternative he sees nothing but the barren and unhappy cross-breed of Conservatism, a party 'whose rule it is to consent to no change until it is clamorously called for, and then instantly to yield;' which treats our institutions as we do our pheasants, preserving only to destroy them. Lyle, we are expressly told, is one of the three people who do most to influence the ripening mind of the hero.

Coningsby had been told by the mysterious stranger at the inn that the age of ruins was past, and had been asked if he had seen Manchester; and he had also been told that 'adventures are to the adventurous.' To Manchester he accordingly goes on his way from Beaumanoir to Coningsby Castle, where his grandfather expects him; and there for several days he devotes himself to the wonders of industry and machinery. Among other things, he visits the model factory of Millbank, and makes the acquaintance of the father and beautiful young sister of his Eton friend Oswald. The elder Millbank has his own reasons for hating Lord Monmouth, and he has also peculiar opinions about the aristocracy as a whole, which he expounds to the astonished Coningsby. The English aristocracy has, he points out, no special quality to mark it off from other classes; it is not richer, better informed, wiser, or more distinguished for public or private virtue,

---

[1] Garendon Towers. [2] Ambrose Lisle Phillips; *vide* p. 195.

than the class to which Millbank himself belongs. It
cannot even claim birth as a ground of distinction ;
Millbank has never heard of a peer with an ancient lineage.
The Wars of the Roses made an end of the Norman Barons,
and the three main sources of the existing peerage of
England, and in his opinion disgraceful ones, are 'the
spoliation of the Church, the open and flagrant sale of
honours by the elder Stuarts, and the boroughmongering
of our own times.' Certainly Disraeli cannot be accused
of flattering in this novel, or in the next, as we shall see,
the class of which he aspired to be the political leader.

At Coningsby Castle, to which we now proceed, we are
shown indeed a side of aristocratic life in which Disraeli
finds scope for some of his most effective satire—grandeur
without heart or soul, ostentatious luxury, riot and confusion, 'nothing of the sweet order of a country life,' a
scene in which Coningsby has constantly to practise the
lesson he has lived long enough to learn, that it is unwise
to wish to have everything explained. Here he finds
abundant food for the thoughts that are fermenting in
the depths of his mind, and the fermentation is stimulated
by his encountering again the stranger of the forest inn,
whom he now learns to know by the name of Sidonia.
Sidonia is a Hebrew of immense fortune, in the prime of
youthful manhood and with an athletic frame which
sickness has never tried ; affable and gracious, but, though
unreserved in manner, impenetrable beneath the surface ;
and yet with a rare gift of expression, and an intellect that,
matured by long meditation, and 'assisted by that
absolute freedom from prejudice which is the compen-
satory possession of a man without a country,' enables
him to fathom, as it were by intuition, the depth of
every question, however difficult or profound.

Sidonia had exhausted all the sources of human knowledge ;
he was master of the learning of every nation, of all tongues
dead or living, of every literature, Western and Oriental. He
had pursued the speculations of science to their last term, and
had himself illustrated them by observation and experiment.

He had lived in all orders of society, had viewed every combination of nature and of art, and had observed man under
every phasis of civilisation. He had even studied him in the
wilderness. The influence of creeds and laws, manners, customs, traditions, in all their diversities, had been subjected to
his personal scrutiny.

Sidonia, in fact, is a type of pure intellect, and he has
one great deficiency for which this prepares us. He is a
man without affections—not, indeed, heartless, for he is
susceptible of deep emotions, and capable of great and
unostentatious acts of kindness. But the individual
never touched him ; woman is to him a toy, man a
machine.

The lot the most precious to man, and which a beneficent
Providence has made not the least common ; to find in another
heart a perfect and profound sympathy ; to unite his existence
with one who could share all his joys, soften all his sorrows,
aid him in all his projects, respond to all his fancies, counsel
him in his cares, and support him in his perils ; make life
charming by her charms, interesting by her intelligence, and
sweet by the vigilant variety of her tenderness ; to find your
life blessed by such an influence, and to feel that your influence
can bless such a life : this lot, the most divine of divine gifts,
that power and even fame can never rival in its delights, all
this nature had denied to Sidonia.

Sidonia's function in the novel is to educate Coningsby,
who in his turn is to educate the New Generation. He
teaches Coningsby to look for the future of England in
what is more powerful than laws and institutions—in the
national character ; and to see the menace to her position
rather in class hostility and other signs of a decline of
the national character than in those more obvious changes
of political institutions to which it is the fashion of the
age to ascribe undue importance. How are the elements
of the nation to be again blended together ? Not by
new dispositions of political power, nor even by insistence
on those economic causes of which so much is heard, but
which are always secondary in their operation. Since the
peace there has been in England an attempt to reconstruct

society on a purely rational basis, a basis of material motives, the principle of utility. It has failed, and was bound to fail, for mankind is governed, not by reason, but by imagination.

' We are not indebted to the Reason of man for any of the great achievements which are the landmarks of human action and human progress. It was not Reason that besieged Troy ; it was not Reason that sent forth the Saracen from the Desert to conquer the world ; that inspired the Crusades ; that instituted the Monastic orders ; it was not Reason that produced the Jesuits ; above all, it was not Reason that created the French Revolution. Man is only truly great when he acts from the passions ; never irresistible but when he appeals to the imagination. Even Mormon counts more votaries than Bentham.'

' And you think, then, that as Imagination once subdued the State, Imagination may now save it ?'

' Man is made to adore and to obey : but if you will not command him, if you give him nothing to worship, he will fashion his own divinities, and find a chieftain in his own passions.'

' But where can we find faith in a nation of sectaries ? Who can feel loyalty to a sovereign of Downing Street ?'

' I speak of the eternal principles of human nature, you answer me with the passing accidents of the hour. Sects rise and sects disappear. Where are the Fifth-Monarchy men ? England is governed by Downing Street ; once it was governed by Alfred and Elizabeth.'

In another famous chapter Sidonia discourses on the gifts and achievements of his race, and pleads for their emancipation. He is no political sentimentalist, and to illiberality as such he has not the slightest objection if it be an element of power ; but he thinks it impolitic in the last degree to make it the interest of a powerful class to oppose the institutions under which they live. The Jews as a race are monarchical in sentiment, deeply religious, and essentially Tories ; yet their present disabilities drive them into the same ranks as the levellers and latitudinarians; and every generation they must become more powerful and more dangerous to the society which provokes their hostility.

' Do you think that the quiet humdrum persecution of a
decorous representative of an English university can crush
those who have successively baffled the Pharaohs, Nebuchad-
nezzar, Rome, and the Feudal ages ?   The fact is, you cannot
destroy a pure race of the Caucasian organisation. It is a
physiological fact ; a simple law of nature, which has baffled
Egyptian and Assyrian Kings, Roman Emperors, and Christian
Inquisitors.   No penal laws, no physical tortures, can effect
that a superior race should be absorbed in an inferior or be
destroyed by it. . . .

' Pure races of Caucasus may be persecuted, but they cannot
be despised, except by the brutal ignorance of some mongrel
breed, that brandishes fagots and howls extermination, but is
itself exterminated without persecution, by that irresistible law
of Nature which is fatal to curs.'

In every great intellectual movement in Europe the
Jews have played and play a principal part. The first
Jesuits were Jews ; that mysterious Russian diplomacy
which so alarms Western Europe is organised by Jews ;
Jews almost monopolise the professorial chairs of
Germany, and are there preparing that mighty revolution
of which so little is known in England as yet, but which
will, in fact, be a second and greater Reformation.
Neander is a Jew ; Wehl is a Jew. Jews are to be found
among the leading Ministers in nearly every state in
Europe. Soult is a Jew ; so also were some of his most
famous colleagues among Napoleon's Marshals—Masséna,
for example. All modern philosophy springs from
Spinoza ; and if the Jews cannot in the present show
great poets or great orators, they have had them in the
past. To-day their passionate and creative genius, the
nearest link to Divinity, debarred by human tyranny
from developing in other fields, has found in music, which
is almost an exclusive Jewish privilege, a medium for its
expression. In the history of the lords of melody you
find the annals of Hebrew genius ; and ' almost every
great composer,[1] skilled musician, almost every voice that

---

[1] To a generation for which Mendelssohn and Meyerbeer were the great
lights above the musical horizon, this statement may have seemed less
astonishing than it seems to us. Joachim, who was a pure Jew, and as proud
of his race as Disraeli himself, could speak with more authority ; and in

ravishes you with its transporting strains, springs from our tribes.'

From Coningsby Castle we pass to Cambridge, where we see Coningsby again surrounded by his Eton friends. At the end of their first year came the general election that followed the death of William IV., and they had the satisfaction of helping to win a great victory for the Conservative cause in the borough of Cambridge, where its champion was an old Etonian. On the day the member was chaired they met in Coningsby's rooms to talk over their triumph.

' By Jove !' said the panting Buckhurst, throwing himself on the sofa, ' it was well done ; never was anything better done. An immense triumph ! The greatest triumph the Conservative Cause has had. And yet,' he added, laughing, ' if any fellow were to ask me what the Conservative Cause is, I am sure I should not know what to say.'

' Why, it is the cause of our glorious institutions,' said Coningsby. ' A Crown robbed of its prerogatives ; a Church controlled by a commission ; and an Aristocracy that does not lead.'

' Under whose genial influence the order of the Peasantry, " a country's pride," has vanished from the face of the land,' said Henry Sydney, ' and is succeeded by a race of serfs, who are called labourers, and who burn ricks.'

' Under which,' continued Coningsby, ' the Crown has become a cipher ; the Church a sect ; the Nobility drones ; and the People drudges.'

' It is the great constitutional cause,' said Lord Vere, ' that refuses everything to opposition ; yields everything to agitation ; conservative in Parliament, destructive out-of-doors ; that has no objection to any change provided only it be effected by unauthorised means.'

' The first public association of men,' said Coningsby, ' who have worked for an avowed end without enunciating a single principle.'

' And who have established political infidelity throughout the land,' said Lord Henry.

conversation with Sir Charles Stanford he once commented on the curious fact that, while the Jews had great names in literature, science, and philosophy, music, for which in a sense their gift was so exceptional, ' did not possess one Jewish composer of the absolutely first rank ' (Studies and Memories, by C. V. Stanford, p. 131).

' By Jove !' said Buckhurst, ' what infernal fools we have
made ourselves this last week !'

' Nay,' said Coningsby, smiling, ' it was our last schoolboy
weakness. Floreat Etona, under all circumstances.'

' I certainly, Coningsby,' said Lord Vere, ' shall not assume
the Conservative Cause, instead of the cause for which
Hampden died in the field, and Sydney on the scaffold.'

' The cause for which Hampden died in the field and Sydney
on the scaffold,' said Coningsby, ' was the cause of the Venetian
Republic.'

' How, how ?' said Buckhurst.

' I repeat it,' said Coningsby. ' The great object of the
Whig leaders in England from the first movement under
Hampden to the last most successful one in 1688, was to
establish in England a high aristocratic republic on the model
of the Venetian, then the study and admiration of all speculative politicians. . . .'

' The Whigs are worn out,' said Vere, ' Conservatism is a
sham, and Radicalism is pollution.'

A vacation visit by Coningsby to his grandfather in
Paris gives an opportunity for the introduction of those
pictures of Parisian society to which allusion has already
been made. In Paris Coningsby meets again, and falls
in love with, Edith Millbank, his Eton friend's sister, now
grown into a beautiful woman ; but though his love is
returned, the feud between Lord Monmouth and Mr.
Millbank is a barrier. This feud is deeper than ever, for
Millbank has just succeeded in thwarting the haughty
noble in some of his most cherished ambitions, snatching
from him a Naboth's vineyard close to Coningsby Castle,
and winning from his creature Rigby the representation
of the neighbouring borough. The lovers exchange vows,
but Coningsby is dismissed by Millbank ; and presently
Lord Monmouth, ignorant of all that has happened, sends
for his grandson, in anticipation of a general election, to
arrange that he should come forward as Millbank's
opponent. The scene that follows between the old
generation and the new is one of the best in the book :

' You are most kind, you are always most kind to me, dear
sir,' said Coningsby, in a hesitating tone, and with an air of

great embarrassment, ' but, in truth, I have no wish to enter Parliament.'

' What ?' said Lord Monmouth.

' I feel that I am not yet sufficiently prepared for so great a responsibility as a seat in the House of Commons,' said Coningsby.

' Responsibility !' said Lord Monmouth, smiling. ' What responsibility is there ? . . . All you have got to do is to vote with your party. . . .'

' You mean, of course, by that term what is understood by the Conservative party.'

' Of course ; our friends.'

' I am sorry,' said Coningsby, rather pale, but speaking with firmness, ' I am sorry that I could not support the Conservative party.'

' By —— !' exclaimed Lord Monmouth, starting in his seat, ' some woman has got hold of him, and made him a Whig !'

' No, my dear grandfather . . . nothing of the kind, I assure you. No person can be more anti-Whig.'

' I don't know what you are driving at, sir,' said Lord Monmouth, in a hard, dry tone. . . .

' What I mean to say is, that I have for a long time looked upon the Conservative party as a body who have betrayed their trust. . . .'

' Well, between ourselves, I am quite of the same opinion. . . . But what is the use of lamenting the past ? Peel is the only man ; suited to the times and all that ; at least we must say so, and try to believe so ; we can't go back. And it is our own fault that we have let the chief power out of the hands of our own order. It was never thought of in the time of your great-grandfather, sir. And if a commoner were for a season permitted to be the nominal Premier to do the detail, there was always a secret committee of great 1688 nobles to give him his instructions.'

' I should be very sorry to see secret committees of great 1688 nobles again,' said Coningsby.

' Then what the devil do you want to see ?' said Lord Monmouth.

' Political faith,' said Coningsby, ' instead of political infidelity.'

' Hem !' said Lord Monmouth.

' Before I support Conservative principles,' continued Coningsby, ' I merely wish to be informed what those principles aim to conserve. . . .'

' All this is vastly fine,' said Lord Monmouth ; ' but I see no means by which I can attain my object but by supporting Peel. After all, what is the end of all parties and all politics ?

To gain your object. I want to turn our coronet into a ducal
one, and to get your grandmother's barony called out of
abeyance in your favor. It is impossible that Peel can
refuse me. . . . It gratifies me to hear you admired and to
learn your success. All I want now is to see you in Parliament. A man should be in Parliament early. There is a
sort of stiffness about every man, no matter what may be his
talents, who enters Parliament late in life ; and now, fortunately, the occasion offers. You will go down on Friday ;
feed the notabilities well ; speak out ; praise Peel ; abuse
O'Connell and the ladies of the Bedchamber ; anathematise
all waverers ; say a good deal about Ireland; stick to the Irish
Registration Bill, that's a good card ; and, above all, my dear
Harry, don't spare that fellow Millbank. Remember, in
turning him out you not only gain a vote for the Conservative
cause and our coronet, but you crush my foe. Spare nothing
for that object ; I count on you, boy.'

' I should grieve to be backward in anything that concerned
your interest or your honour, sir,' said Coningsby, with an air of
great embarrassment.

' I am sure you would, I am sure you would,' said Lord
Monmouth, in a tone of some kindness. . . .

' But I claim for my convictions, my dear grandfather, a
generous tolerance.'

' I can't follow you, sir,' said Lord Monmouth, again in his
hard tone. . . . ' You go with your family like a gentleman ;
you are not to consider your opinions, like a philosopher or a
political adventurer.'

' Yes, sir,' said Coningsby, with animation, ' but men going
with their families like gentlemen, and losing sight of every
principle on which the society of this country ought to be
established produced the Reform Bill.'

' D—— the Reform Bill !' said Lord Monmouth ; ' if the
Duke had not quarrelled with Lord Grey on a coal committee,
we should never have had the Reform Bill. . . .'

' You are in as great peril now as you were in 1830,' said
Coningsby.

' No, no, no,' said Lord Monmouth ; ' the Tory party is
organised now ; they will not catch us napping again : these
Conservative Associations have done the business.'

' But what are they organised for ?' said Coningsby. ' At
the best to turn out the Whigs. And when you have turned
out the Whigs, what then ? . . . What we want, sir, is not to
fashion new dukes and furbish up old baronies, but to establish
great principles which may maintain the realm and secure the
happiness of the people. Let me see authority once more
honored ; a solemn reverence again the habit of our lives ; let

me see property acknowledging, as in the old days of faith,
that labor is his twin brother, and that the essence of all
tenure is the performance of duty ; let results such as these
be brought about, and let me participate, however feebly, in
the great fulfilment, and public life then indeed becomes a
noble career, and a seat in Parliament an enviable distinction.'

'I tell you what it is, Harry,' said Lord Monmouth, very drily,
' members of this family may think as they like, but they must
act as I please. . . . You will [behave], I doubt not, like a man
of sense,' he added, looking at Coningsby with a glance such
as he had never before encountered, ' who is not prepared to
sacrifice all the objects of life for the pursuit of some
fantastical puerilities.'

Coningsby remains firm in his resolution not to contest
an election with Edith's father, and not long afterwards
Lord Monmouth suddenly dies, leaving the bulk of his
vast fortune to an illegitimate daughter whom Coningsby
has befriended in ignorance of their relationship. The
disinherited grandson is consoled by Sidonia, who treats
wealth with a disdain not easy for a millionaire, but easier
for Disraeli in spite of his extravagant taste for splendour
and display. Sidonia insists that mere possessions are
one of the smallest elements in happiness, that Coningsby's
loss of his inheritance is only a conventional misfortune,
not a real calamity. Coningsby is now free ; that is to
say—and here we may suppose that Disraeli speaks from
the heart—free if he is not in debt. There are two careers
between which he can choose. One is diplomacy ; but
' a diplomatist is a phantom.' 'I always look upon
diplomatists as the Hebrews of politics ; without country,
political creeds, popular convictions, that strong reality
of existence which pervades the career of an eminent
citizen in a free and great country.' There remains that
other and nobler career, the Bar, and Coningsby resolves
to try for the Great Seal.

In the solitude of his chambers, and away from the
sustaining influence of Sidonia, he lapses into despair,
but a walk through the ' mighty streets ' restores his
equilibrium.

Whether he inherited or forfeited fortunes, what was it to
the passing throng ? They would not share his splendor, or
his luxury, or his comfort. But a word from his lip, a thought
from his brain, expressed at the right time, at the right place,
might turn their hearts, might influence their passions, might
change their opinions, might affect their destiny. Nothing
is great but the personal. As civilisation advances, the
accidents of life become each day less important. The power
of man, his greatness and his glory, depend on essential
qualities. Brains every day become more precious than
blood. You must give men new ideas, you must teach them
new words, you must modify their manners, you must change
their laws, you must root out prejudices, subvert convictions,
if you wish to be great. Greatness no longer depends on
rentals, the world is too rich ; nor on pedigrees, the world is
too knowing.

'The greatness of this city destroys my misery,' said
Coningsby, ' and my genius shall conquer its greatness !'

This conviction of power in the midst of despair was a
revelation of intrinsic strength. It is indeed the test of a
creative spirit. From that moment all petty fears for an
ordinary future quitted him. He felt that he must be prepared for great sacrifices, for infinite suffering ; that there
must devolve on him a bitter inheritance of obscurity, struggle,
envy, and hatred, vulgar prejudice, base criticism, petty
hostilities, but the dawn would break, and the hour arrive,
when the welcome morning hymn of his success and his fame
would sound and be re-echoed.

From such thoughts, we may believe, Disraeli many a
time himself drew consolation in the darker moments of
his career ; but he is not content to leave his hero to live
by fortitude alone. In the midst of the general election
of 1841, in which all his friends are candidates, and which
was to be an epoch in his own life, Coningsby finds himself
a solitary student in the Temple, cut off from the chance
of action. But suddenly his prospects change, and fortune, which has been buffeting him, begins to shower her
favours. Millbank, coming to a better understanding of
things which he had misconstrued, retires from the contest
in which he is engaged with Rigby, and nominates
Coningsby, who is triumphantly elected. He also bestows
on Coningsby the hand of his daughter, and provides for
the happy pair an ample establishment. Presently, more-

over, the frail and unhappy girl who had inherited the bulk of Lord Monmouth's vast wealth dies, and bequeathes the whole of it to Coningsby. Thus overladen, in Disraeli's customary manner, with all the goods of fortune, he is left with his friends on the threshold of public life.

Will they maintain in august assemblies and high places the great truths which, in study and in solitude, they have embraced ? Or will their courage exhaust itself in the struggle, their enthusiasm evaporate before hollow-hearted ridicule, their generous impulses yield with a vulgar catastrophe to the tawdry temptations of a low ambition ? Will their skilled intelligence subside into being the adroit tool of a corrupt party ? Will Vanity confound their fortunes, or Jealousy wither their sympathies ? Or will they remain brave, single, and true ; refuse to bow before shadows and worship phrases ; sensible of the greatness of their position, recognise the greatness of their duties ; denounce to a perplexed and disheartened world the frigid theories of a generalising age that have destroyed the individuality of man, and restore the happiness of their country by believing in their own energies, and daring to be great ?

Coningsby can be regarded either as a work of art or as the manifesto of Young England. The attempt to disengage the politics from the story will best be reserved till we are in a position to deal with *Sybil* at the same time ; but Young England has its place, and a most important place, in the scheme of the novel even as a work of art. 'Some serious creed, however misty and indefinite, is required,' it has been well said,[1] 'to raise the mere mocker into a genuine satirist ;' and just such a creed Young England supplies. Disraeli in *Coningsby* has given us a picture of the great world of the thirties, painted with all his feeling for the gorgeous and spectacular, and a gallery of political portraits painted with perfect insight, sympathy, and comprehension. He has reproduced in this gallery every type that is mean or ridiculous in politics : the Tapers and Tadpoles ; the ' twelve-hundred-a-yearers ' ; the candidates who present themselves

[1] By Sir Leslie Stephen.

to the Liberals of Darlford : ' Mr. Donald Macpherson
Macfarlane, who would only pay the legal expenses—he
was soon despatched ; Mr. Gingerly Browne, of Jermyn
Street, the younger son of a baronet, who would go as
far as £1,000 provided the seat was secured ; Mr. Juggins,
a distiller, £2,000 man, but would not agree to any annual
subscriptions ; Sir Baptist Placid, vague about expenditure, but repeatedly declaring that " there could be no
difficulty on that head "; he, however, had a moral objection to subscribing to the races, and that was a great
point at Darlford ;' the Lord Fitzboobys, the Jawster
Sharps, down even to the Bully Blucks and Magog Wraths,
the *condottieri* leaders of the Liberal and Conservative mobs.
All these he renders with the discernment of a master, and
the coolest detachment in the presence of every variety
of knavery and baseness. But he has the defects of his
qualities, and just as his love of splendour often lures him
into meretriciousness, so his detachment is sometimes
carried to the point of flippancy, or even cynicism. He
was, however, no mere cynic, and as the total effect of
the picture is not meretricious, but stately and imposing,
so it is not flippant or cynical, but serious and inspiring.
Nothing that is ignoble in politics is evaded, but the
ignoble is never treated in the spirit of the photographic
realist, and we have always the romantic ideal of Young
England to serve as a resting-place for faith and a centre
of illumination, and to give harmony and elevation to the
picture as a whole. Bad as things are, the lofty enthusiasm of the New Generation is to set everything right.

If the creed of Young England had been less vague and
shadowy, if the purpose of the novel had been political
in any crude or narrowly partisan sense, the result must
have been failure from the point of view of art. But
Young England was less a party than a spirit in the air,
or at most a revival of Disraeli's early dream, the dream
that haunts the youth of every generation, of a party
truly national rising above all factious aims and limitations.   The wisdom which Sidonia pours out to Coningsby

is not politics at all, or the politics of the Empyrean in its
detachment, not only from party, but even from nationality and from everything but race. To this serene
wisdom Coningsby and his friends add a wisdom of their
own in which we can distinguish two different elements.
One is the boyish sentimentalism, the taste for mere
ritual, the maypoles and church architecture, for which
Smythe, or more often Manners, is really responsible, and
which Disraeli, we may believe, never took very seriously.
The other is pure Disraeli, the Disraeli we already know
in the *Vindication* and his speeches, with his peculiar
political creed compounded in equal measure of Tory and
Radical elements, and his comparative indifference to
the conventional party divisions. Thus, the politics of
Young England are so broad and disinterested as to save
the novel from all suspicion of mere party pamphleteering.
From his central point of view the author surveys the
scene with judicial impartiality, and awards praise and
blame with due discrimination. He was depicted in
Punch as the infant Hercules strangling, one in either
hand, the twin serpents Whig and Tory ; and certainly
Whigs and Tories are alike made to suffer under the lash
of his satire.

The politics as a rule are woven so deftly into the
texture of the story as not to be obtrusive, though sometimes, especially when Coningsby is speaking, they
degenerate into a lecture, and one feels that the longer
digressions by the author represent a gritty residuum of
unassimilated matter. For all his sense of humour,
Disraeli can be over-solemn when his pet ideas are in
question ; but he has a curious and refreshing habit that
atones for such transgressions. If he has no self-conscious
fears of making himself absurd, he is always ready to
anticipate the laugh against himself. We see this in the
dialogue between Lord Monmouth and Coningsby given
above ; and we see it again in the account of Sir Joseph
Wallinger's simple-minded perplexity at the views of the
New Generation, or in the sly allusion to a speech by

Buckhurst ' denouncing the Venetian constitution, to the
amazement of several thousand persons, apparently not a
little terrified by this unknown danger.'

As regards the principal characters, Coningsby himself
is not altogether successful. He is hardly a living moving
figure, and at times he smacks both of the prig and the
bore. Little attempt is made to preserve the resemblance
to Smythe, who was very far from being either. Sir
Leslie Stephen has remarked that Disraeli's youthful
heroes in his early novels are creative, and that in the
later they tend to become merely receptive. We see the
change in *Coningsby*, and the explanation is that the
nominal hero has ceased to be the real. Coningsby derives
his wisdom from Sidonia, and Sidonia, not Coningsby, is
in fact the central figure in the whole intellectual movement of the novel. Sidonia is said to have been suggested
by a member of the Rothschild family, and the resemblance in many points is too obvious to have been accidental ; he is, as it were, an ideal Rothschild, a Rothschild
equipped not only with great wealth, but with a penetrating and all-embracing intellectual vision. Sidonia is
indeed a god, and perhaps as near to the deity of Disraeli's
religion as we are ever likely to get. There is in him, of
course, much of Disraeli himself. Like Disraeli, and unlike the Rothschilds, he is of the stock of the Sephardim,
the descendant of the ' Nuevos Christianos ' of Arragon ;
and when we are told that he ' observed everything, but
avoided serious discussion,' and ' if you pressed him for
an opinion took refuge in raillery ' ; or that, at the end
of a long appeal addressed to him by Rigby, 'he only bowed
his head and said " Perhaps," and then, turning to his
neighbour, inquired whether birds were plentiful in
Lancashire,' we recognise authentic traits from the manner
of his creator.

Henry Sydney and Buckhurst are much more real and
true to life than Coningsby. Lord Monmouth is finely
conceived and admirably drawn, and is a far more
interesting and attractive figure than either his original

or Thackeray's Lord Steyne. Heartless, self-indulgent and devoid of scruple as he is, he has a certain grandeur of his own as the type of Sulla-like patrician, arrogant but dignified, sublimely selfish, but also self-sufficient, and alike in good and evil fortune undaunted in his bearing. There has been no keener or more effective satirist than Disraeli of the vices and follies of the aristocracy which he so much admired ; and that partly because of his very admiration. Sympathy gave him insight, comprehension, and tolerance, and he remains cool and collected where Thackeray, for instance, is apt to go off in a sputter of moral indignation which defeats its own purpose. We see in Rigby how Disraeli's own work is marred where animus enters. As a picture of the sycophant, Rigby is perhaps overdrawn, and is certainly overdrawn as a portrait of Croker. That very unimpressive, it may be disagreeable, but from all that appears quite honourable man, had the bad fortune to incur the bitter enmity of two such opposite men of genius as Disraeli and Macaulay. Macaulay was so obviously extravagant in his injustice that it has recoiled upon himself. Disraeli's animosity, of which we have seen the origin, was much less violent, but violent enough in contrast to his usual cool detachment to lead him into something that resembles an artistic blunder.

Of the women, Edith Millbank is not altogether a success. Lady Theresa Sydney is entirely uninteresting, but Lady Everingham, her sister, is the best woman in the book. In a different style, Mrs. Guy Flouncey, who is an anticipation of Becky Sharp, is very good, too.

She came [to Coningsby Castle] with a wardrobe which, in point of variety, fancy, and fashion, never was surpassed. . . . At first the fine ladies never noticed her, or only stared at her over their shoulders ; everywhere sounded, in suppressed whispers, the fatal question, ' Who is she ?' After dinner they formed always into polite groups, from which Mrs. Guy Flouncey was invariably excluded. . . . It was, indeed, rather difficult work the first few days. . . . But Mrs. Guy Flouncey . . . had confidence in herself, her quickness, her ever ready accomplishments, and her practised powers of attraction. And she was right. She was always sure of an ally the moment the gentlemen appeared. . . . Somehow or other, before a week was passed, Mrs. Guy Flouncey seemed the soul of everything, was always surrounded by a cluster of admirers, and with what are called ' the best men ' ever ready to ride with her, dance with her, act with her, or fall at her feet. The fine ladies found it absolutely necessary to thaw ; they began to ask her questions after dinner. Mrs. Guy Flouncey only wanted an opening. She was an adroit flatterer, with a temper imperturbable, and gifted with a ceaseless energy of conferring slight obligations. She lent them patterns for new fashions, in all which mysteries she was very versant ; and what with some gentle glozing and some gay gossip, sugar for their tongues and salt for their tails, she contrived pretty well to catch them all.

Disraeli is usually happier in his slighter sketches of women than in his more elaborate pictures. He begins well with the Princess Lucretia, who ' generally succeeded in conveying an impression to those she addressed that she had never seen them before, did not care to see them now, and never wished to see them again ; and all this, too, with an air of great courtesy ' ; but her character when developed passes into melodrama.

The habit of Parliamentary speaking has seldom a good effect on literary style, and seven years in the House of Commons had not improved Disraeli's. He rarely rises in *Coningsby* or the subsequent novels to the highest level, for instance, of *Contarini Fleming*. There is less simplicity and directness, more affectation, and, in the matter of solecisms, more carelessness than ever. It is one of the many contradictions in Disraeli's mind and character that, in spite of his strong grasp of fact, his keen sense of the ridiculous, and his intolerance of cant, he never could quite distinguish between the genuine and the counterfeit either in language or sentiment. His taste for fine writing in an artificial style shows no diminution, and his displays of mawkish sentimentalism, as, for instance, in the love passages between Coningsby and Edith, jar on us the more as they no longer have the excuse of youth and inexperience. On the other hand, years and maturity of mind have developed that pregnant and aphoristic quality which was in his style from the first, and is one of its greatest merits. Disraeli may not be a great moralist, but he is a great master of the art of life in a less lofty sense, and from every chapter of *Coningsby* it would be possible to cull illuminating maxims on this lower plane of wisdom.

To Sarah Disraeli.

Thursday [*May*].

Lord Ponsonby [1] is so ' enchanted with Sidonia ' that we are all to dine together at the Lionel [Rothschild]s' on Sunday. There is no particular news except that Bradshaw, the last of the school of Brummell, has read a book, and it is called *Coningsby*. Twice on our way to Longmans in Paternoster Row we were congratulated. Once by Tom Jones [?], who almost embraced M. A.; which she returned, although she denies it. He was ' not surprised to find in Paternoster Row the most successful author of the day.'

[*June* 13.]

Yesterday we dined with B. Wall, and had a most exquisite dinner in a most refined and sumptuous house, and with the most charming society. I sat next to Sydney Smith, who was delightful : we had besides Lady Morley and Luttrell and Labouchere and G. Smythe and Punch Greville [2] and Lord Melbourne. I don't remember a more agreeable party ; it sprang from *Coningsby* and from Sydney Smith's wish to make my acquaintance. His wife was there, M. A. says a very agreeable person, and Lady Stepney.

Coningsby keeps moving—about 40 a day on average. We are preparing for a third edition, having only 400 or so on hand of the second, and the demand being steady.

From Henry Hope.

May 18.

To tell you how much I admire the story, the style, the terrible power of wit and sarcasm . . . would merely be to repeat what the newspapers say, but there is besides a spirit of daring and chivalry in attacking people who have always been deemed bugbears . . . which much delights and refreshes me. . . .

---

[1] Viscount Ponsonby, 1770(?)-1855, a well-known diplomatist, brother of Sir William Ponsonby who was killed at Waterloo.

[2] Charles Greville, the diarist.

It diverts me much to hear the comments of our friends.
' Dreadfully personal !' says one ; ' What fun Tadpole and
Taper are !' says Ernest Bruce ; ' How like Fitzbooby is !' says
somebody else ; ' Bonham has not appeared,' says another,
and if the species ever committed suicide it would be said of
him. . . . I saw Lord Lyndhurst, who appeared to enjoy the
book beyond measure, and told me of an instance in which
he had heard Rigby set Lord Eldon right on law and the Duke
of Wellington on military matters on one day.

The following reminiscences relating to Croker are
from a manuscript of Disraeli's written in the sixties :

In 1849 there was a grand dinner given in Merchant Taylors'
Hall to inaugurate the new organisation of the ' Protectionist
Party ' under the leadership of Lord Derby and myself.   Tom
Baring was in the chair.   On his right Lord Derby, myself on
his left, and then there were alternately peers and commoners.
The Duke of Northumberland, whom I did not then know,
was to have sate next to me : but his Grace was unwell and
prevented attending at the last moment.   The commoner
next to his Grace's seat was Mr. Croker.   He was requested
by the directors of the fête to sit up next to me.   It was
rather embarrassing : but Mr. Croker and myself were not
socially acquainted.   I had never seen him since I was a boy.
Nor was he the person who ought to assume that a character
in one of my books, which he deemed odious, was intended for
himself.   He behaved like a man of the world : informed me
that he had had the pleasure of, he hoped, the friendship of my
excellent father, talked generally about the political situation,
warmed into anecdote, and made himself agreeable.   I
treated him with great consideration, and spoke enough, but
not too much, and took care never to break into cordiality,
which I should have done under ordinary circumstances with
so eminent a man, met under such conditions.

When I made my speech after dinner, I observed he nodded
his head frequently in approbation, and gave other signs of
sympathy, and perhaps stronger feeling.   I thought all this
on his part a very good performance, and that he had extricated
himself out of an embarrassing position with dexterity and
some grace.   A year or two afterwards—February, 1851—I
had brought forward a great agricultural motion on the
burthens of land, had rallied great numbers, had been beaten
by the Government in a full House, by only 15 or 16 votes, or
even less ; had made a great statement at the commencement
of the debate which lasted some days, and had concluded by a
brilliant reply which made much noise at the time, and was

doubly effective from the capital division that followed. I was standing in the hall of the Carlton, which was rather full, reading a letter, when a person came up to me and put his hand on my arm, and said : ' The speech was the speech of a statesman, and the reply was the reply of a wit.' It was Croker.

I was surprised, and murmured something about *laudari a laudato,* but he had vanished. He had too much good taste to remain.

Years after this George Smythe brought me, one morning, a letter from Croker, who had long been hopelessly ill, to his father, Lord Strangford (Camoens), with whom Croker had been at college, and always chums ; and this letter, if it meant anything, meant a formal reconciliation with me : it seemed even an interview. I remember in the letter this passage : ' Why he attacked me I never could discover, and know no more the cause than I know the man who shot Mrs. Hampden !'

I behaved as kindly as I could under the circumstances : but I could not listen to interviews, or reconciliations, or explanations. It was too late, and my sensibilities, which had [been] played upon in my earlier life, too much required nursing. I told George Smythe to manage the result with the greatest consideration for Croker's feelings and situation ; and there it ended.

The moral I draw from all this is that men of a certain age like the young ones who lick them. I think, now, that Croker was quite sincere at the Merchant Taylors'.

CHAPTER VIII.

DIVERGING FROM THE GOVERNMENT.

1844–1845.

Though when the session of 1844 began Disraeli had already been six years in Parliament, we may doubt whether he had yet attained to any high position in the favour of the House of Commons. The successes in debate which he reported from time to time with so much complacency to his sister had failed to produce the cumulative effect that might have been expected. He had shown qualities that would have won him influence and promotion as a Minister, and if he had been taken into the Ministry in 1841 progress would have been easy ; but an open and visible check such as he then received is more often than not fatal to a Parliamentary career, and in his case recovery was rendered more difficult by the dubious reputation which, taking its origin from his early political escapades and his affectations of dress and manner, still clung to him persistently. Exclusion from the Government had the appearance of setting the seal on this reputation, and for the moment he seemed to lose much of the ground he had won.

Nor, in spite of all his gifts, had he yet acquired the authentic House of Commons manner. He had courage and originality, unbounded cleverness, and that most effective weapon—' dangerous, though most effective,' he calls it in *Endymion* '—the power of sarcasm. But all these are gifts which require supreme tact for their judicious display in Parliament, and in Parliamentary tact he was

at first a little wanting. Englishmen in general, and the
House of Commons in particular, hate everything that
savours of pretentiousness and presumption ; and though
Disraeli, we may believe, was no more of an egoist than
many who had greater art in concealing their foible,
there was an element of pretentiousness and presumption
in his speeches which the House of Commons resented.
The oracular manner, which became a positive asset when
he had reached a high position, tended to delay his ascent.
He was too didactic in tone, and his cleverness, though
great, was too ostentatious. It was often amusing, sometimes impressive ; but, then, he was a man of letters, from
whom cleverness was to be expected, and as an assembly
of practical Englishmen the House of Commons knew
better than to take such a person seriously.

The House, it has been said, hates a man who makes it
think. Disraeli had evolved a political philosophy of his
own, and had been lavish of its wisdom ; but a still greater
master of political philosophy had learnt by bitter experience how little such an instrument profits in Parliament, and where it failed in the hands of Burke, Disraeli
could hardly expect to wield it with success. The very
qualities which give lasting interest to his early speeches
probably tended, as with Burke in every period of his
career, to make them ineffective at the moment of
delivery. The House of Commons has developed a
peculiar style of its own, of which exaggerated verbiage
and a deliberate indirectness are the dominant characteristics. But these are qualities which are entirely alien to
good and lasting literature, and so House of Commons
speeches, when they have served their immediate purpose,
are rarely good reading. Peel and Gladstone, who were
the great exponents of the Parliamentary manner, are
altogether intolerable in the cold pages of Hansard ; and
Disraeli himself, when he had once fully acquired that
manner, becomes much less readable in his speeches in
the House than in his speeches in the country.

His best Parliamentary speeches are those of the

middle period, when the quality of thoughtfulness, the breadth of view, and the literary finish which he had shown from the first, are combined with ease and freedom and an appearance of spontaneity. In the session of 1844 he seemed suddenly to catch the peculiar intonation of Parliamentary debate, and, without sacrificing what was best and most characteristic in his own style, to attune it completely to the ear of the House of Commons. The Irish speech in February, though still a little too didactic, marked a great advance in Parliamentary manner. Occupied with *Coningsby*, he was less active than usual in the business of the House, only speaking on two other occasions of any importance in the course of the session ; but the advance was maintained in these subsequent efforts, and henceforward his command of the House was complete.

One fact stands out conspicuously about the three speeches of the session : they exhibit a continuous divergence from the Government. The first, in February, as we have seen, was comparatively friendly ; the second, in April, was bantering in tone, but could hardly be called hostile; the third, in June, was openly rebellious. When Peel paid his compliment to the Irish speech in February, his sister, Mrs. Dawson, wrote to Mrs. Disraeli :

I was delighted with my brother's speech, and with no part of it more than that in which he alludes to Mr. Disraeli in a complimentary strain. I wish very much that the next time Mr. Disraeli sees my brother he would put out his hand to him. They are both reserved men, and one must make the first advance ; the other would accept it most gladly.

Whether Disraeli's hand would have been accepted gladly or not, it seems never to have been offered, and after the momentary approach to a better understanding the two men began to drift apart again. 'A Parliamentary leader who possesses [the faculty of inspiring enthusiasm] doubles his majority ; and he who has it not may shroud himself in artificial reserve and study with undignified arrogance an awkward haughtiness, but he will never-

theless be as far from controlling the spirit as from captivating the hearts of his sullen followers.' In this sentence
in *Coningsby* there was an obvious fling at Peel, though
his name was not mentioned. But Disraeli was not
touchy, and the 'artificial reserve' and 'awkward
haughtiness' would have counted for less if they had not
been supplemented by deeper causes of division. The
question at issue was more than a mere question of
outward demeanour. Where two men have their faces
set in opposite directions divergence is inevitable.

There was nothing in which Young England was more
thoroughly in earnest, or that did more to give a wide
popularity to its ideas, than its devotion to the cause of
social reform. In this matter Disraeli was no less sincere
than Manners himself.

There is no subject [he said, speaking to his constituents in
the summer of this year] in which I have taken a deeper
interest than the condition of the working classes. Long before
what is called the 'condition of the people question' was dis-
cussed in the House of Commons, I had employed my pen[1] on
the subject. I had long been aware that there was something
rotten in the core of our social system. I had seen that while
immense fortunes were accumulating, while wealth was increasing to a superabundance, and while Great Britain was
cited throughout Europe as the most prosperous nation in the
world, the working classes, the creators of wealth, were steeped
in the most abject poverty and gradually sinking into the
deepest degradation.[2]

The new Poor Law, he added, of ten years before
represented 'a philosophical attempt' by the Whigs to
remedy these evils, and the new Poor Law was still one
of the centres of contention between opposing schools of
thought. Its opponents had not been silenced by the
overwhelming defeat which they suffered in the House
of Commons in Disraeli's first session.[3] *The Times* with
great pertinacity continued to expose and denounce the
iniquities of the new system, and Dickens, in *Oliver Twist*,

---

[1] He was perhaps thinking of *Popanilla*.
[2] *Shropshire Conservative*, Aug. 31, 1844.   [3] See p. 80.

did much by his picture of life in the new union work-houses to fan the agitation.   The Act of 1834 was a pro-visional measure, and when the Whig Government in their last session introduced a Bill for its renewal for ten years, Disraeli had the courage to move the rejection, and was able to muster more than fifty supporters.[1]   The Bill was subsequently lost through the dissolution of Parliament, and there is no doubt that in the elections Peel, though he himself had never given to the agitation the slightest encouragement, owed a good deal of his success to the unpopularity which the Whigs had incurred by their Poor Law, and to the definite pledges that were taken by many of his supporters to vote for its amend-ment or total abolition.   The new Government, however, showed little eagerness to do anything for the fulfilment of these pledges.   Graham, who as Home Secretary was the Minister responsible, was still completely dominated by the *laisser aller* principles of his Whig or Liberal days, and was, if possible, even less sympathetic than Peel. By relaxing in some respects the severity of the adminis-tration, introducing some amendments, and promising others, he persuaded the House of Commons in 1842 to renew the Act for five years ; but the hopes of many Tories were deeply disappointed, and the Ministry for some sessions had to encounter a persistent agitation in the House, which estranged them from a section of their natural supporters, and helped to drive them along that path of approximation to their Manchester opponents which they were too ready to tread.   Anxious at this time to avoid all appearance of hostility to Peel, Disraeli held aloof, never speaking on the subject, and very rarely voting ;[2] but he did not change his opinions.   Better times began in 1843 or 1844, and these, aided by the improve-ments introduced under pressure of the continuous agita-tion, gradually reconciled the country to the new system ;

---

[1] *Hansard*, Feb. 8, 1841.
[2] In one division in Committee in 1842 (June 27) he voted against the Government.

but as late as 1847, when the Act again expired, Disraeli spoke and voted against the Bill for its renewal.

If the new Poor Law was typical of the remedies put forward by one school of doctors for the social evils of the time, the factory legislation, which was now loudly demanded, was no less typical of the remedies which the other and Tory school suggested. The fight over the Poor Law and the fight over the question of factory reform both tended to become incidents in the larger struggle now raging between the landed gentry and the manufacturers. The country party, seeing in the misery of the factory workers the opportunity for a counter-attack on the assailants of their own position, were the more ready to apply those legislative remedies to which their traditions predisposed them ; the factory masters in their turn pointed to the condition of the agricultural labourers as an illustration of the practical working of socialistic theories, and insisted on their own cure for all social evils—the free admission of corn. Disraeli, though he had no doubt in which camp he would be found, as usual steadily surveyed the whole situation from a central point of view.

I beg to be understood [he said to his constituents in justifying his votes in favour of factory legislation] that I do not join in the absurd cry against the manufacturing interest of the country. I respect the talents, the industry, the indomitable energy, of that powerful class, and I acknowledge them as the primary source of our wealth and greatness ; and although I am not blind to the fact that great distress, and perhaps tyranny, exists in the system, I fear—for I was born[1] and have lived in an agricultural county—I fear, nay I am sure, that the condition of the agricultural labourers cannot be cited to the confusion of the manufacturing capitalists.[2]

In the matter of factory reform even more conspicuously than in the matter of the Poor Law, Graham and the Government showed that their sympathies were with

---

[1] Whether this misstatement is to be put down to rhetoric or to momentary forgetfulness it is needless to inquire.

[2] Speech at Shrewsbury, Aug. 28, 1844.

Manchester. Continuing his great campaign against the
oppression of the industrial poor, Lord Ashley in 1840
procured the appointment of a commission to inquire into
the facts as to the employment of women and children ;
and two years later the famous report dealing with mines
and collieries made its appearance. The horrors revealed
by this lurid document gave so great a shock to the
conscience of the nation that Ashley in the same session
was able, though receiving little help from the Government, to carry a Bill excluding women and young children
from the mines altogether. A second report dealing with
trades and manufactures was issued by the commission
in 1843, and Graham himself in this session, spurred on
by Ashley and an insistent public opinion, introduced a
Bill for the regulation of factory labour. It contained
also provisions for the education of factory children, and
one of those storms that suddenly arise when religious
education comes into question caused its abandonment ;
but it was reintroduced in 1844 with the education
clauses omitted. Beside certain restrictions on the
employment of children, Graham's Bill proposed to limit
the labour of ' young persons '[1] to twelve hours a day ; but
the factory reformers had long been insisting that ten
hours were sufficient, and the bulk of the Tory majority,
if left to themselves, were disposed to agree with them.
The Government, however, threw the whole weight of
their influence into the scale of the mill-owners ; and
though Ashley in committee twice succeeded[2] in defeating them by narrow majorities on the question of
twelve hours, he failed, also by a narrow majority, to
carry ten hours as a substantive proposal. It was
expected that the compromise of eleven hours would be
adopted, but the Government were unyielding. They
withdrew their Bill, introduced another, and when Ashley
again proposed his ten-hours amendment, Graham informed the House that if it were carried it would be his

[1] Boys from thirteen to eighteen, and girls up to twenty-one.
[2] March 15 and 22.

duty to seek a private station ; and when it seemed
doubtful, in view of his great unpopularity, whether this
might not be regarded by the Tory members as a blessing,
Peel himself got up and stated that if the question were
decided against them he also would retire. Against such
a threat as this Ashley could make no headway, and he
was beaten in the division [1] by nearly two to one.

Disraeli and Young England[2] supported Ashley throughout the struggle. Disraeli remained silent, but he told
his constituents later that he was anxious to speak before
the last fatal division, and was prevented by the excitement from obtaining a hearing. Most of the official Whigs
voted with Ashley—some of them, like Palmerston, from
sincere interest in the question ; others, no doubt, with an
eye to mere party advantage. Macaulay, who in his
youth had treated Sadler so unworthily, and who had
now become a convert, was, we may hope, among the
former. Bright was a bitter advocate for the mill-
owners throughout, and with him were most of the
Radical free traders ; but Cobden stood aside, watching
with secret joy the embarrassment of the Government,
and feeding himself inwardly with the prescient hope
' that men like Graham and Peel would see the necessity
of taking anchor upon some sound principles, as a refuge
from the socialist doctrines of the fools behind them.' [3]
When Graham and Peel had found the anchorage he
desired, the fools behind them, freed from the constraint
of their leadership, acted in obedience to their natural
instincts, and carried the Ten Hours Bill before the end
of this Parliament.

The occasion for Disraeli's second speech of the session
was a personal dispute. Ferrand, the member for
Knaresborough, who, as we have seen, had affiliations
with the Young England group, was one of the most
zealous of the Tory social reformers, strenuous and out-

---

[1] May 13.
[2] With the exception of Smythe. He was under constant pressure from
his father to support Peel, and this may have determined his vote.
[3] Morley's *Cobden*, I., p. 302.

spoken both in support of the Ten Hours Bill and in
opposition to the new Poor Law. He had become involved on the latter subject in an endless controversy with
Graham about a report from a Poor Law official called
Mott, with regard to which there were grounds for a
suspicion of chicanery ; and in a speech in the country he
had roundly accused Graham of having procured a false
report in order to crush an opponent, and also of having
induced the chairman of an election committee to give a
partial vote in order to deprive the great enemy of the
new Poor Law, Walter of *The Times*, of his seat in
the House of Commons. Graham made the charges a
question of privilege, and Disraeli, who had been a
member of the election committee, intervened in the
debate with a speech which delighted the House by its
wit and adroitness. Without attempting to justify
Ferrand or his charges, he pleaded in his behalf against an
injudicious penalty, and he contrived before he sat down
to make fun of all concerned—of Peel, of Graham, of
Stanley, and even of the House itself—and yet carry
his audience with him. The hon. member, he thought,
had a very bad case, and, he added, greatly daring, a
still worse tribunal ; but the House only laughed. He
had heard the hon. member himself, the Home
Secretary, and the Prime Minister, all three discourse on
the subject of the great Mott case,[1] but he never could
annex a definite idea to any single circumstance of that
most complicated transaction. Something in it there
certainly was — there was a case, there was a subcom-
missioner, a report that was quoted and not printed,
a commissioner that was quoted and dismissed. No one,
however, believed, in spite of the suspicious circumstances,
that the Secretary of State in his exalted position would
pervert his power for so slight an object. But because a
mere member of Parliament, supposing himself engaged

---

[1] The controversy about the report lasted for several years, and ever
afterwards, both in Parliament and the press, was known as ' the great Mott
case.'

in a contest with a powerful Government, had taken an extreme view, was a man like the right hon. gentleman to come with that demure countenance which he could so well put on, and say that the State was in danger, and 'that the House of Commons must interfere to vindicate the reputation of this, I believe still strong, though not popular Ministry ?'[1] The Prime Minister, he thought, had treated the subject in the-right way when, with that historical research and that unrivalled memory for which he was famed, he had referred to the case of the bottle conjurer ;[2] but after he had set this good example it was surprising to find him followed by the noble lord (Stanley) in such a different strain.

There is always something chivalric about the noble lord, and one cannot but admire him when hastening to the rescue of his right hon. friend the Secretary of State. But . . . I could not suppress my surprise at seeing him get up, and, in his zeal to inform the hon. member for Knaresborough, first denounce his statements as calumnies, and then charge him with having made those statements knowing them to be calumnious. That is the model by which the hon. member will profit when he returns to the House . . . and we shall find his speeches hereafter distinguished for all that amenity of manner and that choice selection of conciliatory phrase which have hitherto distinguished the speeches of the noble lord. The noble lord declares the hon. member is an intentional calumniator. . . . How will he substantiate that assertion ? Better than the hon. member has substantiated his ? The noble lord in this case, as in so many others, first destroys his opponent, and then destroys his own position. The noble lord is the Prince Rupert of Parliamentary discussion ; his charge is resistless ; but when he returns from the pursuit he always finds his camp in the possession of the enemy (cheers and laughter).

The name clung to Stanley, and to this day he is best known as the Parliamentary Rupert. It was now again the turn of Graham, and the mockery became malicious :

---

[1] This sally, we are told, was received with ' roars of laughter.'
[2] Peel's speech had contained a reference to ' the public performer who undertook to compress himself into a quart bottle.'

As if all these great guns were not sufficient to sink this unfortunate craft, then comes the Secretary of State to keep up the solemn inspiration of the farce, and rising tells us, ' This is the British House of Commons. This is not a hustings. Gentlemen may tell lies upon the hustings, but gentlemen may not tell lies in the British House of Commons.' This is the political morality of the Secretary of State. Now, I entirely differ from the right hon. gentleman on this point. I certainly do not think that gentlemen ought to tell lies in the House of Commons, but I also think hon. gentlemen ought to be as careful in what they say on the hustings. I even go farther than that : I say that hon. gentlemen ought not to make pledges on the hustings which they do not mean to keep in the House of Commons. I don't think that a gentleman on the hustings, for example, ought to denounce the new Poor Law, and then come into the House of Commons and vote for it. I call that corrupt and unprincipled conduct; and if there be any gentleman in this House who has been guilty of that conduct, why, he may rise in his place and propose a vote of censure on me for saying so (cheers and laughter).

A more genial laugh at Peel brought the speech to a conclusion :

No attempt by this House, whether right or wrong in the beginning, from the time of Sacheverell to our friend Mr. Stockdale, to run down an individual has ever succeeded or has ever terminated to their advantage. Remember what another Sir Robert—not a greater man than our Sir Robert, but still a most distinguished one—said with respect to the case of Dr. Sacheverell. He said he had had ' enough of roasting a parson ' ; and I think the right hon. gentleman, taking as he did the great historical view of the case, the bottle conjurer view of the case, might really, after what has occurred, allow the matter to drop, feeling assured that the hon. member has received a great moral lesson, and that when he appears on the hustings in future he will, not adopting the distinction of the Secretary of State, be almost as cautious there as he is in the House of Commons.[1]

He sat down, we are told, amid loud and continued cheering, and, whether or not in deference to the advice he had given, the House eventually contented itself with

[1] *The Times*, April 25, 1844.

a formal resolution that Ferrand's imputations were
wholly unfounded and calumnious.

From Henry Hope.

April 25.

MY DEAR DISRAELI,

I cannot resist the temptation of expressing to you the
delight I felt at reading your speech of last night. Any
remark from me on the beauty of the composition or the
keenness of the wit would be superfluous, and almost impertinent; but independently of that there is about it a high
feeling which pleases me more than I can tell—tearing off
the mask from hypocrites, exposing the turbulence of bullies,
and showing, what I so long have felt, that the measure of
public virtue and public sympathy was the plausibility and
power of the assailants and assailed.

Ever yours,

HENRY T. HOPE.

In May Peel had succeeded in compelling the House of
Commons to reverse its decision on the question of the
Factory Bill, and in June he repeated the performance on
a question of sugar duties. Skilful finance, aided by two
good harvests and a revival of trade, had at last produced
a surplus, and the Budget of this year proposed among
other changes a reduction of these duties. Sugar was
then, as often before and since, a political explosive; it
had caused the fall of the Whigs in 1841, and Peel's proposals were regarded by many of his supporters as resem-
bling too closely those which he had then resisted. This
section of the Conservative members, anxious to increase
the preference to free-grown sugar from the colonies over
foreign slave-grown sugar, combined with the Opposition,
and carried[1] against the Government an amendment
reducing the duties on all free-grown sugar. Young
England[2] voted in the majority, though Disraeli, 'out of
his great personal regard for the Prime Minister,' as he
told his constituents later, gave his vote in silence; while
Cobden and Bright and the orthodox free traders, dis-

---

[1] June 14. The figures were 241 to 221.
[2] All except Cochrane.

liking the sugar-growers as allies of the landed gentry, and notwithstanding the fact that the amendment implied a step in the direction of free trade, supported the Government. In those days, it must be remembered, the House of Commons had not been reduced to that dependence on the Ministry to which we are now accustomed, and such incidents as the acceptance of this amendment were not uncommon ; but Peel determined to insist on his original proposals, and summoned a party meeting to consider the situation. At this meeting, according to Gladstone, he 'stated his case in a speech which was thought to be haughty and unconciliatory ;'[1] and although the open dissentients, among whom were Disraeli and Ferrand, were only five or six, the general tone was so bad that Peel wrote to the Queen to prepare her for the defeat of the Government.[2]

Disraeli also seems to have believed that the Government were doomed. The original division had been on a Friday, and on the Monday following the House of Commons was to be asked to rescind its vote. On the Sunday night Cam Hobhouse met the Disraelis at dinner at Baron Lionel de Rothschild's, the party, which included Lord and Lady Lansdowne and Lord and Lady John Russell, having, it seems, been made to bring Disraeli and the Whig leaders together. Disraeli told Hobhouse that he believed the Ministers would be out by five o'clock the next day, and he thought the Whigs would have no difficulty in filling their places.

He said Ireland was no obstacle ; we could govern it although the Tories could not. The Corn Laws might be settled as well by us as by Peel ; and as to the Poor Law, some modification must be made by anyone who could govern. . . . Peel had completely failed to keep together his party, and must *go*—if not now, at least very speedily. He said Russell was one of the very few men in the House of Commons who had a *strong will* and was fit to govern. He thought nothing of Stanley ; Graham he admired for his capacity.[3]

---

[1] Morley's *Gladstone*, I., p. 644.   [2] Parker's *Peel*, III., p. 153.
[3] *Lord Broughton's Recollections*, VI. p. 114.

On the Monday, Peel, who was usually, Disraeli told his constituents, 'the most prudent of orators if not of statesmen,' made a speech so unconciliatory as to draw a vigorous protest even from the faithful Sandon. 'His own friends said afterwards that they were astonished at the want of caution, the want of temper, and the arrogant and imperious tone he adopted on this occasion.' Disraeli himself made a speech, the third of the session, which produced a great effect. 'I could not silently,' he explained in his subsequent justification, 'obey the imperious mandate, and I warmly and passionately and quite unpremeditatedly expressed my feelings on the subject.' For a second time within a month, he told the House of Commons, they had been placed in a position which no one on either side could call other than degrading ; for a second time they were asked to repeal a solemn decision. To rescind one vote in the session was, he really thought, enough ; he did not think they ought to be called on to endure this degradation more than once a year. The Prime Minister should introduce some Parliamentary tariff for the regulation of their disapproval ; he ought to tell them the bounds within which they were to enjoy their Parliamentary independence. His was not the most agreeable way of conducting the affairs of the country ; it was not the most constitutional. He had a horror of slavery, but it seemed to extend to every place except the benches behind him. 'There the gang is still assembled, and there the thong of the whip still sounds.' At this gibe, Hobhouse tells us, 'there was a tremendous cheer, and Peel, Stanley, and Graham, sat in most painful silence and submission to the rebuke amidst the applause of many near and all opposite to them. I never saw them look so wretched.'[1]

The Prime Minister, Disraeli proceeded, deserved a better position in the eye of the country than one which he could only maintain by menacing his friends and dealing out threats to keep them to their allegiance.

[1] Broughton, VI., p. 118.

The right hon. gentleman came into power upon the strength of our votes, but he relies for the permanence of his Ministry upon his political opponents. He may be right—he may even be to a certain degree successful in pursuing the line of conduct which he has adopted, menacing his friends and cringing to his opponents ; but I for one am disposed to believe that in this case his success will neither tend to the honor of the House nor to his own credit. I therefore, for one, must be excused if I declare my determination to give my vote upon this occasion as I did on the former occasion, and . . . it only remains for me to declare, after the mysterious hint which fell from the right hon. baronet in the course of his speech, that if I, in common with other hon. members, am called upon to appear again upon the hustings, I shall at least not be ashamed to do so, nor shall I feel that I have weakened my claims upon the confidence of my constituents by not changing my vote within forty-eight hours at the menace of a Minister.

He sat down amid cheers that were loud and sustained, and till near the close of the debate it seemed almost certain that the Government would be beaten. But Lord Howick intervened from the front Opposition bench with a blundering free trade speech, and Stanley, seizing the opportunity with his customary readiness, appealed to Tory sentiment in an adroit party reply, and restored the fortunes of the day. The House rescinded its vote by a majority of twenty,[1] and the Government were saved. It was Stanley's last great appearance in debate in the House of Commons, for at the close of this session he was called to the Upper House by his own desire, and seven years before, in the order of nature, he succeeded to his father. Disraeli probably gave no more than a passing thought to his removal at the time, but it was none the less an event that a few years later was to prove decisive in its influence on his own political career.

[1] The figures were 253 to 233. Disraeli and his friends voted in the minority, even Cochrane, who had at first voted with the Government, now declaring that, as the question at issue had become the independence of the House, he could no longer support them. On the day after the division Queen Victoria wrote to her uncle, the King of the Belgians : ' We were really in the greatest possible danger of having a resignation of the Government without knowing to whom to turn, and this from the recklessness of a handful of foolish half " Puseyite," half " Young England " people ' (*Letters of Queen Victoria*, ch. 13).

To Sarah Disraeli.

HOUSE OF COMMONS,
July 9.

MY DEAREST SA,

I have been intending to write every day, but in the struggle of existence have daily postponed it. M. A. has, I think, written frequently ; therefore when we meet you will have the map of our life tolerably fresh in your memory. . . .

At Bearwood we found all the Walters, his married daughter and her husband, the Ferrands, John Manners, Smythe, Cochrane. We came up on Monday by the 2 o'clock train from Twyford, the most beautiful day for sylvan scenery. And at night we went to the Waverley Ball, which would have been as fine a thing as possible had not the illusion been marred, or rather destroyed, by numerous gentlemen in black coats and white cravats, and among them Lord Wilton and some of the first dandies.

Ld. Castlereagh as a Bedouin chief was very accurate and undiscoverable ; young Hogg as Lovell in *The Antiquary* bore the belt, I think, of the beaus, beyond Cantelupe as Cœur de Lion and Granby as Quintin [*sic*] Durward, not Quintin Dick, which it was reported he represented.

Smythe's book[1] was published on Saturday, but as yet its fate is undecided, though I think it will not rank among the stillborn.

In the course of the month I hope to see my way in many things, which look on the whole favorable.

Manchester has invited me to take the chair at their literary meeting, which delights M. A. much and is a *coup :* and the Buck[ingham]s to commemorate the majority of Chandos.

Thousand loves to all.
Your affectionate
D.

Before going to Manchester he had ' three fatiguing days of triumph ' at Shrewsbury.

To Mrs. Disraeli.

SHREWSBURY,
Aug. 27.

Wherever I go, I hear of nothing but ' Mrs. Disraeli,' and why she did not come, and when she will come. When the railway is finished, then they count on seeing her very often. Among the shopkeepers, whom I wish most to please, your

[1] *Historic Fancies.*

name and memory are most lively and influential. ' Such a
gay lady, sir ! You never can have a dull moment, sir !'—and
I tell them all that you are a perfect wife as well as a perfect
companion, and that, separated from you for the first[1] time
after five years, we are (alas ! alas !) parted on our wedding
day. The women shed tears, which indeed I can barely
myself restrain. It is only half an hour to post, and I have
come in pretty well, but very tired. A sort of amateur canvass
to-day, calling on all the reputable and influential trades-
people, who seek no other reward for their good offices but
such notice. It is understood, I find, that I am *the tradesmen's
member :* so I don't trouble myself much about the pseudo-
aristocracy and less about the real. The Lawrences, Groves,
Taylors, Lees, are the men. They quite approve as to the
attack on the Government, but a little alarmed in some
quarters, I find, about Popery, monasteries, and John Manners.
This I shall quietly soften down. . . . Our wedding feast must
be on Thursday, but if I die for it I will write you some
verses to-morrow.[2]

Wednesday [Aug. 28].

Yesterday at 8 o'clock to the Bull—a capital meeting. I
made an admirable speech. Enthusiasm very great indeed,
and all malcontents apparently silenced. Taylor the maltster
in the chair. His speech proposing your health a miracle of
rhetoric. He said being your husband was a very good
reason why I was fit to be member for Shrewsbury. Indeed,
the feeling for you here is beyond all imagination. Everybody
enquires after you : high and low. Taylor's speech gave me
a good opening about our first separation and the wedding
day, which is now known all over Shrewsbury. The effect
was very great. . . .
At 8 o'clock to-night a very great meeting at the Lion, some
hundreds and reporters engaged. . . . The only thing that
consoles me for our separation is my strong conviction that
my presence here was absolutely necessary. What might
have injured me, I have now turned to good account. The
feeling of the people is genuine and may be depended on.
They seem all of them quite to appreciate my start this year,
both literary and political.

In his two speeches[3] on this occasion he passed in review
his conduct in Parliament from the time of his previous

---

[1] He forgets the separation in the spring of 1842.
[2] In accordance with an annual custom.
[3] They are reported at length in the *Shropshire Conservative* for Aug. 31,
1844.

visit, immediately after which hostilities to the Government, as we have seen, had begun. The local Conservative paper had welcomed with an exultant shout of 'unqualified satisfaction' the speech on the sugar duties ; and Disraeli's task of defending his present attitude towards the Government proved far easier than the task he had essayed at the time of his previous visit, of defending the support he had up to then given them. The two speeches have been freely quoted in the foregoing pages, but one passage, in which he proclaimed his disinterestedness and independence, must be added here :

I supported the Conservative party as long as they kept to their principles, and when they deserted those principles I voted against them. . . . I have always expressed my feelings with regret when I have differed from the party to which I am attached, but I would rather be nothing than be the mute registrar of the decrees of a Government. The situation of an independent representative is by no means an enviable one. If you sit on the benches behind the Ministers and speak in favor of the Ministers, you are sneered at, and it is said you want a place ; and if you speak against the Ministers you are again sneered at, and it is said you have been refused a place. I can assure you, gentlemen, I am not frightened at these sneers and taunts ; I never asked Sir Robert Peel for a place, and they pass me harmless. When such taunts are used by the Opposition I laugh at them, and consider them as the fair play of party . . . but let Sir Robert Peel, or any of his friends who are likely to know anything of the matter, say that I asked for a place, and I will undertake to give them an answer which shall be perfectly satisfactory.

How he reconciled the statement that he had never asked for a place with the correspondence of September, 1841, there will be a more fitting opportunity hereafter to consider ; but desire for place excluded, there still remained the question of the motive for his exertions, and he faced it with his usual boldness :

There is no doubt, gentlemen, that all men who offer themselves as candidates for public favor have motives of some sort. I candidly acknowledge that I have, and I will tell you what they are : I love fame ; I love public reputation ; I love to live in the eyes of the country ; and it is a glorious thing for a man to do who has had my difficulties to contend against.

A few months before he had written in a higher strain of ' that noble ambition which will not let a man be content unless his intellectual power is recognised by his race . . . the heroic feeling ; the feeling that in old days produced demigods ; without which no State is safe ; without which political institutions are meat without salt ; the Crown a bauble, the Church an establishment, Parliaments debating clubs, and Civilisation itself but a fitful and transient dream.'[1]

To Manchester the Disraelis were accompanied by Manners and Smythe, much to the annoyance of their fathers, the Duke of Rutland and Lord Strangford, who exchanged letters[2] on the subject. ' I lament,' wrote the Duke, ' the influence which Mr. Disraeli has acquired over several of the young British senators, and over your son and mine especially. I do not know Mr. Disraeli by sight, but I have respect only for his talents, which I think he sadly misuses.' Strangford had himself been on terms of intimacy with Disraeli, but he had now, it would appear, begun to harbour doubts as to his former friend's integrity. The doubts may have been engendered by the chagrin with which he watched his son following Disraeli into open opposition, when he hoped to see him repair the ruined fortunes of his house by the aid of Peel's favour. The dialogue between Lord Monmouth and Henry Coningsby has been already given. We seem in this dialogue to hear the authentic voices of the old political order which was passing away, and of that which Young England desired to see in its place, and incidentally we have a wholesome reminder of the realities of politics on which Young England, in its enthusiasm for its own romantic ideal, had boldly declared war, but of which Disraeli, we may be certain, though he could share the enthusiasm, never lost sight. However, on this occasion

[1] *Coningsby*, Bk. V., ch. 1.
[2] *Lives of the Lord Strangfords*, by E. B. de Fonblanque, p. 224.

LORD JOHN MANNERS.

at least romanticism prevailed, and Smythe and Manners supported Disraeli at the Athenæum meeting. It was the culminating point in the glory of Young England. The meeting, Disraeli wrote,[1] was, he believed, 'the largest assemblage ever collected within four walls'; and the three friends made eloquent speeches, which were received with great enthusiasm, and republished in pamphlet form for the benefit of a wider audience. Disraeli's contained a sentence which his sister thought 'sublime,' and which he used afterwards to recall himself with a certain complacency :

Knowledge is like the mystic ladder in the patriarch's dream : its base rests on the primeval earth, its crest is lost in the shadowy splendor of the empyrean ; while the great authors who for traditionary ages have held the chain of science and philosophy, of poesy and erudition, are the angels ascending and descending the sacred scale, and maintaining, as it were, the communication between man and heaven.

Disraeli appears to have stayed in the North for some time, and it was now, probably, that he made that study of the industrial districts of which we see the results in *Sybil*. We find him at Worsley Hall as the guest of Lord Francis Egerton, at Bingley, in the West Riding, as the guest of the Ferrands, and at Fryston as the guest of Monckton Milnes or his father. At Bingley the Ferrands were establishing a system of garden allotments for the benefit of industrial operatives, and endeavouring in other ways to bring classes together ; and there Disraeli made a speech in which he tried to expound the aims of Young England, and insisted on class and party divisions as the crying evil of the time.

We are asked sometimes what we want. We want in the first place to impress upon society that there is such a thing as duty. We don't do that in any spirit of conceit or arrogance ; we don't pretend that we are better than others, but we are anxious to do our duty, and, if so, we think we have a right to call on others, whether rich or poor, to do theirs.

[1] To Lord Londonderry.

If that principle of duty had not been lost sight of for the last fifty years, you would never have heard of the classes into which England is divided. . . .

We want to put an end to that political and social exclusiveness which we believe to be the bane of this country. . . . We don't come out like a pack of pedants to tell you we are prepared to remedy every grievance by the square and rule. . . . It is not so much to the action of laws as to the influence of manners that we must look. . . . But how are manners to influence men if they are divided into classes—if the population of a country becomes a body of sections, a group of hostile garrisons ? . . . We see but little hope for this country so long as that spirit of faction that has been so rampant of late years is fostered and encouraged. We call it a spirit of faction, for the principles on which the parties who nominally divide this country were originally formed have worn out and ceased to exist ; and an association of men, however powerful, without political principles is not a party, but a faction. Of such a state of society the inevitable result is that public passions are excited for private ends, and popular improvement is lost sight of in particular aggrandisement.

At Fryston Disraeli met a young lawyer called Gathorne Hardy, who was to be in later days one of his closest political associates. Hardy has left on record his first impressions of his future chief, and they were not wholly favourable. Disraeli's conversation he found 'far from striking ' ; there was too much striving to be epigrammatic. His judgments of men were ' equally clever and just ' ; but his vanity and self-esteem prevented him from talking freely ' lest he should lose ground.'[1]

To Sarah Disraeli.

Jan. 20, 1845.

You have heard of our sudden expedition to Stowe, and its brilliant success ; her Majesty, Peel, Aberdeen, and all equally distinguishing us by their courtesy. The whole scene sumptuous and a great success for the Duke. The Wednesday before I kept my engagement at Stationers' Hall, where I sat on the right hand of the master, and had to make a speech, which was rather ridiculous, as there were only thirty or forty citizens, grubbing like boys a table of delicacies ; but I seemed

[1] Memoir of Gathorne Hardy, I., p. 53.

to please them, and all came up to be presented in turn to the
great man. Most present were of the time of the first red
sandstone, and before Mercury or Venus were created.

A letter of Mrs. Disraeli's had already conveyed to
Bradenham an account of the party at Stowe :

We were for the first hour in the vestibule, like a flock of
sheep, half lit up, and no seats or fire, only a little hot air
and a great deal of cold wind ; a marble floor. Fancy, dear,
shivering Dizzy, and cross-looking Mary Anne, in black
velvet, hanging sleeves looped up with knots of blue, and
diamond buttons. Head - dress, blue velvet bows and
diamonds. After a time we passed her Majesty and the
Prince, the Duke and Duchess and the rest standing behind,
the Duke giving our names exactly the same as an ordinary
groom, and we making our curtseys and bows. About eleven,
or soon after, her Majesty retired, and then all became joy
and triumph to us. First Sir Robert Peel came to us, shaking
hands most cordially, and remained talking for some time,
then Lord Nugent, introducing his lady, Col. Anson, Sir
James Graham, Lord and Lady de la Warr, Lord Aberdeen.
The Duke almost embraced Dizzy, saying he was one of his
oldest friends ; and then he offered me his arm, taking me
all through the gorgeous splendid scene, through the supper
room and back again, down the middle and up again—
all making way for us, the Queen and your delighted Mary
Anne being the only ladies so distinguished. After this I
retired to a sofa, with the Duchess, who told me that her
Majesty had pointed Dizzy out, saying ' *There's Mr. Disraeli.*'
Do you call all this nothing ? The kind Duchess asked me
to luncheon the next day and to see the Queen's private
apartments.

CHAPTER IX.

SYBIL.

1845.

Sybil; or, The Two Nations, appears to have been begun very soon after the publication of *Coningsby*. 'How are the two nations ?' writes George Smythe in the summer of 1844, the two nations signifying the rich and the poor. With the condition of the rural poor Disraeli had become familiar in his long struggle over the Poor Law, and his visits to the North in the autumns of 1843 and 1844 had shown him the facts of life in the great industrial towns. The publication of the reports of the Children's Employment Commission, and the debates on the Factory Bill in the session of 1844, had fixed attention on the social problem ; and as *Coningsby* treated of party, *Sybil* treated of the people and social conditions. The original design of *Coningsby* had been larger than was then executed.

The derivation and character of political parties ; the condition of the people which had been the consequence of them ; the duties of the Church as a main remedial agency in our present state, were the three principal topics which I intended to treat, but I found they were too vast for the space I had allotted to myself. These were all launched in *Coningsby ;* but the origin and condition of political parties, the first portion of the theme, was the only one completely handled in that work.

Next year, in *Sybil*, I considered the condition of the people. . . . At that time the Chartist agitation was still fresh in the public memory, and its repetition was far from improbable. I had mentioned to my friend, the late Thomas Duncombe, and who was my friend before I entered the House of

250

Commons, something of what I was contemplating ; and he
offered and obtained for my perusal the whole of the correspondence of Feargus O'Connor when conductor of the
Northern Star, with the leaders and chief actors of the Chartist
movement. I had visited and observed with care all the
localities introduced ;[1] and as an accurate and never exaggerated picture of a remarkable period in our domestic history,
and of a popular organisation which in its extent and completeness has perhaps never been equalled, the pages of *Sybil*
may, I venture to believe, be consulted with confidence.[2]

The new novel was published in May, a year after
Coningsby.

To Sarah Disraeli.

May-Day, 1845.

Sybil was finished yesterday ; I thought it never would be ;
the printers were on my heels, and have been for the last
month, but I don't think it can be published till the middle of
the month. . . . I have never been through such a four months,
and hope never again. What with the House of Commons,
which was itself quite enough for a man, and writing 600 pages,
I thought sometimes my head must turn. I have never had
a day, until this, that I have felt, as it were, home for the
holidays.

Sybil made its appearance with a dedication which has
become famous :

I would inscribe this work to one whose noble spirit and
gentle nature ever prompt her to sympathise with the suffering ; to one whose sweet voice has often encouraged, and whose
taste and judgment have ever guided, its pages ; the most
severe of critics, but—a perfect Wife !

Among the odds and ends from Disraeli's pen preserved
by his wife's pious care, there is a bundle of little notes
which he wrote to her while he was composing *Coningsby*
and *Sybil :* reports of his progress, inquiries after her

[1] In his preface to *Sybil* itself, Disraeli stated, with regard to his pictures
of industrial life, that ' the descriptions generally were written from his
own observation ' ; he said nothing of his great indebtedness to the reports of
the Children's Commission, partly, no doubt, because those reports were very
widely known, and still more, perhaps, because a confession that the novel
was founded on a Blue Book would not have been alluring.

[2] General Preface to the Novels, 1870.

health, invitations to a stroll, requests for a glass of wine or permission to smoke a cigar, and one calling her to a consultation—'I wish you would come up and talk a little over a point, if you are not particularly engaged '— which seems to show that his compliment to her taste and judgment was no mere pretence. What was certainly not pretence was his desire that the world should believe in her possession of these and all good qualities. Throughout their married life, when conversing with others, even on subjects beyond the range of her cultivation, he was in the habit, it is said, of bringing her tactfully in by references to her opinions or appeals to her critical judgment ; and woe betide those who fell short in the respect which he himself gave and thought due to her pronouncements !

Sybil received from the critics more praise than even *Coningsby*, and ran through its three editions in the course of the summer. With the critics and with the elect it has remained a favourite ever since. It has been variously praised as 'the sincerest '[1] of Disraeli's novels, as 'the grandest and the most valuable,'[2] and as the foremost in interest both to the student of social history and to the critic of English literature—to the one for its picture of social conditions, and to the other for 'the high comedy of its social and political intrigue.'[3] But it has never really enjoyed the popularity of *Coningsby*. *Sybil* suffers more from being a novel with a purpose, even though the purpose is so high and inspiring. Its real interest is possibly deeper, but it is an interest of classes and of situations, not the interest of personalities that was so piquant in *Coningsby*. When Disraeli is recalled as the creator of the political novel, it is usually *Coningsby*, not *Sybil*, that his readers have in mind.

Sybil, like *Coningsby*, has very little plot, but is a succession of scenes, as *Coningsby* of characters. We begin with a scene of admirable comedy in the golden

---

[1] Lord Morley. [2] Lord Iddesleigh, in his edition of the novel.
[3] H. D. Traill.

saloons of a sumptuous London club, obviously meant for
Crockford's, on the eve of the Derby of 1837. The object
from the first is to emphasise the contrast between the
two nations—between riches and poverty, luxury and
suffering ; between gilded youth of the type of Alfred
Mountchesney, whom we meet at the club, and who
'rather likes bad wine because one gets so bored with good,'
and the miserable toilers whom we afterwards encounter.
In the company of youthful patricians assembled at
Crockford's to discuss the odds on the coming race, we
make the acquaintance of Charles Egremont, the hero of
the novel, a younger brother of the Earl of Marney and
heir-presumptive to the title. An account of the Marney
pedigree and of the origin of the family in the plundering
of the Church by Henry VIII. leads to a long digression
on ' the cause of civil and religious liberty,' the politics of
the Venetian party, the careers of Shelburne and Pitt,
who finally broke their power, and other phases of the
recent political history of England which had not been
presented in *Coningsby*. To all this we shall return.
Then we have the famous scene ' in a palace in a garden,'
the accession of Queen Victoria, which is adroitly made
the occasion for the introduction of the real theme and
purpose of the novel :

In a sweet and thrilling voice, and with a composed mien
which indicates rather the absorbing sense of august duty
than an absence of emotion, THE QUEEN announces her
accession to the throne of her ancestors, and her humble hope
that divine Providence will guard over the fulfilment of her
lofty trust.
The prelates and captains and chief men of her realm then
advance to the throne, and, kneeling before her, pledge their
troth, and take the sacred oaths of allegiance and supremacy.
Allegiance to one who rules over the land that a great
Macedonian could not conquer ; and over a continent of which
even Columbus never dreamed : to the Queen of every sea,
and of nations in every zone.
It is not of these that I would speak ; but of a nation nearer
her footstool, and which at this moment looks to her with
anxiety, with affection, perhaps with hope. Fair and serene,

she has the blood and beauty of the Saxon. Will it be her
proud destiny at length to bear relief to suffering millions, and,
with that soft hand which might inspire troubadours and
guerdon knights, break the last links in the chain of Saxon
thraldom ?

In Charles Egremont and his brother Lord Marney we
have the two contrasted types of aristocrat—the good
and the bad. Marney was ' cynical, devoid of sentiment,
arrogant, literal, hard. He had no imagination, had
exhausted his slight native feeling ; but he was acute,
disputatious, and firm even to obstinacy. He believed
he could pass through existence in adamantine armour,
and always gave you in the business of life the idea of a
man who was conscious you were trying to take him in,
and rather respected you for it, but the working of whose
cold, unkind eye defied you.' His character as a landlord
was revealed by the condition of the rural town of Marney :
a collection of ruined hovels arranged in narrow and
crowded lanes, in which the agricultural labourers lived
amid surroundings of indescribable squalor, till pestilence
or famine released them from their misery. Their sufferings caused no qualms of conscience in Lord Marney.

I wish the people were as well off in every part of the country
as they are on my estate. They get here their eight shillings
a-week, always at least seven, and every hand is at this
moment in employ, except a parcel of scoundrels who prefer
wood-stealing and poaching, and who would prefer wood-
stealing and poaching if you gave them double the wages.
The rate of wages is nothing ; certainty is the thing ; and
every man at Marney may be sure of his seven shillings a week
for at least nine months in the year ; and for the other three,
they can go to the House, and a very proper place for them ;
it is heated with hot air, and has every comfort. . . . The
poor are well off, at least the agricultural poor, very well off
indeed. Their incomes are certain, that is a great point, and
they have no cares, no anxieties ; they always have a resource,
they always have the House. People without cares do not
require so much food as those whose life entails anxieties.

Egremont, unlike his brother, had a generous spirit
and a tender heart. By birth one of the happy few for

whom the world was then made, and by charm of disposition a favourite with all, he had spent an idle youth, and
had barely withstood the efforts of his parents and society
to spoil him ; but a disappointment in love at the age of
twenty-four had arrested him in his career of frivolity
and pleasure, and though, after a period spent in travel
and reflection, he had come back to his old life, it was
with the difference that he was now conscious of wanting an
object.   By the contrivance of his mother, who happened
to be a distinguished ' stateswoman,' he was returned
to Parliament in 1837 ; but it was not there that he was to
find the object he was seeking, but in a chance meeting
with three strangers in the ruins of Marney Abbey.   One
of the strangers was Walter Gerard, who, as Egremont
discovers, was an adherent of the old faith, and, though a
leader of the people, had a refinement of spirit and a feeling
for the past which we should look for in vain in the
typical blatant demagogue or the utilitarian Radical.   His
sense of present-day wrongs did not hinder him from
sympathising with the monks who were so foully driven
from the beautiful abbey they had created :

If the world but only knew what they had lost ! . . .   There
were on an average in every shire at least twenty structures
such as this was ; in this great county double that number :
establishments that were as vast and as magnificent and as
beautiful as your Belvoirs and your Chatsworths, your Went-
worths and your Stowes.   Try to imagine the effect of thirty
or forty Chatsworths in this county, the proprietors of which
were never absent.   You complain enough now of absentees.
The monks were never non-resident.   They expended their
revenue among those whose labor had produced it. . . .
They made the country beautiful, and the people proud of
their country. . . .
As long as the monks existed, the people, when aggrieved,
had property on their side.   And now 'tis all over, and travellers come and stare at these ruins, and think themselves very
wise to moralise over time.   They are the children of violence,
not of time.   It is war that created these ruins, civil war, of
all our civil wars the most inhuman, for it was waged with
the unresisting.   The monasteries were taken by storm, they
were sacked, gutted, battered with warlike instruments,

blown up with gunpowder ; you may see the marks of the
blast against the new tower here.   Never was such a plunder.
The whole face of the country for a century was that of a land
recently invaded by a ruthless enemy ; it was worse than
the Norman Conquest ; nor has England ever lost this character of ravage.   I don't know whether the union workhouses
will remove it.   They are building something for the people
at last.   After an experiment of three centuries, your gaols
being full, and your treadmills losing something of their virtue,
you have given us a substitute for the monasteries.

The second of the three strangers was Stephen Morley,
a socialist editor, eager, high-strung, and fanatical, who
found so much to lament in the world in which he lived
that he could spare no pang for the past ; and the third
was Gerard's daughter Sybil.

Sybil among Disraeli's heroines is like Eva in *Tancred*
or Theodora in *Lothair*—rather, as has been well said,[1]
' the symbol of a great idea ' or the embodiment of a great
enthusiasm than a mere individual, or even the representative of a class.   She stands for the people, for the nation
of the poor, for pity of their sufferings, for their hopes
of redemption.   In an ordinary Chartist heroine there
would have been some strident note of vulgarity or self-
assertion to chill and estrange ; but Sybil, like her father,
is refined and ennobled by her devotion to the old faith,
with its long historical memories, its poetry and romance,
its spiritual mystery, its world-wide charity, and its soul-
subduing power.   Egremont first hears her singing, in
tones of almost supernatural sweetness, the evening hymn
to the Virgin from the Lady's Chapel of the abbey, and
then sees her standing in a vacant and starlit arch in
seraph-like beauty.   From that moment Sybil Gerard is
all the world to him.   Haunted by the memory of her
voice and appearance, he pursues her to Mowbray, a
manufacturing town, where her father is a mill-manager ;
and there, living for a time under an assumed name, he
finds, in conversation with Gerard, with Morley the
socialist, and, above all, with Sybil herself, the mission

---

[1] By Dr. Brandes.

of his life—love of Sybil, and vindication of the wrongs of the poor ; for the two things are one.

Close to Mowbray is a Gothic castle, the seat of Earl de Mowbray, formerly Lord Fitz-Warene, whose Norman name and pedigree are traced with bitter satire to his father, John Warren, a St. James's Street waiter, who had become an Indian nabob and been ennobled by Mr. Pitt. The present peer's mother was the daughter of an Irish Earl, and he himself had married the daughter of a ducal house, and now fully believed in the authenticity of his pedigree. His children had been ' christened by names which the ancient records of the Fitz-Warenes authorised,' and the memory of the waiter was completely obliterated.

Pomp and luxury reign in Mowbray Castle ; in poignant contrast is the misery of the people outside its gates. The career of a Devilsdust, the exactions of the mill-owners Shuffle and Screw, and the picture of the sufferings of the hand-weaver Warner and his starving family, help us to realise the price which England has to pay for her manufacturing greatness. Accompanying Stephen Morley on a mission from Mowbray into some neighbouring mining districts, we are shown other phases of our industrial civilisation. We see a gang issuing from a mine :

Bands of stalwart men, broad-chested and muscular, wet with toil, and black as the children of the tropics ; troops of youth, alas ! of both sexes, though neither their raiment nor their language indicates the difference ; all are clad in male attire ; and oaths that men might shudder at, issue from lips born to breathe words of sweetness. Yet these are to be, some are, the mothers of England ! But can we wonder at the hideous coarseness of their language, when we remember the savage rudeness of their lives ? Naked to the waist, an iron chain fastened to a belt of leather runs between their legs clad in canvas trousers, while on hands and feet an English girl, for twelve, sometimes for sixteen hours a day, hauls and hurries tubs of coals up subterranean roads, dark, precipitous, and plashy ; circumstances that seem to have escaped the notice of the Society for the Abolition of Negro Slavery. Those worthy gentlemen too appear to have been singularly unconscious of the sufferings of the little trappers, which was remarkable, as many of them were in their own employ.

See, too, these emerge from the bowels of the earth ! Infants of four and five years of age, many of them girls, pretty and still soft and timid ; entrusted with the fulfilment of responsible duties, and the nature of which entails on them the necessity of being the earliest to enter the mines and the latest to leave it. Their labor indeed is not severe, for that would be impossible, but it is passed in darkness and in solitude. They endure that punishment which philosophical philanthropy has invented for the direst criminals, and which those criminals deem more terrible than the death for which it is substituted.

We are witnesses of a scene outside a truck-shop which is so harrowing as a picture of cruelty and oppression as to be almost unbearable. And then at the nadir of civilisation we find the squatters' town of Wodgate, with its natural aristocracy of master-workmen, who, though ruthless tyrants, are not unpopular with their vassals ; its ' Bishop ' at the apex, the leader of all in ruthlessness and skill ; and its people without names, morality, or religion, or believing at the best ' in our Lord and Saviour Pontius Pilate, who was crucified to save our sins, and in Moses, Goliath, and the rest of the Apostles.' For this travesty of a creed, as for nearly all that is most startling in Disraeli's pictures of industrial life, there is literal warrant in the Blue Books of the time.

The scene shifts to London in the year 1839, the year of the Chartist petition and of Disraeli's speech thereon. Walter Gerard is a leader in the Chartist Convention, and Sybil is in London with him. In a round of visits to members of Parliament which is made the occasion for the portrayal of a number of amusing types, Gerard meets with Egremont, and discovers that the man whom he had previously known as Franklin, and believed to be a journalist, is an aristocrat, the brother of the tyrant Lord Marney, and presumably, therefore, an enemy of the people. Egremont, however, has been pondering on all that he learnt at Mowbray, and is now in ardent sympathy with the cause of the people—sympathy, that is to say, with their deeper aspirations, combined with faith in the possibility of these aspirations being gradually realised; for he is under no illusion about the crude methods of the demagogues or the crude remedies put forward by the people themselves.

The People are not strong [he says to Sybil]; the People never can be strong. Their attempts at self-vindication will end only in their suffering and confusion. It is civilisation that has effected, that is effecting, this change. It is that increased knowledge of themselves that teaches the educated their social duties. There is a dayspring in the history of this nation, which perhaps those only who are on the mountain tops can as yet recognise. You deem you are in darkness, and I see a dawn. The new generation of the aristocracy of England are not tyrants, not oppressors, Sybil, as you persist in believing. Their intelligence, better than that, their hearts, are open to the responsibility of their position. But the work that is before them is no holiday-work. It is not the fever of superficial impulse that can remove the deep-fixed barriers of centuries of ignorance and crime. Enough that their sympathies are awakened; time and thought will bring the rest. They are the natural leaders of the People, Sybil; believe me they are the only ones.

Sybil, who at first is full of prejudice and suspicion in presence of the newly-discovered aristocrat, and thinks that the gulf between them is impassable, is gradually won over by Egremont's devotion. The awakening and progress of her love for him are treated with the delicacy which Disraeli has always at command in such a situation, and so that no breath of commonplace passion touches a figure so ethereally pure and spiritual in conception. It is Egremont's devotion to the cause she has at heart rather than to herself that awaken's Sybil's interest. The turning-point is his speech on the Chartist petition, in that debate in the House of Commons which had been otherwise so disappointing.

Yes! there was one voice that had sounded in that proud Parliament, that, free from the slang of faction, had dared to express immortal truths : the voice of a noble, who, without being a demagogue, had upheld the popular cause ; had pronounced his conviction that the rights of labor were as sacred

as those of property ; that if a difference were to be established, the interests of the living wealth ought to be preferred ;
who had declared that the social happiness of the millions
should be the first object of a statesman, and that, if this were
not achieved, thrones and dominions, the pomp and power of
courts and empires, were alike worthless.

When the Chartist crisis comes, Egremont is able to
render great services to Sybil, as well as to her father,
who has, however, to undergo a lengthy term of imprison-
ment. Though gratitude is now added to Sybil's other
emotions, Egremont's suit still appears to be hopeless ;
but three years later he wins her consent, after rescuing
her from imminent peril during a strike riot in Lancashire,
in the course of which Gerard and Lord Marney are
killed, and Mowbray Castle sacked and burnt. Egremont by his brother's death has become Earl of Marney ;
and quite needlessly, though in accordance with the
Disraelian practice of piling fortune upon fortune, Sybil
is now herself proved to be of noble blood, and the real
inheritor of the great estates attached to Mowbray Castle.
Before the curtain falls all our other friends are happily
provided for ; and even the tension of the general distress
is relaxed, for, as the author slyly tells us, ' the great
measures of Sir Robert Peel, which produced three good
harvests, have entirely revived trade.'

Sybil has many faults. There are scenes of mere melodrama scattered through its pages ; the dialogues of low
life are often rather Cockney than genuine North-country,
and even regarded as Cockney are not very happy ; and
the character of Morley, the socialist editor, is a great
and obvious failure. He is quite incoherent, at one
moment a kindly and well-meaning theorist, at another
a melodramatic villain. There is no character in the
book so arresting as Sidonia in *Coningsby*, and Sidonia
does not reappear. With his millions, his lack of sympathy, and his purely intellectual outlook, he would have
been completely out of harmony with the spirit and
motive of the novel. The part he played in *Coningsby* is
filled by Sybil herself ; and Sybil, though very winning,

is almost too impersonal and too purely ethereal to awaken the deepest interest.

But the defects of the book are far outweighed by its merits. If Sidonia is missing, our old friends Taper and Tadpole reappear, and delight us by their naïve and elementary plotting. It is, indeed, in the chapters of social and political satire that Disraeli here, as always, is found at his best. Nothing could excel the picture of the scramble for office after the Jamaica division of 1839, with the subsequent disappointment of the hopes of the intriguers by the Bedchamber crisis. Admirable, too, are the great political ladies who 'think they can govern the world by what they call their social influences.' There is first Lady St. Julians, who represents the famous Sarah, Countess of Jersey, and whose theory of political motives is so simple and so cynical.

People get into Parliament to get on ; their aims are indefinite. If they have indulged in hallucinations about place before they enter the House, they are soon freed from such distempered fancies ; they find they have no more talent than other people, and if they had, they learn that power, patronage, and pay are reserved for us and our friends. Well then, like practical men, they look to some result, and they got it. They are asked out to dinner more than they would be ; they move rigmarole resolutions at nonsensical public meetings ; and they get invited with their women to assemblies at their leader's, where they see stars and blue ribbons, and above all, us, who, they little think, in appearing on such occasions, make the greatest conceivable sacrifice. . . . Ask them to a ball, and they will give you their votes ; invite them to dinner, and, if necessary, they will rescind them ; but cultivate them, remember their wives at assemblies, and call their daughters, if possible, by their right names ; and they will not only change their principles or desert the party for you, but subscribe their fortunes, if necessary, and lay down their lives in your service.

Then there is the more attractive Marchioness of Deloraine, who is intended as a portrait of Disraeli's friend Frances Anne, Marchioness of Londonderry.[1]

---

[1] A copy of *Sybil* which he sent to Lady Londonderry led to the revival of a friendship which had been in abeyance since his marriage.

She had great knowledge of society, and some acquaintance with human nature, which she fancied she had fathomed to its centre ; she piqued herself upon her tact, and indeed she was very quick, but she was so energetic that her art did not always conceal itself ; very worldly, she was nevertheless not devoid of impulse ; she was animated, and would have been extremely agreeable, if she had not restlessly aspired to wit ; and would certainly have exercised much more influence in society, if she had not been so anxious to show it.

Thirdly there is Lady Firebrace, from whom nothing appeared to be concealed, either in the inmost mind of the Sovereign, the cabinets of the Whigs, or the clubs of the Tories.

' I would sooner meet any woman in London than Lady Firebrace,' said Mr. Berners ; ' she makes me uneasy for the day ; she contrives to convince me that the whole world are employed behind my back in abusing or ridiculing me.'
' It is her way,' said Egerton ; ' she proves her zeal by showing you that you are odious. It is very successful with people of weak nerves. Scared at their general unpopularity, they seek refuge with the very person who at the same time assures them of their odium and alone believes it unjust. She rules that poor old goose, Lady Gramshawe, who feels that Lady Firebrace makes her life miserable, but is convinced that if she break with the torturer, she loses her only friend.'

Other characters in *Sybil* that live in the memory are Lady Firebrace's husband, Sir Vavasour, the baronet whose great aim in life is the vindication of the rights of his order until his zeal is quenched in the glory of a higher title; Baptist Hatton, the peerage lawyer, and his strangely contrasted brother, the Bishop of Hellhouse Yard ; the Ladies Joan and Maud Fitz-Warene ; Captain Grouse, the parasite, who was

a kind of aide-de-camp of the earl, killed birds and carved them, played billiards with him and lost, had, indeed, every accomplishment that could please woman or ease man, could sing, dance, draw, make artificial flies, break horses, exercise a supervision over stewards and bailiffs, and make everybody comfortable by taking everything on his own shoulders :

and finally the generic portrait of

those middle-aged nameless gentlemen of easy circumstances who haunt clubs, and dine a great deal at each other's houses and chambers ; men who travel regularly a little and gossip regularly a great deal ; who lead a sort of facile, slipshod existence, doing nothing, yet mightily interested in what others do ; great critics of little things ; profuse in minor luxuries, and inclined to the respectable practice of a decorous profligacy ; peering through the window of a club-house as if they were discovering a planet ; and usually much excited about things with which they have no concern, and personages who never heard of them.

Some of the humbler characters are perhaps less surely drawn than those in politics and society ; though, in spite of his love of grandeur, Disraeli had a remarkable power of entering into the minds and feelings of the poor, and exhibits it in many of his pictures of low life in *Sybil.*

'I understand he is crotchety,' says Mr. Egerton of Mr. Charles Egremont. 'Well, that will not do for Peel. He does not like crotchety men,' Mr. Berners replies. This is one of several shots at the Minister which betray Disraeli's growing resentment. Elsewhere, in a bitter aside, he writes of ' the times in which we live . . . when there is no treason except voting against a Minister, who, though he may have changed all the policy which you have been elected to support, expects your vote and confidence all the same.' But most noteworthy of all is the Aristophanic outburst against the solemn humbug of politics, of which Peel was the incarnation, in the following dialogue between ' a gentleman of Downing Street ' and Mr. Hoaxem :

' Well, Mr. Hoaxem,' said the gentleman in Downing Street, as that faithful functionary entered, ' there are some deputations I understand to-day. You must receive them, as I am going to Windsor. What are they ?'
' There are only two, sir, of moment. The rest I could easily manage.'
' And these two ?'
' In the first place, there is our friend Colonel Bosky, the members for the county of Calfshire, and a deputation of tenant farmers. . . .'

'Well, you know what to say,' said the gentleman in Downing Street. 'Tell them generally, that they are quite mistaken; prove to them particularly that my only object has been to render protection more protective, by making it practical, and divesting it of the surplusage of odium; . . . and that as for the income-tax, they will be amply compensated for it, by their diminished cost of living through the agency of that very tariff of which they are so superficially complaining.'

'Their diminished cost of living!' said Mr. Hoaxem, a little confused. 'Would not that assurance, I humbly suggest, clash a little with my previous demonstration that we had arranged that no reduction of prices should take place?'

'Not at all; your previous demonstration is of course true, but at the same time you must impress upon them the necessity of general views to form an opinion of particular instances. As for example, a gentleman of five thousand pounds per annum pays to the income-tax, which by-the-bye always call property-tax, one hundred and fifty pounds a-year. Well, I have materially reduced the duties on eight hundred articles. The consumption of each of those articles by an establishment of five thousand pounds per annum cannot be less than one pound per article. The reduction of price cannot be less than a moiety; therefore a saving of four hundred per annum; which, placed against the deduction of the property-tax, leaves a clear increase of income of two hundred and fifty pounds per annum; by which you see that a property-tax, in fact, increases income.'

'I see,' said Mr. Hoaxem, with an admiring glance. 'And what am I to say to the deputation of the manufacturers of Mowbray, complaining of the great depression of trade, and the total want of remunerating profits?'

'You must say exactly the reverse,' said the gentleman in Downing Street. 'Show them how much I have done to promote the revival of trade. First of all, in making provisions cheaper; cutting off at one blow half the protection on corn, as, for example, at this moment under the old law the duty on foreign wheat would have been twenty-seven shillings a quarter; under the new law it is thirteen. To be sure, no wheat could come in at either price, but that does not alter the principle. Then, as to live cattle, show how I have entirely opened the trade with the Continent in live cattle. . . . This cheapness of provisions will permit them to compete with the foreigner in all neutral markets, in time beat them in their own. It is a complete compensation, too, for the property-tax, which, impress upon them, is a great experiment and entirely for their interests. Ring the changes on great measures and great experiments till it is time to go down and make a House. Your official duties, of course, must not be interfered with. They will take the hint. I have no doubt you will get through the business very well, Mr. Hoaxem, particularly if you be " frank and explicit " ; that is the right line to take when you wish to conceal your own mind and to confuse the minds of others. Good morning !'

'That the author is a man of talent there can be no doubt,' said a reviewer of *Sybil*, 'and scarcely any that if he had deeper passions and a larger heart he would be a man of genius.' Disraeli's most conspicuous limitations as an artist are, indeed, a certain lack of emotional depth, of warmth in his sympathy and geniality in his laughter—all associated with a tendency to look at life too exclusively through the eyes of ambition. But these limitations are less visible in *Sybil* than in any other of his novels. For once he came near forgetting himself in the enthusiasm of occupation with his subject. 'The sincerest of his novels ' is the verdict, already quoted, of one eminent critic. If the satire of the rich and powerful is unsparing, it is relieved by a sympathy with the poor and lowly, of which no one can fail to see the depth and sincerity. Nor, though the attack on the existing order, or, rather, the existing temper, in politics and society is more daring than in *Coningsby*, and the satire more pungent, is there any excess of gloom or bitterness in the book. The most lurid scenes in the panorama of industrial life are relieved by genuine touches of humour and pathos ; and if we are shown the darkness, there is always light to make it visible. Against the mill-owners Shuffle and Screw there is to be set Mr. Trafford ; against the tyrant Lord Marney there is to be set his brother Charles Egremont ; against the Vicar, who was Lord Marney's model of a priest because ' he left everybody alone,' there is to be set Aubrey St. Lys. We see, in fact, the manufacturers, the aristocracy, and the Church, all awaking to a sense of duty in the new generation.

'The author of *Sybil*,' says Lord Morley, 'seems to have apprehended the real magnitude, and even the nature, of the social crisis [brought about by the rapid

growth of an industrial population]. Mr. Disraeli's brood-
ing imaginativeness of conception gave him a view of the
extent of the social revolution as a whole, which was
wider, if it did not go deeper, than that of any other contemporary observer.'[1] To have rightly grasped the
problem was no slight step towards finding a solution.
Disraeli in practice was earnest in his purpose to seek
and find a remedy for the ailment of which his diagnosis
was so sure ; but from the point of view of art it matters
little that the remedy suggested in the novel is not very
definite. Comprehension and cure, he tells us at the end,
go hand in hand ; ' it is the past alone that can explain
the present, and it is youth that alone can mould the
remedial future.' Whatever it be as social or political
theory, the conception of the multitude being emancipated by the energy and devotion of our youth from their
long yoke of bondage, and converted into a privileged
and prosperous people, is in the true romantic manner.
' We live in an age when to be young and to be indifferent
can no longer be synonymous. We must prepare for the
coming hour. The claims of the future are represented
by suffering millions, and the Youth of a Nation are the
trustees of posterity.'

[1] *Life of Cobden*, I., p. 297. Lord Morley proceeds : ' To accidents of his
position in society and necessities of personal ambition, it must, I suppose,
be attributed that one who conceived so truly the seriousness of the problem,
should have brought nothing better to its solution than the childish bathos
of Young England.' This sentence was written more than thirty years ago,
and it is perhaps best regarded as an attempt, by a writer who had just
been betrayed into needless generosity to a political opponent, to restore
the political balance. No one knows better than Lord Morley himself that
to have given a sincere and vivid picture of the social state of England was,
even in the field of practice, a very great achievement ; and whatever point
there may be in the gibe at Young England, Lord Morley does not explain
what Disraeli could have done either as novelist or statesman more than
in fact he did. Before *Sybil* appeared Young England had practically
ceased to exist, but Disraeli's exertions in the cause of social regeneration
run through his subsequent life. Lord Morley in his book proceeds at
once to show that Cobden's *laisser faire* solution, which it was his immediate
business to exalt, left untouched the whole question of the relations between
capital and labour, and that the Factory Acts and other social legislation
which Cobden opposed were necessary to progress. This legislation Disraeli
strenuously supported while he was only a private member ; and when he
finally came to power he put, as we shall see, the coping-stone on the edifice.

CHAPTER X.

THE TORY IDEA.

1844–1845.

Coningsby and *Sybil* are not only works of art, but the manifesto of Young England, and, as such, political documents. Woven into their texture there is a theory of English history and of modern English politics which is nowhere else in Disraeli's works so explicitly developed, though we have seen it in the *Vindication* in an embryonic form. As expounded in *Coningsby* and *Sybil*, it bears some marks of a merely transient bias due to the esoteric influence of Young England ; but in all essentials it represents Disraeli's permanent conception of what may be called the Tory Idea, and of the background of history in which he found that idea ; and it is worth disengaging, as it lies at the root of all his convictions and conduct as a statesman.

Let us begin with the following passage from the concluding pages of *Sybil :*

The written history of our country for the last ten reigns has been a mere phantasma, giving to the origin and consequence of public transactions a character and color in every respect dissimilar to their natural form and hue. In this mighty mystery all thoughts and things have assumed an aspect and title contrary to their real quality and style : Oligarchy has been called Liberty ; an exclusive Priesthood has been christened a National Church ; Sovereignty has been the title of something that has had no dominion, while absolute power has been wielded by those who profess themselves the servants of the People. In the selfish strife of factions, two great existences have been blotted out of the history of England, the Monarch and the Multitude ; as the power of the

Crown has diminished, the privileges of the People have disappeared ; till at length the sceptre has become a pageant,
and its subject has degenerated again into a serf.[1]

The real story opens with an event anterior even to
'the last ten reigns,' the fall of the Papacy in England,
and the simultaneous foundation of the modern English
aristocracy.

It is in the plunder of the Church that we must seek for the
primary cause of our political exclusion. . . . That unhal-
lowed booty created a factitious aristocracy, ever fearful that
they might be called upon to regorge their sacrilegious spoil.
To prevent this, they took refuge in political religionism, and
paltering with the disturbed consciences, or the pious fantasies,
of a portion of the people, they organised them into religious
sects. These became the unconscious Prætorians of their ill-
gotten domains. At the head of these religionists, they have
continued ever since to govern, or powerfully to influence,
this country. They have in that time pulled down thrones
and churches, changed dynasties, abrogated and remodelled
parliaments ; they have disfranchised Scotland, and confiscated Ireland. One may admire the vigor and consistency
of the Whig party, and recognise in their career that unity of
purpose that can only spring from a great principle ; but the
Whigs introduced sectarian religion, and sectarian religion
led to political exclusion.[2]

In the pursuit of their policy of political religionism,
the great families came into conflict with the Crown and
the Church of England, which interposed to save the
Catholics from Puritan persecution, but only brought
upon themselves odium and mistrust. From one point
of view, Charles I. may be regarded as the victim of 'the
dark and relentless bigotry of Calvinism.' If 'he had
hanged all the Catholic priests that Parliament petitioned
him to execute, he would never have lost his crown.'[3]
From another point of view, this 'virtuous and able monarch' laid down his life in the cause of the poor, martyred

because, among other benefits projected for his people, he was
of opinion that it was more for their advantage that the

---

[1] *Sybil*, Bk. VI. ch. 13.   [2] *Coningsby*, Bk. II. ch. 1.
[3] *Ibid.*, Bk. III. ch. 5.

economic service of the state should be supplied by direct taxation levied by an individual known to all, than by indirect taxation, raised by an irresponsible and fluctuating assembly. But, thanks to parliamentary patriotism, the people of England were saved from ship-money, which money the wealthy paid, and only got in its stead the customs and excise, which the poor mainly supply. Rightly was King Charles surnamed the Martyr ; for he was the holocaust of direct taxation. Never yet did man lay down his heroic life for so great a cause: the cause of the Church and the cause of the Poor.[1]

The great object of the Whig leaders from the first movement under Hampden was, in words quoted already, 'to establish in England a high aristocratic republic on the model of the Venetian, then the study and admiration of all speculative politicians.' 'We should have had the Venetian Republic in 1640 had it not been for the Puritans.'[2] Geneva on that occasion prevailed over Venice, but the turn of Venice came in 1688. The Revolution of that year has been much misunderstood. 'That the last of the Stuarts had any other object in his impolitic manœuvres than an impracticable scheme to blend the two Churches there is now authority to disbelieve ' ; nor is it credible 'that the English nation (at all times a religious and Catholic people, but who even in the days of the Plantagenets were anti-papal) were in any danger in his time of again falling under the yoke of the Pope of Rome.'

If James II. had really attempted to re-establish popery in this country, the English people, who had no hand in his overthrow, would doubtless soon have stirred and secured their ' Catholic and Apostolic Church,' independent of any foreign dictation ; the Church to which they still regularly profess their adherence ; and, being a practical people, it is possible that they might have achieved their object and yet retained their native princes ; under which circumstances we might have been saved from the triple blessings of Venetian politics, Dutch finance, and French wars.[3]

[1] *Sybil*, Bk. IV. ch. 1   [2] *Coningsby*, Bk. VII. ch. 4.
[3] *Sybil*, Bk. I. ch. 3.

James's indiscretions gave, however, a colour to the pretext that the cause of civil and religious liberty, ' the cause for which Hampden had died in the field, and Russell on the scaffold,' was once more in danger ; and under this pretext, but really ' alarmed at the prevalent impression that King James intended to insist on the restitution of the Church estates to their original purposes, to wit, the education of the people and the maintenance of the poor,' the great Whig families joined ' in calling over the Prince of Orange and a Dutch army, to vindicate those popular principles which, somehow or other, the people would never support.'[1] Religious liberty, when achieved, ' took the shape of a discipline which at once anathematised a great portion of the nation, and, virtually establishing Puritanism in Ireland, laid the foundation of those mischiefs which are now endangering the Empire.' Civil liberty took the shape of the Venetian constitution, though not without a struggle. William III., when he became King, did not prove a pliant instrument in the hands of the oligarchy.

He told the Whig leaders, ' I will not be a Doge.' He balanced parties ; he baffled them as the Puritans baffled them fifty years before. The reign of Anne was a struggle between the Venetian and the English systems. Two great Whig nobles, Argyle and Somerset, worthy of seats in the Council of Ten, forced their Sovereign on her deathbed to change the ministry. They accomplished their object. They brought in a new family on their own terms. George I. was a Doge ; George II. was a Doge ; they were what William III., a great man, would not be. George III. tried not to be a Doge, but it was impossible materially to resist the deeply-laid combination. He might get rid of the Whig magnificoes, but he could not rid himself of the Venetian constitution. And a Venetian constitution did govern England from the accession of the House of Hanover until 1832.[2]

The motive of ' the Dutch invasion of 1688 ' was on the side of the invaders wholly financial.

---

[1] *Sybil*, Bk. I. ch. 3.   [2] *Coningsby*, Bk. V. ch. 2.

The Prince of Orange had found that the resources of Holland, however considerable, were inadequate to sustain him in his internecine rivalry with the great sovereign of France. In an authentic conversation which has descended to us, held by William at the Hague with one of the prime abettors of the invasion, the prince did not disguise his motives; he said, ' Nothing but such a constitution as you have in England can have the credit that is necessary to raise such sums as a great war requires.' The prince came, and used our constitution for his purpose : he introduced into England the system of Dutch finance. The principle of that system was to mortgage industry in order to protect property : abstractedly, nothing can be conceived more unjust ; its practice in England has been equally injurious. . . . It has made debt a national habit; it has made credit the ruling power, not the exceptional auxiliary, of all transactions ; it has introduced a loose, inexact, haphazard, and dishonest spirit in the conduct of both public and private life ; a spirit dazzling and yet dastardly ; reckless of consequences and yet shrinking from responsibility. And in the end, it has so overstimulated the energies of the population to maintain the material engagements of the state, and of society at large, that the moral condition of the people has been entirely lost sight of.[1]

To William we also owe the tradition of hostility to France which ranks with Venetian politics and Dutch finance as the third of the triple blessings conferred on us by the Revolution. Against these, ' in their happiest days, and with their happiest powers, struggled the three greatest of English statesmen — Bolingbroke, Shelburne, and, lastly, the son of Chatham.' Bolingbroke had been dealt with at length in the *Vindication*, but in a list of twenty English statesmen given in that tract neither Shelburne nor Pitt had even been mentioned. Shelburne, we are told in *Sybil*, is ' one of the suppressed characters of English history.' As early as 1842 Disraeli had discovered that he was ' the most remarkable man of his age,'[2] and he now introduces him as ' the ablest and most accomplished minister of the eighteenth century.' After endeavouring to establish a succession

[1] *Sybil*, Bk. I. ch. 3. [2] See p. 133.

of influence and ideas between Bolingbroke and Shelburne, through Carteret, whose daughter Shelburne had married, he proceeds :

> Lord Shelburne, influenced probably by the example and the traditionary precepts of his eminent father-in-law, appears early to have held himself aloof from the patrician connexion, and entered public life as the follower of Bute in the first great effort of George III. to rescue the sovereignty from what Lord Chatham called ' the Great Revolution families.' He became in time a member of Lord Chatham's last administration ; one of the strangest and most unsuccessful efforts to aid the grandson of George II. in his struggle for political emancipation. Lord Shelburne adopted from the first the Bolingbroke system ; a real royalty, in lieu of the chief magistracy ; a permanent alliance with France, instead of the whig scheme of viewing in that power the natural enemy of England ; and, above all, a plan of commercial freedom, the germ of which may be found in the long-maligned negotiations of Utrecht, but which, in the instance of Lord Shelburne, were soon in time matured by all the economical science of Europe, in which he was a proficient. Lord Shelburne seems to have been of a reserved and somewhat astute disposition : deep and adroit, he was however brave and firm. His knowledge was extensive and even profound. He was a great linguist ; he pursued both literary and scientific investigations ; his house was frequented by men of letters, especially those distinguished by their political abilities or economical attainments. He maintained the most extensive private correspondence of any public man of his time. The earliest and most authentic information reached him from all courts and quarters of Europe ; and it was a common phrase, that the minister of the day sent to him often for the important information which the Cabinet could not itself command. Lord Shelburne was the first great minister who comprehended the rising importance of the middle class, and foresaw in its future power a bulwark for the throne against ' the Great Revolution families.' Of his qualities in council we have no record ; there is reason to believe that his administrative ability was conspicuous ; his speeches prove that, if not supreme, he was eminent, in the art of parliamentary disputation, while they show on all the questions discussed a richness and variety of information, with which the speeches of no statesman of that age except Mr. Burke can compare.[1]

---

[1] *Sybil*, Bk. I. ch. 3.

The place of Burke himself in Disraeli's historical
scheme is explained in the following passage :

The situation of the Venetian party in the wane of the
eighteenth century had become extremely critical. . . .
Whiggism was putrescent in the nostrils of the nation ; we
were probably on the eve of a bloodless yet important
revolution ; when Rockingham, a virtuous magnifico, alarmed
and disgusted, resolved to revive something of the pristine
purity and high-toned energy of the old whig connexion,
appealed to his ' new generation ' from a degenerate age,
arrayed under his banner the generous youth of the whig
families, and was fortunate to enlist in the service the supreme
genius of Edmund Burke.

Burke effected for the whigs what Bolingbroke in a preceding
age had done for the tories : he restored the moral existence
of the party. He taught them to recur to the ancient principles of their connexion, and suffused those principles with
all the delusive splendor of his imagination. He raised the
tone of their public discourse ; he breathed a high spirit into
their public acts. . . . He fought the whig fight with a two-edged
weapon : he was a great writer ; as an orator he was transcen-
dent. In a dearth of that public talent for the possession of
which the whigs have generally been distinguished, Burke
came forward and established them alike in the parliament
and the country. And what was his reward ? No sooner had
a young and dissolute noble, who, with some of the aspirations
of a Cæsar, oftener realised the conduct of a Catiline, appeared
on the stage, and, after some inglorious tergiversation, adopted
their colors, than they transferred to him the command which
had been won by wisdom and genius, vindicated by unrivalled
knowledge, and adorned by accomplished eloquence. : . .

Hard necessity made Mr. Burke submit to the yoke, but
the humiliation could never be forgotten. Nemesis favours
genius ; the inevitable hour at length arrived. A voice like
the Apocalypse sounded over England, and even echoed in
all the courts of Europe. Burke poured forth the vials of his
hoarded vengeance into the agitated heart of Christendom ;
he stimulated the panic of a world by the wild pictures of his
inspired imagination ; he dashed to the ground the rival who
had robbed him of his hard-earned greatness ; rent in twain
the proud oligarchy that had dared to use and to insult him ;
and, followed with servility by the haughtiest and the most
timid of its members, amid the frantic exultation of his
country, he placed his heel upon the neck of the ancient
serpent.[1]

    [1] *Sybil*, Bk. I. ch. 3.

Lord Shelburne had been 'the man selected by George III. as his champion against the Venetian party after the termination of the American war.'

The prosecution of that war they had violently opposed, though it had originated in their own policy. First minister in the House of Lords, Shelburne entrusted the lead in the House of Commons to his Chancellor of the Exchequer, the youthful Pitt. The administration was brief, but it was not inglorious. It obtained peace, and, for the first time since the Revolution, introduced into modern debate the legitimate principles on which commerce should be conducted. It fell before the famous Coalition with which ' the Great Revolution families ' commenced their fiercest and their last contention for the patrician government of royal England.

In the heat of that great strife, the king, in the second hazardous exercise of his prerogative, entrusted the perilous command to Pitt. Why Lord Shelburne on that occasion was set aside, will perhaps always remain a mysterious passage of our political history, nor have we space on the present occasion to attempt to penetrate its motives. Perhaps the monarch, with a sense of the rising sympathies of his people, was prescient of the magic power of youth in touching the heart of a nation. Yet it would not be an unprofitable speculation, if for a moment we pause to consider what might have been the consequences to our country if Mr. Pitt had been content for a season again to lead the Commons under Lord Shelburne, and to have secured for England the unrivalled knowledge and dexterity of that statesman in the conduct of our affairs during the confounding fortunes of the French revolution. Lord Shelburne was the only English minister competent to the place : he was the only public man who had the previous knowledge requisite to form accurate conclusions on such a conjuncture ; his remaining speeches on the subject attest the amplitude of his knowledge and the accuracy of his views ; and in the rout of Jena, or the agony of Austerlitz, one cannot refrain from picturing the shade of Shelburne haunting the Cabinet of Pitt, as the ghost of Canning is said occasionally to linger about the Speaker's chair, and smile sarcastically on the conscientious mediocrities who pilfered his hard-earned honors.[1]

During the happier years of Pitt's own career 'the influence of the mind of Shelburne may be traced throughout his policy.'

[1] *Sybil*, Bk. I. ch. 3.

It was Lansdowne House that made Pitt acquainted with Dr. Price, a dissenting minister, whom Lord Shelburne, when at the head of affairs, courageously offered to make his private secretary, and who furnished Mr. Pitt, among other important suggestions, with his original plan of the sinking fund. The commercial treaties of '87 were struck in the same mint, and are notable as the first effort made by the English government to emancipate the country from the restrictive policy which had been introduced by the ' glorious revolution ' ; memorable epoch, that presented England at the same time with a corn-law and a public debt. But on no subject was the magnetic influence of the descendant of Sir William Petty more decided than in the resolution of his pupil to curb the power of the patrician party by an infusion from the middle classes into the government of the country. Hence the origin of Mr. Pitt's famous and long-misconceived plans of parliamentary reform. Was he sincere, is often asked by those who neither seek to discover the causes, nor are capable of calculating the effects of public transactions. Sincere ! Why, he was struggling for his existence ! And when, baffled, first by the Venetian party, and afterwards by the panic of Jacobinism, he was forced to forego his direct purpose, he still endeavoured partially to effect it by a circuitous process. He created a plebeian aristocracy and blended it with the patrician oligarchy. He made peers of second-rate squires and fat graziers. He caught them in the alleys of Lombard Street, and clutched them from the counting-houses of Cornhill. When Mr. Pitt, in an age of Bank restriction, declared that every man with an estate of ten thousand a-year had a right to be a peer, he sounded the knell of ' the cause for which Hampden had died on the field, and Sydney on the scaffold.'

In ordinary times the pupil of Shelburne would have raised this country to a state of great material prosperity, and removed or avoided many of those anomalies which now perplex us ; but he was not destined for ordinary times ; and, though his capacity was vast and his spirit lofty, he had not that passionate and creative genius required by an age of revolution. The French outbreak was his evil dæmon : he had not the means of calculating its effect upon Europe. He had but a meagre knowledge himself of continental politics : he was assisted by an inefficient diplomacy. His mind was lost in a convulsion of which he neither could comprehend the causes nor calculate the consequences ; and, forced to act, he acted not only violently, but in exact opposition to [? accordance with] the very system he was called into political existence to combat ; he appealed to the fears, the prejudices, and the passions of a privileged class, revived the old policy of the oligarchy he had extinguished, and plunged into all the ruinous excesses of French war and Dutch finance.[1]

From the death of the younger Pitt to 1825 'the political history of England is a history of great events and little men.'[2] Among the statesmen that have figured in England since the accession of the present family, 'we may doubt whether there be one, with the exception, perhaps, of the Duke of Newcastle, who would have been a worthy colleague of the council of Mr. Perceval, or the early cabinet of Lord Liverpool.' 'Assuredly the genius of Bolingbroke and the sagacity of Walpole would have recoiled from such men.'

This factious league had shuffled themselves into power by clinging to the skirts of a great minister, the last of Tory statesmen, but who, in the unparalleled and confounding emergencies of his latter years, had been forced, unfortunately for England, to relinquish Toryism. His successors inherited all his errors without the latent genius, which in him might have still rallied and extricated him from the consequences of his disasters. His successors did not merely inherit his errors ; they exaggerated, they caricatured them. They rode into power on a spring-tide of all the rampant prejudices and rancorous passions of their time. From the King to the boor their policy was a mere pandering to public ignorance. Impudently usurping the name of that party of which nationality, and therefore universality, is the essence, these pseudo-Tories made Exclusion the principle of their political constitution, and Restriction the genius of their commercial code. . . .
The peace of Paris found the government of this country in the hands of a body of men of whom it is no exaggeration to say that they were ignorant of every principle of every branch of political science. So long as our domestic administration was confined merely to the raising of a revenue, they levied taxes with gross facility from the industry of a country too busy to criticise or complain. But when the excitement and distraction of war had ceased, and they were forced to survey the social elements that surrounded them, they seemed, for the first time, to have become conscious of their own incapacity. These men, indeed, were the mere children of routine. They prided themselves on being prac-

---

[1] *Sybil*, Bk. I. ch. 3.   [2] *Ibid.*

tical men.   In the language of this defunct school of statesmen,
a practical man is a man who practises the blunders of his
predecessors.

Now commenced that Condition-of-England Question of
which our generation hears so much.   During five-and-twenty
years every influence that can develop the energies and
resources of a nation had been acting with concentrated stimu-
lation on the British Isles.   National peril and national glory ;
the perpetual menace of invasion, the continual triumph of
conquest ; the most extensive foreign commerce that was ever
conducted by a single nation ; an illimitable currency ; an
internal trade supported by swarming millions, whom manufactures and inclosure-bills summoned into existence ; above
all, the supreme control obtained by man over mechanic
power, these are some of the causes of that rapid advance of
material civilisation in England, to which the annals of the
world can afford no parallel.   But there was no proportionate
advance in our moral civilisation.   In the hurry-skurry of
money-making, men-making, and machine-making, we had
altogether outgrown, not the spirit, but the organisation, of
our institutions.

The peace came ; the stimulating influences suddenly ceased ;
the people, in a novel and painful position, found themselves
without guides.   They went to the ministry ; they asked to
be guided ; they asked to be governed.   Commerce requested
a code ; trade required a currency ; the unfranchised subject
solicited his equal privilege ; suffering labor clamored for
its rights ; a new race demanded education.   What did the
ministry do ?

They fell into a panic.   Having fulfilled during their lives
the duties of administration, they were frightened because
they were called upon, for the first time, to perform the functions of government.   Like all weak men, they had recourse
to what they called strong measures.   They determined to
put down the multitude.   They thought they were imitating
Mr. Pitt, because they mistook disorganisation for sedition.[1]

Presently, however, ' the Arch-Mediocrity who pre-
sided, rather than ruled, over this Cabinet of Mediocrities '
began to realise the necessity of importing into his
Ministry talents and knowledge in order to equip it for
the task of government.

The Arch-Mediocrity had himself some glimmering traditions of political science.   He was sprung from a laborious

[1] Coningsby, Bk. II. ch. 1.

stock, had received some training, and though not a statesman, might be classed among those whom the Lord Keeper
Williams used to call 'statemongers.' In a subordinate
position his meagre diligence and his frigid method might
not have been without value ; but the qualities that he possessed were misplaced ; nor can any character be conceived
less invested with the happy properties of a leader. In the
conduct of public affairs his disposition was exactly the reverse
of that which is the characteristic of great men. He was
peremptory in little questions, and great ones he left open.

In the natural course of events, in 1819 there ought to have
been a change of government, and another party in the state
should have entered into office ; but the Whigs, though they
counted in their ranks at that period an unusual number of
men of great ability, and formed, indeed, a compact and
spirited opposition, were unable to contend against the new
adjustment of borough influence which had occurred during
the war, and under the protracted administration by which
that war had been conducted. New families had arisen
on the Tory side that almost rivalled old Newcastle himself
in their electioneering management ; and it was evident that,
unless some reconstruction of the House of Commons could
be effected, the Whig party could never obtain a permanent
hold of official power. Hence, from that period, the Whigs
became Parliamentary Reformers.

It was inevitable, therefore, that the country should be
governed by the same party ; indispensable that the ministry
should be renovated by new brains and blood. Accordingly,
a Mediocrity, not without repugnance, was induced to with-
draw, and the great name of Wellington supplied his place in
council. . . . Another, and a very distinguished Mediocrity,
who would not resign, was thrust out, and Mr. Peel became
Secretary of State. . . . A short time after this, a third
and most distinguished Mediocrity died ; and Canning, whom
they had twice worried out of the cabinet, where they had
tolerated him some time in an obscure and ambiguous
position, was recalled just in time from his impending banish-
ment, installed in the first post in the Lower House, and
intrusted with the seals of the Foreign Office. . . .

The accession of Mr. Canning to the cabinet, in a position,
too, of surpassing influence, soon led to a further weeding of
the Mediocrities, and, among other introductions, to the
memorable entrance of Mr. Huskisson. In this wise did that
cabinet, once notable only for the absence of all those qualities
which authorise the possession of power, come to be generally
esteemed as a body of men, who, for parliamentary eloquence,
official practice, political information, sagacity in council, and

a due understanding of their epoch, were inferior to none that
had directed the policy of the empire since the Revolution.

If we survey the tenor of the policy of the Liverpool Cabinet
during the latter moiety of its continuance, we shall find its
characteristic to be a partial recurrence to those frank principles of government which Mr. Pitt had revived during the
latter part of the last century from precedents that had been
set us, either in practice or in dogma, during its earlier period,
by statesmen who then not only bore the title, but professed
the opinions, of Tories.   Exclusive principles in the constitution, and restrictive principles in commerce, have grown up
together; and have really nothing in common with the ancient
character of our political settlement, or the manners and
customs of the English people.   Confidence in the loyalty of
the nation, testified by munificent grants of rights and fran-
chises, and favor to an expansive system of traffic, were distinctive qualities of the English sovereignty, until the House
of Commons usurped the better portion of its prerogatives.
A widening of our electoral scheme, great facilities to commerce, and the rescue of our Roman Catholic fellow-subjects
from the Puritanic yoke, from fetters which have been
fastened on them by English Parliaments in spite of the pro-
tests and exertions of the English Sovereigns ; these were the
three great elements and fundamental truths of the real Pitt
system.[1]

We must not, however, assume that the Liverpool
Cabinet in the later stages of its career was guided by any
desire to recur to the principles of historical Toryism.

That was not an epoch when statesmen cared to prosecute
the investigation of principles.   It was a period of happy and
enlightened practice.   A profounder policy is the offspring of
a time like the present, when the original postulates of institutions are called in question.   The Liverpool Cabinet uncon-
sciously approximated to these opinions, because from careful
experiment they were convinced of their beneficial tendency,
and they thus bore an unintentional and impartial testimony
to their truth.   Like many men, who think they are inventors,
they were only reproducing ancient wisdom.

But one must ever deplore that this ministry, with all
their talents and generous ardor, did not advance to principles.   It is always perilous to adopt expediency as a guide ;
but the choice may be sometimes imperative.   These statesmen, however, took expediency for their director, when prin-

[1] *Coningsby*, Bk. II. ch. 1.

ciple would have given them all that expediency ensured, and much more.

This ministry, strong in the confidence of the sovereign, the parliament, and the people, might, by the courageous promulgation of great historical truths, have gradually formed a public opinion, that would have permitted them to organise the Tory party on a broad, a permanent, and national basis. They might have nobly effected a complete settlement of Ireland, which a shattered section of this very cabinet was forced a few years after to do partially, and in an equivocating and equivocal manner. They might have concluded a satisfactory reconstruction of the third estate, without producing that convulsion with which, from its violent fabrication, our social system still vibrates. Lastly, they might have adjusted the rights and properties of our national industries in a manner which would have prevented that fierce and fatal rivalry that is now disturbing every hearth of the United Kingdom.

We may, therefore, visit on the *laches* of this ministry the introduction of that new principle and power into our constitution which ultimately may absorb all, AGITATION. This cabinet, then, with so much brilliancy on its surface, is the real parent of the Roman Catholic Association, the Political Unions, the Anti-Corn-Law League.[1]

The dispersion of ' this clever and showy Ministry ' is a fine illustration of the singular influence of individual character—an influence that arises as often from the weakness of the character as from its strength.

One morning the Arch-Mediocrity himself died. At the first blush, it would seem that little difficulties could be experienced in finding his substitute. His long occupation of the post proved, at any rate, that the qualification was not excessive. But this cabinet, with its serene and blooming visage, had been all this time charged with fierce and emulous ambitions. They waited the signal, but they waited in grim repose. The death of the nominal leader, whose formal superiority, wounding no vanity, and offending no pride, secured in their councils equality among the able, was the tocsin of their anarchy. There existed in this cabinet two men, who were resolved immediately to be prime ministers ; a third who was resolved eventually to be prime minister, but would at any rate occupy no ministerial post without the lead of a House of Parliament ; and a fourth, who felt

[1] *Coningsby*, Bk. II. ch. 1.

himself capable of being prime minister, but despaired of the revolution which could alone make him one ; and who found an untimely end when that revolution had arrived.

Had Mr. Secretary Canning remained leader of the House of Commons under the Duke of Wellington, all that he would have gained by the death of Lord Liverpool was a master. Had the Duke of Wellington become Secretary of State under Mr. Canning he would have materially advanced his political position, not only by holding the seals of a high department in which he was calculated to excel, but by becoming leader of the House of Lords. But his Grace was induced by certain court intriguers to believe that the King would send for him, and he was also aware that Mr. Peel would no longer serve under any minister in the House of Commons. Under any circumstances it would have been impossible to keep the Liverpool Cabinet together.[1]

Disraeli's account of Peel's part in the intrigue against Canning has an interest of its own.

We have seen that at any early period of his career, Mr. Peel withdrew from official life. His course had been one of unbroken prosperity ; the hero of the University had become the favourite of the House of Commons. His retreat, therefore, was not prompted by chagrin. Nor need it have been suggested by a calculating ambition, for the ordinary course of events was fast bearing to him all to which man could aspire. One might rather suppose, that he had already gained sufficient experience, perhaps in his Irish Secretaryship, to make him pause in that career of superficial success which education and custom had hitherto chalked out for him, rather than the creative energies of his own mind. A thoughtful intellect may have already detected elements in our social system which required a finer observation, and a more unbroken study, than the gyves and trammels of office would permit. He may have discovered that the representation of the University, looked upon in those days as the blue ribbon of the House of Commons, was a sufficient fetter without unnecessarily adding to its restraint. He may have wished to reserve himself for a happier occasion, and a more progressive period. He may have felt the strong necessity of arresting himself in his rapid career of felicitous routine, to survey his position in calmness, and to comprehend the stirring age that was approaching. . . .

Adopting this view of the position of Mr. Peel, strengthened

[1] *Coningsby*, Bk. II. ch. 1.

as it is by his early withdrawal for awhile from the direction
of public affairs, it may not only be a charitable but a true
estimate of the motives which influenced him in his conduct
towards Mr. Canning, to conclude that he was not guided in
that transaction by the disingenuous rivalry usually imputed
to him. His statement in Parliament of the determining circumstances of his conduct, coupled with his subsequent and
almost immediate policy, may perhaps always leave this a
painful and ambiguous passage in his career ; but in passing
judgment on public men, it behoves us ever to take large and
extended views of their conduct ; and previous incidents will
often satisfactorily explain subsequent events, which, without
their illustrating aid, are involved in misapprehension or
mystery.[1]

The struggle 'between the Duke of Wellington and
"my dear Mr. Canning"' ended unexpectedly in the
victory of Canning ; but death soon removed him, and
after the disappearance of his successor, Lord Goderich,
'the transient and embarrassed phantom,' as he is called
in *Endymion,* the Duke's turn came.

The Duke of Wellington brought to the post of first minister
immortal fame ; a quality of success which would almost seem
to include all others. His public knowledge was such as might
be expected from one whose conduct already formed an important portion of the history of his country. He had a
personal and intimate acquaintance with the sovereigns and
chief statesmen of Europe, a kind of information in which
English ministers have generally been deficient, but without
which the management of our external affairs must at the best
be haphazard. He possessed administrative talents of the
highest order.

The tone of the age, the temper of the country, the great
qualities and the high character of the minister, indicated a
long and prosperous administration. The only individual in
his Cabinet who, from a combination of circumstances rather
than from any intellectual supremacy over his colleagues, was
competent to be his rival, was content to be his successor. In
his most aspiring moments, Mr. Peel, in all probability, aimed
at no higher reach ; and with youth and the leadership of the
House of Commons, one has no reason to be surprised at his
moderation. The conviction that the Duke's government
would only cease with the termination of his public career

---

[1] *Coningsby,* Bk. II. ch. 1.

was so general, that, the moment he was installed in office, the whigs smiled on him ; political conciliation became the slang of the day, and the fusion of parties the babble of clubs and the tattle of boudoirs.

How comes it, then, that so great a man, in so great a position, should have so signally failed ; should have broken up his government, wrecked his party, and so completely annihilated his political position, that, even with his historical reputation to sustain him, he can since only reappear in the councils of his sovereign in a subordinate, not to say equivocal, character ?

With all those great qualities which will secure him a place in our history not perhaps inferior even to Marlborough, the Duke of Wellington has one deficiency which has been the stumbling-block of his civil career. Bishop Burnet, in speculating on the extraordinary influence of Lord Shaftesbury, and accounting how a statesman, so inconsistent in his conduct and so false to his confederates, should have so powerfully controlled his country, observes, ' HIS STRENGTH LAY IN HIS KNOWLEDGE OF ENGLAND.'

Now that is exactly the kind of knowledge which the Duke of Wellington never possessed. . . . Throughout the brief but eccentric and tumultuous annals [of his administration] we see continual proof. . . . In twenty-four months we find an aristocracy estranged, without a people being conciliated ; while on two several occasions, first, the prejudices, and then the pretensions of the middle class, were alike treated with contumely. . . . This administration, which commenced in arrogance, ended in panic. . . . The growl of reform was heard, but it was not very fierce. There was yet time to save himself. His grace precipitated a revolution which might have been delayed for half a century, and need never have occurred in so aggravated a form. He rather fled than retired. He commenced his ministry like Brennus, and finished it like the tall Gall sent to murder the rival of Sylla, but who dropped his weapon before the undaunted gaze of his intended victim.[1]

We now reach a period when the history begins to be politics—the politics in which Disraeli had himself been an actor. The revolution which followed the fall of the Duke of Wellington overthrew the aristocracy, but it did not emancipate either the Crown or the people. Disraeli judged the Reform Act in the light of his doctrine of the

[1] *Sybil*, Bk. I. ch. 3.

Three Estates of the Realm, on which, as we have seen, he had insisted in the *Vindication*.

In England, under the Normans, the Church and the Baronage were convoked, together with the estate of the Community, a term which then probably described the inferior holders of land, whose tenure was not immediate of the Crown. This Third Estate was so numerous that convenience suggested its appearance by representation ; while the others, more limited, appeared, and still appear, personally. The Third Estate was reconstructed as circumstances developed themselves. It was a Reform of Parliament when the towns were summoned.

In treating the House of the Third Estate as the House of the People, and not as the House of a privileged class, the Ministry and Parliament of 1831 virtually conceded the principle of Universal Suffrage. In this point of view the ten-pound franchise was an arbitrary, irrational, and impolitic qualification. It had, indeed, the merit of simplicity, and so had the constitutions of Abbé Sieyès. But its immediate and inevitable result was Chartism.[1]

Bad, however, as was the principle on which the Reform Bill was founded, it was not so much the Bill itself, Sidonia remarks, as the means by which it was carried, that shook the aristocracy. For this result the blame must rest with the Duke of Wellington.

The future historian of the country will be perplexed to ascertain what was the distinct object which the Duke of Wellington proposed to himself in the political manœuvres of May, 1832. It was known that the passing of the Reform Bill was a condition absolute with the King ; it was unquestionable, that the first general election under the new law must ignominiously expel the Anti-Reform Ministry from power ; who would then resume their seats on the Opposition benches in both Houses with the loss not only of their boroughs, but of that reputation for political consistency, which might have been some compensation for the parliamentary influence of which they had been deprived. It is difficult to recognise in this premature effort of the Anti-Reform leader to thrust himself again into the conduct of ʼpublic affairs, any indications of the prescient judgment which might have been expected from such a quarter. . . . Even temporary success could only

---

[1] *Coningsby*, Bk. I. ch. 7.

have been secured by the utmost decision, promptness, and
energy. These were all wanting : some were afraid to follow
the bold example of their leader ; many were disinclined. In
eight-and-forty hours it was known there was a ' hitch.'
The Reform party, who had been rather stupefied than
appalled by the accepted mission of the Duke of Wellington,
collected their scattered senses, and rallied their forces. The
agitators harangued, the mobs hooted. The City of London,
as if the King had again tried to seize the five members,
appointed a permanent committee of the Common Council to
watch the fortunes of the ' great national measure,' and to
report daily. Brooks', which was the only place that at first
was really frightened and talked of compromise, grew valiant
again ; while young Whig heroes jumped upon club-room
tables, and delivered fiery invectives. Emboldened by these
demonstrations, the House of Commons met in great force,
and passed a vote which struck, without disguise, at all rival
powers in the State ; virtually announced its supremacy ;
revealed the forlorn position of the House of Lords under the
new arrangement ; and seemed to lay for ever the fluttering
phantom of regal prerogative.[1]

When the Whigs had triumphed, there was a general
conviction that, ' by a great stroke of state similar in
magnitude and effect to that which in the preceding
century had changed the dynasty,' they had secured to
themselves the government for at least a generation.
Yet before the new Parliament had existed two years,
the Reform Ministry was upset and the Parliament dissolved. The fact is, ' the success of the Reform Ministry,
on their first appeal to the new constituency which they
had created, had been fatally complete.'

No government can be long secure without a formidable
Opposition. It reduces their supporters to that tractable
number which can be managed by the joint influences of
fruition and of hope. It offers vengeance to the discontented,
and distinction to the ambitious ; and employs the energies
of aspiring spirits, who otherwise may prove traitors in a
division or assassins in a debate.

The general election of 1832 abrogated the Parliamentary
Opposition of England, which had practically existed for
more than a century and a half. And what a series of equiv-

[1] *Coningsby*, Bk. I. ch. 7.

ocal transactions and mortifying adventures did the withdrawal of this salutary restraint entail on the party which then so loudly congratulated themselves and the country that they were at length relieved from its odious repression! In the hurry of existence one is apt too generally to pass over the political history of the times in which we ourselves live. The two years that followed the Reform of the House of Commons are full of instruction, on which a young man would do well to ponder. It is hardly possible that he could rise from the study of these annals without a confirmed disgust for political intrigue ; a dazzling practice, apt at first to fascinate youth, for it appeals at once to our invention and our courage, but one which really should only be the resource of the second-rate. Great minds must trust to great truths and great talents for their rise, and nothing else.[1]

Disraeli, we may believe, was not oblivious of the opening which this grave admonition afforded to an enemy for pointed comments on his own career ; but he had not the sort of self-consciousness that shrinks from such a trial. Elsewhere he traces ' all that insubordination, all those distempered ambitions, and all those dark intrigues ' that finally broke up the Whig Government and the Whig party, to a deeper cause than the weakness of the Opposition, to ' the absence of individual influence and of the pervading authority of a commanding mind.' Lord Grey's supremacy was ' the supremacy of a tradition rather than of a fact,' and by the time that he retired his intended successor (Stanley) was no longer in the Whig ranks. And yet Disraeli adds, seizing the opportunity of making graceful reparation to Lord John Russell for the ruthless punishment inflicted on him by Runnymede, that the interval that elapsed between 1835 and 1837 proved that from the first there had been ' in the Whig army one entirely competent to the office of leading a great party, though his capacity for that fulfilment was too tardily recognised.'

Lord John Russell has that degree of imagination, which, though evinced rather in sentiment than expression, still enables him to generalise from the details of his reading and

[1] *Coningsby*, Bk. II. ch. 1.

experience; and to take those comprehensive views, which, however easily deprecated by ordinary men in an age of routine, are indispensable to a statesman in the conjunctures in which we live. He understands, therefore, his position; and he has the moral intrepidity which prompts him ever to dare that which his intellect assures him is politic. He is consequently, at the same time, sagacious and bold in counsel. As an administrator he is prompt and indefatigable. He is not a natural orator, and labours under physical deficiencies which even a Demosthenic impulse could scarcely overcome. But he is experienced in debate, quick in reply, fertile in resource, takes large views, and frequently compensates for a dry and hesitating manner by the expression of those noble truths that flash across the fancy, and rise spontaneously to the lip, of men of poetic temperament when addressing popular assemblies. If we add to this, a private life of dignified repute, the accidents of his birth and rank, which never can be severed from the man, the scion of a great historic family, and born, as it were, to the hereditary service of the State, it is difficult to ascertain at what period, or under what circumstances, the Whig party have ever possessed, or could obtain, a more efficient leader.[1]

We now come to Peel and the organisation of the Conservative party. On the very eve of their return to office in 1834, 'the Tory party, according to those perverted views of Toryism unhappily too long prevalent, was held to be literally defunct, except by a few old battered cronies of office, crouched round the embers of faction which they were fanning, and muttering "reaction" in mystic whispers.'

It cannot be supposed indeed for a moment, that the distinguished personage who had led that party in the House of Commons previously to the passing of the act of 1832, ever despaired in consequence of his own career. His then time of life, the perfection, almost the prime, of manhood; his parliamentary practice, doubly estimable in an inexperienced assembly; his political knowledge; his fair character and reputable position; his talents and tone as a public speaker, which he had always aimed to adapt to the habits and culture of that middle class from which it was concluded the benches of the new Parliament were mainly to be recruited,—all these were qualities the possession of which must have assured a

[1] *Coningsby*, Bk. V. ch. 4.

mind not apt to be disturbed in its calculations by any intemperate heats, that with time and patience the game was yet for him.[1]

Peel had stood aloof from the Duke's impolitic manœuvres of 1832. It would seem, indeed, that from an early period he had 'meditated his emancipation from the political confederacy in which he was implicated, and that he had been continually baffled in this project.'

He broke loose from Lord Liverpool ; he retired from Mr. Canning. Forced again into becoming the subordinate leader of the weakest government in parliamentary annals, he believed he had at length achieved his emancipation, when he declared to his late colleagues, after the overthrow of 1830, that he would never again accept a secondary position in office. But the Duke of Wellington was too old a tactician to lose so valuable an ally. So his Grace declared after the Reform Bill was passed, as its inevitable result, that thenceforth the Prime Minister must be a member of the House of Commons ; and this aphorism, cited as usual by the Duke's parasites as demonstration of his supreme sagacity, was a graceful mode of resigning the pre-eminence which had been productive of such great party disasters. It is remarkable that the party who devised and passed the Reform Bill, and who, in consequence, governed the nation for ten years, never once had their Prime Minister in the House of Commons : but that does not signify ; the Duke's maxim is still quoted, as an oracle almost equal in prescience to his famous query, ' How is the King's government to be carried on ?'[2]

One result of the Duke's tactics was that Peel, who had escaped so often, was caught at last in 1834—the victim of ' short-sighted intriguers who persisted in looking upon a revolution as a mere party struggle, and would not permit the mind of the nation to work through the inevitable phases that awaited it.' ' Had Sir Robert Peel been in England in the autumn of 1834,' the Whig Government might probably never have been dismissed. The dismissal was a ' premature movement which necessarily led to the compact reorganisation of the Liberal party.' Peel probably never believed in the success of his

---

[1] *Coningsby*, Bk. II. ch. 1.   [2] *Ibid.*

administration, and 'its mere failure could occasion him little dissatisfaction ; he was compensated for it by the noble opportunity afforded to him for the display of those great qualities, both moral and intellectual, which the swaddling clothes of a routine prosperity had long repressed.' But though his brief tenure of office 'elevated him in public opinion, and even in the eye of Europe,' the effect of the premature effort on his future position was far from being so satisfactory. If he had waited, he would have ' acceded to power as the representative of a creed, supported by earnest and enduring enthusiasm '; as it was, he came into office as the leader of a confederacy supported only by 'that churlish sufferance which was the result of a supposed balance of advantages in his favor.' He was forced before the time was ripe into attempting to form a great Conservative party on a comprehensive basis '; and that he did his work 'like a dexterous politician, who can deny ?' But let us consider the performance with 'the impartiality of the future.'

The Tamworth Manifesto of 1834 was an attempt to construct a party without principles ; its basis therefore was necessarily Latitudinarianism ; and its inevitable consequence has been Political Infidelity.

At an epoch of political perplexity and social alarm, the confederation was convenient, and was calculated by aggregation to encourage the timid and confused. But when the perturbation was a little subsided, and men began to inquire why they were banded together, the difficulty of defining their purpose proved that the league, however respectable, was not a party. The leaders indeed might profit by their eminent position to obtain power for their individual gratification, but it was impossible to secure their followers that which, after all, must be the great recompense of a political party, the putting in practice of their opinions ; for they had none. . . .

Conservatism was an attempt to carry on affairs by substituting the fulfilment of the duties of office for the performance of the functions of government ; and to maintain this negative system by the mere influence of property, reputable private conduct, and what are called good connexions. Conservatism discards Prescription, shrinks from Principle,[disavows Progress ; having rejected all respect for Antiquity, it offers no redress for the Present, and makes no preparation for the Future. It is obvious that for a time, under favourable circumstances, such a confederation might succeed ; but it is equally clear, that on the arrival of one of those critical conjunctures that will periodically occur in all states, and which such an unimpassioned system is even calculated ultimately to create, all power of resistance will be wanting : the barren curse of political infidelity will paralyse all action ; and the Conservative Constitution will be discovered to be a *Caput Mortuum*.[1]

The old Tory party had possessed definite principles and a definite tradition. It was

the party that resisted the ruinous mystification that metamorphosed direct taxation by the Crown into indirect taxation by the Commons ; that denounced the system which mortgaged industry to protect property ; the party that ruled Ireland by a scheme which reconciled both churches, and by a series of parliaments which counted among them lords and commons of both religions ; that has maintained at all times the territorial constitution of England as the only basis and security for local government, and which nevertheless once laid on the table of the House of Commons a commercial tariff negociated at Utrecht, which is the most rational that was ever devised by statesmen ; a party that has prevented the Church from being the salaried agent of the State, and has supported through many struggles the parochial polity of the country which secures to every labourer a home.[2]

But the Tory party had now ceased to exist, and its place had been taken by ' the great Conservative party,'

that for ten years in an age of revolution had never promulgated a principle ; whose only intelligible and consistent policy seemed to be an attempt, very grateful of course to the feelings of an English Royalist, to revive Irish Puritanism ; who when in power in 1835 had used that power only to evince their utter ignorance of Church principles ; and who were at this moment [1840] in open insurrection against the prerogatives of the English Monarchy ?[3]

[1] *Coningsby,* Bk. II. ch. 5.   [2] *Sybil,* Bk. IV. ch. 14.
[3] *Coningsby,* Bk. VIII. ch. 3.

The final result is that the Liberal revolution of 1832 and the Conservative reconstruction of 1834 have given us two parties : one ' the destructive party ; a party with distinct and intelligible principles : they seek a specific for the evils of our social system in the general suffrage of the population ' ; the other the Conservative party, ' who, without any embarrassing promulgation of principles, wish to keep things as they find them as long as they can.'

Whenever public opinion, which this party never attempts to form, to educate, or to lead, falls into some violent perplexity, passion, or caprice, this party yields without a struggle to the impulse, and, when the storm has passed, attempts to obstruct and obviate the logical and, ultimately, the inevitable results of the very measures they have themselves originated, or to which they have consented.[1]

With regard to the first school, it was hard to have any faith ' in the remedial qualities of a government carried on by a neglected democracy, who, for three centuries, had received no education '; yet if democracy were combated only by conservatism, democracy must triumph, and at no distant date. The men who entered public life at this epoch had to choose between Political Infidelity and a Destructive Creed. That was the dilemma to which we had been brought by nearly two centuries of Parliamentary rule.

But Parliamentary rule would prove no more enduring than other forms of government.

' You will observe one curious trait,' said Sidonia to Coningsby, ' in the history of this country : the depository of power is always unpopular ; all combine against it ; it always falls. Power was deposited in the great Barons ; the Church, using the King for its instrument, crushed the great Barons. Power was deposited in the Church ; the King, bribing the Parliament, plundered the Church. Power was deposited in the King ; the Parliament, using the People, beheaded the King, expelled the King, changed the King, and, finally, for a King substituted an administrative officer. For one hundred

---

[1] *Coningsby*, Bk. VII. ch. 2.

and fifty years Power has been deposited in the Parliament, and for the last sixty or seventy years it has been becoming more and more unpopular. In 1830 it was endeavoured by a reconstruction to regain the popular affection ; but, in truth, as the Parliament then only made itself more powerful, it has only become more odious. As we see that the Barons, the Church, the King, have in turn devoured each other, and that the Parliament, the last devourer, remains, it is impossible to resist the impression that this body also is doomed to be destroyed ; and he is a sagacious statesman who may detect in what form and in what quarter the great consumer will arise.'[1]

Elsewhere we are given a clue to Disraeli's own theory of the identity of ' the great consumer.' ' If the peers have ceased to be magnificoes,' he remarks in his account of the overthrow of the House of Lords in 1832, ' may it not also happen that the Sovereign may cease to be a Doge ? It is not impossible that the political move-ments of our time, which seem on the surface to have a tendency to democracy, may have in reality a monarchical bias.'[2] Sidonia himself, in a later conversation with Coningsby, is more confident and explicit :

The tendency of advanced civilisation is in truth to pure Monarchy. Monarchy is indeed a government which requires a high degree of civilisation for its full development. It needs the support of free laws and manners, and of a widely-diffused intelligence. Political compromises are not to be tolerated except at periods of rude transition. An educated nation recoils from the imperfect vicariate of what is called a repre-sentative government. Your House of Commons, that has absorbed all other powers in the State, will in all probability fall more rapidly than it rose. Public opinion has a more direct, a more comprehensive, a more efficient organ for its utterance, than a body of men sectionally chosen. The Printing-press is a political element unknown to classic or feudal times. It absorbs in a great degree the duties of the Sovereign, the Priest, the Parliament ; it controls, it educates, it discusses. That public opinion, when it acts, would appear in the form of one who has no class interests. In an enlight-ened age the Monarch on the throne, free from the vulgar prejudices and the corrupt interests of the subject, becomes again divine ![3]

1 *Coningsby*, Bk. IV. ch. 13.   2 *Ibid.*, Bk. I. ch. 7.
3 *Ibid.*, Bk. V. ch. 8.

In a conversation with Oswald Millbank, Coningsby develops Sidonia's ideas :

' The only way [said Coningsby] to terminate what, in the language of the present day, is called Class Legislation, is not to entrust power to classes. You would find a locofoco majority as much addicted to Class Legislation as a factitious aristocracy. The only power that has no class sympathy is the Sovereign.'

' But suppose the case of an arbitrary Sovereign, what would be your check against him ?'

' The same as against an arbitrary Parliament.'

' But a Parliament is responsible.'

' To whom ?'

' To their constituent body.'

' Suppose it was to vote itself perpetual ?'

' But public opinion would prevent that ?'

' And is public opinion of less influence on an individual than on a body ?'

' But public opinion may be indifferent. A nation may be misled, may be corrupt.'

' If the nation that elects the Parliament be corrupt, the elected body will resemble it. The nation that is corrupt deserves to fall. . . .'

' Do you then declare against Parliamentary government ?'

' Far from it : I look upon political change as the greatest of evils, for it comprehends all. But if we have no faith in the permanence of the existing settlement, . . . I would accustom the public mind to the contemplation of an existing though torpid power in the constitution, capable of removing our social grievances, were we to transfer to it those prerogatives which the Parliament has gradually usurped, and used in a manner which has produced the present material and moral disorganisation. The House of Commons is the house of a few ; the Sovereign is the sovereign of all. The proper leader of the people is the individual who sits upon the throne.'

' Then you abjure the Representative principle ?'

' Why so ? Representation is not necessarily, or even in a principal sense, Parliamentary. . . . Opinion is now supreme, and Opinion speaks in print. The representation of the Press is far more complete than the representation of Parliament. Parliamentary representation was the happy device of a ruder age, to which it was admirably adapted : an age of semi-civilisation, when there was a leading class in the community ; but it exhibits many symptoms of desuetude. It is controlled by a system of representation more vigorous and comprehensive ; which absorbs its duties and fulfils them more efficiently, and in which discussion is pursued on fairer terms, and often with more depth and information.'[1]

Here, then, we have the suggestion of a new political ideal :

Let us propose to our consideration the idea of a free monarchy, established on fundamental laws, itself the apex of a vast pile of municipal and local government, ruling an educated people, represented by a free and intellectual press. Before such a royal authority, supported by such a national opinion, the sectional anomalies of our country would disappear. Under such a system, where qualification would not be parliamentary, but personal, even statesmen would be educated ; we should have no more diplomatists who could not speak French, no more bishops ignorant of theology, no more generals-in-chief who never saw a field.[2]

There we have 'a polity adapted to our laws, our institutions, our feelings, our manners, our traditions ; a polity capable of great ends and appealing to high sentiments ; a polity which would render government an object of national affection.' There, also, we have the material of a programme and a creed for a rejuvenated Tory party.

In a parliamentary sense, that great party has ceased to exist; but I will believe that it still lives in the thought and sentiment and consecrated memory of the English nation. It has its origin in great principles and in noble instincts ; it sympathises with the lowly, it looks up to the Most High ; it can count its heroes and its martyrs ; they have met in its behalf plunder, proscription, and death. Nor, when it finally yielded to the iron progress of oligarchical supremacy, was its catastrophe inglorious. Its genius was vindicated in golden sentences and with fervid arguments of impassioned logic by St. John ; and breathed in the intrepid eloquence and patriot soul of William Wyndham. Even now it is not dead, but sleepeth ; and, in an age of political materialism, of confused purposes and perplexed intelligence, that aspires only to wealth because it has faith in no other accomplishment, as men rifle cargoes on the verge of shipwreck, toryism will yet rise from the tomb over which Bolingbroke shed his last tear, to bring back strength to the Crown, liberty to the Subject, and to announce that power has only one duty : to secure the social welfare of the People.[3]

[1] *Coningsby*, Bk. VII. ch. 2. [2] *Ibid.*
[3] *Sybil*, Bk. IV. ch. 14.

We began with a passage from the last chapter of *Sybil* ; let us end with another which immediately follows it, and brings the novel to a conclusion :

It is nearly fourteen years ago, in the popular frenzy of a mean and selfish revolution which emancipated neither the Crown nor the People, that I first took the occasion to intimate, and then to develope, to the first assembly of my countrymen that I ever had the honor to address, these convictions. They have been misunderstood, as is ever for a season the fate of Truth, and they have obtained for their promulgator much misrepresentation, as must ever be the lot of those who will not follow the beaten track of a fallacious custom. But Time, that brings all things, has brought also to the mind of England some suspicion that the idols they have so long worshipped, and the oracles that have so long deluded them, are not the true ones. There is a whisper rising in this country that Loyalty is not a phrase, Faith not a delusion, and Popular Liberty something more diffusive and substantial than the profane exercise of the sacred rights of sovereignty by political classes.

That we may live to see England once more possess a free Monarchy, and a privileged and prosperous People, is my prayer ; that these great consequences can only be brought about by the energy and devotion of our Youth is my persuasion. We live in an age when to be young and to be indifferent can be no longer synonymous. We must prepare for the coming hour. The claims of the Future are represented by suffering millions ; and the Youth of a Nation are the trustees of Posterity.[1]

To disengage this theory of English history and English politics, and present it in consecutive form, is at once in some degree to criticise and appraise it. That the history contains an element of paradox is obvious enough ; that it also contains a large measure of truth, originality, and insight, few competent historians would now care to deny. We are beginning to be emancipated from the tyranny of the Whig writers, and Disraeli startles us less than he startled the generation for which his views were first promulgated. One of his objects, indeed, was doubtless to produce a travesty of the rival Whig theory

[1] *Sybil*, Bk. VI. ch. 13.

that held the field, to show that it was perfectly possible to formulate another no less plausible and coherent, in appearance just as water-tight and floating just as securely. We have always in Disraeli's case to guard against the temptation of taking him too literally. An element of subtle irony is usually in his mind even—indeed, especially—when he is most grave and solemn. He likes to be oracular and to ignore the other side ; but he is all the time, we may be certain, perfectly conscious of its existence. Toryism may not be the spirit of light, but it was something to show that it was just as easy so to present it as Macaulay found it easy so to present Whiggery ; and for a generation which was inclined to be excessively self-complacent, and which was peculiarly in mental bondage to existing political fact, it was a salutary discipline to be reminded that the whole history of England might have been different and yet have ended happily, and that we might have been conducted by another and easier route to a similar, or possibly even to a better, end.

Disraeli had the speculative, *a priori* mind which finds pleasure in the exercise of fitting facts to theories ; but in the region of politics and history this type of mind, as long as it is active, flexible, and receptive, is, if not more likely to arrive at truth, more likely to be illuminating than the other laborious type, often overpraised, which clings timidly to detail, and shrinks from independent and imaginative flight. That the facts in Disraeli's history are sometimes wrested to fit the theory there is no need to deny. The process is especially visible in his reconstruction of the history of the seventeenth century. His version of the quarrel between Charles I. and the Parliament is too fanciful to be quite serious, and we may believe that he was here consciously paying tribute to the historical caprices of Manners and Smythe. When we come to the eighteenth century, the elements of caprice in his picture of Bolingbroke, and in the exaltation of Shelburne as Pitt's tutelary genius, are more peculiarly his own. Between Shelburne and Disraeli there is a certain affinity of character which perhaps helps to explain Disraeli's admiration. The words applied to Shelburne—'Deep and adroit, he was, however, brave and firm '—probably made the reader think of Disraeli himself, and the resemblance goes farther. Shelburne, like Disraeli, was far in advance of his time, and to us who know the issue appears to have been nearly always right in the controversies of that age ; yet he inspired among his contemporaries dislike and distrust to a degree which we find it most difficult to explain. He seems not only, like Disraeli, to have been deficient in the faculty of winning the confidence of his fellows, but also, like Disraeli, to have had the unfortunate art of making himself distrusted more even than was justified by anything we can discern in his motives and conduct. At a point, indeed, the resemblance ceases. Shelburne's want of tact and skill in handling men made his career a comparative failure ; Disraeli had even greater disadvantages to contend with, but overcame them all.

As we draw nearer to his own times, Disraeli's history gains in seriousness and value. His estimate of the younger Pitt shows real discernment and insight; though in an account of the two periods of Pitt's career which he gave in later life in a letter[1] to Sir William Harcourt the note of banter and exaggeration seems to become audible :

I do not at all agree with you in your estimate of Pitt's career. It is the first half of it which I select as his title-deed to be looked upon as a Tory Minister—hostility to borough-mongering, economy, French alliance, and commercial treaties, borrowed from the admirable negotiations of Utrecht ; the later half is pure Whiggism; close Parliaments, war with France, national debt and commercial treaties, all prompted and inspired by the arch-Whig trumpeter, Mr. Burke.

When we come to Pitt's successors, and especially to the period between the conclusion of the war and the passage of the Reform Act, Disraeli is illuminating and

[1] 1873. Quoted in Lord Rosebery's *Pitt*, p. 278.

suggestive, and most helpful to an understanding of subsequent English politics. He does not spare the Tory party of that generation, and he makes us realise how easily, with more breadth and statesmanship, they might have guided national progress on safe and conservative lines, and avoided the catastrophic developments which their blunders made inevitable ; yet he effectively dispels the traditional Liberal prejudice, not yet extinct, that all before the Reform Act is a period of Cimmerian darkness, and all that follows light. After 1832 the hegemony of Peel begins, and we are in the disputable region of modern party politics. Disraeli's view of Peel is possibly nearer to that which posterity will adopt than to any that would gain general acceptance even in the present generation. Peel has been fortunate in the treatment he has received from both political parties. Nominally a great Conservative statesman, he has escaped severe criticism from the quarter whence criticism was most natural and necessary : really one of the chief apostles of modern Liberalism, he has been regarded, of course, by Liberals with sympathetic eyes. Peel, to adopt the language of Disraeli's later life,[1] found two parties—one ' exclusive and odious,' the other ' liberal and cosmopolitan,' neither of them national. When the power of the exclusive party had been shattered, it became his business to reconstruct it, and to make it once more a truly national organ of government ; and for a time his labours seemed to be attended with great success. But he was labouring in the spirit of the mere opportunist who was guided by momentary expediency, and who had laid firm hold of no great principle as the distinctive possession of the party he was building up ; and he ended, after espousing the principles of the enemy, by abandoning his task and deserting to the other side.

It is time to come to Disraeli's own conception of Toryism and of the Tory ideal. For him in the political cosmos there are two great realities—the Throne at the

---

[1] 1870. In the General Preface to the Novels.

centre, and the People at the circumference ; and on the maintenance of their normal and unimpeded interaction the health and balance of all depends. 'The privileges of the multitude and the prerogatives of the Sovereign had grown up together, and together they had waned ;' together also they were to be redeemed from the selfish oligarchy which had usurped them, and the not less selfish and only less narrow middle class which had now taken the place of the oligarchy. That, briefly stated, is the Disraelian position. There is no shrinking, as we can see, from democracy as such, though there is a shrinking from a sudden transference of power to a neglected and entirely uneducated democracy. There is, however, a clear perception of the rapid and almost inevitable drift towards democracy which had already begun, and to which Disraeli himself was to give so great an impetus. Since he wrote *Coningsby* and *Sybil*, the whole story of English politics has been the story of the gradual awakening of the multitude below, and of confused attempts to secure attention to their interests and recognition of their privileges. In that his prevision was right, as was also in one sense his prevision that by a parallel process there would come to the monarchy a revival of its prestige. Nothing is more marked than the steady growth of its popularity and indirect influence since the advent of democracy. Disraeli himself did much, when he acceded to power, to foster this growth ; but if he had ever cherished the hope of a formal restoration of direct personal prerogative in the government of the kingdom and the empire, he made no serious attempt to give it fulfilment. He was a dreamer of dreams, but he had also the peculiarly hard grasp of fact to which only the imaginative dreamer can attain, and he saw the impossibility of any movement in that direction. Indeed, on Sidonia's principle that the depository of power in England is always unpopular, such a movement was not desirable, even in the best interests of the monarchy itself.

But if we substitute for the Sovereign the governing

executive which acts in his name and exercises his functions, then the forecast of political developments given
in *Coningsby* has been verified to the letter. Parliament,
as foreshadowed, has rapidly declined, and 'the great
consumer,' if not the Crown, is its reflection, the Cabinet,
to which Parliament transferred the power it had
wrested from the Crown. In a sense, indeed, the Cabinet
is the creature of the House of Commons, which can at
any moment overthrow it ; but only at the suicidal cost of
putting an end to its own existence, and the Cabinet,
while it is in being, has an independent life, and is more
and more monopolising not only the executive power,
but control of legislation and of the House of Commons
itself. The House, in fact, is being crushed between the
upper and nether millstones of the executive and the
people. Coningsby's ideal of a Crown emancipated from
serfdom to Parliament, placed at the apex of a vast
pyramid of municipal and local institutions, and dispensing
government to a people represented by a free press, seems
in a certain perverted sense on the way to being realised ;
but as it approaches realisation it ceases to be an ideal.
The supreme Government, instead of being a thing above
party, is the very incarnation of the spirit of party ; and
so far from having reached a haven of rest, we are obviously in rapid movement to some new goal which is not
discernible.

Disraeli's great merit as a political thinker is his ability
to penetrate through names and appearances to the
realities beneath, with the power he thereby gains of
emancipating us from formula. Sometimes, indeed, he
becomes, before he has finished, the slave of formula himself ; and, like Matthew Arnold, he can repeat a phrase
till he is persuaded that it is more than words, and has
acquired some sovereign virtue of its own. There is a
certain amount of mere formula in the politics of Young
England, in its vague and shadowy programmes, and
even in the statements of its aspirations and ideals. But
the programmes and ideals of one generation are apt to

be consigned to the lumber-room of the next ; and in
Disraeli's exposition of the Tory idea it is not the letter,
but the spirit, that is permanently valuable.   From him
the ethics of Toryism receives its best and deepest expression.   'The feudal system may have worn out, but
its main principle—that the tenure of property should be
the fulfilment of duty—is the essence of good government.   The divine right of kings may have been a plea
for feeble tyrants, but the divine right of government is
the keystone of human progress, and without it governments sink into police, and a nation is degraded into a
mob.'[1]   In a passage such as that, which contains the
kernel of Disraeli's teaching, we feel the sentiment that
gives to Toryism its power over the imagination ; and
for lack of which Liberalism, in spite of its self-confi-
dent and triumphant advance, remains in comparison
mechanical and uninspiring, invested in mediocrity,
stamped with the seal of the commonplace, and profoundly unsatisfying to the deeper spirits of every age.

The following letter shows that Disraeli was at some
pains to verify his theory of a chain of personal influence
connecting Bolingbroke, Shelburne, and Pitt, ' the three
greatest of English statesmen.'

From Lord Lansdowne.[2]

BOWOOD,
Jan. 29, [1845].

MY DEAR SIR,

I can have no hesitation in answering, as far as it is in
my power, your enquiries relating to my father, and with the
greater pleasure as I am already sensible of the justice you
have already done to his views on public questions, and the
favourable spirit in which you have referred to them.

My father did not marry Lord Granville's[3] daughter till
after Lord Granville's death, and, though he had seen him,
was too young to have lived in any habits of intercourse with
him.   He of course knew and heard a great deal about him,

---

[1] General Preface to the Novels, 1870.
[2] The 3rd Marquis, 1780-1863.   His father, Disraeli's Lord Shelburne, was
the first.
[3] Carteret.

and considered him to have been acknowledged the person of his day of greatest talent for debate in the House of Lords, Lord Bolingbroke being incapacitated from sitting.

Then as to Mr. Pitt, my father, having been much connected with Lord Chatham during the last years of his life, knew him from his boyhood ; and I am sure he was a visitor at this place both before and after he came into Parliament, though long before my recollection.

You do not mention the precise object of the work in which, whatever it may be, I am glad to hear you are engaged ; but [if] there are any other points respecting which I could give you information, I shall feel happy to do so when I settle in town next month, where I could refer to my father's papers. . . .

I remain, dear sir,
Your very faithful servant,
LANSDOWNE.

CHAPTER XI.

DISRAELI AND PEEL.

1845–1846.

Coningsby and *Sybil* had sprung from Young England, and were, indeed, its most notable outcome ; but by the time *Sybil* appeared Young England was no more, and Disraeli was winning a fame in comparison with which the greatest literary success is feeble in its resonance. The significance of Young England in the story of his political career has sometimes been overrated. It had supplied him with a motive for the systematic formulation of his political ideas, and led to the development of those ideas in a monarchical direction ; and it had given him for the time something of the position of a leader, and for his life some cherished friends. But there was a good deal in the movement which he had taken over mechanically from his younger associates, and in which he never had his heart, and he did not let it deflect him even for the moment from the path of his ambition. Young England was, in fact, little more than a beautiful dream, and no dream could long detain a man like Disraeli from the world of reality.

In the session of 1844 he had won the ear of the House of Commons, but he had not yet succeeded in winning its confidence. His bad reputation clung to him persistently and impeded his progress. It clung to him all the more because, in subtle combination with high and serious qualities, the element of wayward fantasy in his character was still there, ever tending to renew the sus-

picions which it had helped to engender at the first.
With all his self-complacency, he had too much sagacity
to be under any illusion as to the real situation. He had
now reached the age of forty, and the years as they had
gone by had brought him success of a kind, but not the
success he sought. He had compelled the House of
Commons to listen to him, to laugh with him, and even to
cheer him ; but it cared nothing for his ideas, and he was
making no visible progress to the attainment of the
power for which his ambition craved. The Ministers
had driven him into opposition, and from them he had
no longer anything to hope. His dream of a reconstructed Toryism was clearly past realisation, for Peel
was now marching straight towards Manchester. The
reputation of a brilliant speaker and the homage of a
picturesque coterie were not enough to satisfy a man of his
temper, yet of any higher reward there appeared to be
little prospect.

But he had one supreme quality which neither Ministers
nor the House of Commons, while noting his more obvious
endowments and limitations, had yet learnt to appraise—
the power of patient, unflagging, yet intense resolve.
Everything comes at last, he wrote in *Sybil*, if men are
firm and calm, and will such as his was certain in the
end to carve a way to success. Will in his case was
reinforced by a rare insight in discerning opportunity,
and by a rare courage in seizing opportunity when it
came. Thirty years later, in conversation with Lord
Rowton, he cited in application to the present emergency
the maxim of Cardinal de Retz : ' Il n'y a rien dans le
monde qui n'ait son moment décisif ; et le chef d'œuvre
de la bonne conduite est de connaître et de prendre ce
moment.' Few could have seen that at the beginning
of 1845 the decisive moment had come. The Government, which had been tottering in 1843, had survived
all its troubles, and was now to all appearance stronger
than ever. The country was again prosperous. Peel's
reform of the tariff in 1842 had done something to revive

trade, the development of railways had done a great
deal more, and a series of good harvests had done most
of all.   Disraeli told Lord Campbell, who came up to him
in the lobby at the beginning of the session to ask his
opinion of affairs, that he thought they were in the third
year of the Walpole administration ; and he said the
same thing in a speech in the House itself a few weeks
later.   One seems, indeed, to feel something of his usual
subtle irony lurking in the phrase ; but he confided to
his sister, in the letter in which he reported the conversation with Lord Campbell, that he did not see many
signs of trouble before Peel.   He at once, however,
added the cautious reflection that the storms in Parliament, like squalls in the Mediterranean, rose in a moment.

Probably, indeed, with his strange gift of prescience,
he saw clearly enough that the current on which the
Government were floating must bear them to disaster.
'I have observed,' he had said in *Contarini Fleming*,
'that, after writing a book, my mind always makes a
great spring ;' and as he wrote *Coningsby* and *Sybil* his
eyes had been opened to the realities of the situation.
We have seen in *Sybil*, as compared with *Coningsby*, an
increased distrust of Peel and an increased estrangement
from his policy ; and Disraeli no doubt realised that,
with all its apparent strength, the Peel Ministry was a
house built upon the sand.   At all events, while it stood
his path was barred, and he now determined to advance
to the assault upon it alone, to strike openly and persistently, and extort by sheer aggression from a reluctant
House of Commons the recognition which it had denied
to his more persuasive methods ; and having determined
to strike, he characteristically chose to strike at the
highest, at the First Minister himself.

After all that has preceded, it is hardly necessary to
enlarge on the character and achievements of the statesman whom Disraeli now singled out for attack.   When
an appreciation of Sir Robert Peel at once judicial and
discerning is sought by historians, it is to the man who

overthrew him that they most frequently turn. In the
year after Peel's death Disraeli wrote what follows :

Nature had combined in Sir Robert Peel many admirable
parts. In him a physical frame incapable of fatigue was
united with an understanding equally vigorous and flexible.
He was gifted with the faculty of method in the highest
degree ; and with great powers of application which were
sustained by a prodigious memory ; while he could com-
municate his acquisitions with clear and fluent elocution. . . .
Thus gifted and thus accomplished, Sir Robert Peel had
a great deficiency ; he was without imagination. Wanting
imagination, he wanted prescience. No one was more
sagacious when dealing with the circumstances before him ;
no one penetrated the present with more acuteness and
accuracy. His judgment was faultless provided he had not
to deal with the future. Thus it happened through his long
career, that while he always was looked upon as the most
prudent and safest of leaders, he ever, after a protracted display of admirable tactics, concluded his campaigns by sur-
rendering at discretion. He was so adroit that he could
prolong resistance even beyond its term, but so little foreseeing that often in the very triumph of his manœuvres he
found himself in an untenable position. And so it came to
pass that Roman Catholic emancipation, Parliamentary reform,
and the abrogation of our commercial system, were all carried
in haste or in passion and without conditions or mitigatory
arrangements.
Sir Robert Peel had a peculiarity which is perhaps natural
with men of very great talents who have not the creative
faculty ; he had a dangerous sympathy with the creations of
others. Instead of being cold and wary, as was commonly
supposed, he was impulsive, and even inclined to rashness.
When he was ambiguous, unsatisfactory, reserved, tortuous,
it was that he was perplexed, that he did not see his way,
that the routine which he had admirably administered failed
him, and that his own mind was not constructed to create
a substitute for the custom which was crumbling away.
Then he was ever on the lookout for new ideas, and when
he embraced them he did so with eagerness, and often with
precipitancy. . . . Although apparently wrapped up in himself
and supposed to be egotistical, except in seasons of rare
exaltedness, as in the years 1844-5, when he reeled under the
favour of the Court, the homage of the Continent, and the
servility of Parliament, he was really deficient in self-con-
fidence. There was always some person representing some
theory or system exercising an influence over his mind. In

his ' sallet-days ' it was Mr. Horner or Sir Samuel Romilly ; in later and more important periods it was the Duke of Wellington, the King of the French, Mr. Jones Lloyd—some others—and finally Mr. Cobden. . . .

The Roman Catholic Association, the Birmingham Union, the Manchester League, were all the legitimate offspring of Sir Robert Peel. No Minister ever diminished the power of government in this country so much as this eminent man. No one ever strained the constitution so much. He was the unconscious parent of political agitation. He literally forced the people out of doors to become statesmen, and the whole tendency of his policy was to render our institutions mere forms. In a word, no one with all his conservative language more advanced revolution. In an ordinary period he would have been a perfect Minister, but he was not a Minister for stormy times : he wanted depth, and passion, and resource for such an occasion.

Sir Robert Peel had a bad manner of which he was sensible ; he was by nature very shy, but forced early in life into eminent positions, he had formed an artificial manner, haughtily stiff or exuberantly bland, of which, generally speaking, he could not divest himself. . . . Generally speaking he was never at his ease, and never very content except in the House of Commons. Even there he was not natural, though there the deficiency was compensated for by his unrivalled facility, which passed current with the vulgar eye for the precious quality for which it was substituted. He had obtained a complete control over his temper, which was by nature somewhat fiery. His disposition was good ; there was nothing petty about him ; he was very free from rancour ; he was not only not vindictive, but partly by temperament, and still more perhaps by discipline, he was even magnanimous. For so very clever a man he was deficient in the knowledge of human nature. The prosperous routine of his youth was not favourable to the development of this faculty. It was never his lot to struggle ; although forty years in Parliament, it is remarkable that Sir Robert Peel never represented a popular constituency or stood a contested election. As he advanced in life he was always absorbed in thought, and abstraction is not friendly to a perception of character, or to a fine appreciation of the circumstances of the hour. . . .

As an orator Sir Robert Peel had perhaps the most available talent that has ever been brought to bear in the House of Commons. . . . His statements were perspicuous, complete, and dignified ; when he combated the objections or criticised the propositions of an opponent, he was adroit and acute ; no speaker ever sustained a process of argumentation in a

public assembly more lucidly, and none as debaters have united
in so conspicuous a degree prudence with promptness. In
the higher efforts of oratory he was not successful. His
vocabulary was ample and never mean ; but it was neither
rich nor rare. His speeches will afford no sentiment of surpassing grandeur or beauty that will linger in the ears of
coming generations. He embalmed no great political truth
in immortal words. His flights were ponderous ; he soared
with the wing of the vulture rather than the plume of the
eagle ; and his perorations, when most elaborate, were most
unwieldy. In pathos he was quite deficient ; when he
attempted to touch the tender passions, it was painful. His
face became distorted, like that of a woman who wants to
cry but cannot succeed. Orators certainly should not shed
tears, but there are moments when, as the Italians say, the
voice should weep. The taste of Sir Robert Peel was highly
cultivated, but it was not originally fine ; he had no wit ;
but he had a keen sense of the ridiculous and an abundant
vein of genuine humour. Notwithstanding his artificial
reserve, he had a hearty and a merry laugh ; and sometimes
his mirth was uncontrollable. He was gifted with an admirable organ ; perhaps the finest that has been heard in the
House in our days, unless we except the thrilling tones of
O'Connell. Sir Robert Peel also modulated his voice with
great skill. His enunciation was very clear, though somewhat marred by provincialisms. His great deficiency was
want of nature, which made him often appear even with a
good cause more plausible than persuasive and more specious
than convincing. . . .

One cannot say of Sir Robert Peel, notwithstanding his
unrivalled powers of despatching affairs, that he was the
greatest Minister that this country ever produced, because,
twice placed at the helm, and on the second occasion with
the Court and the Parliament equally devoted to him, he
never could maintain himself in power. Nor, notwithstanding his consummate Parliamentary tactics, can he be
described as the greatest party leader that ever flourished
among us, for he contrived to destroy the most compact,
powerful, and devoted party that ever followed a British
statesman. Certainly, notwithstanding his great sway in
debate, we cannot recognise him as our greatest orator,
for in many of the supreme requisites of oratory he was
singularly deficient. But what he really was, and what
posterity will acknowledge him to have been, is the greatest
Member of Parliament that ever lived.[1]

[1] *Lord George Bentinck*, ch. 17.

In a stray fragment in Disraeli's hand written in the early forties, one finds grouped together under the legend 'Similarity of characters in different ages and countries,' and without other comment, the names Augustus, Pompeius, Peel. The underlying thought may not improbably have been that here were three men all in a sense mediocre, and with little of the eagle quality of the great men of action, yet all in the course of events constrained to play lofty parts. Augustus, heir to the achievements and political ideas of a man of supreme genius, established the most famous monarchy that the world has ever seen ; while, coming into collision with the same man of genius, Pompey was a tragic failure. Peel's career, of course, is at a far lower pitch of dramatic intensity than that of either of the Romans, and the time has hardly come for any attempt at a final estimate of its value and significance. Though nearly two generations have elapsed since his death, his reputation is still involved in current political controversy, and he still suffers from the excessive praise, and in a less degree from the excessive blame, that fall to statesmen while they live. Perhaps he is best regarded as the typical statesman of a middle-class era, with all the excellences and limitations appropriate to the part. A dominant middle class having none of the proud confidence in its own character and ideals that gives to an aristocracy strength and persistence, and not resting like a democracy on the broad basis that endures, is always in a condition of unstable equilibrium, and is never able long to maintain itself in power. Without genius, without ideas, and without imagination, but with a strong business instinct and great practical talents, it aims rather at the establishment of honest and efficient administration than at achievements of creative statesmanship. And so it was with Peel. He was never sure of himself, and was always in a state of uneasy transition or of violent revolt against his own past. Mainly interested in finance and in practical measures of administration, he cared little for the imperial ideas of generations that had preceded and were to follow his own. But, as Mr. Gladstone once remarked, he was the best man of business who was ever Prime Minister ; and he was that not only by virtue of what Disraeli calls his 'unrivalled powers of despatching affairs,' but also by his possession of many of the higher moral qualities of the ideal man of business. There was, indeed, a good deal more of egoism and ambition in his character than has often been recognised, but he was incapable of any petty or ignoble self-seeking ; and in point of industry, rectitude, and devotion to public duty, he set an example which has served permanently to raise the standard of English government. That is a better title to fame than the dubious distinction, which Disraeli assigned him, of having been the greatest Member of Parliament that ever lived.

His weakness as a statesman lay in his failure to understand the significance of a great historic party as an organ of government not easily to be created, not lightly to be destroyed. In his eager pursuit of mere measures he forgot what was more essential than even the greatest measure. He shattered the Conservative party, and not wholly, it would seem, in a spirit of inattention, but acting in some degree on a theory, which he appears to have borrowed from the Court, that party was an evil, and that he could govern better without it. His theory broke down, and he left parties in the state of confusion in which they long remained, and to which, among other evils, that most needless of our foreign adventures, the Crimean War, may not unreasonably be traced. It was to this neglect and disparagement of party connexion that, as we shall see, Disraeli steadily directed his assault in the struggle that now began.

Peel by his tactless arrogance had seemed to invite a declaration of war, and war, if he sought it, he was now to have with a vengeance. The campaign began with a skirmish in the first weeks of the session of 1845. In the course of the previous year the public had been much excited over the famous affair of the opening of Mazzini's letters in the post under a Home Office warrant. On Graham, as Home Secretary, most of the obloquy descended, but as a matter of fact he was only technically responsible, having acted at the instance of the Foreign Secretary, Aberdeen ; and though the particular occasion chosen for the exercise of an invidious but necessary power was singularly unfortunate,[1] neither of the Ministers had in theory exceeded his rights.

Secret committees of the Lords and Commons had investigated the matter, and reported in a sense favourable to the Government ; but when Parliament reassembled, Disraeli's Radical friend, Duncombe, returned to the attack, and demanded a public investigation by a select committee. Lord Howick moved an amendment for an inquiry by a select committee into a new specific charge brought forward by Duncombe, that his own letters had been opened, and this amendment, which had first been suggested by Manners, was seconded by Disraeli. Having accepted the Government's defence on the foreign part of the question, he proceeded to his favourite pastime of mocking Graham and Peel :

The noble lord at the head of the Foreign Office, accurate as he is in the discharge of his duties, is a man of generous impulses, and is much more likely to have erred on the side of leniency than any other. But, even if the noble lord had erred, who could have ventured to criticise his conduct with such a stake on the die ? When that great master of analytical narrative the Secretary of State traced the other night the vast and precise consequences of the non-interception of the letter of Mr. Mazzini, all must have felt he offered a complete vindication under any circumstances of his colleague. The letter sent, the solitary colony in the Mediterranean in commotion, the invasion of Calabria by an expedition of twenty men without arms, Italy in insurrection, the Austrians crossing the Apennines, and the French crossing the Alps, and England, who the right hon. Secretary assures us could not have been a silent spectator in a general war—and all prevented by intercepting the letter of Mr. Mazzini. (Loud cheers

---

[1] The story, however, that it led to the execution of the brothers Bandiera by the Bourbon Government at Naples is now completely disproved.

and laughter.) Certainly, since the celebrated narrative of the *House that Jack Built* never was detail so consecutively precise.

He now came to Peel :

The right hon. gentleman will pardon me for observing it, but he displayed an unusual warmth. I am aware that it by no means follows that the right hon. gentleman felt it. The right hon. baronet has too great a mind, and fills too eminent a position, ever to lose his temper ; but in a popular assembly it is sometimes expedient to enact the part of the choleric gentleman. The right hon. gentleman touched the red box with emotion. I know from old experience that when one first enters the House these exhibitions are rather alarming, and I believe that some of the younger members were much frightened, but I advised them not to be terrified. I told them that the right hon. baronet would not eat them up, would not even resign ; the very worst thing he would do would be to tell them to rescind a vote. (Loud cheering and shouts of laughter.)

Having indulged in these sallies, he hastened to disclaim personal feeling against Graham. Of the Secretary of State he knew nothing but honour, and had experienced nothing but courtesy, a declaration which was received with laughter by the Opposition. When, with equal emphasis, he disclaimed hostility to the Government, he was similarly rewarded with an ironical cheer from Peel. In making the last disclaimer, Disraeli had contrived to sound, whether intentionally or not, the special note of the coming conflict. The First Minister, he said, was superior to all parties ; he governed by pure reason, not by party. They were now in the third year of a Walpolian administration, and party feeling was extinct. This was not a question of confidence, and he therefore hoped that without offence he might give an independent vote. The motion was not brought forward in a hostile spirit, and as far as he was concerned was not supported in a hostile spirit.[1]

Peel was acutely sensitive to ridicule, and speaking

[1] *The Times*, Feb. 21, 1845.

on the following day he took up the insinuation that his
warmth had been simulated :

It is certainly very possible to manifest great vehemence
of action, and yet not to be in a great passion. On the other
hand, it is possible to be exceedingly cold, indifferent, and
composed in your manner, and yet to cherish very acrimonious
feelings. Notwithstanding the provocations of the hon.
gentleman, I will not deal so harshly with him as he has dealt
with me. He undertakes to assure the House that my
vehemence was all pretended, and warmth all simulated.
I on the contrary will do him entire justice; I do believe
that his bitterness was not simulated, but that it was entirely
sincere. The hon. gentleman has a perfect right to support
a hostile motion . . . but let him not say that he does it in a
friendly spirit.

> ' Give me the avowed, the erect, the manly foe ;
> Bold I can meet, perhaps may turn, the blow ;
> But of all plagues, good Heaven, Thy wrath can send,
> Save, save, O save me, from the candid friend !' [1]

The retort was effective, but the quotation very unlucky. Peel's behaviour to Canning was still remembered
by many on both sides of the House, and regarded as
one of the doubtful passages of his life ; and his use of
Canning's well-known lines therefore gave Disraeli an
opening. A week later Duncombe brought the subject
of the opened letters before the House again, and Disraeli
again supported him. He dwelt at length on the relations
between Peel and his Conservative followers, accusing
the Prime Minister of having introduced a system for
preventing fair discussion on questions not of a party
character. The system was established on two principles,
or rather processes—innuendo and imputation ; the insinuation of base motive and the allegation of factious
conduct. He protested against it. The system was not
founded in justice or fair-play ; it was not founded upon
a real understanding of the principles on which party
connexion should exist. It was, in fact, a system of
tyranny, and as degrading to those who exercised it as to
those who endured it.

[1] Hansard, Feb. 21, 1845.

He illustrated its working from the debates on the
present grievance, and gradually, and as it were without
premeditation, he led up to his real object, Peel's reply
to his previous speech. Peel in this reply had complained of the inconvenience of having an unexpected
blow aimed at your right flank while you were engaged
with the enemy in front. Disraeli retorted that the
enemy in front never wished to fight, and that, with a
large party to support him, Peel was in a position in
which he could afford to be indulgent.

There is another reason why he should not adopt this tone
—he should not forget, after all, that a great many of his
supporters were elected on the hustings under very different
circumstances to those under which they sit here. (Loud
cheers from the Opposition benches.) Really a little philosophical consideration from so great a statesman under such
circumstances is the least we might expect. I admit that I
for one was sent here by my constituents to sit on this side.
He may object to me, although I think he has no great occasion
to object that I am sometimes in a different lobby to himself ;
but I was sent to swell a Tory majority—to support a Tory
Ministry. Whether a Tory Ministry exists or not I do not
pretend to decide ; but I am bound to believe that the Tory
majority still remains, and therefore I do not think that it is
the majority that should cross the House, but only the
Ministry. (Loud cheers and much laughter.) I hope that
the right hon. gentleman, on reflection, will take a more con-
descending and charitable view of our conduct than he has
hitherto been pleased to do. I am sure myself I never misin-
terpret the conduct of the right hon. gentleman. I know there
are some who think that he is looking out for new allies. I
never believed anything of the kind. The position of the
right hon. gentleman is clear and precise. I don't believe
he is looking to any coalition, although many of my constituents do. The right hon. gentleman has only exactly to
remain where he is. The right hon. gentleman caught the
Whigs bathing, and walked away with their clothes. (Much
cheering and great laughter.) He has left them in the full
enjoyment of their liberal position, and he is himself a
strict conservative of their garments. (Continued cheers and
laughter.) I cannot conceive that the right hon. gentleman
will ever desert his party ; they seem never to desert him.
There never was a man yet who had less need to find new
friends. I therefore hope all these rumours will cease. I

look on the right hon. gentleman as a man who has tamed
the shrew of Liberalism by her own tactics. He is the political
Petruchio, who has outbid you all.

If we could only induce the right hon. gentleman, therefore,
to take a larger and more liberal view of his Parliamentary
position than he seems to adopt in moments too testy for so
great a man to indulge in, he would spare us some imputations which I assure him are really painful. If the right
hon. gentleman may find it sometimes convenient to reprove
a supporter on his right flank, perhaps we deserve it—I for
one am quite prepared to bow to the rod ; but really, if the
right hon. gentleman, instead of having recourse to obloquy,
would only stick to quotation, he may rely on it it would be
a safer weapon. It is one he always wields with the hand
of a master ; and when he does appeal to any authority, in
prose or verse, he is sure to be successful, partly because he
never quotes a passage that has not previously received the
meed of Parliamentary approbation, and partly and principally
because his quotations are so happy. The right hon. gentleman knows what the introduction of a great name does in
debate—how important is its effect, and occasionally how
electrical. He never refers to any author who is not great,
and sometimes who is not loved—Canning, for example. That
is a name never to be mentioned, I am sure, in the House of
Commons without emotion. We all admire his genius. We
all, at least most of us, deplore his untimely end ; and we all
sympathise with him in his fierce struggle with supreme
prejudice and sublime mediocrity—with inveterate foes and
with candid friends. (Loud cheering.) The right hon.
gentleman may be sure that a quotation from such an
authority will always tell. Some lines, for example, upon
friendship, written by Mr. Canning, and quoted by the right
hon. gentleman ! The theme, the poet, the speaker—what
a felicitous combination ! (Loud and long-continued cheers.)
Its effect in debate must be overwhelming ; and I am sure, if
it were addressed to me, all that would remain would be for
me thus publicly to congratulate the right hon. gentleman,
not only on his ready memory, but on his courageous conscience.[1]

In a contemporary publication[2] there is a description
of Disraeli's Parliamentary manner which helps us to
reconstruct the scene in the House of Commons during
the delivery of this speech :

[1] *The Times*, March 1, 1845.
[2] *Fraser's Magazine*, Feb., 1847.

As an orator Mr. Disraeli cannot be pronounced highly
eloquent. He never abandons himself to his theme, but
always holds it in subjection to his purpose. In both voice
and manner there is much monotony. He wants variety
in action, gesture, expression, and elocution—always excepting when he breathes his sarcastic vein. . . . His whole manner
as an orator is peculiar to himself. It would scarcely be
tolerated in another ; he seems so careless, supercilious, indifferent to the trouble of pleasing. . . . His action, where he has
any, is ungraceful ; nay, what is worse, it is studiously careless
—even offensively so. With his supercilious expression of
countenance, slightly dashed with pomposity, and a dilettante
affectation, he stands with his hands on his hips, or his thumbs
in the armholes of his waistcoat, while there is a slight, very
slight, gyratory movement of the upper part of his body, such
as you will see ballroom exquisites adopt when they condescend to prattle a flirtation. And then, with voice low-
toned and slightly drawling, without emphasis, except when
he strings himself up for his points, his words are not so
much delivered as that they flow from the mouth, as if it were
really too much trouble for so clever, so intellectual—in a
word, so literary a man to speak at all. . . .
So much for his ordinary level speaking. When he makes
his points, the case is totally different. Then his manner
changes. He becomes more animated, though still less so
than any other speaker of equal power over the House. You
can then detect the nicest and most delicate inflexions in the
tones of his voice ; and they are managed, with exquisite art,
to give effect to the irony or sarcasm of the moment. . . . In
conveying an innuendo, an ironical sneer, or a suggestion of
contempt, which courtesy forbids him to translate into words
—in conveying such masked enmities by means of a glance,
a shrug, an altered tone of voice, or a transient expression of
face, he is unrivalled. Not only is the shaft envenomed, but
it is aimed with deadly precision by a cool hand and a keen
eye, with a courage fearless of retaliation. He will convulse
the House by the action that helps his words, yet leave nothing
for his victims to take hold of. He is a most dangerous
antagonist in this respect, because so intangible. And all the
while you are startled by his extreme coolness and impassi-
bility. . . . You might suppose him wholly unconscious of the
effect he is producing ; for he never seems to laugh or to
chuckle, however slightly, at his own hits. While all around
him are convulsed with merriment or excitement at some of
his finely-wrought sarcasms, he holds himself, seemingly, in
total suspension, as though he had no existence for the ordinary
feelings and passions of humanity ; and the moment the

shouts and confusion have subsided, the same calm, low, monotonous, but yet distinct and searching voice, is heard still pouring forth his ideas, while he is preparing to launch another sarcasm, hissing hot, into the soul of his victim.

With the aid of this writer we can almost see Disraeli standing with pale face and impassive manner as he delivers his philippic ; hear the tone of every sentence as it falls from his lips ; and follow the emotions of his audience as it listens, now perplexed, now expectant, now hilarious. We have first the low, level speaking in no way remarkable that makes the preparation ; the gradual development of the theme of Peel's disregard of party, till it leads to the great strokes of the bathing and the shrew ; then, when the House has been wrought up to a high pitch of excitement, the sudden descent by the speaker, who is alone grave and unmoved, to the low level again ; the feigned humility of his readiness to bow to the rod, and the seeming compliment to Peel's mastery of quotation ; Peel nervous and expectant, the House still puzzled ; the stealthy approach to the position from which the spring is to be made ; the name which is the keyword dropped as if by accident—' Canning, for example ' ; Peel visibly uncomfortable ; the House beginning to be excited ; the drawling allusion to Canning's fierce struggle with ' sublime mediocrity '— perhaps aimed at Peel, though all are still doubtful—and ' with— candid friends '—when the pause, the inflexion of the speaker's voice, and the direction of his glance, convert doubt into certainty ; and then the culminating blow, ' Some lines upon friendship written by Mr. Canning, and quoted by the right honourable gentleman !' and, where a lesser artist would have spoilt all by some crudity of comment, only the restrained but mordant words : ' The theme, the poet, the speaker—what a felicitous combination !'

The effect of the speech on the House was stupendous. ' It would have made you cry with delight,' wrote George Smythe to Mrs. Disraeli, ' to have heard the thunders of

cheering '; and the excitement at the close was so great
that it was some time before Graham, who rose to follow,
could make himself heard. When he was able to proceed,
he professed to rejoice that the time was now come when
they were to have from the member for Shrewsbury open
and avowed rebellion instead of covert mutiny. Peel
spoke later, and hoped that Disraeli, ' having discharged
himself of the accumulated virus of the last week,' now
felt more at ease. He would not condescend to reciprocate personalities. The hon. member must have been
aware in 1841 of his relations with Mr. Canning, and
ought not to have waited for a quotation from a poem
before withdrawing his confidence ; and so forth in the
same vein.

To Sarah Disraeli.

HOUSE OF COMMONS,
Half-past six [*Monday, March* 3].

MY DEAREST SA,
    I much regretted I could not get out on Saturday to send
you a line from myself as to the great scene in the Commons
the night before, from which that respectable assembly has
not yet recovered. There never was an instance of a trip
being succeeded by such a leap ; and the only thing I have
now which can give you an idea of it is a sketch by Horace
Walpole of a sudden ebullition by the elder Pitt in a drowsy
House. As for P[eel], he was stunned and stupefied, lost his
head, and, vacillating between silence and spleen, spoke much
and weakly. Never was a greater failure ! Assuring me that
I had not hurt his feelings, that he would never reciprocate
personalities again, having no venom—The bell !
                                                            D.

His sister had already sent to Mrs. Disraeli her account
of the joy and excitement at Bradenham ; of the old
blind father's delight with the ' bathing,' the ' taming of
the shrew,' and ' the tremendous closing personality ' ;
and of his sitting by her murmuring, ' The theme, the poet,
the speaker !' ceaselessly as she wrote.

About a fortnight later Disraeli advanced to the attack
again. Amid the general prosperity of the country, the

agricultural interest alone was still in a state of depression. Wheat, which in 1843 had been over sixty shillings, was now down to forty-five, and Cobden, who had never based his case for the repeal of the Corn Laws on an expectation of low prices, thought he saw his opportunity. He had once condemned Peel for proposing to lower prices by his simplification of the tariff, 'instead of aiming to maintain them by enlarging the circle of exchange '; and he now moved for an inquiry into the effect of the Corn Laws on agriculture, and made a highly successful speech on similar lines of argument. Peel, who had already been almost completely mastered by Cobden's *a priori* theory, listened, it is said, with ever lengthening face, till, crumpling up the notes he had been taking for a reply, he turned to Sidney Herbert, who sat next him on the bench, and said : 'You must answer this, for I cannot.'[1] Herbert obeyed, and in the course of his answer made the unlucky remark that it was ' distasteful to the agriculturists to come whining to Parliament at every period of temporary distress.' But Cobden's motion was defeated, Disraeli voting with the Government.

A few days later, however, the question was reopened by a county member with a motion that in the disposal of the surplus due regard should be paid to the necessity of affording relief to the agricultural interest, and Disraeli supported him. Peel, having failed to secure any of the commercial treaties of which he had held out hopes in 1842, had now abandoned reciprocity, and was engaged in a second revision of the general tariff, which represented a great concession to the Manchester theory and a great advance towards the system which in the modern phrase is called ' insular free trade.' While the opinions of the Ministers had been in a state of flux, Disraeli had not changed his standpoint ; he still clung to the central position from which he could see all around him, and he was as little moved by the abstract reasoning of Cobden and his friends on the one side as by the narrow selfishness

---

[1] Morley's *Cobden*, I., p. 318.

of the bigoted protectionists on the other. Lord John
Russell in the present debate had just made a speech
in the high *a priori* vein. Disraeli reminded him that
protection was an expedient, not a principle, and that
the question was therefore not to be settled by quotations
of abstract dogmas. Alluding to Cobden's speech of a
few days before, he said it was a speech not easily to be
forgotten by anyone who heard it ; but the real problem
was, Would they have protection, or would they have,
not free trade, for that was not the alternative, but a
system of free imports ? Cobden had convinced himself
that if we dispensed with protection the rest of the world
would speedily follow our lead ; and Disraeli thus placed
his finger precisely on the spot where Cobden's theories
broke down.

Coming to the immediate question, he recalled the
debate and division on a similar resolution moved in 1836
in a Whig House of Commons by his friend Lord Chandos ;
reminded several Ministers of their votes on that occasion ;
and with an allusion to the complaints made by his
agricultural friends of the present conduct of the Prime
Minister, and an ironical declaration that these complaints
were unreasonable, he reached his peroration :

There is no doubt a difference in the right hon. gentleman's
demeanour as leader of the Opposition and as Minister of the
Crown. But that's the old story ; you must not contrast
too strongly the hours of courtship with the years of possession.
'Tis very true that the right hon. gentleman's conduct is different. I remember him making his protection speeches. They
were the best speeches I ever heard. It was a great thing
to hear the right hon. gentleman say : ' I would rather be the
leader of the gentlemen of England than possess the confidence
of Sovereigns.' That was a grand thing. We don't hear
much of ' the gentlemen of England ' now. (Great cheering.)
But what of that ? They have the pleasures of memory—
the charms of reminiscence. They were his first love, and,
though he may not kneel to them now as in the hour of
passion, still they can recall the past ; and nothing is more
useless or unwise than these scenes of crimination and reproach, for we know that in all these cases, when the beloved
object has ceased to charm, it is in vain to appeal to the

feelings. (Great laughter.) You know that this is true.
Every man almost has gone through it. My hon. friends
reproach the right hon. gentleman. The right hon. gentleman
does what he can to keep them quiet ; he sometimes takes
refuge in arrogant silence, and sometimes he treats them
with haughty frigidity ; and if they knew anything of human
nature they would take the hint and shut their mouths. But
they won't. And what then happens ? What happens under
all such circumstances ? The right hon. gentleman, being
compelled to interfere, sends down his valet, who says in the
genteelest manner: ' We can have no whining here.' And
that, sir, is exactly the case of the great agricultural interest
—that beauty which everybody wooed and one deluded.
There is a fatality in such charms, and we now seem to
approach the catastrophe of her career. Protection appears
to be in about the same condition that Protestantism was in
in 1828. The country will draw its moral. For my part, if
we are to have free trade, I, who honour genius, prefer that
such measures should be proposed by the hon. member for
Stockport than by one who through skilful Parliamentary
manœuvres has tampered with the generous confidence of a
great people and a great party. For myself, I care not what
may be the result. Dissolve, if you please, the Parliament
you have betrayed, and appeal to the people, who, I believe,
mistrust you. For me there remains this at least—the opportunity of expressing thus publicly my belief that a Conservative Government is an organised hypocrisy.[1]

' No report,' says a contemporary journalist, writing
of this speech, ' can give an idea of the effect produced
in the House of Commons. The manner of the delivery,
the perfect intonation of the voice, the peculiar looks of
the speaker—all contributed to a success that we believe
to be perfectly unparalleled. No man within our recollection has wielded a similar power over the sympathies
and passions of his hearers.'[2] The sentence at the close
denouncing a Conservative Government as ' an organised
hypocrisy ' called forth, as we are told by Disraeli himself,
a demonstration of ' tumultuous sympathy ; but the
cheers,' he adds, ' were in a great degree furnished by
the voices opposite, and the Tory gentlemen beneath
the gangway who swelled the chorus did so with downcast

[1] Hansard, March 17, and *The Times*, March 18, 1845.
[2] *Weekly Chronicle*, March 23, 1845.

eyes, as if they yet hesitated to give utterance to feelings
too long and too painfully suppressed.'[1] Peel, speaking
later, again protested that he would not engage in a war
of personal recrimination ; but he recalled Disraeli's
speech in defence of the tariff of 1842, and bitterly declared that he then held the panegyric in the same
estimation as he at present held the attack.

The House had now begun to await Disraeli's risings
on the tiptoe of expectation. The writer quoted on a
previous page unfolds the drama of the situation as it
gradually developed—the complacency with which Peel
sat at first in his place, confident in his strength and
despising his assailant ; the cool audacity with which
Disraeli advanced to the attack on a reputation established
by a long career of Parliamentary triumph ; the comparative indifference which the House at first displayed, rising
gradually to the point of malicious curiosity, and then
changing into a sustained excitement and attention as it
began to be manifest that Disraeli was working on a
deliberate plan.

For him to rise late, in a stormy debate, cool, even to
iciness, amidst the fever-heat of party atmosphere around,
was suddenly to arrest all passions, all excitement, all murmurs
of conversation, and convert them into one absorbing feeling
of curiosity and expectation. They knew not on whom to
fix their watch—whether on the speaker, that they might not
lose the slightest gesture of his by-play, or whether they
should concentrate their attention on his distinguished victim,
whom he had taught them almost to regard with levity. The
power of the orator was more confessed, perhaps, in the
nervous twitchings of Sir Robert Peel, and his utter powerless-
ness to look indifferent, or to conceal his palpable annoyance,
than even in the delirious laughter with which the House
accepted and sealed the truth of the attacks—followed, in
justice, let us add, by a sort of compunction that they should
thus have joined in ridiculing their former idol.

Peel, said Mr. Gladstone nearly half a century later,
only tried once to answer, but 'failed utterly ' ;[2] his

---

[1] *Lord George Bentinck*, ch. i.
[2] *Notes from the Life of an Ordinary Mortal*, by A. G. C. Liddell, p. 271.

personal followers, afraid alike of the assailant and the
assailed, did not dare to intervene ; and Disraeli was
thus left to march unmolested from triumph to triumph.

The occasion of the next philippic, the last of this
session, was furnished by Ireland. Peel's attempts to
find a policy for that country had now led to something
definite. The Whigs had persisted in regarding the Irish
difficulty as purely political, or at the utmost religious,
and had concentrated their energies on political and religious questions, such as the reform of corporations and
the position of the Irish Church. Peel in a moment of
insight had seemed to divine the truth that the trouble
was really agrarian, and had appointed the Devon Commission, whose report, if it had been acted upon, would
have averted unnumbered woes, social and political. But
before the report appeared O'Connell's triumph in the
House of Lords, and the rapid growth of the Repeal
movement, impressed the Minister with the importance
of finding a policy that would be speedier in its action.

The tranquillity which might result from a reformed tenure
of the soil must, if attainable, be a distant blessing, and at
present he saw only the obstacles to its fulfilment. . . . He
required a policy for the next post and the next division.
There was in his view only one course to take, to outbid his
predecessors as successfully in Irish politics as he was doing
in taxes and tariffs. He resolved to appropriate the Liberal
party of Ireland, and merge it into the great Conservative
confederation which was destined to destroy so many things.
He acted with promptitude and energy, for Sir Robert Peel
never hesitated when he had made up his mind. His real
character was very different from his public reputation.
Far from being timid and wary, he was audacious, and even
headstrong. It was his cold and constrained demeanour
that misled the public. There never was a man who did
such rash things in so circumspect a manner . . . and so Sir
Robert Peel, without a qualm, suddenly began to govern
Ireland by sending it ' messages of peace.'[1]

One of the messages of peace was the famous Maynooth
Bill. Since the time of Perceval a grant of £9,000 had

[1] *Lord George Bentinck*, ch. 7.

been voted annually to Maynooth, the Roman Catholic
seminary for the education of priests, and Peel now
proposed to convert this grant into a permanent endowment of £30,000 a year. In introducing the Bill, he urged
that the principle was already conceded, and justified
the increase by dwelling on the wretched condition of the
students, who at present had to be maintained on £23
a year, a sum too small to allow them even separate beds.
But this tactful presentation of the case did not avail to
appease Protestant feeling, which was soon roused to
such fury that no one but Peel himself could have made
headway against the storm. The Bill had already cost
him the services of Gladstone, who had resigned at the
beginning of the session, not disapproving, but feeling
bound by declarations in his book on *State and Church*.
Gladstone had explained his resignation in a speech
which puzzled his best friends, and caused Disraeli to
write to his sister, 'He may have an *avenir*, but I
hardly think it'; and when the second reading came, he
made the puzzle greater by declaring himself dissatisfied
with Peel's temporising arguments and supporting the
Bill on the very principle of concurrent endowment
which he had formerly denounced. When he sat down
Disraeli rose, but, giving way for the moment to the heir
to the Norfolk dukedom, he was chosen next by the
Speaker out of half a dozen competitors, in obedience
to loud calls from all parts of the House.

They had been told, he said, in the speech that introduced the Bill, that there were three courses open to them.
He had never heard the Prime Minister bring forward
a measure without making the same confession. In a
certain sense, and looking to his own position, he was
right.   There was the course he had left ; there was the
course he was pursuing ; and there was usually the course
he ought to pursue. The right. hon. gentleman sent
them back to precedents. With him a great measure
was always founded on a small precedent ; he always
traced the steam-engine back to the tea-kettle. In the

present case he appealed to the action of Mr. Perceval and
some odd vote in a dusty corner from which he inferred
that the principle was admitted.

Now, I deny that it is admitted, even in the limited sense.
In the first place that was a temporary vote, and this is not ;
in fact, it is a permanent one. But I will not make that the
ground of opposition. I will go to the arguments founded on
circumstances of the late President of the Board of Trade
[Gladstone]. I am astonished that he seems in his argument
so completely to have supplanted principles. I looked upon
the right hon. gentleman as the last paladin of principle, the
very abstraction of chivalry ; and, when a question was
raised which touched the elementary principle of constitutional
settlement and ecclesiastical arrangement, I never believed
that it would be the right hon. gentleman who would come
down and give the House the small change of circumstances
to settle this great account. (Laughter and cheers.)

He then dealt at some length with Gladstone's plea
for concurrent endowment, the positions of the two men
being curiously the reverse of those they were to occupy
a quarter of a century later on the question of the Irish
Church. The right hon. gentleman was a subtle casuist,
said Disraeli, but what was the result of his adroit argumentation ? That the principle upon which the State
had hitherto been connected with religion in this country
was now worn out, that they must seek a new principle,
and that the Government which he had left because he
supported it had discovered a new principle. But wherein
did their new principle differ from that which underlay
the measures proposed by the Whig Government, opposition to which was the bond of union of the Conservative
party and the foundation of the Conservative theory ?
Where were they to stop in the application of the new
principle ? Why should they stop ? They found their
Erastian system crumbling under their feet ; were they
to adopt a pantheistic principle, and was any body of
sectarians who could satisfy Downing Street to have a
claim for endowment ? He had no great confidence in
the cure of souls in that quarter, and he could conceive

nothing more at variance with the feelings of this country than a police surveillance over the religious ordinances of the people. He denied that in the existing order the Church of England was the creature of the state. The alliance between them had been formed and was maintained on equal terms ; and if it were attempted to introduce a species of Prussian discipline in ecclesiastical affairs, the people of this country would never submit to such a system.

That alone was a sufficient ground for opposition to the Bill, but he had other reasons for opposing it. He opposed it on account of the manner in which it had been introduced, and also on account of the men by whom it had been brought forward. He did not think the gentlemen who were now seated on the Treasury bench were morally entitled to bring such a measure forward. It involved a principle against which they had all along signally struggled. Because they had crossed the floor and abandoned with their former seats their former professions, had they a right to ask the House to look to the merits of their measures and forget themselves and their protestations ? Such pretensions led to the question whether party, as a political instrument, was to continue to govern them. To object to party government was nothing more or less than to object to Parliamentary government. A popular assembly without parties—500 isolated individuals—could not stand five years against a Minister with an organised government without becoming a servile senate. Here was a Minister who habitually brought forward as his own measures those very schemes and proposals to which, when in Opposition, he always avowed himself a bitter and determined opponent. The result was the country was left without an Opposition, and they heard the low murmurs of the people because there was no exponent in that House of a great national opinion. On constitutional grounds he might say that the noble lord (John Russell), the hereditary leader of the Whig party, which founded Parliamentary government, ought, even though he approved of it, to oppose the present measure.

He hoped he would not be accused of 'bandying personalities' in making observations which were in entire and complete relation to the motion before the House. Certainly they lived in strange times, when a person in so eminent a position as that of First Minister of the Crown could stop Parliamentary criticism by calling it 'personality.' This system of putting down Parliamentary discussion had been tried in another place, but he did not know that the position occupied by 'another place' in the public estimation was one of which the House of Commons was particularly ambitious. It was not Radicalism, it was not the revolutionary spirit of the nineteenth century, that had consigned the place in question to illustrious insignificance ; it was Conservatism and a Conservative dictator. The same arts that had broken the spirit of 'another place' might lower the tone of the House of Commons ; as the one had been drilled into a guard-room,[1] the other might be degraded into a vestry. If they chose to maintain a Government that announced no distinctive principles, and an Opposition that did not oppose, he was certain that no degree of spirit could resist the influence of such a system.

If you are to have a popular Government, if you are to have a Parliamentary administration, the conditions antecedent are, that you should have a Government which declares the principles upon which its policy is founded, and then you can have on them the wholesome check of a constitutional Opposition. What have we got instead ? Something has risen up in this country as fatal in the political world as it has been in the landed world of Ireland—we have a great Parliamentary middleman. (Immense cheering.) It is well known what a middleman is ; he is a man who bamboozles one party, and plunders the other (great laughter), till, having obtained a position to which he is not entitled, he cries out : 'Let us have no party questions, but fixity of tenure.' I want to have a commission issued to inquire into the tenure by which Downing

---

[1] The Duke of Wellington, it will be remembered, was leader of the House of Lords.

Street is held. I want to know whether the conditions of
entry have been complied with, and whether there are not
some covenants in the lease which are already forfeited. I
hope I shall not be answered by Hansard. I am not surprised
the right hon. gentleman should be so fond of recurring to
that great authority ; he has great advantages ; he can look
over a record of thirty, and more than thirty, years of an
eminent career. But that is not the lot of everyone, and I
may say, as a general rule, I am rather surprised that experienced statesmen should like to recur to that eminent
publication. What, after all, do they see on looking over a
quarter of a century or more even of their speeches in Hansard ? What dreary pages of interminable talk, what predic-
tions falsified, what pledges broken, what calculations that
have gone wrong, what budgets that have blown up ! And
all this, too, not relieved by a single original thought, a single
generous impulse, or a single happy expression ! Why,
Hansard, instead of being the Delphi of Downing Street, is
but the Dunciad of politics. But I want something more
than quotations from Hansard to account for how parties have
been managed in this House. It is a system so matter-of-fact
and yet so fallacious, taking in everybody, though everybody
knows he is deceived ; so mechanical, and yet so Machiavellian
that I can hardly say what it is, except a humdrum hocus-
pocus, in which the order of the day is read to take in a nation.

If it were a vote which concerned the social and political
equality of the Roman Catholic population, he would go
as far as any man, perhaps farther than many. But no
one pretended that that was now the question. This
measure was not flattering to the pride of the Roman
Catholics or solacing to their feelings. It was not a
great grant ; he thought it was a mean, a meagre, and a
miserable grant.

If the Roman Catholic priesthood are to be educated by the
State, it must be something greater than the difference between £23 and £28, something higher than the difference
between three in a bed and two. That is not the way in which
I would approach a reverend priesthood. I cannot believe,
therefore, that the Roman Catholic gentlemen, on reflection—
and I hope they will have time for reflection—will vote for
this measure, when they consider what it is. Who is he who
introduces it ? It is the same individual whose bleak shade
fell on the sunshine of your hopes for more than a quarter of

a century. Will not these considerations affect you ? What
if it be a boon ?—I deny that it is one—but if it were such a
boon as it is said to be, would you accept it from hands
polluted ? It is not from him you ought to accept it—not
from him who, urged on, as he reluctantly admitted, by a
fatal State necessity, accompanied the concession of your
legitimate political claims by the niggardly avowal that he
was obliged to concede them.

As for the Whigs, he was almost in despair of appealing
to their hereditary duties, their constitutional convictions,
or their historical position, but he should have thought
that the noble lord was weary of being dragged at the
triumphal car of a conqueror who did not conquer him
in fair fight. He hoped, then, for their aid, and the aid
of the Roman Catholic gentry, in opposing this measure,
as well as for the aid of those who would reject it on
exclusive Protestant principles or on the general principle
he had tried to uphold against state interference.

But, whatever may be the various motives and impulses
which animate these different sections of opinion, there is at
least one common ground for co-operation—there is one ani-
mating principle which is likely to inspire us all. Let us in
this House re-echo that which I believe to be the sovereign
sentiment of this country ; let us tell the people in high places
that cunning is not caution, and that habitual perfidy is not
high policy of state. On that ground we may all join. Let
us bring back to this House that which it has for so long a
time past been without—the legitimate influence and salutary
check of a constitutional Opposition. That is what the
country requires, what the country looks for. Let us do it
at once in the only way in which it can be done, by dethroning
this dynasty of deception, by putting an end to the intolerable
yoke of official despotism and Parliamentary imposture.
(Loud cheers.)[1]

Hobhouse, who was watching the scene from the front
bench opposite, has recorded his impressions during the
delivery of this speech :

Peel hung his head down, changing colour and drawing his
hat over his eyes ; and Graham grinned a sort of compelled

[1] *The Times*, April 12, 1845.

smile, and looked a good deal at me, who happened to be just opposite, to see how we took the attack. Our front row was well behaved, but Russell and Palmerston and George Grey whispered to me, ' It is all true ' ; and even Ellice laughed, and Macaulay[1] looked happy. The speech was listened to with profound attention, and spoken without the slightest hesitation or reference to notes.[2]

Disraeli said subsequently that it was his opposition to the Maynooth Bill that broke up Young England, and as a matter of fact Smythe and Manners both supported the Government ; but the same thing had happened on the agricultural motion which was the occasion of the previous philippic, and the soul was out of Young England before the Maynooth speech was delivered.[3]

To Lord Carrington.

HOUSE OF COMMONS,
April 15, 1845.
MY DEAR LORD,

I am meditating the moment that Parliament will permit me to make a visit to Berlin ; and I am afraid that I must not appear there except in a red coat. If your lordship would therefore kindly appoint me one of your lieutenants, I will endeavour to maintain the honor of the cloth at foreign Courts, and shall feel extremely obliged to you.

The petitions this afternoon *re* Maynooth are more numerous than ever, and the debate has the aspect of a long protraction.

Ever, my dear Lord,
Your obliged and faithful servant,
B. DISRAELI.

Eight years earlier, when the Whigs were in office, Disraeli, through Lord Chandos, had unsuccessfully tried

---

[1] Macaulay himself in the debate made an attack on Peel, which, though in some respects it sounds like an echo of Disraeli's, is really more violent : ' Did you think,' he asked, ' when you went on, session after session, thwarting and reviling those whom you knew to be in the right, and flattering all the worst passions of those whom you knew to be in the wrong, that the day of reckoning would never come ? It has come. There you sit, doing penance for the disingenuousness of years.'

[2] *Lord Broughton's Recollections*, VI., p. 140.

[3] Maynooth, it may be noted, was equally disruptive in its effect on the Manchester School, Cobden voting with the Government, and Bright against.

BENJAMIN DISRAELI, 1844.

to obtain the coveted red coat. He got it on the present occasion, but the visit to Berlin was not, it would seem, paid till after the lapse of a generation ; when, though he had garments in his wardrobe even more resplendent, he was great enough in himself to be content to make his impression by ostentatious simplicity.

To Sarah Disraeli.

CASSEL,
Sept. 17.

We are here without having had the slightest intention of coming. But hearing that the place had beauty and seclusion, we agreed to pitch our tent here, if we could find any sort of accommodation. This was difficult, as it is an extremely savage place ; few of the inhabitants, and none of the humbler classes, talk French. There is no library, bookseller's shop, nor newspaper of any sort ; they never heard of *Galignani*, and I hardly know whether the majority of the people are conscious of the three glorious days. It is quite French Flanders ; their provisions come from Holland ; the Hôtel de Ville was built by the Spaniards, and religion is supreme. The country around is rich, and the landscape a vast panorama, and as the place is high, we conclude it is healthy. We have taken a house for a month and have hired a Flemish cook, who, Mary Anne desires me to tell my mother, stews pigeons in the most delicious way : eggs, cloves, and onions, ending in a red-brown sauce, a dish of the time of the Duke of Alva. Fruit and poultry plentiful and cheap. Six fowls for 5 francs, meat 6d. per pound. We crossed from Dover to Boulogne, a very rough passage. Our first walk at Boulogne we found *Sybil affiché* in a large placard, ' Disraeli's New Novel,' in every window. We travelled from Boulogne *en voiture* to this place, sleeping the first night at St. Omer.

CASSEL,
Oct. 26.

The tragedy of Ely Cathedral[1] has shaken me to the centre. It is vain to speak of such a catastrophe : impossible not to think of it. Since the death of the Duke of Orleans, no sudden end has been more terrible.

I get up at half-past five, and don't find it difficult, going to bed by nine. The effort was great at first, and the house very unmanageable. You cannot expect any news from us ;

---

[1] Disraeli's cousin, George Basevi (1794-1845), the well-known architect, had been killed by falling from the belfry.

we know no one and hear nothing, except from you. I have been able to write very regularly, and made better progress than usual, which is encouraging. Your life is as secluded as our own, yet you always make your letters interesting. We have a pretty garden, which gives us mignonette and Alpine strawberries ; and the autumn there is mellow, fine, and mild, though we live on the top of a mountain. We look upon a most charming landscape, and can see thirty or forty miles ahead, and the sea, on a clear day. We now see *Galignani* regularly, and an unknown Englishwoman—Miss King, as I observe by the direction of her paper—sends me the *Illustrated Times*, and another unknown, *Bell's Life*.

D.

By the beginning of December the Disraelis are in Paris, in their old quarters in the Rue de Rivoli.

To Baron Lionel de Rothschild.

HÔTEL DE L'EUROPE, RUE DE RIVOLI,
Dec. 3, 1845.

MY DEAR BARON,

The journals of to-day give us the interesting information of the birth of your son.[1] I hope he will prove worthy of his pure and sacred race, and of his beautiful brothers and sisters. We are anxious to hear that Madame Lionel is as well as we could all wish, and that you are happy.

We arrived here on Sunday, after having passed more than two months in a perfect solitude at Cassel, French Flanders, a rich rural country. My wife walked 300 miles in two months, of which she is very proud, and by which she has much benefited. She had no companions, except those boxes of books at which you laughed, and which are all exhausted. We rose every morn at half-past five, and retired at half-past nine : our greatest adventure the discovery of a village.

Yesterday I had the honor of a very long and interesting audience of his Majesty. The fate of the English Ministry, the Oregon question, and what the King calls ' the commercial crisis,' the staple of our talk. They seem, all three, much to disquiet him. I apprehend that, though the Corn Laws must eventually break up the Government, it will not sink before one bad harvest. The movement of Lord John was able, and absolutely required by the interests of the Whig party. He was resolved that Peel should no longer jockey him.

[1] Mr. Leopold de Rothschild.

The King told me that it was not true, as frequently stated, that the arbitration of the Oregon question had ever been proposed to him. He seemed to think that it would have been well if it had been so, but that it was now too late. The American Government is a *mauvaise plaisanterie*, for it governs nothing except the Customs-houses. It has no more influence over the Western States, than over Devonshire or Dorset. . . .

I have not yet seen a human being here ; nor have we even left a card, except yesterday at your families. The weather is soft and charming. . . .

Ever, dear Lionel,
Yours sincerely,
B. DISRAELI.

Events during the autumn had been hastening on in England, and this letter has anticipated. Disraeli's onslaughts of the previous session had produced no visible effect on the position of the Ministry, as he himself confesses.

Practically speaking, the Conservative Government at the end of the session of 1845 was far stronger than even at the commencement of the session of 1842. If they had forfeited the hearts of their adherents, they had not lost their votes, while both in Parliament and the country they had succeeded in appropriating a mass of loose, superficial opinion not trammelled by party ties, and which complacently recognised in their measures the gradual and moderate fulfilment of a latitudinarian policy both in Church and State. Their position was also aggrandised and confirmed by a conviction then prevalent, and which it is curious to observe is often current on the eve of great changes, that the Ministry of Sir Robert Peel were the only body of men then competent to carry on affairs.[1]

The Opposition, he adds, was split into sections, the condition of the Whig party absolutely forlorn, and the Anti-Corn-Law League nearly reduced to silence. ' The Manchester confederates seemed to be least in favour with Parliament and the country on the very eve of their triumph.'

But the weather during the summer and autumn was

[1] *Lord George Bentinck*, ch. i.

bad. In reply to an inquiry by Disraeli as to the harvest, his sister wrote from Bradenham in the middle of October :

It rains here so much that I do not think a dove would find a dry spot to rest upon. It cannot be called autumn, for nearly all the leaves have been washed off the trees these weeks past. ˉIt is a very bad harvest—half the ear blighted, the yield consequently very short. . . . There is a good deal of corn out here still, and a great deal in the North, which must be entirely spoilt. But our present despair and every-one's is ' the potato cholera.'

The potato disease was first reported from the South of England ; but it soon declared itself in Ireland, where there was far more at stake, and before the end of October the accounts became alarming. ' This mysterious but universal sickness of a single root ' was, in fact, to quote *Endymion*, to ' change the history of the world.' Peel summoned the Cabinet for October 31, and it met four times in the course of a week. ' " There is no gambling like politics," said Lord Roehampton, as he glanced at *The Times*. " Four Cabinets in one week ; the Government must be more sick than the potatoes." '[1] During the last couple of years Peel's mind had been gradually mastered by Cobden's abstract reasoning, and he had completely changed his views on the question of the tariff. He had hoped there would be no need for a public recantation during the term of the existing Parliament, which had been expressly returned to support him as a protectionist Minister ; and towards the close of the session of 1845 he had stated in Parliament on three different occasions that his policy was one of gradual relaxation of duties, and that he could not consent to the total and immediate abolition of the Corn Laws. But the failure of the potato crop upset all his plans. Something had to be done, and his judgment of what was required by the practical emergency was affected by the fermentation proceeding in his mind. In the first days of realising that scarcity was threatened in Ireland, he wrote to his Lord Lieu-

[1] *Endymion,* ch. 82.

tenant : ' The remedy is the removal of all impediments to the import of all kinds of human food—that is, the total and absolute repeal for ever of all duties on all articles of subsistence.'[1]   When the Cabinet met, the policy he proposed was to open the ports at once by an Order in Council, call Parliament together to sanction the Order, and then proceed after Christmas with a Bill for the permanent modification of the Corn Laws.   He was supported in these proposals only by Aberdeen, Graham, and Sidney Herbert.   Stanley, who alone had much acquaintance with Ireland, showed their futility as a measure of relief, pointing out quite truly that what was required by the Irish cottiers was, not reduction of price, but the absolute means of purchase ; that the two great crops of the small farmers in Ireland were potatoes and oats ; and that at the moment when they had lost one it was proposed to relieve them by reducing the price of the other.   After its four meetings, the Cabinet separated early in November without having reached a decision.

It was now that Lord John Russell, watching the proceedings from Edinburgh, and divining the perplexity of Ministers, divining also, no doubt, that the clothes of the Whigs were again in danger of being stolen, executed the movement to which Disraeli alludes in his letter to Baron Rothschild.   Without consultation with any of his colleagues, he issued a manifesto to his constituents in the City of London proclaiming the gravity of the crisis, condemning the inertness of the Government, and on his own side abandoning the fixed duty to which the Whigs had hitherto clung, and ranging himself with Cobden as an advocate of total repeal.   The movement has often been praised as bold, but is perhaps better described as rash,[2] and it certainly, as we shall see, proved a constant cause of embarrassment to the Whigs in the subsequent session. The manifesto, though dated November 22, did not appear

---

[1] Parker's *Life of Peel*, III., p. 224.
[2] Even Disraeli, who commended it in his letter to Baron Rothschild, soon came, as we shall see, to regard it as a great blunder.

in *The Times* till November 27, and the Cabinet had
begun a fresh series of meetings on November 25.
Russell's letter had, of course, an effect on their deliberations, but the effect would appear to have been greatly
exaggerated.[1] Peel, though he recognised that the policy
of opening the ports might now seem to have been
adopted at the dictation of the Whig leader, was ready
to go on if supported by a united Ministry ; but he had
been determined from the first that their next step must
be the virtual repeal of the Corn Laws, and it was his
determination that told with his colleagues, not the
Edinburgh letter. The Duke of Wellington, though not
persuaded of the necessity of action, announced that it
was his intention to support the Prime Minister ; and the
majority who had gone with Stanley a few weeks before
now followed the Duke's lead. Even Stanley, when he
found that he stood almost alone, took two days for
reflection, and then offered to consent to suspension of
the Corn Laws if suspension alone was intended.

But when he was told that the temporary emergency of
apprehended scarcity in Ireland was not to lead to a remedy
commensurate in duration with the expected evil, but was
to be made the groundwork of suspending, for the purpose
of not re-enacting, the Corn Law, he felt that he could not
take that course consistently with his own feelings as an
honourable man ; and that, with such ulterior views, to
propose to Parliament to sanction the opening of the ports
would be to lead those who were disposed to support the
Government into a snare. He said that he had tried to
school himself into the belief that, under certain circumstances, the interests of the country might require even a
sacrifice of personal and public character, but he had failed
in bringing himself to so humiliating a conclusion.[2]

The fatal Cabinet meeting was on December 4 ; and
The Times of that day had contained an announcement
that the Government had decided to call Parliament
together for the first week in January, and propose total

---

[1] Among others by Disraeli in his *Lord George Bentinck*, writing without
documents that have now become accessible.
[2] *Lord George Bentinck*, ch. 2.

repeal. This announcement, which, it is now known, was
founded on information that came from Aberdeen,
caused great public excitement ; and it probably did not
tend to restore harmony in the divided Cabinet. Peel
waited a day after Stanley's ultimatum, and then told
his colleagues that he thought it impossible to go on ;
and on the 6th he went to the Queen and tendered his
resignation. Russell, who was sent for, did not at first
either accept or decline, so Peel's resignation was not at
once made effective. It did not become public for nearly
a week, and the situation remained ambiguous for nearly
a fortnight in all, while Russell was on the way from
Edinburgh to Osborne or engaged in consulting his friends
as to the possibility of forming a Government.

To Lord John Manners.

HÔTEL DE L'EUROPE, RUE DE RIVOLI,
Dec. 17.

MY DEAR LORD JOHN,

What is going to happen ? After living three months in
profound solitude in a Flemish wilderness, really never having
conversed with a single being or even read a journal, I arrived
here a fortnight ago, and found myself in a political atmosphere of fever heat. The King sent for me the day after my
arrival, and from that moment I have conversed with none
but Ministers and Ambassadors, of all parties and all countries,
and all equally distracted.

As I see you are at Melton, furiously hunting, this will
reach you. Where is G. S[mythe] ? I have not heard from
him for months, and expected to find him here, but in vain.
Has he gone on to Stamboul ? If not, and in England, I
wish you would send him a line and beg him to write to me,
or come over.

I heard last night from a good quarter that the Whigs
had resolved to decline the enterprise. The King inquired
whether Gladstone, who is not compromised in the 'four
Cabinet Councils in one week,' could not lead the *personnel*
of the Commons, with the Duke in the Lords. It is quite
clear that the feeling in favor of protection is much stronger
than was supposed by many, and that it will be impossible
to carry repeal.

Conjecture is quite baffled here in high places. In lower
ones there is a general opinion that Peel will return in triumph ;

but this appears to me a superficial conclusion, and I cannot but believe it highly improbable. At all events he has lost his prestige. Every resignation weakens a Minister, and is almost as foolish a thing as frequent Cabinet Councils. No one will now talk of a Walpolian Government ; yet he might have completed his term. I am told that a month ago Thiers said : ' If it be a *real* famine, Sir Robert will be a great man, and will command his party ; but if it be a *false* famine, and he tries to play tricks, he is lost.' Now, I think it is a false famine ; and the question is not ripe enough for his fantastic pranks. He is so vain that he wants to figure in history as the settler of all the great questions ; but a Parliamentary constitution is not favorable to such ambitions : things must be done by parties, not by persons using parties as tools — especially men without imagination or any inspiring qualities, or who, rather, offer you duplicity instead of inspiration. Pray write.

Ever yours,
D.

The King inquired a great deal about Gladstone of me. It was evident that his name had recently been suggested to his Majesty by some high quarter. I told the King that he was quite equal to Peel, with the advantage of youth.

Meanwhile Disraeli, in Paris, had been endeavouring to simplify the problem before Russell by smoothing the way for the return of Palmerston to the Foreign Office.

To Lord Palmerston.

[PARIS,
Sunday, December 14.]

MY DEAR LORD,
M. Guizot invited me to a private conversation on Friday evening on the intelligence which had arrived from London that morning. In some casual talk previously with the Duc Decazes I had ascertained that it was M. Guizot's opinion that Sir Robert Peel would be restored to power *dans une quinzaine ;* M. Guizot did not express this opinion to me, but he elicited mine that the return of Sir Robert Peel, assuming the supposed causes of his retirement to be correct, was highly improbable.

Yesterday the King, whom I have had the honor occasionally to see during the throes of the last fortnight, during which, though anxious, he seemed confident as to Peel's triumph, sent for me to St. Cloud. I found his Majesty grave and

calm, more ready to listen than to talk, very consecutive
and keeping to the point [and not in any degree indulging
in those amusing but rambling details which sometimes
distinguish his conversation].[1] His Majesty told me that
Guizot had mentioned at the morning Council that he had
seen me on the previous eve ; his Majesty's belief in Peel had
evaporated : he repeated more than once that Guizot was
disabused of his idea that Peel would return ; that every
resignation weakened a Minister, and was almost as silly a
thing as frequent Cabinet Councils. After some conversation
on this head, the probable materials of the new Ministry, etc.,
the King, assuming that there would be a Whig Government,
spoke to me very much of your lordship's accession to
office.

Your lordship is doubtless aware of the apprehensions which
the people of this country entertain on that subject, and
therefore I will not dwell on them. Your lordship is a man
of too great experience and of too great a mind either to
exaggerate or to depreciate the importance of such circumstances. Being not unfamiliar with the subject, it was in
my power to discuss it in all its bearings, and to make those
representations to the King, and enter into those explanations and details, which were desirable. I impressed on his
Majesty with delicacy, but without reserve, that your lordship was our first Foreign Minister who had taken the French
intimacy as an avowed element of our national policy, and
that the original want of cordiality had not been manifested
by you ; that from your frank character you required frankness and decision ; that if these were not wanting on the part
of the French Government I felt sure that your lordship
would never take a litigious view of the policy of France, but
would rather assist in any fair development of its external
influence, which had for its object to popularise the throne
and satisfy the public. There followed on the part of the King
before repeated explanations of Spanish and Egyptian affairs,
but expressed with gravity, much earnestness, and clearness.

This conversation lasted about half an hour, when the
King, rising, said : [' We must not lose all the music.' There
was a concert.][2] 'There are persons here to whom I must
give a word, but do not go, as I wish to speak to you again.'
Accordingly, about half-past ten o'clock, the concert having
finished [which, by-the-by, was very choice, as there was
no one but the Court],[2] His Majesty approached me, and

---

[1] In the draft from which this letter is given, the words in brackets are
lightly erased.

[2] The words in brackets are pencilled interpolations, apparently of a
ater date.

invited me to follow him into his cabinet. He said, the moment we were seated : ' What you have said of Lord Palmerston has given me much pleasure. I have been thinking of it. I feel also persuaded that Peel cannot be brought back again in triumph ; and if he were to return, he is no longer the same man. I will not deny I regret Lord Aberdeen. But if Lord Palmerston will enter the administration without *rancune*, and with a friendly disposition, all may be well. I consider that affairs are very serious. It is not isolated questions now—Spain, Turkey—as before. Isolated questions settle themselves. Or even American, the same. It is the state of the Continent that occupies me.' His Majesty then entered at great length on this subject. I perceived that the state of Germany disquiets him, and that he believes that a vast revolutionary movement in Central Europe is not to be avoided. Approaching midnight his Majesty dismissed me.

Notwithstanding my attempts at brevity, my letter has already grown much longer than I intended, and I have not even yet expressed its purpose. It is this : I suspect, from many circumstances, that a sort of cry of (affected terror) will be raised up in England against your lordship, sure to be re-echoed here, which may add to the embarrassments of your Government, which I doubt not are sufficient without it. Do not you think some means might be devised to terminate this for ever ? Had you made your projected visit to Paris,[1] and become known to this impressionable people, all would have been right. But now that is, of course [illegible]. I do not think that any mere representation by the Press will effect the purpose. These representations are important when they reiterate and amplify the words of some eminent personage, but the world requires the reality of the individual for the original impulse. On the meeting of Parliament, under circumstances which render developments of policy on the part of a Government not unusual, it would not be difficult to arrange something which would elicit a satisfactory exposition. I am sure I should be very happy to assist you in this respect, were I present ; but if the Parliament be summoned speedily, I do not think I shall be tempted to quit this agreeable residence—especially as the great object of my political career is now achieved. However, you would not find much difficulty in devising the requisite machinery.

Our Embassy here, I am credibly informed, have been left perfectly in the dark. Lord Cowley has dislocated his shoulder, but ' Lord ' Hervey, as the Deputies call him, was

---

[1] Palmerston visited Paris the following Easter, and succeeded by his social tact in dispelling for the moment the prejudice against him.

active at Guizot's levée on Friday, assuring all that the Whigs can never form a Government while St. Aulaire wrings his hands and shrugs his shoulders like a doctor, and asks in a whisper what you can do against *la majorité des Lords*.

I see no change in the King since 1842, and I know, from an authentic quarter, that his health is perfect.

From Lord Palmerston.

3, CARLTON TERRACE,
Dec. 18, 1845.

MY DEAR SIR,

I am extremely obliged to you for your letter of the 14th, which I was accidentally prevented from answering yesterday. I thank you very much for the just explanation which you have given to the King and Guizot and others of my feelings and policy in regard to France, and you may confidently speak in the same sense on the subject to anybody with whom you may converse upon it. I have the strongest conviction that the great foundation of the foreign policy, both of an English and of a French Government, ought to be a cordial and sincere good understanding between England and France ; and though two great and independent nations must from time to time have on particular subjects somewhat separate views and interests, I can see no reason why, with a right good-will on all sides, that cordial good understanding should not be firmly maintained ; and it will always [be] my anxious endeavour to use any power which I may possess to accomplish so important a purpose.

Nothing is yet finally settled, but I should think that before many hours have elapsed it will be known which of the three possible Governments the country is to have : John Russell's, Peel's, or a Protection Cabinet. Whatever may be the allurements of Paris, I think you will hardly refrain from being in your place on so curious and interesting an occasion as the opening of the approaching session of Parliament.

My dear sir,
Yours sincerely,
PALMERSTON.

It is worth while to add Disraeli's account of this transaction in his *Lord George Bentinck :*[1]

About this time Louis Philippe of Orleans, King of the French, exercised a great influence over public affairs. This

[1] Ch. 14.

Prince had entirely identified himself with the Peel administration. There existed between his Majesty and the English
Minister not only a sentiment of sympathy, but one of reciprocal
admiration. Each believed the other the ablest man in their
respective countries; their system of government was the
same, to divert the public mind from political change by the
seduction of physical enjoyment, and to neutralise opinion
in the pursuit of material prosperity ; finally, they agreed in
another point, that their tenure of power was as interminable
as the nature of things admitted, and that it was insured
by mutual co-operation.

No one was more amazed and more alarmed by the breaking
up of the Conservative Government in November, 1845, than
the King of the French. With the quickness of perception
which with him always seemed rather instinct than thought,
he instantly trembled before a long vista of war and revolution.
His fears of Lord Palmerston were fed by all the diplomacy
of Europe, and especially by the connexions of the late
Conservative Cabinet, who still hoped that the repugnance
of the European Courts to the appointment of that Minister
might, in conjunction with the domestic weakness of the Whig
party, yet bring back the game to Sir Robert.

One to whom the King had disburdened his mind in an
hour of intolerable anxiety, and from whom his Majesty
asked that counsel which circumstances permitted to be
given, tried to relieve him from these bugbears of state, in
a truer appreciation of the position than those around him
cared to encourage. It was represented to the King that
a cordial understanding between the two countries had
become a necessity for every English administration ; that
the Parliament and the people of England would never
support a Minister whom they believed to be inclined to
treat the French connexion with levity or disregard ; and
that it was especially the interest of the Whigs in their present
feeble condition to prove to the country that they took office
with no prejudice against their neighbours. With these views,
and in order at once to relieve his mind, it was suggested to
the King that through the medium of some private friend it
might be wise to make an effort to disembarrass this question
of the personal complications with which it had been the
interest of certain individuals too long to invest it ; and that
he should seek for some frank explanation of the feelings
with respect to France with which the new English Minister
returned to office.

The King, who was a man of great impulse, grasped at the
suggestion, and acted upon it immediately. The appeal was
promptly attended with the most satisfactory results, and

the King of the French, with a countenance radiant with
smiles, was assuring the whole diplomatic circle that he was
never less uneasy as to the prospects of Europe, and that
Lord Palmerston had resumed office with a determination to
act cordially with France, when, to the astonishment of his
Majesty, he learnt that Lord John Russell had resigned his
mission, in consequence of an absurd and really discreditable
intrigue against Lord Palmerston by a portion of his own
party, on the plea that his appointment to the Foreign Office
would endanger our friendly relations with the Tuileries.

It was not till December 18 that Russell definitely
undertook the task of forming a Government, and he
abandoned it on the following day. All who were to be
his colleagues had agreed to the total repeal of the Corn
Laws ;[1] but Lord Grey,[2] who was to have the Colonial Office,
refused to join a Ministry in which Palmerston should be
Foreign Secretary. 'The intrigue,' says Disraeli, 'was
neither contrived with dexterity nor conducted with
temper, but it extricated the Whig leader from a false
position. . . . He endured the mortification of confessing
to his Sovereign his inability to serve her, and handed
back with courtesy the poisoned chalice to Sir Robert.'[3]

Peel accepted it eagerly, and set about the task of recon-
structing his Government. Stanley remained obdurate,
but Peel was not, like Russell, to be frightened by the loss
of his Minister for the Colonies. The Duke of Wellington,
with his curious habit of carrying ideas of military discipline into the sphere of constitutional government,
thought it his duty ' to fall in,' only giving vent to his
feelings in the characteristic comment : ' Rotten potatoes
have done it all ; they put Peel in his damned fright.'[4]
The other Ministers, except Stanley, again followed the
Duke's lead ; and Gladstone[5] came back to take Stanley's

---

[1] So Russell wrote to Cobden. See Morley's Cobden, I., p. 345.
[2] The Lord Howick of previous chapters. He had succeeded on the
death of his father in the course of the present year.
[3] Lord George Bentinck, ch. 2.
[4] The Greville Memoirs, under date Jan. 13, 1846.
[5] Disraeli, in his Maynooth speech, had described him as ' one who had
quitted the Cabinet for some reason not given, and might join it again in
circumstances equally obscure.' In the rearrangement of minor offices,
George Smythe became Under-Secretary for Foreign Affairs.

place. At the end of all the tumult it seemed likely that the schism would end with Stanley's retirement, and that the Government would resume its course hardly, if at all, weakened. Peel himself was fully convinced that he would carry his party with him in abolishing the Corn Laws ; and Disraeli a few years later gave it as his opinion that if he had called the party together, and taken them into his confidence, they would again have followed his lead.[1] But, whether as a result of excessive assurance or of a disposition that was naturally autocratic and secretive, the Minister chose the course of haughty isolation ; and the outcome was far different.

The warmest admirers of Sir Robert Peel have never attempted to deny that there is much in his conduct during this crisis that calls for explanation. Quite apart from any question as to the intrinsic merits of the great measure which he now proceeded to pass stands the question of the manner in which he precipitated the crisis, and of his right to be the principal agent in carrying the measure through. Here the judgment of his contemporaries was decisively against him. Melbourne dining at Windsor, when the subject was referred to, broke out indignantly, regardless of the Queen's feelings : ' Ma'am, it's a damned dishonest act !'[2] Even Cobden thought it was wrong to ask the Protection Parliament to violate its pledges, and years after Peel's death still held that his conduct was difficult to defend.[3] Peel had once before, on the question of Catholic emancipation, broken faith with his party ; and, instead of feeling that it was undesirable to repeat the experiment, he seems rather to have been encouraged by its comparative success to expect an equally easy course on the present occasion. While condemning the lack of wisdom and foresight that he had shown in his attitude to the Catholic claims, most historians have conceded that he had the justification in that matter of a real and urgent necessity for his sudden change of

[1] Broughton, VI., p. 228.   [2] Greville, Jan. 13, 1846.
[3] Morley's *Cobden*, I., p. 348.

front ; and, according to the legendary view, he had a similar justification in the matter of the Corn Laws. Precisely, it is said, as in 1829 he sacrificed consistency and character to the public duty of averting revolution, so in 1846 he sacrificed them again to the great national need created by the Irish famine. The legendary view will hardly bear examination in the light of the facts. It was the potato disease indeed that set the train of events in motion, but poor Ireland was afterwards little thought of in the matter.[1] No one has ever been able to show that the repeal of the Corn Laws did anything to alleviate the horrors of the Irish famine, while the injury that it caused to permanent Irish interests is obvious and confessed. It was soon found, as a matter of fact, that the extent of the potato disease had at first been exaggerated, and the real crisis in Ireland did not come till the following season ; and so completely in the meantime had the pretence of an immediate emergency been abandoned, that the Act carried by Peel retained substantial duties[2] on corn for a period of years.

But on any view of the gravity of the Irish situation in the winter of 1845, an Order in Council suspending the Corn Laws was all that was called for, and to this even Stanley, as we have seen, would have assented. It had been the frequent practice to suspend duties in times of scarcity, as the Minister himself showed ; and if he had been content with this remedy, no charge of breaking faith could fairly have been brought against him. Peel harped, indeed, on the difficulty of renewing the Corn Laws once they were suspended, but this harping only suggests the embarrassment of a man who was conscious

[1] Croker, who knew both Ireland and Peel, wrote to Graham under date Feb. 21, 1846 : ' Ireland has no more to do with the grand convulsion than Kamschatka, and I think facts will show hereafter that the only way that Ireland is concerned in the revolution is that the measures taken in England, and for English views and no other, have increased the dangers and misery of Ireland ' (*Croker Papers*, III., p. 64).

[2] Ten shillings the quarter when the price was under 48s., sinking to four shillings when the price was above 53s. These duties were subsequently suspended during the crisis of the famine, but their suspension only serves to strengthen the argument.

that his real object had from the first been to get rid of
the Corn Laws for ever. 'If we open the ports,' he asked,
'do you expect us to guarantee that they will ever be
closed again ?'   As Manners answered in debate, no one
on the Tory side had looked for such a guarantee. 'Suspend the Corn laws, open the ports, and leave it to the
good sense of the English people to decide whether they
should be closed again.'[1]   All, in fact, that was needed
to keep the Cabinet and party together was that Peel
should refrain from an explicit declaration of his intention
to go out of his way to violate his pledges.

The truth is, Peel had got entangled in the meshes of an
economic theory, and was in a state of intense intellectual
discomfort and excitement. The real crisis was in his
own mind rather than in the facts. Peel was a typical
Englishman of the middle classes from which he sprang,
with their practical concrete intellect and a certain scorn
and incapacity for theoretical principles ; and theory
had her revenge by mastering him periodically. His
justification in practice on this occasion has been that the
English people followed him into the same prison-house
of economic dogma, and have remained there in tolerable
contentment ever since. But for anyone who retains his
freedom of mind moral dogma will seem to have a higher
validity than economic ; and whether he thinks the repeal
of the Corn Laws a good thing or a bad, he will find it
hard to discern any such pressing necessity for their
repeal at the particular moment chosen as to justify a
statesman in violating his pledges and breaking up his
party.

Let it be granted, however, that Peel, whether with
sufficient warrant or not, was honestly convinced that the
instant repeal of the Corn Laws was imperatively necessary, and there is still something in his conduct that
requires explanation. He himself admitted more than
once in the House of Commons that he was not the right
person to propose such a measure, but excused himself

---

[1] Hansard, Feb. 17, 1846.

on the ground that he only undertook the task because
of the failure of the Whig leader to form an administration. On one occasion, waxing warm, he even said that
to suggest that he had wished to interfere with the
settlement of the question by Lord John Russell was
'as foul a calumny as a vindictive spirit ever dictated
against a public man.'[1] Disraeli in reply then and
always pressed the question why, if this were so, he tried
to induce his own Cabinet to adopt the policy of repeal
a week before he gave the opportunity to Russell. No
answer was ever given, and none[2] is easily conceivable.
In spite of Peel's protestations, the conclusion irresistibly
suggested by the whole transaction is that he was anxious
from first to last to keep the matter in his own hands.
If he had shown half the determination to avoid the
breach of faith involved in his repealing the Corn Laws
himself that he showed to get the Corn Laws somehow
repealed, he could have secured both objects. He
acquiesced far too readily in Russell's failure to form a
Government. If the Corn Laws were to be repealed,
Russell was the man clearly designated for the task. By
his Edinburgh letter he had invited the country to entrust
it to him ; and in the majority by which the Bill was
actually carried, if we take the test of the second reading,
his followers were to Peel's as two to one. The excuse
which he gave for his desertion of the Queen was wholly
inadequate,[3] and would not have held against a little

[1] Hansard, June 12, 1846.

[2] The answer suggested by Gladstone (Morley, I., p. 286), that the measure
proposed by Peel at the beginning of December was less sweeping than
that to which he was eventually led, is devoid of substance. In his
Cabinet Memorandum of December 2, Peel expressly recommended such a
modification of the Corn Laws ' as would secure the ultimate and not remote
extinction of protective duties.'

[3] So it seemed to Peel himself. He wrote to Lord Heytesbury (Parker,
III., p. 289) that Russell had thrown up the task on which he entered for
no better reason than ' that one intemperate and headstrong man objected
to another gentleman having one particular office.' It has been urged,
indeed, that the Whigs could not have carried the Corn Bill through the
House of Lords ; but Peel himself thought otherwise, as he expressly wrote
to the Queen (on Dec. 12, 1845 : Parker, III., p. 242), so he cannot be given
shelter under this plea. In any case, Russell could have met the immediate
emergency by an order of suspension, and thrown on the opposite party
the responsibility of refusing the sanction of Parliament.

resolution on the part of the retiring Minister. The
Whigs[1] were, of course, glad that Peel, in Disraeli's words,
should have the glory and the odium of settling the
question ; but Peel himself, it is clear, was more attracted
by the glory than repelled by the odium.

Here, indeed, the latent egoism of his character came
into play. Disraeli's judgment in his letter[2] to Manners
is expressed in harsher terms than he would have used
at a later date, but it contains a large element of truth.
That there was no petty or deliberate self-seeking in
Peel's motives everyone would agree, but to a man of his
type temptation presents itself in forms more subtle.
Like many other statesmen with long experience of office,
he had begun to think, not, perhaps, that he was indispensable, but that all the great things that had to be done
could best be done by himself. Ambition combined with
the fermentation in his mind to lead him astray, and he
sacrificed his pledges and his party to a supposed urgent
necessity that had no real existence. He made the higher
obligation of preserving good faith in political life sub-
servient to the lower of repealing the Corn Laws, and
both his character as a man and his reputation as a
statesman must suffer in consequence.

Parliament met on January 22. In the House of
Lords the Duke of Wellington, by a curious manœuvre,
deprived Stanley of the opportunity of explaining his
resignation ; but in the House of Commons the Prime
Minister made a long statement, of which Disraeli gives
us a graphic account in his *Lord George Bentinck*.[3] While
the House was on the tenters for the explanations of the
crisis, Peel plunged into a tedious fat cattle speech,
discoursing at great length on the price of flax and wool,
salt beef, and domestic lard ; inquiring 'whether employment, low prices, and abundance, contributed to the

---

[1] Not all of them, however, believed that they were wise in shirking
their duty. ' We stayed in,' said Macaulay, ' when we ought to have gone
out ; and now we stay out when we ought to have gone in ' (Greville,
Dec. 23, 1845).
[2] See p. 337.   [3] Ch. 3.

diminution of crime,' and gravely stating that ' he would no longer resist the inference that they did—as if any human being ever resisted the inference '; and then closing ' this eulogium of the effect of low prices ' with a demonstration that all preceding reductions of the tariff had greatly increased the prices of the articles affected.

Some fine judges have recognised in all this only the artifice of a consummate master of the House of Commons, lowering the tone of an excited assembly by habitual details, and almost proving by his accustomed manner of addressing them that, after all, he could have done nothing very extraordinary. When a senate after a long interval and the occurrence of startling transactions assembles, if not to impeach, at least to denounce, a Minister, and then are gravely anointed with domestic lard, and invited to a speculation on the price of salt pork, an air of littleness is irresistibly infused into the affair from which it seems hopeless to extricate the occasion.

Finally the speaker slid into a long and confused narrative of the Cabinet Councils and their consequences ; and concluded with a fierce reply to threats of mutiny that had been heard from some of his own followers.

Turning round with great scorn to his former supporters, and with an expression of almost malignant haughtiness, he exclaimed : ' I see constantly put forth allusions to the power of those men to remove me from office.' He should therefore define the relation in which he conceived himself to stand with respect to party and to his Sovereign. But dilating on the latter point with considerable feeling, and full, perhaps, of an important subject which he was fast approaching, he entirely forgot the former and on this occasion far more interesting topic. He concluded by a vindication of what he held to be true Conservative policy in his best style ; earnest without being solemn, and masculine without turgidity. Yet the well-considered conclusion contained a somewhat portentous confession for a Conservative Minister of England —that ' it was no easy task to insure the united action of an ancient monarchy, a proud aristocracy, and a reformed House of Commons.'

Peel was followed by Russell with what Disraeli calls the authentic statement of Whig disasters '; and when

Russell sat down, in a House tame and dispirited, and with the country members unorganised, helpless, and dumb, the debate nearly collapsed.

It seemed that the curtain was about to fall, and certainly not to the disadvantage of the Government. In their position the first night of the session passed in serenity was comparatively a triumph. With the elements of opposition, however considerable, so inert and desponding, the first night might give the cue to the country. Perceiving this, a member, who, though on the Tory benches, had been for two sessions in opposition to the Ministry, ventured to rise and attack the Minister. The opportune in a popular assembly has sometimes more success than the weightiest efforts of research and reason. The Minister, perhaps too contemptuous of his opponents, had not guarded all his approaches. His depreciation of those party ties by which he had risen, in an assembly, too, in which they are wisely reverenced ; his somewhat ostentatious gratitude for the favour of successive Sovereigns ; his incautious boast that his Conservative Government had discouraged sedition and extinguished agitation, when it was universally felt that he was about to legislate on the most important of subjects in deference to agitation ; and, above all, his significant intimation that an ancient monarchy and a proud aristocracy might not be compatible with a reformed House of Commons—at least, unless he were Minister— offered some materials in the handling of which the least adroit could scarcely fail. But it was the long-constrained passion of the House that now found a vent far more than the sallies of the speaker that changed the frigid silence of this senate into excitement and tumult.

The speaker was, of course, Disraeli himself. He began by explaining that, as an early day was to be appointed for the discussion of the great question, he would not at this moment have intruded on the House but for the peculiar tone of the Prime Minister's speech. He admired a Minister who said that he held power to give effect to his own convictions, and he had no doubt that in the present case the convictions were conscientious. But, looking to all the circumstances, he must say that the Minister, however conscientious, was very unfortunate, and that he ought to be the last man in the world to turn round and upbraid his party in the tone of menace he had adopted.

Sir, there is a difficulty in finding a parallel to the position of the right hon. gentleman in any part of history. The only parallel which I can find is an incident in the late war in the Levant, which was terminated by the policy of the noble lord opposite. I remember when that great struggle was taking place, when the existence of the Turkish Empire was at stake, the late Sultan, a man of great energy and fertile in resources, was determined to fit out an immense fleet to maintain his empire. Accordingly a vast armament was collected. The crews were picked men, the officers were the ablest that could be found, and both officers and men were rewarded before they fought. (Much laughter.) There never was an armament which left the Dardanelles similarly appointed since the days of Solyman the Great. The Sultan personally witnessed the departure of the fleet ; all the muftis prayed for the expedition, as all the muftis here prayed for the success of the last general election. Away went the fleet, but what was the Sultan's consternation when the Lord High Admiral steered at once into the enemy's port. (Loud laughter and cheers.) Now, sir, the Lord High Admiral on that occasion was very much misrepresented. He, too, was called a traitor, and he, too, vindicated himself. ' True it is,' said he, ' I did place myself at the head of this valiant armada ; true it is that my Sovereign embraced me ; true it is that all the muftis in the empire offered up prayers for the expedition ; but I have an objection to war. I see no use in prolonging the struggle, and the only reason I had for accepting the command was that I might terminate the contest by betraying my master.' (Tremendous Tory cheering.)

It was all very well for the right hon. gentleman to say : ' I am the First Minister '—he might as well, by-the-by, adopt the phraseology of Walpole, and call himself the sole Minister, for his speech was rich in egoistic rhetoric ; it was all very well for him to come forward and say : ' My sentiments are magnanimous, my aim is heroic, and, appealing to posterity, I care neither for your cheers nor your taunts ' ; but how did he acquire his position, how did he obtain power to turn round on his supporters and treat them with contempt ?

Well do we remember on this side of the House—perhaps almost with a blush—well do we remember the efforts which we made to raise him to the bench on which he now sits. Who does not remember the ' sacred cause of protection '— the cause for which Sovereigns were thwarted, Parliaments dissolved, and a nation taken in ? Delightful indeed was it to have the right hon. gentleman entering into all his confidential details when, to use his courtly language, he ' called ' upon his Sovereign. Sir, he called on his Sovereign, but would his Sovereign have called on the right hon. baronet, if, in 1841, he had not placed himself, as he said, at the head of the gentlemen of England ? (loud Ministerial cheers)— that well-known position, to be preferred to the confidence of Sovereigns and of courts. It is all very well for the right hon. baronet to take this high-flying course ; but I think myself—I say it without any wish to achieve a party triumph, for I believe I belong to a party which can triumph no more ; for we have nothing left on our side except the constituencies which we have not betrayed (loud cheering) ; but I do say that my idea of a great statesman is of one who represents a great idea—an idea which may lead him to power, an idea with which he may connect himself, an idea which he may develop, an idea which he may and can impress on the mind and conscience of a nation. That, sir, is my notion of what makes a man a great statesman. I do not care whether he be a manufacturer or a manufacturer's son. That is a grand —that is indeed an heroic—position. But I care not what may be the position of a man who never originates an idea— a watcher of the atmosphere, a man who, as he says, takes his observations, and when he finds the wind in a certain quarter trims to suit it. Such a person may be a powerful Minister, but he is no more a great statesman than the man who gets up behind a carriage is a great whip. (Tremendous cheering and laughter.) Certainly both are disciples of progress. Perhaps both may get a good place. (More laughter.) But how far the original momentum is indebted to their powers, and how far their guiding prudence applies the lash or regulates the reins, it is not necessary for me to notice.

The right hon. gentleman, giving it as his own recommendation that he had served four Sovereigns, asked them to follow him. Follow him ! Who was to follow him, or why was anybody to follow him, or where was anybody to follow him to ? What did he mean to do—this great statesman who talked with a sneer of an ancient

monarchy and a proud aristocracy, and told them they
were but drags on the wheel, and he the only driver ?
He told them he was still a Conservative, for had not,
he asked, his Government put down agitation ?

Sir, I confess when I heard this, that great as undoubtedly
are the powers of Parliamentary face of the right hon. gentleman (loud laughter)—I confess, sir, that I was thunderstruck.
I could forget the agitated councils called without a cause
and dismissed without a consequence, the candid explanation
of the situation of his Cabinet—his admission that the only
man in that body who dared to speak the truth differed from
him ; the almost humble confession that he had been misled
in his information ; that his Viceroy, who, being a diplomatist,
communicated his principal information in a postscript, had
caused such false impressions in the Cabinet that the Secretary of State was obliged to send a courier for an explanation—
all these frank details I could afford to admire in one who
has taken up so lofty a position as the right hon. baronet
says he has taken, and who can afford to speak the truth.
But, really, when he told us that his Conservative administration had put down agitation, when he said this in the face
of the hon. member for Stockport [Cobden], in the face of the
hon. member for Durham [Bright]—then, sir, I confess that
the right hon. baronet did manage to achieve the first great
quality of oratory, that he did succeed in making an impression on his audience ! Put down agitation ! Will he rise
and deny that he is legislating or about to legislate with direct
reference to agitation ? (Loud cheers.) What other excuses
has he, for even his mouldy potatoes have failed him, even
the reports of his vagrant professors have failed him.
Sir, I remember, in the midst of a great revolution, when
all the principles of our social system were called into question,
when we heard much of the inconvenience of ancient mon-
archies and proud aristocracies, when it was necessary to
invent some means, to devise some expedient, to manage
reformed constituencies—well do I remember that great
mind which was to control divided counsels, to guide a
distracted people, delivering itself of that oracle which rang
so solemnly over the land, ' Register, register, register.'
(Loud cheers.) Register, some thought, to save the Corn
Laws, some to save the monarchy, some to save the Church.
(Loud cheers). We went on registering, and the right hon.
gentleman went on making protection speeches—a great
orator before a green table, beating a red box. (Laughter.)
Then he showed us the sovereign passion—we were to register

to make him a Minister. The statesman who opposed
Catholic Emancipation against arguments as cogent as any
which the gentlemen of the League can now offer, in spite
of political expediency a thousand times more urgent than
that which now besets them ; always ready with his arguments
and amendments ; always ready with his fallacies, ten thousand
times exploded ; always ready with his Virgilian quotations to
command a cheer — the moment that an hon. and learned
gentleman was returned for the county of Clare, then immediately we saw this right hon. gentleman not ashamed to recall
his arguments, not ashamed to confess that he was convinced,
but telling us, on the contrary, he should be ashamed if he had
not the courage to come forward and propose a resolution
exactly contrary to his previous policy. And so is it always
with the right hon. gentleman. Nursed in the House of
Commons, entertaining no idea but that of Parliamentary
success, if you wish to touch him to the quick, you must
touch him on the state of the poll. (Cheers and laughter.)

It was really too much for a Minister with such a
career to talk to them in high-pitched language about his
lofty spirit, about posterity and the love of fame.

What an advantage to a country to be governed by a Minister
who thinks only of posterity ! The right hon. gentleman has
before assured us that he and his colleagues are only thinking
of the future. Who can doubt it ? Look at them. Throw
your eyes over the Treasury bench. See stamped on every
ingenuous front ' the last infirmity of noble mind.' They are
all of them, as Spenser says, ' imps of fame.' They are just
the men in the House you would fix upon as thinking only
of posterity. The only thing is, when one looks at them,
seeing of what they are composed, one is hardly certain
whether ' the future ' of which they are thinking is indeed posterity or only the coming quarter-day. (Cheers and laughter.)
I should like to know what posterity may think of a Cabinet
which resigns office because it cannot support a policy, and
accepts office for the same reason. (Loud cheers.) In the
history of England, in the history of parties, I defy any man,
I defy even the right hon. member for Edinburgh [Macaulay],
with his disciplined memory and cultivated mind—I defy
any man learned in British history to adduce me a case
parallel to this.
And what is to be the result ? If ' coming events cast their
shadows before,' I suppose no gentleman in a sane state of
mind can doubt it. We resisted the moderate proposal of

the Whigs. We rejected it, confiding in the experience of
that practised individual—the gentleman who has served
four Sovereigns. (Loud laughter.) We were blind enough to
believe that a gentleman of such great ability, of such long
experience, who had had such immense advantages, could not
make very gross and palpable blunders. We accepted him
for a leader to accomplish the triumph of protection, and now
we are to attend the catastrophe of protection. (Loud laughter.)
Of course the Whigs will be the chief mourners. (Loud laughter.)
They cannot but weep for their innocent, although it was an
abortion (loud cheers and laughter); but ours was a fine
child. Who can forget how its nurse dandled it, fondled
it ? (Loud laughter.) What a charming babe ! Delicious little
thing ! so thriving ! (Loud laughter.) Did you ever see such
a beauty for its years ? This was the tone, the innocent
prattle; and then the nurse, in a fit of patriotic frenzy, dashes
its brains out (loud laughter), and comes down to give master
and mistress an account of this terrible murder. The nurse,
too, a person of a very orderly demeanour, not given to
drink, and never showing any emotion, except of late, when
kicking against protection.

Away with this talk about going down to Windsor and
finding that Lord John this or Lord William that could not
form a Ministry, and saying : ' Then I must form one, and
bring all my colleagues to support measures of which they
do not approve.' Was that the constitution that governed
England ? If so, the sooner they could get rid of such a
constitution, the better. He could understand an absolute
Sovereign in a country of high civilisation governing
through a council of state, selected by his arbitrary but
intelligent will from the ablest men of the country ;
but the House of Commons still formed a part of the
constitution, though if the principles they had just
heard from the Prime Minister were once admitted, it
must soon cease to count. Six hundred men met together
without the sympathy of great ideas, to wield all the
power of a country, with all the patronage at the
command of one man appointed by the Sovereign to
direct them as he willed—who could doubt what the
result would be ?

If you had a daring, dashing Minister, a Danby or a Walpole, who tells you frankly, ' I am corrupt, and I wish you to be corrupt also,' we might guard against this ; but what I cannot endure is to hear a man come down and say : ' I will rule without respect to party, though I rose by party ; and I care not for your judgment, for I look to posterity.' Sir, very few people reach posterity. And who amongst us may arrive at that destination I presume not to vaticinate. Posterity is a most limited assembly. Those gentlemen who reach posterity are not much more numerous than the planets. But one thing is quite evident, that whilst we are appealing to posterity—while we are admitting the principles of relaxed commerce—there is extreme danger of our admitting the principles of relaxed politics. I advise, therefore, that we all—whatever may be our opinions about free trade—oppose the introduction of free politics. Let men stand by the principle by which they rise, right or wrong. I make no exception. If they be in the wrong, they must retire to that shade of private life with which our present rulers have often threatened us. . . . It is not a legitimate trial of the principles of free trade against the principle of protection if a Parliament, the majority of which are elected to support protection, be gained over to free trade by the arts of the very individual whom they were elected to support in an opposite career. It is not fair to the people of England.

The Opposition would err if they admitted the principle that they were to support any man who acted on their opinions. A Minister in the position of the right hon. gentleman was not the Minister who ought to abrogate the Corn Laws.

Whatever may be the fate of Government : whether we are to have a Whig administration or a Conservative; whether the noble lord or the right hon. gentleman is to wield the sceptre of the state—whatever, I say, may be the fate of Cabinets (and they are transitory and transient things, things which may not survive the career of many men in this House), on Parliament as an institution, and still a popular institution in this country, is dependent, and not upon the Government, the consideration of the vast majority of the members of this House. Do not, then, because you see a great personage giving up his opinions—do not cheer him on, do not give so ready a reward to political tergiversation. Above all, maintain the line of demarcation between parties, for it is only by maintaining the independence of party that you can maintain the integrity of public men, and the power and influence of Parliament itself.

The cheers at the close lasted for several minutes, and the effect of the speech did not end when the cheers died away. It helped greatly to foster the rising spirit of revolt among the country members, and preparations were at once begun for organising resistance. Disraeli's bold example of rebellion had told at last, and his warfare against the Government was no longer to be solitary.

CHAPTER XII.

THE OVERTHROW OF PEEL.

1846.

The preparations for resistance were arrested for a moment by a rumour launched by the Duke of Wellington, that the Government meant to offer the agricultural interest such countervailing advantages as would completely reconcile it to the modification of the Corn Laws. As the actual proposals were to be explained to the House of Commons in a few days, it was decided to wait for details. Peel's speech unfolding his plan is described by Disraeli as eminently characteristic.

This remarkable man, who in private life was constrained and often awkward, who could never address a public meeting or make an after-dinner speech without being ill at ease, and generally saying something stilted or even a little ridiculous, in the senate was the readiest, easiest, most flexible and adroit of men. He played upon the House of Commons as on an old fiddle. And to-night the manner in which he proceeded to deal with the duties on candles and soap, while all were thinking of the duties on something else ; the bland and conciliatory air with which he announced a reduction of the impost on boot-fronts and shoe leather ; the intrepid plausibility with which he entered into a dissertation on the duties of foreign brandy and foreign sugar ; while visions of deserted villages and reduced rentals were torturing his neighbours, were all characteristic of his command over himself and those whom he addressed.[1]

Eventually the House learnt that there was to be a total repeal of the Corn Laws, though three years were

[1] *Lord George Bentinck,* ch. 4.

to elapse before the ports were to be really open. The measures of compensation, of which so much had been heard, turned out to be trivial readjustments of expense between the counties and the national exchequer ; and as far as Ireland was concerned—' and " if there were any part of the United Kingdom which was to suffer by the withdrawal of protection," the Minister " had always felt it would be Ireland " '—a remission of local taxation similar in amount and character. ' No degree of rhetorical skill could invest with any semblance of substance these shadowy schemes of compensation.' A feeling of blank disappointment ran along the Conservative benches; indignation resumed its sway ; and the Tory magnates and county members at once resumed their arduous enterprise of creating a third party.

The leading spirit among them was Lord George Bentinck, second son of the Duke of Portland, and a man better known for his prowess in the hunting-field, and his devotion to the turf, where he reigned as ' lord paramount,' than for his activity as a politician. He had, to use his own expression, ' sat in eight Parliaments without having taken part in any great debate.' In his youth he had been private secretary to Canning, who was his uncle by marriage ; and, following the friends of Canning into the Whig camp, he had supported the Reform Bill, but had subsequently seceded from the Whigs with Stanley. He had been trained as a soldier, and, apart from his lack of serious political education and experience, he suffered from a certain rigidity of character that became the soldier better than the politician. But he was now in the prime of life, and, in addition to a noble presence and his rank and social standing, he had many of the qualities of which leaders are made—a vehement and imperious spirit, unflinching courage, a mind of great native vigour directed by a will that never knew submission, and the reputation for unbending rectitude that wins the confidence of men. Of frank and severely truthful nature himself, he was fiercely intolerant of

anything like deception ; and it was a sense of betrayal
rather than any motive drawn from selfish or class
interests that stirred him to unwonted exertions on the
present occasion. He had trusted Peel implicitly, and,
as he afterwards confessed, when Disraeli, in the session
of 1845, ' predicted and denounced the impending
defection of the Minister, there was no member of the
Conservative party who more violently condemned the
unfounded attack, or more readily impugned the motions
of the assailant.'[1] On the eve of the meeting of Parliament he wrote to Lord Stanley : ' I agree with Gladstone
(in 1843), and think that to unsettle the Corn Law of
1842 " would be dishonourable to Parliament as well
as to the Government," and, therefore, if anything is
said about Corn Laws in the Queen's speech, if no better
man can be found, I mean to move an amendment.'
' I keep horses in three counties,' he said to a political
opponent, ' and they tell me that I shall save fifteen
hundred a year by free trade. I don't care for that :
what I cannot bear is being sold.' His activity in
organising the third party at once led to the suggestion
that he should accept the position of leader ; but he shook
his head ' with an air of proud humility that was natural
to him,' and said : ' I think we have had enough of
leaders ; I shall remain the last of the rank and file.'

Such was the man with whom Disraeli now found
himself in the closest relations. When the Session began
the two were not, it would seem, even acquainted with
each other ; but a common political purpose soon brought
them together, and in no long time they were fast friends
as well as allies. Bentinck's social position made him
the better fitted for playing ostensibly the first part in
the control of the new movement ; but Disraeli showed
his usual power of winning the confidence of those with
whom he was brought into close contact, and was soon
established as Bentinck's chief counsellor and lieutenant.
With his commanding will and vehement character,

[1] *Lord George Bentinck*, ch. 2.

Lord Geo. Bentinck.

from an engraving by Belli after Lane.

Bentinck was not the man to be the mere puppet he is sometimes represented as having been ; but Disraeli, we may believe, with his greater knowledge and experience, his patient tact in the management of men, his remarkable freedom from jealousy and his power of self-suppression, was able throughout to guide his friend much as he desired. At all events, the combination worked with great smoothness, and Bentinck, who quarrelled with many, seems never, to the day of his death, to have had even a moment of angry difference with Disraeli.

The new party, from the nature of the case, was an army without officers, and the first business was to organise a Parliamentary staff and make preparations for a Parliamentary campaign. The motion for going into committee on the Minister's proposals was down for February 9, and the Government no doubt hoped that the occasion would pass with nothing worse than one of Disraeli's now customary ebullitions. But when the appointed day came, an amendment was moved from the Protectionist benches that the House should go into committee that day six months, and the lately forlorn party showed unexpected powers of sustaining the debate. New speakers were brought forward, and those who had already ventured were encouraged to try again. At the end of the fifth night the Prime Minister rose and made a speech to divide on ; but no division came. Disraeli spoke on the eighth night, and it was not till the twelfth that, after lasting three full Parliamentary weeks, the debate came to an end. It was wound up by Bentinck in a speech of great length, packed with detail, and delivered, as Disraeli says, in a style of ' dignified diffidence.' When the division was called, the West India and shipping interests deserted the land and supported the Minister ; but even so the Protectionist amendment was only defeated by a majority of 97 in a House of 581. No more than 112 of their usual supporters voted with the Government, while 242 voted against them. Peel, in fact, had lost control of the Conservative party, and the knell of his Ministry was rung.

Disraeli's speech was long and in an entirely different vein from the speech on the Address and the philippics of the previous session. Pledging himself to meet the question on its merits, he first lodged a protest against the Prime Minister's appeal from party to public opinion. Party, said Disraeli, was public opinion embodied, and his quarrel with the Prime Minister was not that he had deferred too much to public opinion, but that he had outraged it by preventing its legitimate action. The right hon. gentleman had said that their business was not to discuss party, but to meet an emergency and to construct a system. That was where he went wrong in his very first step : a system should be permanent, an emergency was temporary. With regard to the emergency, he and his friends were prepared to do for Ireland every-thing that human judgment could devise ; but they could not understand the Prime Minister's position. He was prepared to open the ports, and had shown by a rapid review of economic policy that they had often been opened, and beneficially opened. There was no difficulty about that ; the real difficulty was that he was not prepared to close them again. He had resolved, in fact, from the first that the existing system of corn and provision laws should cease — as was shown, indeed, by his proposing his present measures in Council, and insisting on their adoption before the idea could have been conceived by any other human being.

As we have seen more than once, Cobden·was always certain that, if we abandoned protection, other countries would speedily follow our example. Peel could never make up his mind whether this was probable or not, or even whether it was necessary to the success of his measure. In his last speech he had argued that they had been relaxing protection for more than thirty years, and the country was now more flourishing than ever.

It flourishes, retorted Disraeli, because you have given
to its trade a just, a judicious, and a moderate protection.

The whole speech only proved the advantage of the principle
of a moderate protection ('Oh!'). I am sorry, sir, to have
excited that groan from a free trader in distress. (Great
laughter.) I want to ask the right hon. gentleman a very
important question : Does he believe that he can fight hostile
tariffs with free imports ? That is the point ('Hear, hear!').
'Hear, hear!' from the disciples of the school of Manchester![1]
A most consistent cheer ! They have always maintained they
can ; and if their principles are right, as they believe they are
—as I believe they are not—I can easily understand that, their
premises being assumed, they may arrive at that conclusion.
They believe they can fight hostile tariffs with free imports,
and they tell us very justly : 'Let us take care of our imports,
and everything else will take care of itself.' But is that the
conviction of the right hon. gentleman ? We want to know
that, because, if that be his conviction, why all these elegies
over defunct diplomatic negotiations to preserve commercial
treaties ? If he believes that we can meet hostile tariffs with
free imports, he need not trouble himself about commercial
treaties. But if the right hon. gentleman does not believe
that, if he has not the conviction of the school of Manchester,
then he is not justified in offering this measure.

They were told that great things would follow from
a good example—that the Americans were on the point
of changing their tariff, that Prussia was shaken, that
the French were votaries of free trade. Let him offer
them some facts. Did the House understand the power
of the manufacturing interest—the protected interest
in America ? In 1840 there were 800,000 manufacturing
operatives in the United States, and since 1840 under
their tariff there had been the greatest development of
manufacturing industry known in the history of the
country. When he was told that Prussia was shaken,
he could only say that he had just been reading a book
about Prussia, published within the month, from which

---

[1] According to Cobden himself (in Elliot's *Life of Goschen*, I., p. 75), the
phrase 'the Manchester school,' which passed into general use as a title for
his party, was invented by Disraeli ; and this was not improbably the first
occasion when it was heard.

he found that that country was most obstinately determined in its resistance to free trade, and till he was given
a more detailed account of the shaking he must remain
sceptical. With regard to France, he could speak with
some knowledge of her public men, and with the exception
of an occasional individual who attempted to humour
an English Minister he did not believe that there was a
single leading statesman in France who was not in favour
of a high restrictive policy. There was only one way of
gaining any relaxation of the French mercantile system,
and that was by diplomacy ; but they now proposed to
open their ports without condition, and France had no
longer an object to negotiate for. It all came to this, that
if the right hon. baronet was not prepared to meet hostile
tariffs with free imports he had no ground to stand on.

On other aspects of their measure Peel and his colleagues
were no less undecided, and Disraeli was not slow to note
their inconsistencies. The Secretary at War,[1] he said,
who had addressed the House as a martyr when he was
only a convert, had asserted that the fallacy of cheap
bread was now discarded by all parties ; the Secretary of
State[2] on the following night had declared that unless the
question before the House involved a cheaper and more
abundant supply of food to the people there was no
question before them. He was not surprised that there
should be such distraction in their councils when there
was such discord in their speeches. The Secretary at
War asked what they feared from free imports—where
were they to come from ? He had investigated the
subject as well as he could, and he had not the slightest
doubt that when this system was established they could
get from the corn-growing countries any quantity of
corn they liked. It was idle to say that capital and
railways were wanting ; both would be supplied. There
was no fallacy so great as to suppose that when there
was an established market here prices would rise in
proportion to the demand. The examples of tea and

[1] Sidney Herbert.   [2] Graham.

cotton showed prices continually falling as the demand increased. The Secretary at War asked them again, Why all this agitation about a mere question of the repeal of a duty on one article of imports ? He forgot that last year it was a social revolution ; and even now they were told by the consistent Secretary of State that if they refused to pass this measure they would bring upon England anarchy, misery, and ruin.

I have observed that ever since the right hon. baronet [Graham] has been a Minister of a Conservative Cabinet he has annually brought forward a very extensive measure, which has as regularly produced great alarm and excited great odium in the country ; and that the right hon. gentleman, alarmed at his own proceedings, has ended by withdrawing the measure. Bold in opposition, not too scrupulous, it seems somewhat extraordinary that the responsibilities of office should bring to him, not prudence, but panic. (Renewed cheers and laughter.) And these are the Ministers who turn round and say : ' You are alarmed at our measure, but you will not suffer at all except from your own panic.' Why, they are the children of panic, they are an alarmist Cabinet. (Loud cheers.) I know not from what cause, but fright is stamped on their very forehead—whether it arises from a deficiency of food in Ireland or a superabundance of suffrages in Lancashire.[1]

He had now something to say on the question of protection, and he began by showing historically that England in her commercial arrangements had generally taken the middle course. Protection in England had never been protection to every branch of native industry. We had once had a commercial system founded on principle, definite in its details, and, in a certain sense, beneficial in practice—the colonial system. At an earlier date there had been a very liberal system of commerce with the Continent ; but in the middle of the eighteenth century our foreign trade had been sacrificed to the upholding of our colonial system. The range of our transactions had thereby been curtailed ; but our merchants were compensated by more secure markets and

---

[1] In allusion to a by-election that had been lost by the Government.

larger profits. When we lost our principal colonies, Mr. Pitt saw that it was necessary to establish a new system—a large system of commercial intercourse on the principle of reciprocal advantage. This in turn was upset by the revolutionary war ; but the moment the war was over they had gone back to the Pitt system, under the guidance of Lord Liverpool, Mr. Huskisson, and at a later date the present Prime Minister. He himself had given a conscientious vote for the Prime Minister's tariff as embodying a system of moderate and judicious protection in complete harmony with what he thought were their true commercial principles. If they sought examples of a different policy, they would see in Spain the effects of absolute prohibition, and in Turkey the effects of absolute free trade. In the one case un-bridled competition had been as pernicious as excessive protection in the other.

The Prime Minister had said there was a *prima facie* case in favour of free trade. He never cared much about *prima facie* cases ; it would be just as easy for him to say that there was a *prima facie* case in favour of protec-tion, for to protect the industry of our fellow-subjects was *prima facie* desirable. He could find in the speeches of the gentlemen of the League no single reasonable objection to the principle involved. Their arguments had per-petually changed ; they began by promising cheap bread to the labourer, and had ended by promising high rents to the landlord. They said that protection aimed at two objects—to feed the people and to employ the people—and that it had failed in both. Had it failed ? Fifty years ago we could not feed the people ; the population had since doubled, and in average years we could now feed them, and at a lower rate of cost. Nowhere in the world was there any great breadth of land with an agriculture to be compared to that of Great Britain. It was only natural that it should be so, for the land of England received the tribute of the world. There was not an Englishman in any of our colonies, not a resident at the Court of any Indian Prince, whose great ambition was not to return, purchase land, and become a justice of the peace or deputy-lieutenant. ' Riding on elephants, surrounded by slaves, he is always dreaming of quarter-sessions.' Our territorial constitution, which had conferred on the possession of land an honour peculiar to itself, would always secure the investment of capital in the soil of England.

But look, said the gentlemen of the League, at the condition of the peasantry : has protection provided them with sufficient employment ? It was not there alone that he had tried to call attention to the condition of the peasantry ; but when they came with their cool assumptions and daring charges, he asked what was the condition of the peasantry before the protective system was instituted ? Worse even than at present. He might just as well take them to Stockport or Manchester, show them human suffering and human degradation, and say, Competition has done this ; but he knew that these were exceptional cases, and that the industry of Lancashire was a noble and well-ordered industry, and he could not condescend to such vile arts of faction. In the same way, if protection had given the peasant of Wiltshire seven shillings a week, it had equally given the peasant of Lincolnshire an ample remuneration. He found the people employed, though not so well as he could wish ; their condition in many instances bad, but superior generally to that of the other nations of Europe ; and he could not assent to the bold assumption that they would improve their condition by introducing foreign labour into competition with theirs, or that they would elevate their character by diminishing their wages.

He had endeavoured not to make a mere Corn Law speech. He had never rested his defence of the Corn Laws on the burdens to which the land was subject. There were heavy burdens on the land, but the land had great honours, and he who had great honours must also have great burdens. He wished his friends to bear in

mind that their cause must be sustained by principles
of high policy, and he would venture feebly and slightly
to indicate those principles. In every country, he said,
it was the first interest of the state to maintain a balance
between the two great branches of national industry ;
that was a principle which had been recognised by all
great Ministers for the last two hundred years. But he
went farther, and said that in England there were special
reasons why they should not only maintain the balance,
but give a preponderance—he did not say a predominance,
which was not the proper word—to the agricultural
branch ; and the reason was that in England they had a
territorial constitution.

You have thrown upon the land the revenues of the Church,
the administration of justice, and the estate of the poor ;
and you value that territorial constitution, not as serving to
gratify the pride or pamper the luxury of the proprietors of
the land, but because in that constitution you, and those
whom you have succeeded, have found the only security for
self-government ; and, more than that, the only barrier to
that system of centralisation which has taken root and
enslaved the energies of surrounding nations. (Great cheering.)
That is why I have ever supported, and that is why I will
still support, this principle of preponderance. My constituents are not landlords ; they are not aristocrats ; they
are not great capitalists ; they are, in fact, the children of
industry—born only to employment; but they believe not
only that their material interests are involved in a system
which favours native industry, by insuring at the same time
real competition, but also that their social and political
interests are involved in a system under which their rights
and liberties have been guaranteed ; and I agree with them.
I know these are old arguments; but I know also that they
are strong, and that it is necessary they should not be forgotten. (Continued cheering.)
I know we are told, and by one [Cobden] who on this
subject should be the highest authority, that we shall derive
from this great struggle not merely the repeal of the Corn Laws,
but the transfer of power from one class to another—to one
distinguished for its intelligence and wealth, the manufacturers
of England. My conscience assures me that I have not been
slow in doing justice to the intelligence of that class ; I do not
envy them their wide and deserved prosperity, but I must

confess my deep mortification that in an age of political regeneration, when all social evils are ascribed to the operation of class interests, it should be suggested that we are to be rescued from the alleged power of one class only to sink under the avowed dominion of another. I for one, if this is to be the end of all our struggles—if this is to be the great result of this enlightened age—I for one protest against the ignominious catastrophe. I believe that the monarchy of England, its sovereignty mitigated by the power of the established estates of the realm, has its root in the hearts of the people, and is capable of securing the happiness of the people and the power of the state. If this be a worn-out dream—if indeed there is to be a change—I for one, anxious as I am to maintain the present polity of this country, ready to make as many sacrifices as any man for that object—if there is to be this great change, I for one hope that the foundations of it may be deep, the scheme comprehensive, and that, instead of falling under such a thraldom, under the thraldom of capital, under the thraldom of those who, while they boast of their intelligence, are more proud of their wealth —if we must find new forces to maintain the ancient throne and immemorial monarchy of England, I for one hope we may find that novel power in the invigorating energies of an educated and enfranchised people. (Loud and long-continued cheers.)[1]

Having been content with this comparatively sedate speech on the great question, Disraeli a few days later delighted the House by a return to his more characteristic style. Roebuck, the Radical member for Bath, had made enemies in all parties by indulging a bitter tongue, and a personal wrangle of which Ferrand, as usual, was the centre, but in which Roebuck was involved, gave Disraeli an opportunity of reading him a lesson. In a rather inflated speech, Roebuck had laid stress on the resolution against Ferrand passed in a previous session. Disraeli followed, and remarked that a more ridiculous resolution never had been passed, and that he believed the Prime Minister, who had a natural taste for humour, was keenly sensible of the fact. Neither he nor the Home Secretary had originated the proceedings ; they originated

[1] Hansard , Feb. 20, 1846 ; and *The Times* and *Morning Post*, Feb. 21, 1846.

in the quarter where the most disagreeable proceedings naturally originated—with the member for Bath, who now dilated upon them with all the dramatic effect worthy of a minor theatre. ' Sir,' the speaker added with imperturbable gravity, ' I have not had any resolution passed yet against me, and if my hon. friend had taken my advice never to abuse anybody (shouts of laughter), but rather to resort to such language as our English tongue and the forms of the House permit for the expression of opinion, he would never have been in the position in which that resolution, I think, unjustly placed him.' The member for Bath himself was in the habit of infringing the rules of the House by imputing motives most corrupt, most sinister, and most ungentlemanlike.

Some of my hon. friends have noticed it ; I never have. I always felt that in this world you must bear a good deal (great laughter), and that even in this indulgent though dignified assembly, where we endeavour, as far as possible, to carry on public affairs without any unnecessary acerbity— still, we must occasionally submit to some things which the rules of this House do not permit. I could, no doubt, easily have vindicated my character ; but that would only have made the hon. member for Bath speak once or twice more, and, really, I have never any wish to hear him. (Loud cheers and laughter.) I have had the most corrupt motives imputed to me. But I know how true it is that a tree must produce its fruit—that a crab tree will bring forth crab apples (loud laughter), and that a man of meagre and acid mind, who writes a pamphlet or makes a speech, must make a meagre and acid pamphlet or a poor and sour speech. (Shouts of laughter.) Let things, then, take their course. But, for the member for Bath—extraordinary purist as he is—I think that he, though now assuming the functions of general instructor, as formerly of general accuser, would do well to profit by his own precepts, and eschew his melodramatic malignity and Sadler's Wells sort of sarcasm. (Loud and general laughter and cheering.)[1]

---

[1] This speech, which was delivered on the night of the Corn Law division before the resumption of the chief debate, is also notable as having led to the public reconciliation between Cobden and Peel. Bright had accused Ferrand of having charged the League with abetting assassination, and had talked of a prosecution. Disraeli recalled the fact that a similar charge had been made in the House of Commons itself ' by the very distinguished

Roebuck sought his revenge in season and out of season for the remainder of the session. On one occasion he went out of his way to recall the old affair of Disraeli's appearing at Wycombe with Hume and O'Connell as his sponsors. To this 'arranged impromptu' Disraeli replied as usual, that he had never changed his opinions.

I am not in a condition to have had hereditary opinions carved out for me, and all my opinions, therefore, have been the result of reading and thought. I never was a follower of either of the two great aristocratic parties in this country. My sympathies and feelings have always been with the people from whom I spring ; and when obliged as a member of this House to join a party, I joined that party with which I believe the people sympathise. I continue to hold substantially the same opinions as I have always professed ; and when the hon. member talks of my going 'into his camp,' I never heard that he had a camp. How the solitary sentry talks of his garrison ! He a leader of the people ! In my opinion there is no greater opponent of real democracy than a modern Liberal ; and as to popular principles, I believe they are never more in danger than when they are professed by political economists. Three months of solitude for an attack on the consistency of my political opinions ! never was any senator struck with a rhetorical paralysis more remarkable ; never was anything more malignant, and certainly never was anything more futile.[1]

After the defeat of the protectionist amendment on the principle of the new proposals, Disraeli and Bentinck made it their object to delay the Government measures so that they should not reach the House of Lords before the Easter adjournment. Time appeared to be on their side. The chapter of accidents might at any moment cause the fall of a Government which had no majority for anything except its tariff policy. The failure of the potato crop was proving to have been exaggerated, and if the course of events should dispel panic it was possible

---

individual at the head of the administration.' Why not prosecute him ? Here was an antlered monarch of the woods : why hunt small deer ? Peel rose afterwards and explained that it had been his intention to relieve Cobden completely of the imputation he had put upon him by a misapprehension ; Cobden accepted the disavowal ; and peace was established.

[1] Hansard, May 8, 1846.

that the House of Lords might have the courage to reject
the Bill when eventually it reached them. There was
no excitement in the country in favour of the new policy,
and a good deal of excitement among the farmers against
it. The Ministerial changes had led to a number of
by-elections ; and Lord Ashley and other members who
had been elected as protectionists, more sensitive as to
their pledges than the Minister and his colleagues, thought
it right to vacate their seats. Nearly every vacant seat
was carried against the Government. Lord Lincoln,
who had been promoted to the office of Chief Secretary,
was defeated through the influence of his father, the Duke
of Newcastle, and Gladstone through the same influence
left without a seat for the remainder of the Parliament.

Thus encouraged, the protectionists gathered confidence
and force. Bentinck, who still persisted in refusing to
accept the formal position of leader, was indefatigable
in debate and in all the work of organisation that properly
falls to a leader. The resolutions on which the Government's Bills were to be based abounded in detail, and
several weeks were consumed in getting them through
committee. It was not till March 27 that the Bill for
the repeal of the Corn Laws was read a second time, and
the majority for the Government had now sunk to 88.
Disraeli, who at this time appears to have been in poor
health, and soon afterwards was definitely ill, took no
part in the debate of four nights that preceded ; and its
only remarkable feature was a speech by Palmerston, in
which, after an abstract eulogy of free trade, he astonished
the free traders by unfurling the standard of a moderate
fixed duty.

The cheers suddenly stopped ; and a member for a metropolitan district who had been applauding vociferously whispered to a neighbour : ' He has spoilt a capital speech ; what
could have induced him to bring in a fixed duty !' Penetrating
member for a metropolitan district ! As if the ' capital
speech ' had been made for any other purpose than to introduce the very declaration which you looked upon as so
damaging ! There is diplomacy even in debate : Lord

Palmerston threw a practised and prescient eye over the disturbed elements of the House of Commons, and two months afterwards, when a protectionist Ministry on moderate principles (principles moderate and not fixed) was not impossible, the speech of the noble lord was quoted by many as a rallying-point.[1]

How disturbed the elements were, and how uncertain the protectionist position, in spite of the good division, is shown by a letter from Stafford O'Brien to Disraeli on the following day. ' I am altogether unsanguine,' he writes, ' as to our compactness, and I believe that we shall go to pieces so fast that it will soon be a question how far we shall be authorised in maintaining ourselves as a party at all.' In political history, when we look beneath the surface, we find the key to most events in personal will and influence ; and here there is no exception. Nothing could seem more natural and inevitable now than the permanence of the party which seceded from Peel ; as a matter of fact, but for the exertions of Disraeli and Bentinck it would either never have been born at all or its life would have been brief and flickering, and the resistance to the Minister have speedily collapsed.

Fortune rarely fails to favour a bold and determined policy, and the protectionist leaders now began to be helped by a blunder of which the Minister had been guilty. The distress in Ireland during the winter, not severe enough to produce the paralysis of famine, had been severe enough to provoke a serious outbreak of agrarian crime ; and in the Queen's speech at the beginning of the session a measure for the protection of life had been promised. A month had been allowed to elapse, and then, in fulfilment of this promise, a stringent ' Coercion ' Bill had been brought into the House of Lords. It had been supported there by the Whigs as well as by the Tories, but had been passed through its stages in a

[1] *Lord George Bentinck,* ch. 6. Palmerston wrote to Disraeli on March 29, in reply to some note, probably, of congratulation : ' I could not refrain from affording one " pitying tear to grace the obsequies " of fixed duty. Many would, I am persuaded, be glad to revive it ; but to all appearance its life seems entirely extinct.'

leisurely fashion ; and, reaching the Commons in the middle of March, had been allowed to remain dormant till after the Corn Bill had received its second reading. If such a measure as the Coercion Bill was needed at all, it was obviously needed at once, and ought to have been pressed through both Houses with all the force of the Government in the first weeks of the session. Probably in that case it would have met with little resistance ; but the opportunity was missed. Peel, in fact, had put forward two opposite remedies for the troubles in Ireland, but inverted their logical order. His passionate eagerness in the matter of the Corn Bill had blinded his judgment, and led him into an error of political strategy which was to pursue him throughout the session, and finally cause his overthrow.

The first reading of the Coercion Bill was to be taken in the Commons on March 30, and before the appointed day the protectionists met to consider the course to be adopted. With assassination rife, and the Whigs, as was supposed, already committed to the Bill by their leaders in the Lords, the result was never in doubt. Disraeli alone urged them to pause before they gave a Government, ' against which they were arrayed in circumstances of urgent and unusual opposition,' the striking proof of confidence that would be involved in their pledging themselves to support such a measure ; but his arguments, as he tells us, ' though received with kindness, elicited little sympathy.' Bentinck, marking the general feeling, intervened with the adroit suggestion that they should make their support conditional on the Minister's proving his sincerity by pressing forward with the Coercion Bill in preference to every other measure ; and this suggestion, promising the advantage of an indefinite delay of the Corn Bill, was adopted with enthusiasm.

Thus authorised, Bentinck made an arrangement with the Government Whip by which the third reading of the Corn Bill was to be postponed till after Easter, and the protectionists were to support the Government in pushing forward the Coercion Bill. For some reason Peel repudiated this arrangement, and, while adhering to his determination to give the Coercion Bill a first reading at once, refused his assent to the postponement of the Corn Bill. Meanwhile the Whigs, though feeling no dislike for coercion as such, decided to insist that the Corn Bill should have precedence, and the Government suddenly found themselves in a false and dangerous position. They had in the same breath to argue that the urgency of the Coercion Bill made it necessary to postpone everything till its principle had been affirmed, and to promise that, if this Bill had once been granted a first reading, it should not be allowed to interfere with the progress of the Corn Bill. Even so, on the night of the 30th, though supported by all the protectionists present, they only escaped defeat, on a dilatory amendment moved from the Whig benches, by a majority of 39.

The division of the House of Commons between free traders and protectionists had now ceased to be paramount, and for the next three months the fate of the Government hung on a nice balance of factions. There were about 120 Peelites, the old guard of the Government; a rather more numerous body of Radicals and O'Connellites, who were opposed to coercion on principle; perhaps 150 Whigs, who, though not opposed to coercion, wished the Corn Bill to have precedence; and 250 protectionists, who wished the order of the Bills reversed. In this situation the Irish members began a course of obstruction, and when the Easter adjournment came, though all the Government time had been given to the Irish Bill, it had not received a first reading. The obstinate Minister even announced that, when the House met again in the middle of April, he would proceed with it again till the stage was completed.

The Irish members glanced defiance, and the protectionists could scarcely conceal their satisfaction. The reputation of Sir Robert Peel for Parliamentary management seemed to be vanishing; never was a Government in a more tottering

state ; and the Whigs especially began to renew their laments
that the Edinburgh letter and its consequences had prevented
the settlement of the corn question from devolving to the
natural arbitrator in the great controversy, their somewhat
rash but still unrivalled leader, Lord John Russell.[1]

In such a situation intrigue was, of course, rife.

The lovers of compromise, always the strongest party in
this country, were now active. Why did not the Whigs step
in and settle the question in a spirit consistent with all their
previous declarations, which even the protectionists would
now willingly accept ? A moderate fixed duty was the Whig
policy ; it would save the honour of the landed party ; it would
meet the scientific objections of those economical authorities
who, however favourable to interchange, were of opinion that
it was injurious to encounter hostile tariffs by free imports ;
it might prove a fruitful source of revenue ; finally, it would
permit the formation of a strong Government, and the Whigs
would only be in their natural position as the leaders of the
aristocracy of the country.[2]

Perhaps foreseeing the possibility of some such development, Disraeli, as the reader may have noticed, had
during the last couple of years greatly moderated the
violence of his attacks on the Whigs, had treated Russell
with some deference both in his novels and in the House
of Commons, and with Palmerston had even contrived
to establish a sort of friendship. When intrigue was going,
Disraeli was not likely to be wholly without a hand in it,
but his papers throw little light on his activities at this
moment. Such evidence as is to be gleaned from them
indicates that he was anxious for the formation of a
strong Government, and the only possible basis for such
a Government was an arrangement between Whigs and
protectionists. If Palmerston, not Russell, had been
leader of the Whigs, there can be very little doubt that
such an arrangement would have been effected, and that
Peel would have fallen.

The Whigs were sufficiently patriotic not to shrink from
office ; they were as a party both from feeling and conviction

unanimous in favour of a fixed duty ; Lord Palmerston's speech was still ringing in the ears of the House of Commons, and not to run the risk of its being forgotten his lordship had properly taken care to have it printed ; they were sure under the circumstances of the unanimous support of the Irish members, who would have got rid at the same time of the Corn and the Coercion Bills ; they would have received from the landed interest a permanent support ; and if Lord George Bentinck had entered the new Cabinet, which many among the Whigs talked of and desired, he would have only reverted to that ancient political connexion of which his house for generations had been one of the main props.[1]

A junction between the two aristocratic parties, the Whigs and the protectionists, leaving Peel, if he liked, to join forces with the middle - class Liberals under Cobden, with whom he was now most in sympathy, would have been the best and healthiest outcome of the situation. It would have anticipated in a sense a rearrangement which was delayed till 1886, and averted much of the confusion of the intervening period. But Russell, embarrassed by his Edinburgh letter, which had been intended to embarrass others, and even more, perhaps, by his engagement with the Queen to support Peel in a settlement of the Corn Laws, proved an insuperable obstacle, and the plan came to nothing.

Another combination was possible, however, which we may believe was not without attractions for Disraeli. The protectionists and the Irish members together formed a clear majority of the House, and united would be able to defeat the Government. O'Connell, the Irish leader, still, indeed, clung to his old allies the Whigs, and was anxious to hasten the passing of the Corn Bill in order to facilitate their return to power ; but O'Connell was now at the end of his career, and his influence almost gone. The younger generation, whose aims were national and social rather than religious and political, had no particular love either for the Whigs or the Corn Bill ; and they were at present in a state of fury against Peel. They had long been familiar with Disraeli's broad views on the

[1] *Lord George Bentinck*, ch. 11.

subject of Ireland ; and in the debate on the Coercion
Bill Bentinck had made a speech that attracted their
attention, and proved that his views were as liberal as
Disraeli's. This was before Easter, and after the holidays,
while the debate on the Coercion Bill was still dragging
slowly along, Smith O'Brien, who was the leader of the
Young Ireland party in the House, made overtures to
Bentinck. In order to clear the air, O'Brien by arrangement rose in his place, and, accepting the protectionist
position that the Government had no right to couple the
question of Irish famine with the question of free trade
—nay, accusing the Prime Minister of a singular want of
candour in putting forward the famine as a pretext for
what was clearly not an Irish but an English measure—
he asked whether Bentinck and his friends would support
a Bill to suspend the existing Corn Laws with respect to
Ireland, so as to admit grain duty-free. Bentinck, who
had just at last been persuaded to accept the formal
office of leader, made a statesmanlike reply. He argued
against the assumption that O'Brien's suggested remedy
would afford any relief, pointing out that corn was still
being exported from Ireland, and that its price there was
lower than the price in England of foreign corn in bond ;
and insisting very justly that the real trouble in Ireland
was not the want of food, but the want of money to buy
it, and that the only immediate remedy was to break the
rigid rules of political economy and make provision for
the needy. But he wished to dispel the illusion that the
protectionist party stood between the people of Ireland
and their food ; and if the Irish members proposed a
suspension of the Corn Laws, he and his friends, though
convinced of the futility of such a measure, were willing
to support it.

The story at once went round that a compact had been
arranged between the protectionists and the Irish members, and the Government and the free traders took
serious alarm. Cobden presently rose and rated the
protectionists in vigorous style ; threatening them with

dissolution, at which they only cheered, and reminding O'Brien and Bentinck that there were other parties to be consulted on the proposition they were making. 'There are the people of England—I don't mean the country party, but the people living in the towns, and who will govern this country.' At this Peel was supposed to cheer ; and Disraeli, rising after Cobden, said he had defined the people, with whose indignation he threatened them, as those who lived in towns, and the Prime Minister, who had once been proud of being the head of the gentlemen of England, had cheered that definition. Peel jumped up and exclaimed : 'I totally deny it'; whereupon Disraeli said : 'The right hon. gentleman totally denies it. If he means to say that anything I stated is false, of course, I sit down.' Peel remained silent, and a scene of confusion and excitement followed till at length satisfactory explanations were exchanged and all again became tranquil.

The incident, however, had a sequel. The Prime Minister's brother, Colonel Jonathan Peel, coming up to Disraeli in the House when peace had been restored, said : 'There shall be no doubt as to what *one* person thinks of your assertion, and *I* say it *is* false.' The last duel in England had not yet been fought, and Disraeli at once placed the matter in the hands of Bentinck, who called on Peel to retract. He was referred by Peel to a friend,[1] and Disraeli went to bed to prepare for a visit to Wormwood Scrubbs with pistols in the morning ; but a conference between the seconds late at night at White's Club led to the withdrawal of the offensive expression, with an ample apology. Disraeli was supposed to have behaved well throughout the affair.[2]

[1] Captain (afterwards Admiral) Rous. The apology in Bentinck's hand and signed by him and Rous, is preserved among Disraeli's papers. There have been stories of a challenge from Sir Robert Peel himself, but this incident appears to be their only foundation ; though Disraeli in later years told Lord Rowton that ' Sir Robert was a very " fightable " man, and wished to challenge me often, but was restrained by Lord Granby and others.'

[2] See Broughton's *Recollections*, VI., p. 168, where Brougham, in the midst of some vulgar abuse, gives his testimony to this effect.

It was now the last week of April, and the Coercion Bill was still awaiting its first reading, while the Corn Bill had not been heard of for a month. The general feeling was that the situation had become critical, and Peel himself saw that he must make a great effort to end the deadlock. When the House next met he spoke on the Coercion Bill, and, alluding to insinuations that the Government were becoming indifferent to the progress of the Corn Bill, said that he was more than ever determined to carry the Corn Bill through ; that his opinions indeed had changed in the course of the debates, but the change was that restrictions which he had at first believed to be impolitic he now believed to be unjust. A sense of their injustice precluded any compromise, and he would be perfectly ready to testify, by any public act, the sincerity of his intentions. This was generally interpreted as a threat of dissolution, but Bentinck was undismayed. He never would believe that Peel would dissolve, because, ' whatever might be the national decision as to the principle of policy which was to be adopted, he was convinced that the whole body of the present men in office, at least with rare exceptions, must lose their seats.' The Whigs, however, were frightened by the threat of dissolution, and Young Ireland was discouraged by the loss of its leader, Smith O'Brien, who had been imprisoned by the House for refusing to serve on a railway committee. A few days after this speech of Peel's the division on the Coercion Bill was taken at last, and the first reading carried by a great majority. Neither Whigs nor protectionists had yet advanced to a position of hostility to the principle, and Russell and Bentinck, and most of their followers, voted with the Government. Disraeli walked out of the House.

The way was now clear for the Corn Bill again, but on the motion to go into committee Bentinck demanded an explanation of Peel's remark that he now regarded the Corn Laws as not only impolitic, but unjust. In rallying his colleagues and attempting to rally his followers after

Russell's failure in December, Peel[1] had justified his course by the assurance that the only alternative to a free trade Conservative Ministry was a Government dominated by Cobden. The position which he assumed at the meeting of Parliament ' was that of the patriotic individual who by great sacrifices had succeeded in preventing Cobden from becoming a Minister.' But the revolt of his followers had entirely changed his tone, and his declaration that the repeal of the Corn Laws was a matter of justice rather than of policy marked a fresh approximation to the Manchester League which greatly irritated the protectionists. His reply to Bentinck on the present occasion did not diminish their irritation.

Both sides of the House listened with no little astonishment while the Minister, with an apparent interest in the subject which it would have been supposed novelty could have alone inspired, recapitulated all those arguments which for years the Anti-Corn-Law League had presented to the consideration, not only of the community, but even of the House of Commons, in every form which Ingenuity could devise and a versatile and experienced rhetoric illustrate and enforce. But when, with an air of discovery, he availed himself of one of the most subtle but certainly not least hackneyed tactics of Mr. Cobden, and, in order to depreciate the importance of wheat-growing, called upon the House to take the map of Great Britain, and divide the island by a line from Inverness to Southampton, and observe that, generally speaking, to the westward of the line the country had no interest in the restrictions on the importation of wheat, the gentlemen who had left their agricultural constituents in the lurch because they had been told that, unless Sir Robert Peel were permitted to repeal the Corn Laws, Mr. Cobden might actually become a Minister, began to ask themselves whether, after all, such an event would not have been the honestest arrangement of the two. Unlike the Corn Laws, the exclusion of Mr. Cobden might have been

---

[1] See, for instance, his letter to the Queen, in *Queen Victoria's Letters*, under date Dec. 21, 1845 : ' Sir Robert Peel . . . has written very strongly to the Duke [of Buccleugh], stating that the present question is not one of Corn Law, but whether your Majesty's former servants or Lord Grey and Mr. Cobden shall constitute your Majesty's Government. Sir Robert Peel defied the wit of man to suggest now another alternative to your Majesty.'

politic, but, 'after the discussion of the last three months,'
it certainly seemed unjust.[1]

Disraeli in the course of the evening happily ridiculed
'the fervour of Peel's mimetic rhetoric.' Taking up a
remark of the Minister's that the debate was unexpected,
he said :

Though not prepared for a debate, I can scarcely say that
is an excuse for not being prepared to answer the speech of
the right hon. baronet. That is not a speech heard now for
the first time. It has been heard in other places, in different
localities, and, I may be permitted to add, from a master-
hand. That speech has sounded in Stockport ; it has echoed
in Durham.[2] There has been on the stage of the classical
theatre a representation of it on the finest scale, and, as is
usual in such cases, the popular performance is now repeated
by an inferior company. Especially, when I heard the line
drawn which marks on the map the corn-growing districts
of Great Britain, I thought I might say, as I hear sometimes
said on railway committees upon rival lines, 'That is surely
the line of the hon. member for Stockport' (Mr. Cobden).

But, in spite of Disraeli's wit and Bentinck's zeal and
energy, the Minister, backed by the Whigs, now made
steady progress, and the Corn Bill soon reached the stage
of third reading. It was read a third time on May 15,
after a debate of three nights, by a majority of 98 in a
House of 560. Disraeli on the last night made the speech
of the debate. According to the fashion of the time, it
was a speech of great length, occupying no less than
three hours in the delivery, and throughout its greater part
it was a closely-reasoned performance on the lines of the
speech in February. Clinging to his central position, he
had little difficulty in showing the contradictions in
which the theorists of free trade were involved by their
a priori dogmas ; and many of his own arguments are
curious anticipations of the arguments that have become
familiar during the revival of the controversy in the last
ten years. He believed, for instance, 'that the effect

---

[1] *Lord George Bentinck*, ch. 12.   [2] Bright's constituency.

of the present Corn Laws was to raise the price of the necessaries of life in this country ' ; but he also believed ' that they increased in an infinitely greater ratio the purchasing powers by the community of the necessaries of life.' He believed, again, that it could be ' laid down as a principle of commerce, that where an article could be progressively produced to an indefinite extent, precisely as the demand increased the price would decrease.' Even the colonial argument was touched upon. ' I am not one of those who think it the inevitable lot of the people of Canada to become annexed to the United States. Canada has all the elements of a great and independent country, and is destined, I sometimes believe, to be the Russia of the new world. . . . But I will ask the gentlemen of Manchester to consider what may become of the trans-atlantic market for their manufactures if the whole of that continent belong to one power.' All this was lit up by occasional flashes of Disraelian wit : the suggestion, for instance, of a limbo for political economists, to which their exhausted arguments and exploded fallacies might be consigned after serving their turn ; the picture of the member for Lincoln placing the arch-fiend of political economy on the celebrated tower that overlooks the city, to take a survey of the agriculture spread out before him ; and the often-quoted description of Cobden and his friends : ' I find that a body of men have risen in this country eminent for their eloquence, distinguished for their energy, but more distinguished, in my humble opinion, for their energy and their eloquence than for their knowledge of human nature or for the extent of their political information.'

This led him on to the conclusion of the speech, which was a long and sustained invective against Peel. The Anti-Corn-Law League had been successful, he said, because the party who were hostile to their ideas had not unnaturally slumbered at their posts, trusting to their leaders—to those who had clambered into power by accepting, or rather by eagerly seeking, the trust of guarding them—to one who in this way had obtained the greatest place in the country, and at that moment governed England. More than a year ago he had said in his place that protection appeared to him to be in about the same state that Protestantism was in in 1829. His friends, he remembered, were very indignant at that assertion, but they had since been so kind as to observe that, instead of being a calumny, it was only a prophecy. But with that very humble exception the Prime Minister, he thought, had been completely successful in deceiving his party to the very last moment. How ingenuous was his conduct he left the House to decide ; but was it not strange that after all his Machiavellian manœuvres, when he met them at last, he acted as if they had deserted him, instead of his having deserted them ? Who could forget those tones and that indignant glance ?

> Vectabor humeris tunc ego inimicis eques :
> Meæque terra cedet insolentiæ :[1]

which was as much as to say : ' I, a protectionist Minister, mean to govern England by the aid of the Anti-Corn-Law League ; and as for the country gentlemen, why, I snap my fingers in their faces.'

Yet even then the right hon. gentleman had no cause to complain of his party. It is very true that, on a subsequent occasion, 240 gentlemen recorded their sense of his conduct. But then he might have remembered the considerable section of converts that he obtained, even in the last hour. (Loud laughter.) Why, what a compliment to a Minister— not only to vote for him, but to vote for him against your opinions (much cheering), and in favour of opinions which he had always drilled you to distrust. (Loud cheers.) That was a scene, I believe, unprecedented in the House of Commons. Indeed, I recollect nothing equal to it, unless it be the conversion of the Saxons by Charlemagne, which is the only historical incident that bears any parallel to that illustrious occasion. (Great cheers and laughter.) Ranged on the banks of the Rhine, the Saxons determined to resist any further movement on the part of the great Cæsar ; but when the Emperor appeared, instead of conquering he converted

---

[1] Horace, *Epod.* XVII., 74, 75.

them. How were they converted ? In battalions—the old chronicler informs us they were converted in battalions and baptised in platoons. (Roars of laughter.) It was utterly impossible to bring these individuals from a state of reprobation to a state of grace with a celerity sufficiently quick. When I saw the hundred and twelve fall into rank and file, I was irresistibly reminded of that memorable incident on the banks of the Rhine. (Loud cheers.)

He must say, in vindication of the right hon. gentleman, that a great injustice had been done him throughout these debates. He had been accused of foregone treachery, of long-meditated deception, of always having intended to abandon the opinions by which he rose to power.

Sir, I entirely acquit the right hon. gentleman of any such intention. I do it for this reason : that when I examine the career of this Minister, which has now filled a great space in the Parliamentary history of his country, I find that between thirty and forty years, from the days of Mr. Horner to the days of the hon. member for Stockport, that right hon. gentleman has traded on the ideas and intelligence of others. (Loud cheering.) His life has been a great appropriation clause. (Shouts of laughter and cheers.) He is a burglar of others' intellect. Search the Index of Beatson, from the days of the Conqueror to the termination of the last reign, there is no statesman who has committed political petty larceny on so great a scale. (Renewed laughter.) I believe, therefore, when the right hon. gentleman undertook our cause on either side of the House, that he was perfectly sincere in his advocacy ; but as, in the course of discussion, the conventionalisms which he received from us crumbled away in his grasp, feeling no creative power to sustain him with new arguments, feeling no spontaneous sentiments to force upon him conviction, the right hon. gentleman, reduced at last to defending the noblest cause, one based on the most high and solemn principles, upon the ' burdens peculiar to agriculture '[1]—the right hon. gentleman, faithful to the law of his nature, imbibed the new doctrines, the more vigorous, bustling, popular, and progressive doctrines, as he had imbibed the doctrines of Mr. Horner —as he had imbibed the doctrines of every leading man in this country for thirty or forty years, with the exception of the

[1] The words in inverted commas, we are told, were uttered in a tone of sarcasm that elicited very great laughter.

doctrine of Parliamentary reform, which the Whigs very wisely led the country upon, and did not allow to grow sufficiently mature to fall into his mouth.

The right hon. gentleman told them that he did not feel humiliated. It was impossible for anyone to know what were the feelings of another ; but this he would tell him, that, though he might not feel humiliated, his country ought to feel humiliated. Was it grateful to the pride of England that her foremost citizen should be one of whom it might be said, as Dean Swift said of another, that ' he was a gentleman who had the perpetual misfortune to be mistaken '? Even now in this the last scene of the drama, when the party which he had unintentionally betrayed was to be intentionally annihilated, faithful to the law of his being, he was going to pass a project which it was a matter of notoriety was not of his own invention.

After the day that the right hon. gentleman made his first exposition of his scheme, a gentleman well known in this House, and learned in all the political secrets behind the scenes, met me, and said : ' Well, what do you think of your chief's plan ?' Not knowing exactly what to say, but, taking up a phrase which has been much used in the House, I observed : ' Well, I suppose it's a " great and comprehensive " plan.' ' Oh !' he replied, ' we know all about it ! It was offered to us ! It is not his plan ; it's Popkins's plan !' (Peals of laughter from all parts of the House.) And is England to be governed, and is England to be convulsed, by ' Popkins's plan ?' (Cheers and laughter.) Will he go to the country with it ? Will he go with it to that ancient and famous England that once was governed by statesmen—by Burleighs and by Walsinghams ; by Bolingbrokes and by Walpoles ; by a Chatham and a Canning—will he go to it with this fantastic scheming of some presumptuous pedant ? (Great cheering.) I won't believe it. I have that confidence in the common sense, I will say the common spirit of our countrymen, that I believe they will not long endure this huckstering tyranny of the Treasury bench (loud cheers)—these political pedlars that bought their party in the cheapest market, and sold us in the dearest. (Enthusiastic cheering.)

I know, sir, that there are many who believe that the time is gone by when one can appeal to those high and honest impulses that were once the mainstay and the main element of the English character. I know, sir, that we appeal to a people debauched by public gambling, stimulated and encouraged by an inefficient and a short-sighted Minister. I know that the public mind is polluted with economic fancies—a depraved desire that the rich may become richer without the interference of industry and toil. I know, sir, that all confidence in public men is lost. (Great cheering.) But, sir, I have faith in the primitive and enduring elements of the English character. It may be vain now, in the midnight of their intoxication, to tell them that there will be an awakening of bitterness ; it may be idle now, in the springtide of their economic frenzy, to warn them that there may be an ebb of trouble. But the dark and inevitable hour will arrive. Then, when their spirits are softened by misfortune, they will recur to those principles that made England great, and which, in our belief, will only keep England great. (Prolonged cheers.) Then too, sir, perchance they may remember, not with unkindness, those who, betrayed and deserted, were neither ashamed nor afraid to struggle for the ' good old cause '— the cause with which are associated principles the most popular, sentiments the most entirely national, the cause of labour, the cause of the people, the cause of England !

' Mr. Disraeli,' it is recorded, ' here resumed his seat amid cheers which for duration and vehemence are seldom heard within the walls of Parliament.' It was eight years since he had told them that the time would come when they would hear him.

From Lord Ponsonby.[1]

May 15, 1846.

MY DEAR DISRAELI,

' A cat may look at a king, and a country parson may praise a Bishop.' Such is the beginning of a letter from Sydney Smith to the Bishop of Oxford.

Fortified by the above assertion of right, I will venture to praise you. I heard your speech—all but the first few minutes. It lasted, they say, three hours, and when it was over I wished it to last three hours more. I thought your argument admirably managed, and perfectly sound in essence, and I doubt if any classic orator of Rome or England ever did anything so well as you crucified Peel. Had I been him, I would have rushed at and murdered you, or run home and hanged myself.

[1] See note, p. 225.

John Russell tired me in a quarter of an hour, and I left the House dissatisfied.

I never in my life heard any speech so much cheered as yours was ; I never saw so much effect produced by one. I think you will no longer talk of flying your country ; I think you will no longer talk of difficulties of position, but will feel that you were born to the foremost rank of its chiefest ornaments and leaders. From the first of my acquaintance with you I felt your power.

Tell Mrs. Disraeli that I wish her joy.

Yours most truly,

PONSONBY.

Hobhouse also bears his testimony to the great impression made by the speech :

His conclusion for a good twenty minutes was a steady philippic against Peel, which was very powerful indeed, and produced a great effect on all parts of the House. Peel looked miserable, and his brother Jonathan more wretched still, and bursting with mortification ; even Macaulay told me he thought the effect very powerful, and the speech the best Disraeli ever made. Russell, who followed, was unable to go on for some time on account of the prolonged cheering ![1]

The final cheer is recalled by Disraeli himself in a note of the sixties reminiscent of an incident to which the speech gave rise.

After my great speech in 1846, on the second [sic] reading of the Bill for the repeal of the Corn Laws, and which was followed by the loudest and the longest cheer that ever was heard in the House of Commons, a gentleman who was obliged to be a protectionist, but no friend of mine, but very much of Sir R. Peel, met O'Connell in the lobby, and asked him what he thought of my speech. ' I should have said,' replied the great Dan, ' that it was one of the ablest speeches I ever heard in the House of Commons, but for the invective.' ' Ah !' said the protectionist, shaking his head and looking quite mournful at the mention of the sacrilege. ' But for the invective,' continued O'Connell, ' and that made it incomparable.'

' What a sell !' said Lord March, who heard it and came and told me.

[1] Broughton, VI., p. 170.

The speech was followed by another incident which has become too celebrated. Peel, who had an angry reception[1] from the members of the country party, spoke later in the evening, and, after the customary prelude that he would not condescend to bandy personalities, remarked that, when he entered on his present course from a sense of public duty, he foresaw that it would expose him to many serious sacrifices; but the smallest of all the penalties which he then anticipated were the continued venomous attacks of the member for Shrewsbury.

Sir, I will only say of that hon. gentleman, that if he, after reviewing the whole of my public life—a life extending over thirty years previously to my accession to office in 1841—if he then entertained the opinion of me which he now professes; if he thought I was guilty of these petty larcenies from Mr. Horner and others, it is a little surprising that in the spring of 1841, after his long experience of my public career, he should have been prepared to give me his confidence. It is still more surprising that he should have been ready, as I think he was, to unite his fortunes with mine in office, thus implying the strongest proof which any public man can give of confidence in the honour and integrity of a Minister of the Crown.

The retort was not overwhelming; nor was the taunt very chivalrous, though the provocation may have excused it. Disraeli might well have remained silent; or, still better, if he had risen and frankly told the story of his application to Peel in 1841, in which there was nothing really discreditable, he would, in all probability, have carried the House with him, and effectually have turned the tables on his antagonist. But, frightened, we may believe, by a consciousness that his character did not stand high, he for once lost his head, and grievously blundered. Rising after Peel, he asked for a moment's attention to the

---

[1] 'When he talked of honour and conscience' (Greville tells us under date May 21, 1846), 'they assailed him with shouts of derision and gestures of contempt. Such treatment in a House of Commons, where for years he had been an object of deference and respect, nearly overcame him. The Speaker told me that for a minute or more he was obliged to stop; and, for the first time in his life, probably, he lost his self-possession, and the Speaker . . . expected him to burst into tears.'

' peculiarly personal ' subject of the Prime Minister's
insinuation, and then embarked on a shambling and
obviously embarrassed statement, of which, however, the
general effect is only too clear. He began by denying
that his opposition to the Government had been inspired
by personal motives, pointing out, fairly enough, that
he had supported them for two years, and that his first
step in opposition had only been taken when his constituents in 1843 called on him to explain his views on
protection. He then proceeded :

I understand the insinuation of the right hon. gentleman,
if it meant anything, to be this—that my opposition, or, as
he called it, my ' envenomed opposition ' to him, was occasioned by my being disappointed of office. Now, having been
for five years in opposition to the late Government, an active,
though I well know not an influential, supporter of the right
hon. gentleman, and having been favoured by him with an
acknowledgment of his sense of my slight services, I do not
think there would have been anything dishonourable for me
if, when the new Government was formed in 1841, I had been
an applicant for office. It might have been in good taste or
not, but at least there would have been nothing dishonourable ; but I can assure the House nothing of the kind ever
occurred. I never shall—it is totally foreign to my nature—
make an application for any place. But in 1841, when the
Government was formed . . . an individual possessing, as I
believe him to possess, the most intimate and complete
confidence of the right hon. gentleman called on me and
communicated with me. There was certainly some conversation—I have certainly never adverted to these circumstances, and should not now unless compelled, because they
were under a seal of secrecy confided in me. There was some
communication, not at all of that nature which the House
perhaps supposes, between the right hon. gentleman and me,
but of the most amicable kind. I can only say this—it was
a transaction not originated by me, but which any gentleman,
I care not how high his honour or spirit, might entertain to-
morrow.

After an allusion to the rumours of interested motives
that were put in circulation from the moment that he
began to criticise the Government, he concluded :

I never asked a favour of the Government, not even one of those mechanical things which persons are obliged to ask . . . and, as regards myself, I never directly or indirectly solicited office. . . . It is very possible if, in 1841, I had been offered office, I dare say it would have been a very slight office, but I dare say I should have accepted it. I have not that high opinion of myself as to suppose that the more important offices of the Government would have been offered to my acceptance; but I can only say that I am very glad I did not accept it. But with respect to my being a solicitor of office, it is entirely unfounded. Whatever occurred in 1841 between the right hon. gentleman and myself was entirely attributable to the intervention of another gentleman, whom I supposed to be in the confidence of the right hon. baronet, and I dare say it may have arisen from a misconception.

Peel was content to rejoin that he had not attributed personal motives for Disraeli's opposition. He had only asked why, if Disraeli really believed he deserved the character he had given him to-night, he should in 1841 ' have intimated to me that he was not unwilling to give me that proof of confidence that would have been implied by the acceptance of office.' The impression in the House was that Disraeli had better have remained silent, and there the matter ended.

Of the mysterious ' individual ' of Disraeli's speech, and his ' communication ' from Peel, authorised or not, in 1841, we know nothing besides. It might conceivably have been someone—Lyndhurst or another—who endeavoured to soothe Disraeli's feelings by hinting at the real difficulties in the way of Peel's giving him office ; but there is no reason to think that if we knew more the whole transaction would wear any very different aspect. We have already seen that as early as 1844 Disraeli denied before his constituents that he had ever asked Peel for office, and it is impossible to believe that in the short space of three years he could have forgotten his letter of 1841.[1] Speaking among his constituents, he might have thought he was safe from challenge ; but it

[1] There is nothing in Disraeli's papers to indicate that he kept a copy of this letter.

is very hard to understand how he could have risen in the House of Commons, and, with his position clearly before his eyes, have taken the terrible risk of Peel's crushing him for ever by producing the correspondence.[1] By way of meeting this difficulty, it has been pointed out that in the letter of 1841 there is no explicit request for office, and that it might therefore have been just possible to reconcile it with the speech of 1846. But the House of Commons would have been little impressed by such ingenious refinements, and Disraeli himself, to do him justice, in his moments of complete self-possession would have scorned to seek shelter beneath them. ' The general effect is the thing '—that is his own canon ; and though some element of mystery may remain in this affair, the general effect is clear enough. Having asked Peel for office in 1841, Disraeli in 1846, not to press the other occasion, publicly denied that he had done so ; and he must pay the full penalty. Let the politician who is without sin in the matter of veracity cast the first stone.

Though the Corn Bill had now been carried through the House of Commons, the fate of the Government and all their measures still hung in the balance. A week after the great division they had a narrow escape. The Ten Hours Bill, which had proved so embarrassing to Peel and Graham a couple of years before, had been introduced again ; and though the whole weight of their influence was again thrown into the scale against it, they only succeeded in defeating it by a majority of ten.[2] The bulk of the Whigs and protectionists voted for the Bill against the Peelites and Manchester Liberals ; and this was so obviously the natural division of parties that the attempts were now renewed to give it permanent recognition.

A nobleman, whose services have been since prematurely lost to the country, and whose excellent sense, imperturbable

[1] Lord Rosebery (*Sir Robert Peel*, p. 9) has a story of Peel's searching among his papers for Disraeli's letter late into the night of the affair in the House of Commons. The correspondence was first published long after Disraeli's death, in the late Mr. Parker's Life of Sir Robert Peel.
[2] 203 to 193.

temper, and knowledge of mankind, had for many years exercised a leading influence in the councils of the Whigs, and always to their advantage, was extremely anxious that by a reconstruction in this spirit an end should be put to that balanced state of parties which, if permitted to continue, frustrated the practicability, and even the prospect, of a strong Government. What he wished particularly to accomplish was, to see Lord George Bentinck in the new Whig Cabinet. But though this eminent individual conducted his negotiations under the happiest auspices, for Lord George Bentinck entertained for him great personal regard, and was united to his son by ties of very warm and intimate friendship, his object was not attained.[1]

The nobleman was Lord Bessborough,[2] who was afterwards Russell's Lord Lieutenant, and who, in addition to the personal ties to which Disraeli alludes, was as an Irishman attracted by Bentinck's Irish policy. His kinsman, Lord Ponsonby, who, as we have seen, had conceived a high opinion of Disraeli's powers, had been labouring throughout the session for the formation of a strong Government on the basis of an understanding between Whigs and protectionists ; and through him Disraeli had for some time been in communication with Bessborough and his friends. The intrigue on the present occasion was hatched, according to Greville,[3] at Palmerston House, and the plan was to transform the Corn Bill in the Lords by the introduction of a fixed duty. It was not yet realised how insuperable was the obstacle presented to this plan by Russell's engagements ; but Russell, when he heard of it, promptly summoned a meeting of the Whig peers at Lansdowne House, and told them that it was inconsistent with his personal and political honour. The result was reported to Hobhouse by Palmerston, who was present, as ' All unanimous against the Bill and all unanimous not to oppose it.' A few days later, on May 28, the Lords passed the second reading by the ample and unexpected majority of 47.

When the Houses adjourned for Whitsuntide, the

---

[1] *Lord George Bentinck,* ch. 14.   [2] The 4th Earl, 1781 to 1847.
[3] Under date June 1, 1846.

outlook, which at Easter had been so full of hope for the protectionists, had become very gloomy. Few now thought of defeating the Corn Bill, and it was even a question whether it would be possible to secure the defeat of the Government when the Corn Bill had become law. After their majority in the Lords, Ministers themselves began to be sanguine that they would escape for this session, and it was far from easy to see how they were to be caught. A direct vote of censure would probably not be supported by the Liberal wing of the Opposition ; and, as it would appear to be conceived in the interest of the Whigs, it would have the effect of driving back many of the rebellious Conservatives to the Ministerial fold. Other courses suggested presented similar difficulties.

Thus it happened that, although for several weeks the persons most adroit in such affairs had been planning the overthrow of a Government which was only supported by one-sixth of the members of the House of Commons, the Whitsun recess had closed, and Parliament had again re-opened, without apparently any approximation to the means which were to accomplish their purpose. The Bill for the repeal of the Corn Laws could not be carried through the House of Lords until the end of June ; and until that measure was secured the Whigs and their Liberal allies were not pre-pared to strike. What opportunity would they have of dealing the blow after June ? There was no reason why the Govern-ment, having carried their measure, might not rapidly wind up the session and prorogue Parliament. Was it probable that at the end of another month, the Government having achieved their great object, those who were conspiring their overthrow would be richer in their resources or more felicitous in their expedients than at the present moment, when ven-geance, ambition, the love of office, and the love of change, all combined to advance and assist their wishes ?

At length Disraeli succeeded in persuading Bentinck that the only chance lay in the course he had urged from the first—opposition to the Coercion Bill. Both Russell and Bentinck, as we have seen, had supported the first reading—Russell, as Disraeli tells us, ' entrapped by the precipitate acts and indiscreet admissions of his colleagues in the House of Lords,' and Bentinck, ' though warned against taking a course which was in itself foreign to his policy with respect to Ireland, seduced into the proceeding by the irresistible temptation of securing delay in the progress of the Corn Bill.' Russell had since prepared for a retreat, artificially enough, by quarrelling with some of the vital clauses, and hinting that it would be fairer to oppose the second reading than to mutilate the Bill ; but Bentinck's position was much better. He had made it a condition of his support that the Government should show they were in earnest by pressing forward with the Bill, and nearly three months had now elapsed since it came down from the House of Lords, and it had only been advanced one stage. The second reading was to be taken on June 8, and the indications were that the Whigs would oppose. In this matter, of course, they would have the Irish and Radicals with them, and if a moderate number of protectionists could be induced to vote against the Bill, the defeat of the Government was certain. But at first the omens were unfavourable. Before the debate began, Bentinck, in a rapid council of his friends, suggested the plan of opposing the Bill, but Disraeli alone supported him. The others all thought the movement must fail, and bring discredit upon them. When the rejection was moved from the Whig benches, Bentinck, sitting with Disraeli by him, was still undecided. At the end of the first speech he left Disraeli in charge, and went out to confer with one of his whips. When he came back, he reported :

There are no means of calculating at this moment how our men will go, but he agrees with us. It may be perilous, but if we lose this chance the traitor will escape. I will make the plunge, and as soon as I can   There is a rumour that Lord John is hardly up to the mark. I suppose he has heard that our men will not vote against the Bill. Now, if I speak early and strongly, it will encourage him to be decided.

He made the plunge during the evening. In the course of a vehement speech, he reminded Peel that he was now

what he had once proudly declared he would never consent
to be—a Minister on sufferance, ' supported by none but
his forty paid janissaries and some seventy other rene-
gades, one-half of whom, while supporting him, expressed
their shame of doing so.' They were told now by the
Minister that it would have been base and dishonest in
him if he had concealed his opinions after he had changed
them ; but he remembered with sorrow when his illustrious
relative Canning was ' chased and hunted to death '
by the right hon. baronet, who refused to support his
Ministry on the ground that it was favourable to Catholic
emancipation. That was in 1827 ; yet in 1829 he told
the House of Commons that he had changed his opinions
on that subject in 1825, and had communicated the
change of opinion to Lord Liverpool. Did he not therefore by his own verdict stand convicted of conduct that
was base and dishonest ?

This speech, of course, raised the temperature of the
debate. Sidney Herbert at once followed in an acrimonious
vein, and was foolish enough to offend both protectionists
and Whigs by talk of secret negotiations, for which he had
nothing better than vague rumour to offer as his warrant.
By the end of the night the field of battle was fixed ;
the Government were pledged to stand by their measure ;
Russell and Bentinck were both pledged to oppose it ;
and a good many protectionists had been irritated into
sympathy with a policy of which at first they were inclined
to disapprove. For a moment it seemed even possible
that the Government might fall before the Corn Bill was
through the Lords ; but this the Whigs were determined
to avoid, and it became the problem to postpone the
critical division till the Corn Bill was safe.

An episode that developed out of Bentinck's speech
helped to fill up the time. When the Irish debate was
resumed four days later, Peel spoke effectively, dwelling,
in the tones of sorrowful indignation which he knew how
to command, on the licence of Bentinck's language ;
denying unequivocally the charge that in 1829 he had

avowed a change of opinion in 1825, which he subsequently
concealed in 1827 ; and concluding with the declaration
to which allusion has already been made, that it was a
foul calumny to suggest that he had wished to rob
Russell of his right to settle the corn question. Bentinck
seems to have made his reference to Peel's supposed avowal
in 1829 on the spur of the moment, as to a fact that was
verified by his own recollection and accepted by all
who were familiar with the events of that time. He was
not prepared for Peel's denial ; but he now turned to the
records, and found that though the words of the speech
of 1829, on which his case rested, did not appear in the
report in Hansard, which admittedly had been revised,
they appeared in *The Times* and in another publication
called the *Mirror of Parliament*. Other corroborative
evidence was also obtained, and as by the rules of the
House Bentinck could not speak again in the Irish debate,
he handed this material for a reply to Disraeli.

Disraeli employed it in what Hobhouse calls a ' very
powerful speech,' defending his friend and maintaining
the charge against Peel in a manner ' exceedingly effective.'[1] On the subject of the Coercion Bill, he remarked
that there had been no attempt to account for the fact
that only now, in the month of June, were they asked
to read it a second time. He insisted that even though
Bentinck had changed his attitude on the Bill, there was
a world of difference between his conduct and the conduct
of the Minister who had drawn a parallel between the two.
Bentinck had violated no confidence and betrayed no
trust ; he had not with practised duplicity supplanted a
candidate on the hustings by promising to vote for the
very measure he was coming to Parliament to oppose.
As a matter of fact, he had given the Government the most
exact notice of what he intended to do. Coming to Peel's
declaration that it was a foul calumny to suggest that
he had wished to anticipate Russell in the settlement of
the corn question, the speaker proved that the original

[1] Broughton, VI., p. 178.

author of the so-called calumny was the First Minister himself. With regard to Bentinck's strong language, he had no difficulty in showing that similar language had been used ' by men of great light and leading, by the greatest statesmen, and orators that England ever produced,' one passage he cited from Fox containing the very word ' janissaries ' applied exactly as Bentinck had applied it.

The noble lord [he proceeded], the member for Lynn—I say it in his presence, for I know he is superior to any petty offence on the subject—the noble lord, if he has any characteristic more than another, it is his total absence of affectation and pretence. The noble lord never comes here but he always tells us that he does so most unwillingly, and that he has been pressed against his will into the position he now occupies. He always tells us : ' I am no ripe scholar, I am not a practised statesman, I am not an orator ; cannot you get someone else than me ? I was bred a soldier ; I never aspired to more than the reputation of a high-spirited and honourable English gentleman.' That is the character of the noble lord, and I believe he has attained his utmost wishes. I must say it not in his praise ; for I think, with his great abilities and his high station, it is a deficiency in such a man ; but the fact is that he is not ambitious. Anyone who knows him intimately, knows that the idea—and it is a legitimate idea—of his rising in the State is foreign to his nature, and never entered his mind. (Loud cheers.) The noble lord may have expressed himself with unusual warmth and vigour. With no pretensions, as he tells us, as an orator, speaking from the heart, I am not sure but the very vigour of his brave honesty is worth all the modern eloquence with which we are so often favoured, when we have all those pompous plausibilities, all those solemn adroitnesses, all those ' damnable iterations,' all those stale sophisms and solemn commonplaces, which are held up by the name of modern eloquence.

He then produced the evidence in support of the Canning charge, and concluded :

Sir, I think I have answered the elaborate attack of the right hon. gentleman on the noble lord—his attack on my noble friend's consistency, his attack on his Parliamentary language, his attack upon the imputation my noble friend made upon him as to the conduct of the right hon. gentleman

to Mr. Canning.　But I trust I have done more than vindicate
my noble friend.　I trust I have put in its true and intelligible
light that mysterious passage which has so long perplexed the
politicians of Europe, and which the right hon. gentleman
on Friday night so elaborately explained for the benefit of
the rising generation.　I am not surprised that, closely connected with Mr. Canning as he was, my noble friend should
have expressed himself as he did.　The feeling to which he
gave utterance is shared by all who have had intercourse
with Mr. Canning.　I never saw Mr. Canning but once, when
I had no expectation of being a member of this House, but I
can recollect it but as yesterday, when I listened to the last
accents—I may say the dying words—of that illustrious
statesman.　I can recollect the flash—the lightning flash—of
that eye, and the power of that imperial brow.　But, sir,
when shall we see another Mr. Canning—a man who ruled
this House as a man rules a high-bred steed, as Alexander
ruled Bucephalus (a laugh), of whom it was said that horse
and man were alike proud.　I thank that hon. gentleman
for his laugh.　The pulse of the national heart does not beat
as high as once it did.　I know the temper of this House is
not as spirited and brave as it was, nor am I surprised, when
the vulture rules where once the eagle reigned.　(Loud cheers.)
The right hon. gentleman once said that Ireland was his great
difficulty.　I ask the right hon. gentleman why Ireland was
his great difficulty, and whether, if he had acted with frankness to Mr. Canning in reference to his communication with
Lord Liverpool in 1825, Ireland would have been his great
difficulty.　This the right hon. gentleman must feel at the
present moment, when we are about again to divide on an
Irish question—a division which may be fatal to the endurance
of his power—he must feel that it is a nemesis that dictates
this vote and regulates this decision, and that is about to
stamp with its seal the catastrophe of a sinister career.　(Loud
and continued cheering.)

Peel, who, according to Hobhouse, was ' completely
knocked down,' asked the House at the close to suspend
judgment on the Canning charge ; but a few days later
he made his defence, and carried all before him.　Never,
says Disraeli, was there a more successful explanation.
Its success, perhaps, was rather owing to the high character of the man, and to his adroitness in handling the
case than to the solid merits of his argument or its
completeness as an answer to the evidence on the other

side. He proved conclusively that the report in the *Mirror
of Parliament* was founded on that in *The Times*, so
that it could not be cited as independent testimony ; but
he left much unexplained. There is no doubt that a belief
had been allowed to establish itself that Peel had used
the words which Bentinck afterwards brought against
him, that they had been referred to in the House of
Commons, and that neither Peel nor his friends attempted
to correct them ; equally, no doubt, that the words were
out of correspondence with the facts, and that, whether
spoken or not, they did not represent the speaker's intention. Disraeli himself sums up the incident with ' the
full admission that, though Lord George Bentinck was
perfectly justified in making the particular charge which
he advanced, it was without real foundation.' We may
feel a little sceptical on the point of Bentinck's justification. Justification there certainly was in the sense of a
good deal of evidence ; but even if the charge had been
proved, the taste and wisdom of raking up such a story in
the middle of a great struggle on other issues twenty years
later would have remained very doubtful.[1] ' In passing
judgment on public men,' Disraeli himself had written
with reference to this very question of the relations
between Peel and Canning, ' it behoves us ever to take
large and extended views of their conduct '; and one
could wish that he and Bentinck had left the Canning
charge alone.[2] Their best excuse is that they blundered
into it without forethought, under guidance of the blazing
passions of this ' sad, fierce session.'

[1] There is, however, no justification except pardonable bad temper for
Peel's description of the affair, in a letter to the Queen (*Queen Victoria's
Letters*, June 22, 1846), as ' a foul conspiracy concocted by Mr. Disraeli and
Lord George Bentinck in the hope and belief that from the lapse of time
or want of leisure in Sir Robert Peel to collect materials for his defence, or
the destruction of documents and papers, the means of complete refutation
might be wanting.' Bentinck, who was mainly responsible, certainly
believed the charge ; and whatever we may think of his judgment, he was,
if possible, more incapable of an act of deliberate baseness than even Peel
himself.

[2] Disraeli seems to have had some such feeling as this himself when he
dissuaded Bentinck, six months later, from reopening the question on some
fresh evidence that was forthcoming. See *Lord George Bentinck*, ch. 15,
where the story of the Canning episode is told at length.

A few days after the termination of the Canning episode, on June 25, the Corn and Customs Bills finally passed the House of Lords ; and on the same night[1] the division on the Coercion Bill was taken in the Commons. The result seems to have been doubtful up to the last moment.

The managers for the Government were certain of the support of a very large portion of the protectionist party. They were induced to believe that many of that party would avoid the division, but that very few indeed would bring themselves to vote against a Bill which they had already stoutly supported. The protectionists were very discreet and their tactics extremely close ; the party was never better managed than on this division.

A hundred protectionists voted with the Government, and about eighty abstained. Disraeli has given a famous epic catalogue of the others who defiled before the Minister to the hostile lobby—' the Manners, the Somersets, the Bentincks, the Lowthers, and the Lennoxes '; and those gentlemen of England of whom a few years before he had been so proud of being the leader—' Sir Charles Burrell, Sir William Jolliffe, Sir Charles Knightly, Sir John Trollope, Sir Edward Kerrison, Sir John Tyrrell, and Sir John Yarde Buller.'

They trooped on : all the men of metal and large-acred squires, whose spirit he had so often quickened and whose counsel he had so often solicited in his fine Conservative speeches in Whitehall Gardens : Mr. Bankes, with a Parliamentary name of two centuries, and Mr. Christopher from that broad Lincolnshire which protection had created ; and the Mileses and the Henleys were there ; and the Duncombes, the Liddells, and the Yorkes ; and Devon had sent here the stout heart of Mr. Buck—and Wiltshire, the pleasant resence of Walter Long. Mr. Newdegate was there, whom Sir Robert had himself recommended to the confidence of the electors of Warwickshire, as one of whom he had the highest hopes ; and Mr. Alderman Thompson was there,

[1] This has often been described as an ' extraordinary coincidence,' but, as will be clear from the foregoing narrative, it was neither a coincidence nor extraordinary.

who, also through Sir Robert's selection, had seconded the
assault upon the Whigs, led on by Sir John Buller. But the
list is too long ; or good names remain behind.

Over seventy protectionists followed Bentinck and
Disraeli, and with the Whigs, the Radicals, and the
Irishmen, they were more than sufficient.

When Prince Metternich was informed at Dresden, with
great ostentation, that the Emperor had arrived, ' Yes ; but
without his army,' was the reply. Sir Robert Peel was still
First Minister of England, as Napoleon remained Emperor for
a while after Moscow. Each perhaps for a moment had indulged in hope. It is so difficult for those who are on the
pinnacle of life to realise disaster. They sometimes contemplate it in their deep and far-seeing calculations, but it is
only to imagine a contingency which their resources must
surely baffle ; they sometimes talk of it to their friends, and
oftener of it to their enemies, but it is only as an insurance
of their prosperity and as an offering to propitiate their
nemesis. They never believe in it.

The news that the Government were not only beaten, but
by a majority so large as 73, began to circulate. An in-
credulous murmur passed it along the Treasury bench.

' They say we are beaten by 73 !' whispered the most important member of the Cabinet in a tone of surprise to Sir
Robert Peel.

Sir Robert did not reply, or even turn his head. He
looked very grave, and extended his chin, as was his habit
when he was annoyed and cared not to speak. He began to
comprehend his position, and that the Emperor was without
his army.

Cobden tried to persuade Peel to dissolve rather than
resign, hailing him as the personification of the ' idea of
the age,' and assuring him of success if he placed himself
at the head of a great middle-class party. ' There must,'
he wrote, ' be an end of the juggle of parties, the mere
representatives of traditions, and some man must of
necessity rule the state through its governing class. The
Reform Bill decreed it ; the passing of the Corn Bill has
realised it.' Peel was more alive to ' the serious risk of
defeat ' if he essayed such an enterprise, and, weary
besides, preferred to resign. He announced his resigna-

tion on June 29 in a speech in the House of Commons which has often been quoted since with sympathy and approbation, but which was generally condemned at the time as an error of taste and judgment. He irritated the Whigs by a long commendation of the acts of his own Government, and he deeply offended his late followers by a glowing eulogy of Cobden, whom only six months before they had been asked to regard as such a danger to the State that he must be kept out of power even at the expense of a surrender of their convictions. There was, however, a certain dramatic fitness, in spite of the inconsistency, in his paying homage at such a moment to the real author of his policy. He concluded with the famous passage in which he talked of leaving a name that might be execrated by monopolists, but would sometimes, he hoped, be remembered with good-will in the abodes of those whose lot it was to labour, when they should recruit their exhausted strength with abundant and untaxed food, the sweeter because it was no longer leavened by a sense of injustice.

Peel was overthrown, but his policy prevailed. In its origin it was not suggestive either of foresight or of circumspection, but the stars in their courses fought for it. The great development of steam and railways that was proceeding when it was adopted, and the gold discoveries in California and Australia that soon followed, led to a mighty growth of national prosperity with which the new system from the first became identified in the public mind ; and the period of almost continuous war that presently began, and lasted till the seventies, long concealed its chief weakness by postponing the injury to English agriculture which Disraeli and his friends had predicted. Thus favoured by fortune, the new fiscal system became firmly established, and England has now been faithful to it for two generations. It was long almost a heresy to attempt even to criticise it, but that day is past. We can see now that a statesman of wider vision than Peel—such a statesman as Disraeli if he had

had the position and influence—might have done all that
was needed in 1846 in the interest of English industry
and the town population, while safeguarding our agriculture against the disasters that overtook it in the last
quarter of the nineteenth century ; that he might have
settled the corn question, not, as Peel did, by 'a precipitate
and violent scheme,' but while maintaining the continuity
of national policy and preserving what was best in the
traditions of the old commercial system.   Cobden and his
school were devoid of the historic sense, and when Peel fell
under their influence he broke completely with the past.
Breaking with the past, he lost control of the future. It was
not he who committed us to the industrial line of growth,
but it was he who committed us apparently past recall.
The repeal of the Corn Laws was the first decisive step
in that policy of sacrificing the rural life of England to a
one-sided and exaggerated industrial development which
has done so much to change the English character and
the English outlook, and which it may not impossibly
be the business of subsequent generations to endeavour
to retrace.

Up to a certain point Peel's policy in the forties was
a natural and legitimate development of what had
gone before, and a development in the direction of real
free trade. Up to that point he was supported by
Disraeli ; but when he abandoned Adam Smith and Pitt
and Huskisson, and leagued himself with Cobden,
Disraeli deserted him.   Disraeli's views on trade were
liberal from the first, and remained liberal to the end,
but he never became, like Peel, the slave of a formula.
He is the one conspicuous statesman of that generation,
it might almost indeed be said, or of the two generations
that followed, who, as I have tried to make clear, kept
his mind free on the question of the tariff, realised its
essentially concrete and practical character, and sought
guidance in history and a comprehensive survey of the
commerce of his day. He perceived and pointed out
the huge miscalculations on which Cobden and Peel

were basing their system of free imports, and in spite of which it has prospered. He knew there would be a great development of oversea production to overwhelm our agriculture, and he knew that other nations would never voluntarily acquiesce in our insular ideal of being the workshop of the world, and throw open their ports in obedience to our example. Nor, when he refused to be blinded by the fanaticism of free imports, did he pay any tribute to the fanaticism of protection. Throughout the great controversy he saw the issue steadily and saw it whole, saw it above all in its political bearings, and never deviated to the right or to the left from the middle course which his judgment had prescribed. In all his speeches on the subject it would be hard to point to two sentences which are inconsistent with each other either in the letter or in the spirit. If Peel had taken Disraeli for his guide, or, indeed, if he had only continued on the lines on which he began and on which Disraeli would have supported him, he might have identified his name with a system of free trade of which, after the lapse of two generations, the United Kingdom would not have been the solitary adherent among the nations of the world.

It is said, indeed, that if Disraeli had been taken into the Government in 1841 he would never have turned against Peel. That may be true, for the whole course of events would then have been different ; but that it is true in any sense discreditable to Disraeli is the merest affectation. If his character had stood higher, nothing would ever have been heard of the particular charge implied. I have set forth with some minuteness the sequence of events from the beginning of the Peel Parliament as it touches the question, and the reader can judge for himself. Disraeli supported the Peel Government for two years after his exclusion ; he diverged from it first on a clear question of principle and under pressure from his constituents ; and he only entered on a course of systematic opposition when it had become manifest that on the one hand Ministers were drifting away from the principles on which they had come into power, and which he himself had upheld, and on the other that they had established an ostracism against him, and were determined to deprive him of a field for the exercise of his genius. He was conscious of great political gifts, of seeing deeper and farther than the mediocrities, ' sublime ' or simple, by whom he was surrounded. Was he tamely to submit to the prejudices of men who had no remarkable pre-eminence of intellect or vision, and who were now passing under the influence of a school of political thought against which his whole career is a protest and a struggle ? If he had so allowed himself to be effaced, he would only have been a weaker, hardly a better, man. He did nothing that has not been done with far less justification by statesmen of the highest character in every age and country. If his revolt against the Government differed from a thousand other political incidents of the same order which we accept as a matter of course, the difference was not in motive ; it was in a certain absence of cant and virtuous pretence which was peculiar to himself, in the patience and self-restraint with which he waited for the appropriate moment, the discernment and daring with which he seized it when it came, the genius with which his warfare was conducted, and the overwhelming success by which it was attended.

The measure for the repeal of the Corn Laws has been canonised by English opinion, and the story of the events that led up to its passage has more often than not been told by men who can see only wisdom and virtue on the side of its advocates, wickedness, or at the best folly, on the side of its opponents. Coming up for trial with an indifferent reputation before such a court, Disraeli has been judged with censorious harshness, whereas Peel, with a friendly jury and a good reputation, has been let off too lightly. We have been asked to recognise in Peel an example of noble self-sacrifice postponing to the call of duty the luxury of a merely selfish consistency ; in Disraeli an example of inconsistency equally or more flagrant, and sinning against the light for the gratification of personal malice. This judgment may now be seen to stand in need of revision ; on the face of it, indeed, it is essentially shallow. Anyone can feel the implicit drama of the struggle between the two men, and there can be no great drama with the right all on one side. Here, at all events, the right was divided, and the struggle inevitable—inevitable, that is to say, if Peel was to be Peel and Disraeli Disraeli. On the question of consistency from the political point of view, enough perhaps has been said to show that the advantage is not on the side of Peel ; and even from the moral standpoint some may now feel that in these transactions at least he has no marked superiority over his antagonist. Disraeli certainly was no moral hero, but Peel's claims to be so regarded are not most wisely based on his dealings with the Corn Laws. Disraeli's falsehood in the House of Commons stands, of course, against him, and helps to give a colour to the worst interpretations his enemies can place on his character and motives. Morally Peel was incapable of an error such as that ; but with his furtive and unstable mind, his remarkable powers of self-deception, and his debater's instinct for the merely specious as an efficient substitute for the truth, he was very far from being a pattern of straightforwardness and candour. There is not only a moral but an intellectual integrity, and in the intellectual virtue Peel was as much the inferior of Disraeli as in the moral he was his superior.

When he had once decided to strike, Disraeli struck very hard, but, if the prejudice had not been against him and on the side of Peel, few would say unfairly. The weapons of ridicule and sarcasm which he mainly employed were those which were best fitted to penetrate the armour of oily evasion in which his antagonist had encased himself, and they were employed with deadly precision ; but except possibly in the Canning episode, where he was not the prime mover, the attacks did not transgress the bounds of taste and judgment. And though Disraeli could be ruthless and rarely failed to exact a penalty for injuries that were done him, he was free from mean rancour and he knew how to spare the fallen. When his object was accomplished, the Government overthrown, the organised hypocrisy at length swept away, and a path cleared for his own ambition and the triumph of his own ideas, he held his hand and struck no more. From the moment that he had succeeded in driving Peel from office, he never uttered another offensive word against him.

APPENDIX.

MEMORANDUM FOR THE KING OF THE FRENCH, 1842.

PAGE 150.

VERY CONFIDENTIAL NOTE ON THE MEANS OF RESTORING THE UNDERSTANDING BETWEEN FRANCE AND ENGLAND, ENTRUSTED TO GENERAL BAUDRAND.

The writer of this memorandum has observed with deep attention the characters and circumstances in France which exercise an influence on the relations between the two countries. He has that knowledge of the actors and motives of the political world of England which years of thought and action and intimate intercourse with the chiefs of parties can alone give ; and he cannot resist the conviction that the system at present pursued for the purpose of maintaining the connexion between the two countries is one which must inevitably terminate in disaster and failure.

Unquestionably the genius of a great Prince, eminently fertile in resource and strengthened by an unprecedented experience of life, may for a long time baffle the catastrophe. But what is the consequence of this policy ? The energies of the founder of the dynasty are wasted in acts hostile to the popularity of the dynasty. The English connexion, instead of consolidating the throne, which was its original intent and is its natural bias, menaces and enfeebles it. Stripped of a thousand circumstances which lay (*sic*) upon the surface and distract the superficial, this is the real point which should occupy the thought of every friend of the King, and I will add of every friend of France and England.

The present system, then, entails upon the two countries a general condition of frigid and professional connexion broken by episodes of suspicion, misconception, irritation, courtly phrases, adroit diversions, little acts of concerted courtesy, and war.

Before the writer details the measures which in his opinion might revive and permanently retain the feelings that existed between the two countries ten years since, and establish between France and England a genuine and hearty alliance, he would make one observation on the feelings of the two nations in respect to this great result.

He perceives that in France the enlightened classes are generally in favor of the English connexion, but that the great body of the nation is hostile to England. In England, on the contrary, the great body of the people is friendly to France, while the superior classes look to France with no cordiality. Yet there is reason to believe that in neither instance is this hostility the result of the ancient prejudices of the two nations. In England it is habit; in France it is passion. The reason of the class in England must therefore be instructed, the vanity of the class in France must therefore be soothed.

In the opinion of the writer there are three measures which would materially tend to revive, and if assisted by a judicious policy on the part of France would absolutely and speedily restore, a genuine and hearty alliance between the two countries.

1st. On the very night that the English Parliament meets an influential member who has the ear of the House should give public notice of his intention of inviting the consideration of the House of Commons on the earliest occasion to the state of the relations between England and France.

It should be observed that in the whole course of the last twelve eventful years, during which England has witnessed her foreign system changed and reconstructed, the intimate alliance between herself and France announced one day as the only basis of her policy, and the English Minister who had avowedly entered into wars to baffle Russian intrigue, and promoted men to embassies for having written anti-Russian pamphlets, repudiating on another day that same French alliance and acting with Russia in violation of France,—during all these long years of confused and contradictory conduct, not a single debate has ever taken place on the principles on which the foreign policy of England should be established.[1] The Parliament of England, absorbed in domestic struggles, has been left with respect to its foreign affairs without a principle to guide and without knowledge to enlighten it. But these domestic struggles are over, and a new generation has entered the House of Commons to add its quota to the great aggregate of national [illegible].

---

[1] The memorandum is given from a very rough draft, and this Thucydidean sentence is the best that can be made of an excessively blotted passage.

A clear and comprehensive statement at this moment in the English Parliament of the great question of the English and French alliance would produce a marvellous effect. It would teach men to think. It would give principles to that vast majority who must be led. It would open new considerations of paramount interest. It would give a train to expressions which would touch the heart of the French people. It would afford an opportunity to a great section of the Opposition to repudiate the late policy of Lord Palmerston. It would be a signal to England that a new era was at hand. It would above all force from the English Minister, not merely complimentary phrases, but a declaration in detail which would echo in every Cabinet in Europe.

2ndly. Previous to the meeting of the English Parliament a party should be organised which in respect to the external policy of England should be systematically opposed to the Russian system. The Government of Sir Robert Peel is at this moment upheld by an apparent majority in the Commons of 90 members. It is known that among these 90 are between 40 and 50 agricultural malcontents who, though not prepared to commence an active opposition, will often be absent on questions which, though not of vital, may yet be of great importance to the Minister. It is obvious, therefore, that another section of Conservative members, full of youth and energy and constant in their seats, must exercise an irresistible control over the tone of the Minister. Sympathising in general with his domestic policy, they may dictate the character of his foreign, especially if they appeal to a conviction which at the bottom of Sir R. Peel's heart responds to their own. Such a party would strengthen him against the menacing applications of M. de Brunow : it would soon dispel Lord Aberdeen's mystical hallucinations of German nationality.

When the writer of this note states that such a party can be formed, he speaks with an absolute knowledge of his subject. A gentleman has already been solicited to place himself at the head of a Parliamentary party which there is every reason to believe would adopt the views on the Foreign Policy of England referred to, a party of the youth of England, influenced by the noblest views and partaking in nothing of the character of a Parliamentary intrigue ; and if he has not at once accepted an offer which it is known he esteems the greatest honor that he ever received, it is only because next to the responsibility of forming a Government is in his opinion that of leading a party.

It is right to state that it is calculated that the leadership of a Parliamentary party in England involves an extra expenditure of a very great amount. This circumstance is mentioned only to show that no one would heedlessly contemplate such a contingency. For no other purpose, for it would only express the common feeling of every English gentleman, were it stated, that if this expenditure were the sole qualification for the office there would be an universal rivalry to supply it.

The third measure which the writer recommends is a comprehensive organisation of the Press of England in favor of the French and English alliance. This power so vast, but the management of which is so frequently neglected and so generally misunderstood even by English Ministers, is of itself, if skilfully conducted, capable of effecting great things ; but whenever it has chanced to be combined with a Parliamentary power its influence has invariably been irresistible. Great interests sensible of the power of the Press, and unable to analyse it, often appropriate to themselves the columns of a popular journal, and are surprised that the effect is not proportionate to their expectations. But a single journal, however ably conducted, is only an organ. Recognised to be an organ, it ceases to be an authority. Its moral influence merges in its official character. The monitor that counsels the people of England to view France with a glance of affection and confidence, to believe that the power and prosperity of France will secure the empire and increase the wealth of England, must speak in journals of every school of politics, and sound in every district. It is with a machinery of this description that the ideas of a single man, acting upon latent sympathies which only require development, soon become the voice of a nation. Independent of the extreme difficulty which most men must experience in effecting such an arrangement, many have been dissuaded from the attempt by the impression that the result could only be obtained by vast expenditure. This idea is completely erroneous. Thousands and tens of thousands, indeed, have sometimes been blunderingly thrown away on the mismanagement of a single organ, but the Press of England is not in a gross and general sense corrupt. The writer will, if desired, draw up a confidential note on the organisation of the Press, and furnish a plan which may be carried into practice. Indeed, if it cannot be put in practice without his aid, he will undertake its fulfilment. At all events he will consent, when the organisation has taken place, to exercise the same general supervision that Lord Palmerston now exercises over the anti-Gallic Press.

These are the measures which, if carried into effect simultaneously and with energy, would, in the opinion of the writer, materially tend to produce the great result desired by all those who believe that in the international union of France and England depend, not merely their material prosperity, but ultimately their existence as Powers of the first class. These plans may perhaps seem vast, but they are not visionary. They are, on the contrary, essentially practical. They are even to the minutest element necessary to their success digested and matured, and it is believed that the influence and intellect of an individual can at this moment carry them into effect.

INDEX

END OF VOL. II.

BILLING AND SONS, LTD., PRINTERS, GUILDFORD